Interpersonal Psychoanalysis and the Enigma of Consciousness

Edgar A. Levenson is a key figure in the development of interpersonal psychoanalysis whose ideas remain influential. *Interpersonal Psychoanalysis and the Enigma of Consciousness* builds on his previously published work in his key areas of expertise such as interpersonal psychoanalysis, transference and countertransference, and the philosophy of psychoanalysis, and sets his ideas into contemporary context. Combining a selection of Levenson's own writings with extensive discussion and analysis of his work by Stern and Slomowitz, it provides an invaluable guide to how his most recent, mature ideas may be understood and applied by contemporary psychoanalysts in their own practice.

This book explores how the rational algorithm of psychoanalytic engagement and the mysterious flows of consciousness interact; this has traditionally been thought of as dialectical, an unresolvable duality in psychoanalytic practice. Analysts move back and forth between the two perspectives, rather like a gestalt leap, finding themselves listening either to the "interpersonal" or to the "intrapsychic" in what feels like a self-state leap. But the interpersonal is not in dialectical opposition to the intrapsychic; rather a manifestation of it, a subset. The chapters pick up from the themes explored in *The Purloined Self*, shifting the emphasis from the interpersonal field to the exploration of the enigma of the flow of consciousness that underlies the therapeutic process. This is not the Freudian Unconscious nor the consciousness of awareness, but the mysterious Jamesian matrix of being. Any effort at influence provokes resistance and refusal by the patient. Permitted a "working space," the patient ultimately cures herself. How that happens is a mystery wrapped up in the greater mystery of unconscious process, which in turn is wrapped into the greatest philosophical and neurological enigma of all—the nature of consciousness.

Interpersonal Psychoanalysis and the Enigma of Consciousness will be highly engaging and readable; Levenson's witty essayist style and original perspective will make it greatly appealing and accessible to undergraduate and postgraduate students of psychoanalysis and psychoanalytic psychotherapy, as well as practitioners in these fields.

Edgar A. Levenson, M.D., is Fellow Emeritus, Training, Supervisory Analyst and Faculty at the William Alanson White Institute. He is Adjunct Clinical Professor of Psychology at the NYU Graduate Studies Division, Honorary Fellow at the Postgraduate Center for Mental Health, Honorary Member of the American Psychoanalytic Association, Life Fellow of the American Academy of Psychoanalysis, and Distinguished Life Fellow of the American Psychiatric Association. Winner of the 2006 Mary S. Sigourney Award, he is author of over 110 publications, including *Fallacy of Understanding* (1972), *The Ambiguity of Change* (1983) and *The Purloined Self* (2016).

Alan Slomowitz, Ph.D., is a graduate of the William Alanson White Institute of Psychiatry, Psychoanalysis and Psychology. He is a Supervisor of Psychotherapy at the White Institute, on the Editorial Board of *Contemporary Psychoanalysis*, and the Internet Editor of the Contemporary Psychoanalysis in Action blog. Dr. Slomowitz edited the new release of *The Purloined Self* (2016) with Dr. Levenson. Dr. Slomowitz is in private practice in psychoanalysis and psychotherapy in New York City.

"Much like the subject matter of this wonderful book, Edgar Levenson is an enigma. Even though he has published for over fifty years, his work is continuously contemporary. Even though he is the most well-known and subtle theorist of interpersonal psychoanalysis, he is a decisive critic of theory and theorizing. Levenson has made a truly original contribution to our understanding of psychoanalytic process, but at the same time, he has repeatedly warned against codifying this understanding into a specific technique of method or treatment. He has always been our foremost student and authority on process, and much like analytic process itself, Levenson eludes capture. He describes the ineffable nature of our work in a way that continues to change, to evolve, never settling onto a single set of concepts that might be elevated to a new orthodoxy. He challenges us to think anew, to experience with a fresh awareness never reduced to our conceptualizations.

In this new book, we see Levenson's work at a new level of maturity, leapfrogging over the pervasive conundrums of our field today. Psychoanalysis across the world is finally coming to terms with concerns raised by Levenson since the beginning of his work. Current international interest in intersubjectivity, mutual influence, field phenomena, the limits of understanding and the importance of negative capacity have been continued interests for Levenson, raised in response to the fixity of a psychoanalytic theorizing that has not taken into account the effects of theory in process itself. This is Levenson's purview. But in his recent work, Levenson moves further, situating internal private experience in relation to the intersubjective, proposing a nuanced reflection on the role of perception in psychoanalytic process, offering as always a perspective that subtends dichotomies, but that here also finds new integrations without ever simply settling for making sense.

One finds a unique pleasure in the *encounter* with Levenson. More than any other psychoanalyst, we read what Levenson writes, and we have an incarnation of his presence. Reading becomes an experience with him, a process in itself. We find ourselves shifted, in spite of ourselves, out of our familiar stance of knowing into an experience of being, into an encounter with the ineffable, always tilted from familiar moorings in a way that leads us to consider, and more importantly, to experience our work afresh. This is the Levenson idiom, one that offers a rare opportunity to play with him as he pursues psychoanalytic process and the enigmatic nature of experience."

—**Jack Foehl, Ph.D., ABPP**, Training & Supervising Analyst, Boston Psychoanalytic Society and Institute, Supervisor and Faculty, Massachusetts Institute for Psychoanalysis and Harvard Medical School, Associate Professor (Adjunct) NYU Postdoctoral Program in Psychotherapy and Psychoanalysis

PSYCHOANALYSIS IN A NEW KEY BOOK SERIES

DONNEL STERN
Series Editor

When music is played in a new key, the melody does not change, but the notes that make up the composition do: change in the context of continuity, continuity that perseveres through change. Psychoanalysis in a New Key publishes books that share the aims psychoanalysts have always had, but that approach them differently. The books in the series are not expected to advance any particular theoretical agenda, although to this date most have been written by analysts from the Interpersonal and Relational orientations.

The most important contribution of a psychoanalytic book is the communication of something that nudges the reader's grasp of clinical theory and practice in an unexpected direction. Psychoanalysis in a New Key creates a deliberate focus on innovative and unsettling clinical thinking. Because that kind of thinking is encouraged by exploration of the sometimes surprising contributions to psychoanalysis of ideas and findings from other fields, Psychoanalysis in a New Key particularly encourages interdisciplinary studies. Books in the series have married psychoanalysis with dissociation, trauma theory, sociology, and criminology. The series is open to the consideration of studies examining the relationship between psychoanalysis and any other field—for instance, biology, literary and art criticism, philosophy, systems theory, anthropology, and political theory.

But innovation also takes place within the boundaries of psychoanalysis, and Psychoanalysis in a New Key therefore also presents work that reformulates thought and practice without leaving the precincts of the field. Books in the series focus, for example, on the significance of personal values in psychoanalytic practice, on the complex interrelationship between the analyst's clinical work and personal life, on the consequences for the clinical situation when patient and analyst are from different cultures, and on the need for psychoanalysts to accept the degree to which they knowingly satisfy their own wishes during treatment hours, often to the patient's detriment.

For a full list of all the titles in the Psychoanalysis in a New Key series, please visit the Routledge website.

Recent titles in this series:

Vol. 39 *The Voice of the Analyst: Narratives on Developing a Psychoanalytic Identity* Edited by Linda Hillman and Therese Rosenblatt

Vol. 38 *Interpersonal Psychoanalysis and the Enigma of Consciousness* Edgar A. Levenson and Edited by Alan Slomowitz

Vol. 37 *The Organizational Life of Psychoanalysis: Conflicts, Dilemmas, and the Future of the Profession* Kenneth Eisold

Vol. 36 *Nonlinear Psychoanalysis: Notes from Forty Years of Chaos and Complexity Theory* Robert M. Galatzer-Levy

Vol. 35 *A Beholder's Share: Essays on Winnicott and the Psychoanalytic Imagination* Dodi Goldman

Interpersonal Psychoanalysis and the Enigma of Consciousness

Edgar A. Levenson
Edited by Alan Slomowitz

LONDON AND NEW YORK

First published 2018
by Routledge
2 Park Square, Milton Park, Abingdon, Oxon OX14 4RN

and by Routledge
711 Third Avenue, New York, NY 10017

Routledge is an imprint of the Taylor & Francis Group, an informa business

© 2018 Edgar A. Levenson

The right of Edgar A. Levenson to be identified as author of this work
has been asserted by him in accordance with sections 77 and 78 of the
Copyright, Designs and Patents Act 1988.

All rights reserved. No part of this book may be reprinted or
reproduced or utilised in any form or by any electronic, mechanical, or
other means, now known or hereafter invented, including photocopying
and recording, or in any information storage or retrieval system,
without permission in writing from the publishers.

Trademark notice: Product or corporate names may be trademarks or
registered trademarks, and are used only for identification and
explanation without intent to infringe.

British Library Cataloguing in Publication Data
A catalogue record for this book is available from the British Library

Library of Congress Cataloging in Publication Data
Names: Levenson, Edgar A., author. | Slomowitz, Alan., author.
Title: Interpersonal psychoanalysis and the enigma of consciousness /
Edgar A. Levenson ; edited by Alan Slomowitz.
Description: Abingdon, Oxon ; New York, NY : Routledge, 2018. |
Series: Psychoanalysis in a new key book series ; 38 | Includes
bibliographical references and index.
Identifiers: LCCN 2017005805| ISBN 9781138692404 (hardback : alk.
paper) | ISBN 9781138692411 (pbk. : alk. paper) | ISBN 9781315532394
(epub) | ISBN 9781315532387 (mobipocket/kindle)
Subjects: LCSH: Psychoanalysis. | Interpersonal psychotherapy. |
Consciousness.
Classification: LCC RC504 .L483 2018 | DDC 616.89/17—dc23
LC record available at https://lccn.loc.gov/2017005805

ISBN: 978-1-138-69240-4 (hbk)
ISBN: 978-1-138-69241-1 (pbk)
ISBN: 978-1-315-53241-7 (ebk)

Typeset in Times New Roman
by Florence Production Ltd, Stoodleigh, Devon, UK

Contents

Foreword DONNEL STERN	x
Preface ALAN SLOMOWITZ	xii
Acknowledgments EDGAR LEVENSON	xvii
Introduction	xx

PART I
The unfolding of Interpersonal Psychoanalysis, from Interpersonal Psychiatry to Interpersonal Psychoanalysis   **1**

1	An interpersonal therapist (1998)	3
2	Back to the future: the new psychoanalytic revisionism (1991)	9
3	Harry Stack Sullivan: from Interpersonal Psychiatry to Interpersonal Psychoanalysis (1992)	26
4	Shoot the messenger: interpersonal aspects of the analyst's interpretations (1993)	43
5	A Monopedal version of Interpersonal Psychoanalysis (1995)	57

viii Contents

| 6 | The last shall be first: some observations on the evolution of interpersonal psychoanalysis (2002) | 63 |

| 7 | Fifty years of evolving interpersonal psychoanalysis (2006) | 72 |

PART II
Psychoanalytic process

81

8	Standoffs, impasses, and stalemates (1991)	83
9	Mistakes, errors, and oversights (1992)	91
10	Beyond countertransference: aspects of the analyst's desire (1994)	108
11	Aspects of self-revelation and self-disclosure (1996)	125
12	Psychoanalytic love and therapeutic despair (2000)	138
13	On seeing what is said: visual aids to the psychoanalytic process (2003)	144
14	The enigma of the transference (2009)	161
15	Psychoanalysis and the rite of refusal (2012)	178

PART III
The philosophy of psychoanalytic theory and practice

185

16	The uses of disorder: Chaos theory and psychoanalysis (1994)	187
17	The politics of interpretation (1996)	206
18	Awareness, insight, and learning (1998)	225
19	The enigma of the unconscious (2001)	237
20	Freud's dilemma: on writing Greek and thinking Jewish (2001)	252
21	Creativity, genius, and divine madness (2001)	269

22	Oh what a blow that phantom gave me: observations on the rise of virtual desire (2007)	277
23	Deeper, wider: some comments on the Gill/Bromberg correspondence (2011)	286
24	Lost in translation (2011)	293
25	Psychoanalysis, the uncanny, and the banalization of evil (2016)	298

Epilogue: interview with Edgar Levenson by Irwin Hirsch and Victor Iannuzzi (2005) — 305
Bibliography of Edgar A. Levenson, M.D. — 310
Index — 317

Foreword

I have known Edgar Levenson since I began my psychoanalytic training at the William Alanson White Institute in New York City in 1976. Ed is about 25 years older than I am, and so when I arrived as a 27-year-old, he was already in the shank of his career. It has been a very long career, and he is still in the shank of it.

At that time, Levenson was Director of Clinical Services at the Institute, and he ran the weekly Tuesday meetings in the Clinic, in which candidates presented their work with analytic and psychotherapy patients, and more senior analysts came to present whatever they were thinking about at the time. If you know Levenson's work, you can imagine how stimulating those meetings were.

Before long, though, I understood that Levenson was a good deal more than Director of Clinical Services. I read *The Fallacy of Understanding* (1972) during my first year at White, and when it appeared in 1983, I read *The Ambiguity of Change*. These books are among the most significant contributions to American psychoanalysis. In them, Levenson more or less singlehandedly created the recognition that the analyst's subjectivity is crucial. (Levenson himself will tell you that everything he has ever said he learned from Edward Tauber, his analyst. As much as I admired Tauber myself, I can't agree.) Prior to Levenson's work, the analyst's subjectivity had not really been theorized, or had been theorized as countertransference in the problematic sense. There were exceptions of course—Winnicott, Searles, Benjamin Wolstein, Edward Tauber, Janet Rioch, Sarah Tower, Margaret Little, Paula Heimann, and others—but Levenson was the first to make the analyst's subjectivity the core of a psychoanalytic point of view. In so doing, he also brought the first generation of interpersonal psychoanalysis—Sullivan, Fromm, and Thompson—into the modern era.

That is, he is responsible, with Benjamin Wolstein, for the existence of contemporary interpersonal psychoanalysis. But most of all, Levenson deserves to be known as a unique writer, the author of a perspective that should be identified with him alone. He has been the greatest contemporary influence on my own work, and I know that Philip Bromberg, Darlene Ehrenberg, and many of our colleagues feel the same way.

In 2005 I had the pleasure of republishing Ed's first two books, *The Fallacy of Understanding* and *The Ambiguity of Change*, in the *Psychoanalysis in a New Key* book series. Recently, Ed's classic collection of articles *The Purloined Self*, first published in 1991, appeared in this same series. And now I am honored most of all to offer a collection of articles by Edgar Levenson that have never before appeared in book form. *Interpersonal Psychoanalysis and the Enigma of Consciousness* is composed of work by Levenson that has appeared since *The Purloined Self*. We are all lucky and grateful that Alan Slomowitz edited this collection, as well as *The Purloined Self*. Without his devotion to the task, neither book would have appeared.

In this collection Levenson elaborates on the themes that have preoccupied him from the beginning: the creation and development of interpersonal psychoanalysis, the analyst's use of his/her own experience, and most of all, the nature of psychoanalytic process. Levenson is impatient with the imposition of meaning on experience, labeling it "metapsychology." He believes that new meanings, thoughts, and feelings come about unpredictably, and by themselves, once the treatment deconstructs the old patterns and narratives. The creation of instability is Levenson's aim; interpretations designed to create new meanings are less interesting, and certainly less profound.

There is no recipe, no theory of technique, for deconstruction. Levenson shows us, and convinces us, that we never know exactly what we are doing, or why whatever we did made the difference it did. Or *whether* what we did made the difference. Or even what the difference was that we thought the treatment made! Levenson never stands still. The ground is always shifting under his feet, and under ours as we read him.

You will enjoy these essays. They are unlike the writing of anyone else in psychoanalysis. Levenson is not only profound, he is also a brilliant literary stylist. And he is funny. You will laugh out loud sometimes as you read this book, and you will often smile ruefully. You will be glad you read it.

Donnel B. Stern, Ph.D.

New York

Preface

For the second time in a year I have had the privilege to edit a book by Edgar Levenson, perhaps the premier theorist and exponent of Interpersonal Psychoanalysis for over 50 years. Dr. Levenson's ubiquitous turn from "what does it mean" to "what is going on around here" still echoes in his writings. As you will also notice Dr. Levenson added an important subtext to his famous aphorism, "try not to be helpful." This is his playful variation of the Hippocratic oath of "do no harm." This book, *Interpersonal Psycho-analysis and the Enigma of Consciousness*, contains selected papers of Dr. Levenson's writings since the publication of *The Purloined Self* in 1991, and newly reissued by Routledge in 2016. Since he continues to write and we could not include all of his papers in this volume we may well have to publish a fifth book in a couple of years.

In this book, we have taken a different approach in organizing the chapters. We grouped chapters into three distinct parts. Our goal was to add additional theoretical coherence to the book and to demonstrate how Dr. Levenson's thinking has both evolved yet stayed on point over the years. The chapters appear in chronological order within each part, with one exception, the very first chapter of the first part, "The Unfolding of Psychoanalysis: From Interpersonal Psychiatry to Interpersonal Psycho-analysis." The first chapter, titled "An Interpersonal Therapist," was initially published in 1998 in a book called *Why I Became a Therapist?* and is unlikely to have been widely read by many of us. This chapter wonderfully captures Dr. Levenson at his best and gives us a window into the personal and professional circumstances of his life. He describes not "why" he became an analyst but "how" he became one. Although he does tell us that perhaps his father was exasperated by all his "why's" of childhood.

In the first chapter Dr. Levenson sets the stage for all that will follow. He writes, "I became a skeptic . . . that the truth of all knowledge must always be in question, and that true inquiry was a process of doubting." Toward the end of this chapter, Dr. Levenson writes about becoming an analyst: "I think I fell into it, through a congeries of converging needs, and corrections of errors made in my life choices . . ." Echoing the theme in his first book, *The Fallacy of Understanding*, he writes "That therapy consists of just such a series of falling into enactments with the patient (transformations) and then creative extrications" (Levenson, 1972). And so Dr. Levenson embarks on his journey of how he views the work and theory of Harry Stack Sullivan as the foundations of Interpersonal Psychoanalysis. At the same time he explores and explains why Sullivan's thinking is not per se psychoanalysis. Participant-observation is crucial but not enough. One needs inquiry, transference-countertransference, dreams and memories as well as the "transformation of that data as it is processed in a nonlinear fashion" by both the patient and the analyst. This involves the use of the detailed inquiry in a deconstructive way, viewing transference-countertransference as a field of inattended interpersonal transactions and an enactment of the material under discussion.

All of the chapters in this book have been previously published. However, as with the first chapter, several of them were first published in books or journals that are not widely known or are no longer available. Chapter 5, "A Monopedal version of Interpersonal Psychoanalysis," was first published in 1995 in a short-lived journal, *The Review of Interpersonal Psychoanalysis*. Here Dr. Levenson succinctly (while standing on one foot so to speak, see the article!) states his definition of Interpersonal Psychoanalysis: "Interpersonal psychoanalysis may be defined as the science of omissions." This is an interpersonal event, as it means "something is *left out* in a discourse between people." Echoing Rabbi Hillel: The rest is commentary.

Part II, "Psychoanalytic Process," groups articles focused more specifically on psychoanalytic praxis with particular emphasis on the key topics of transference and countertransference. In Chapter 8, "Standoffs, Impasses and Stalemates," Dr. Levenson "suggests that psychoanalysis works by showing the patient how it *doesn't* work when the therapist sets out to help the patient with some problems." People enter therapy because they actually desire to "perfect their neurosis" and not to change. As analysts we must recognize that we are pressing on what (quoting Wynn in 1958) he calls the "rubber fence" that surrounds every family. We build networks of inattentions and dissociations to avoid losing the sense of security from our caregivers and resulting loss of self-esteem. Our function as analysts is using the detailed inquiry to challenge the boundaries of the family narrative. We try and see what is not supposed to be seen and speak what is not to be spoken. However, and this is most crucial, our goal is to not have the patient submit to our views, but rather feel free to challenge us, ask us the unaskable, "to wonder what the therapist does not see or allow to be seen." Without a heightened awareness of our own participation then "psychoanalysis becomes an attempt to influence the patient . . . And influence is never fully benign . . ."

In Chapter 10, "Beyond Countertransference: Aspects of the Analyst's Desire," Dr. Levenson reiterates his key insight "that the interaction of the therapist and patient always enacts the problem under inquiry. Interpretation is simultaneously a transferential enactment. Analyzing this enactment as a reiterative replay of the problem is what carries the therapeutic leverage." The last chapter of this part, "Psychoanalysis and the Rite of Refusal," provides a summary. He addresses what he calls the failures of our efforts, the "refusal" of the patient. He lists five: fear of influence (wanting change but not to *be* changed), fear of helplessness, fear of expulsion (from the group/family), fear of growing up (staying forever young), and the joy of blowing things up (the dark irrational aspects of human desire).

Part III, "The Philosophy of Psychoanalytic Theory and Practice," contains many different chapters, a number of which appeared in books and not in psychoanalytic journals. Chapter 19, "The Enigma of the Unconscious," and almost the title of this book, opens with McLuhan's famous quote that Dr. Levenson has used several times: "We don't know who discovered water, but we do know it wasn't a fish." As analysts we must always acknowledge that we are immersed in our world and changed by it. We are all tapping into a creative and cohesive, but largely out-of-awareness process taking place between analyst and patient. "We do not cure; we do our work and cure happens." This out-of-awareness is not a result of repression but rather because most thought is unconscious, inattended. Dr. Levenson writes: "I think we cure people by tapping into and participating in a largely unconscious—with a bubble of awareness—process . . . The mind is a field phenomenon, a network, a web . . . It takes others to extend that network and the extension may be, in itself, restorative." This bubble of awareness and how it expands and contracts is the very *Enigma of Consciousness*. It is obscure and perhaps ultimately unknowable. Dr. Levenson has shifted in his thinking, now believing this enigma represents his belief that the binary of conscious/unconscious or intrapsychic/interpersonal are false dichotomies. These bubbles of consciousness rise to the surface and burst with more right behind. We find ourselves trying to grasp or catch the bubbles, much like the young child who excitedly blows bubbles, runs gleefully after them and just as she grasps them, they burst and are gone. And so she starts over again, much as we fall into an enactment, unravel it only fall into the next one.

Chapter 20, "Freud's Dilemma, On Writing Greek and Thinking Jewish," highlights the schism in psychoanalysis between the classical and interpersonal perspectives. This is the split between those who believe in one Truth and those that believe in the Many. The Greeks (through Plato) believed there was one true answer. The rabbis of the Talmud believed in an infinity of meanings. This is another critical aspect of psychoanalysis. It "does not reach for understanding, it pursues the singularity of the patient's experience, wherever it might lead." We can augment and facilitate this process without needing to conceptualize it clearly. Psychoanalytic positions need to be fluid. Textual fluidity and open-endedness are the essence of our work. The conceptual and theoretical splits and dichotomies are not really so stark and rigid.

An added gem to this book is the Epilogue—an excerpt of a wide-ranging interview with Dr. Levenson by Irwin Hirsch and Victor Iannuzzi. The interview and a number of articles by colleagues was published in a special edition of *Contemporary Psychoanalysis* in 2005. We are pleased to provide a link that will give readers of this book free access to the entire issue.

The link to the interview is: www.tandfonline.com/doi/abs/10.1080/00107530.2005.10747269

This link also appears at the end of the Epilogue as well as the link to special issue of *Contemporary Psychoanalysis*.

This Preface cannot do justice to the wonderful breadth and depth of Dr. Levenson's clinical and theoretical writing and thinking, to his truly unique, powerful, and influential perspective on psychoanalysis. His writings demonstrate a broad range of reading and thinking across the Psychoanalytic spectrum. While he draws on Freud, Klein, Sullivan, Fromm, Thomson, Kohut, Bion, Lacan, Gill, literature and philosophy, he is his own voice. He is serious and thoughtful and simultaneously playful and full of wit and charm. His voice has defined Interpersonal Psychoanalysis for over 50 years.

I am honored to have another opportunity to thank Dr. Donnel Stern, Editor, *Psychoanalysis in a New Key* Book Series, for giving me this unique and rewarding opportunity to work with Dr. Levenson. Working with Dr. Levenson is a combination of detailed effort (just like the inquiry) as well as intense joy. For me this was an intellectual and clinical journey that I did not want to end. Dr. Levenson is gracious and collegial, wonderful and inspiring. I will greatly miss our meeting every few weeks to discuss the book and review our progress. I hope he decides to publish that fifth book.

Alan Slomowitz, Ph.D.
New York

Acknowledgments

I want to express my heartfelt appreciation to the two people without whom this book would never have been realized. First, to Don Stern, editor of the *Psychoanalysis in a New Key* book series, whose support, encouragement, and dogged persistence mobilized me to finally move on this project: and second, to Alan Slomowitz, inestimable editor of both this compendium and the reissued *The Purloined Self*, who conceptualized, organized, and did the hard work of bringing it to production. They are both my treasured colleagues at the William Alanson White Institute that has been for over six decades my professional home, intrinsic to my life and my creative development.

Edgar Levenson, M.D.

Permissions

The chapters listed below were originally published in *Contemporary Psychoanalysis and Psychoanalytic Dialogues*. They are reprinted with permission from Taylor & Francis, LLC:

Chapter 3   1992   Harry Stack Sullivan: from interpersonal psychiatry to interpersonal psychoanalysis.

Chapter 4   1993   Shoot the messenger: interpersonal aspects of the analyst's interpretations.

Chapter 6   2002   The last shall be first: some observations on the evolution of Interpersonal Psychoanalysis.

Chapter 7   2006   Fifty years of evolving Interpersonal Psychoanalysis.

Chapter 8   1991   Standoffs, impasses, and stalemates.

xviii Acknowledgments

Chapter 9	1992	Mistakes, errors, and oversights.
Chapter 10	1994	Beyond countertransference: aspects of the analyst's desire.
Chapter 11	1996	Aspects of self-revelation and self-disclosure.
Chapter 13	2003	On seeing what is said: visual aids to the psychoanalytic process.
Chapter 14	2009	The enigma of the transference.
Chapter 15	2012	Psychoanalysis and the rite of refusal.
Chapter 16	1994	The uses of disorder: Chaos theory and psychoanalysis.
Chapter 17	1996	The politics of interpretation.
Chapter 18	1998	Awareness, insight, and learning.
Chapter 19	2001	The enigma of the unconscious.
Chapter 20	2001	Freud's dilemma: on writing Greek and thinking Jewish.
Chapter 23	2011	Deeper, wider: some comments on the Gill: Bromberg correspondence.
Chapter 24	2011	Lost in translation.
Epilogue	2005	Levenson, E.A., Hirsch, I., Iannuzzi, V., Interview with Edgar Levenson.

Reprinted with kind permission from Jason Aronson:

Chapter 1	1998	An interpersonal therapist. In J. Reppen (Ed.). *Why I Became A Psychotherapist*. New Jersey: Jason Aronson, pp. 209–214.
Chapter 21	2001	Creativity, genius and divine madness. In J. Petrucelli and K. Stuart (Eds). *Hungers and Compulsions*. New Jersey: Jason Aronson, pp. 233–244.

Reprinted with kind permission from *Contemporary Psychotherapy Review:*

Chapter 2	1991	Back to the future: the new psychoanalytic revisionism.

Reprinted with kind permission from *The Review of Interpersonal Psychoanalysis:*

Chapter 5	1995	A Monopedal version of Interpersonal Psychoanalysis.

Reprinted with kind permission from *The Journal of the American Psychoanalytic Association:*

Chapter 12   2000   Psychoanalytic love and therapeutic despair.

Reprinted with kind permission from Taylor & Francis, LLC:

Chapter 25   2016   Psychoanalysis, the uncanny, and the banalization of evil. In J. Petrucelli and S. Schoen (Eds). *Unknowable, Unspeakable and Unsprung: Psychoanalytic Perspectives on Truth, Scandal, Secrets and Lies.* London, New York: Routledge, pp. 209–215.

The following quotes were used with permission:

Chapter 10, Excerpt from T.S. Eliot (1936), reprinted with kind permission from *The Wasteland* from *Collected Poems* 1909–1962 by T.S. Eliot. Copyright 1936 by Houghton Mifflin Harcourt Publishing Company. Copyright © renewed 1964 by Thomas Stearns Eliot. Reprinted by permission of Houghton Mifflin Harcourt Publishing Company. All rights reserved.

Excerpt from T.S. Eliot (1936), from *The Wasteland* from *Collected Poems* 1909–1962 by T.S. Eliot. Copyright 1936 by Houghton Mifflin Harcourt Publishing Company. Copyright © renewed 1964 by Thomas Stearns Eliot. Reprinted with kind permission by Faber and Faber Limited, UK, with non-exclusive gratis permission in the English language throughout the World Excluding US from Print and EBook.

Chapter 25, Excerpt from Rilke, R.M. (1923/2001), *Duino Elegies*, Reprinted with kind permission by North Point Press.

Chapters 6 and 25, Excerpt from Dostoevsky (1961). Excerpt(s) from *Notes from the Underground* by Fyodor Dostoyevsky, translated by Andrew MacAndrew, translation copyright © 1961, renewed © 1989 by Andrew MacAndrew. Used by permission of New American Library, an imprint of Penguin Publishing Group, a division of Penguin Random House LLC. All rights reserved. *Notes from the Underground.* Reprinted with kind permission of Signet Classics.

Introduction

Being now into my tenth decade, I'd held some hope of finally understanding how psychoanalytic therapy worked. I do believe I have attained a relatively clear sense of the praxis, the Act; but what it acts *on* is another story altogether. How psychoanalytic praxis affects its changes must remain somewhat obscure, since it touches upon the enigma of human consciousness. The paradigmatic shift in psychoanalytic thinking that came with interpersonalism was the acknowledgment that consciousness is coconstructed; that is, that a person's sense of being in the world and what that world is, is constructed in interaction with others, most notably parental figures, but also siblings, teachers, friends, social groups, and the very sociocultural surround. Compare the penetrating gaze of an infant and a dog. The dog is trying to figure out what you want; the infant is trying to determine who or what you are. From infancy, through childhood, into adolescence and adulthood, the developing person depends on other's affirmations, assessments, and reflected appraisals in order to develop a worldview; generally referred to as sense of self, identity, or consciousness.

Underlying it all is a superordinate narrative that the person creates in order to understand what is going on out there and how to engage it. This narrative is, in Isaiah Berlin's application of Kant's term, "a crooked piece of timber," indeed (Berlin 2013). It is riddled with misinformation and, more significantly, omissions, inattentions, dissociations; the latter being enforced and thus not accessible to easy correction. They fall under the rubric of mystifications, originally a Marxist term, applied to psychoanalysis by R.D. Laing; a not-knowing, not-seeing what is there to be seen that is interpersonally induced (Laing, 1967). In H.S. Sullivan's version, the threat of becoming aware of anything that would provoke severe anxiety in the other, results in mystification, denial. Sullivan may have over-emphasized the "contagious" aspect of anxiety. I suspect that the profoundest anxiety results from the archaic fear of expulsion, exclusion, and loss of the necessary other, from the breast to the tribe. Ultimately, for whatever reason, one does not see what is there to be seen. It is necessary to close the eyes! [1]

Clearly there are limitations to trying to live according to the constraints of the narrative. Psychoanalysis providing an enriching of the person's ability to grasp the nuances of interaction would allow more flexibility; it would be, in essence, a semiotic education that would enrich the person's armamentarium of perceptions and responses. Neurosis is a kind of banality and psychoanalysis is at once a re-education and a corrective experience.

What is it then that the analyst does? If the sine qua non of medical practice is Hippocrates, "First do no harm"; the equivalent dictum in psychoanalytic practice is "Try hard *not* to be helpful." The patient tells her story: the analyst listens and inquires. The intent of this detailed inquiry is not to clarify, create a better narrative, provide a more lucid explanation; but, rather, to *unpack* the narrative, to reveal the gaps, the absences, the avoidances, the signs of distress when taboo areas are approached.

The therapist's inquiry becomes participation. It is impossible to listen neutrally, to not bring one's own self-narrative and blind spots into play. Therein lies the birth of transference and countertransference as seen in interpersonal therapy—not distortion projected onto, but mutual mystifications mutually constructed and sustained. For me, the most astonishing part of the psychoanalytic interaction is the way what is talked about comes to be simultaneously *played out* between the therapist and patient, with remarkable consistency if one is looking for it. Speech is behavior. This uncanny confluence of minds has been described by neuropsychologists as right brain talking to right brain, which is, I believe, a bit over-concretized but does define the trope (Siegel, 1999).

Still, all this is a précis of our algorithm, what we do when we do what we know how to do. How and why the patient responds or does not is much harder to designate. This is not to deny that character and constitution exist and are relevant, nor that there is attachment experience, needs, and drives. But I cannot see restitution or repair as sufficient, although it is certainly a significant, albeit collateral, event in therapy.

We are the acolytes of the patient's process, her flow of consciousness. We see this mysterious process emerging in a kaleidoscopic way, as issues emerge and drift away, as focuses come and go, as dreams and associations—both the patient's and ours—reveal the turning of internal wheels. But ultimately, change does not come at our bidding.

How do the rational algorithm of psychoanalytic engagement and the mysterious flow of consciousness interact? We have traditionally thought of it as dialectical, an unresolvable duality in our praxis (Foehl, 2016). One moves back and forth between the two perspectives, rather like a gestalt leap (see Rubin figures). That is to say, one finds oneself listening either to the "interpersonal" or to the "intrapsychic" in what feels like a self-state leap.

The fallacy lies in what I believe is an entirely false dichotomy. The interpersonal is not in dialectical opposition to the intrapsychic; but is rather a manifestation of it, a subset. These are the issues that have intrigued and occupied me and, that, I trust, are addressed in the following chapters.

Note

1. This, of course, a reference to Freud's dream after his father's death; "it is requested to close the eyes." Opening the eyes, the third eye, has been an almost universal metaphor for consciousness, awareness (see Levenson 1983).

References

Berlin, I. (2013). *The Crooked Timber of Humanity: Chapters in the History of Ideas*. Princeton, NJ: Princeton University Press.

Foehl, J.C. (2016). Hedgehogs at the gate. *Contemporary Psychoanalysis*, 52(3): 434–456.

Laing, R.D. (1967). *The Politics of Experience*. New York: Pantheon Books.

Levenson, E. (1983). *The Ambiguity of Change: An Inquiry into the Nature of Psychoanalytic Reality*. New York: Basic Books.

Siegel, D.J. (1999). *The Developing Mind: Towards a Neurobiology of Interpersonal Experience*. New York: Guilford Press.

Part I

The unfolding of Interpersonal Pyschoanalysis, from Interpersonal Psychiatry to Interpersonal Psychoanalysis

Chapter 1

An interpersonal therapist[1]

Gregory Bateson (1979) said that the point of the probe is always in the heart of the explorer; that is, every voyage of discovery leads back to the self. As I understand it, this is the theme of this book, namely, how the therapist's own life experience inhabits and defines his or her theoretical and clinical understandings.

In the process of thinking about this issue, an iconic memory popped into my mind. Iconic memories are those highly stylized and persistent accounts we have of our lives, memories that loom like monoliths through the mists of the past. Their tangibility is deceptive, however, inasmuch as they seem very clear to us until they are stressed, and then they fracture and deconstruct in very odd ways.

My iconic memory, par excellence, is of being in a synagogue with my father. I was, I suppose, about 8 years old. My father was not a religious man. He was, rather, a sort of diffident Marxist, unlike several of my uncles who were really rabid and unregenerate Stalinists. We were in synagogue because my mother—who did not entirely believe in God, but was afraid of Him—thought that my father should do his paternal duty and take me there. It was an Orthodox synagogue with the women upstairs, the entire service in Hebrew, and notably lacking any of the choral effects, organ music, or other chic, "reformed," *goyish* elaborations that would have sent my grandfather spinning in his grave.

At any rate, there came a point in the service when the doors of the Ark, which contains the sacred scrolls, were opened, and the members of the congregation covered their bowed heads with their prayer shawls, and looked fixedly at the floor. "Don't look," said my father. "Why not?" I asked (already a troublemaker). "Because you'll die on the spot," he said.

4 Unfolding of Interpersonal Psychoanalysis

That's like telling a kid not to touch wet paint. So, I glued my eyes to the floor, dreading their inexorable upward drift. I would look! I would see! And that would be the end of little Edgar.

I did, however, sneak a sidelong look at my father, and to my absolute horror, he was staring straight ahead, totally unperturbed! I can—to this day—still see with total clarity the tiny red capillaries in his eyes. Now, that's where the iconic memory ends. I don't know whether I then looked, or if I expected him to drop dead, or if I decided that he must be immune to God's vengeance. I don't know why he constrained me in such a draconian fashion (a variant of the Old Testament story of the Hebrew who rushed forward to steady the unbalanced Ark and was killed on the spot for his troubles). Was he exasperated with my endless whys? Was he kidding? In his Freudian Unconscious (not a concept either of us was cognizant of at that time) did he hope I'd drop dead? Did I hope he'd drop dead? The more I think about the incident, the less clear it becomes. As I said, this heavy over-determination is a cardinal characteristic of iconic memories.

So I became a skeptic. Or, maybe I became a disenchanted kid, and later a skeptic. The ancient Greek skeptics were defined by their belief that the truth of all knowledge must always be in question, and that true inquiry was a process of doubting. There is no absolute truth, and inquiry into the premises of belief is more fruitful than belief itself. This is, I think, not the same as Jewish skepticism, wherein truth is not given by authority, but must be arrived at individually.[2] I suspect, but I am not sure, that the classic skepticism is more austere. Truth remains always elusive and in question.

Somewhat later, I found myself sympathetic to the anthropologist Kluckhohn's (Kluckhohn and Murray, 1953) claim that every culture is defined by pervasive and profoundly unexamined premises about the nature of time, space, and reality. This led me quite naturally to the cultural relativism current in the 1940s and 1950s, when anthropologists Benedict, Mead, Whorf, Lee, and Sapir were questioning the ethnocentricity of Western man and his view of "primitive" cultures.

Ethnology seemed to me to be a very attractive career, but I'd already gone through medical school, the usual route for bright, but uninspired, Jewish boys in a world that did not, in 1943, permit very many other options. I might add that my father was a physician, which certainly influenced my choice. I really did not have much ambition beyond getting into a medical school, which seemed nigh on impossible, and, when to my surprise, I found myself to be a newly minted M.D., I didn't quite know what to do with it. I was too prone to panic to make a good surgeon and internal medicine seemed like a depressing and overly intellectualized business.

After my internship, a residency in neurology became available, so I took it. I then spent 2 years (1948–1950) in the Army Medical Corps, mostly in Berlin. The army, in its inimitable fashion, had no category for neurologists, so I was designated a neuropsychiatrist, and a neuropsychiatrist I became. On my return to the States, I entered psychoanalytic training, quite possibly my first entirely proactive career move, a decision that seemed to me then, and seems to me now, an enterprising and creative way to do what I wished without admitting that after all those years of unremitting and agonistic striving, medicine was not what I really wanted to do. Nor was I about to go live in a straw hut and eat witchetty grubs (for all I know, Margaret Mead lived on tinned foie gras, but that's not what I'd been led to believe). Oh—and also I needed a personal analysis rather badly, although I didn't quite admit that to myself. Undergoing a "training analysis" seemed like a face-saving way to get therapy, since psychoanalytic treatment, in those presumably less enlightened days, was not considered an entirely acceptable undertaking. Being an analyst was somewhat like being a syphilologist—treating the disease was OK, having it was not.

I applied to the William Alanson White Institute because of its strongly cultural orientation, particularly manifest in Erich Fromm's teaching. I was not as aware of Harry Stack Sullivan's teachings, nor of Clara Thompson's. The White Institute's position was a heady amalgam of the views of these three innovators—Fromm's social (Marxist) psychology; Thompson's Ferenczi-derived, democratized psychoanalysis; and Sullivan's interpersonal psychiatry (note, *not* psychoanalysis), which was heavily influenced by Adolf Meyer's institutional psychiatry. Moreover, White was decidedly different from the New York Psychoanalytic Institute. Candidates were considered colleagues, dissension and challenge were appreciated, and psychologists were accepted for training.[3] I must confess that, although apprised of it, I had no real interest in the intense political struggle taking place between White and the American Psychoanalytic Association.[4]

I wish I could claim that becoming an analyst was the culmination of a sequence of focused experiences, but I think I fell into it, through a congeries of converging needs, and corrections of errors made in my life choices. Is it chance or destiny? Actually, I suspect it is how many people

6 Unfolding of Interpersonal Psychoanalysis

arrive at their destinations. This echoes the theme of my first book, *The Fallacy of Understanding*, that therapy consists of just such a series of falling into enactments with the patient (transformations) and then creative extrications (Levenson, 1972). That is, therapy consists of a backward reaching process: getting into messes, recognizing and delineating them, and then working one's way through and out—not so dissimilar to how one arrives at one's life. Regardless of metapsychological differences, all analysts meticulously monitor their deviation from the standardized technique, their lapses from ideal participation, be it neutrality or authentic interaction. Therapy is a series of lapses and corrections. Isn't that what countertranference is all about? I do not believe that a therapist stays ahead of the patient, leading him or her to the promised land. Sullivan would certainly agree; wasn't it what he had in mind when he said, "God keep me from a clever psychoanalyst."

It would appear, again in retrospect, that it was not incidental that I gave so much space in *The Ambiguity of Change* to Freud's dream the night before his father's funeral (Levenson, 1983). According to Krüll (1979), it was quite possibly the key to Freud's critical abandoning of his seduction theory. In the dream he reads on a board the following message: "It is requested to close the eyes." As I pointed out, it is intriguing that the priestesses of the Eleusian mysteries were called *mystes* and were bound to secrecy. "Mystery" is from the Greek *myein*—to close the eyes! It was nothing short of a blessing for me to discover a community of psycho-analysts who thought, *pace* little Edgar, that opening one's eyes was desirable, and moreover, that raising one's eyes—subjecting authority to a good, hard look—was not a likely invitation to instant death.

Were I to be in a Freudian institute—assuming I'd survived—I would still remain a skeptic. One can no more change one's characterological style than a leopard can change its spots. Even the White Institute has its share of constitutional conservatives, crypto-Freudians. But I suppose that had I been in the New York Psychoanalytic in the fifties, they would have wished I'd looked up at the wrong time in the service.

It is consistent with my avowed skepticism to be skeptical of the usual explanations of how one becomes anything. So I have elided life experiences that helped shape my path: teachers, books, experiential epiphanies. I like to think that I have become what I always was. My historical tradition is a variety of Jewish freethinking, with an outsider's sense of irony and play, a lack of conviction about authority, and a traditional entitlement to question what I am told. The post-World War II explosion of interest in cultural perspectivism, the foment of intellectual activity that takes place occasionally in the world (Renaissance Italy, Berlin in the twenties, Paris in the thirties, and New York in the post-World War II diaspora) was current when I returned from the army after a 2-year breather, an involuntary yet very welcome interlude in a lifetime of dogged study. It was, as I have indicated, an easy step into psychoanalysis, which was then an honored and, believe it or not, relatively well-remunerated profession. Philip Lehrman, who was an early Freudian and a close friend of my father, told me that in the early days of psychoanalysis, he paid patients 25 cents a session to come to be analyzed. No such sacrifices were required of me. I was paid 15 dollars a session, which was ample recompense in those halcyon days.

Sometimes, though, in the hour of the wolf, I wonder if indeed I became what I was or whether I became what I am. Is adult personality an evocation of a unique core self, or are there, as Sullivan suspected, many selves, many outcomes? Would I have become the same person had I done something else? Is there, in a parallel universe, another me, the successful cosmetic surgeon or scriptwriter, driving a Mercedes and wearing gold chains? It is certainly more comforting to stick to my original conceit—that there is a core personality, which is, one hopes, approximated, however inchoately, over time—even if I sound a bit like the parrot in Woody Allen's movie who sings, "I've Got to Be Me."

Notes

1. First published in 1998, in *Why I Became a Psychotherapist*, Ed. J. Reppen. New Jersey, Jason Aronson, pp. 209–214.
2. See Handelman (1982) for an interesting exegesis of Rabbinic thought in psychoanalysis.
3. At that time, 1952, on a somewhat compromised basis, but shortly thereafter on full parity.
4. Times have, indeed, changed. In 1994 I was made an honorary member of the American Psychoanalytic Association.

References

Bateson, G. (1979). *Mind and Nature: A Necessary Unity*. New York: Dutton.
Handelman, S. (1982). *The Slayers of Moses: The Emergence of Rabbinic Interpretation in Modern Literary Theory*. Albany, NY: State University of New York Press.

8 Unfolding of Interpersonal Psychoanalysis

Kluckhohn, C., and Murray, H.A. (1953). Personality formation: the determinants. In *Personality in Nature, Society and Culture*. New York: Knopf, pp. 53–67.

Krüll, M. (1979). *Freud und sein Vater*. Munich: C.H. Beck.

Levenson, E. (1972). *The Fallacy of Understanding*. New York: Basic Books.

Levenson, E. (1983). *The Ambiguity of Change: An Inquiry into the Nature of Psychoanalytic Reality*. New York: Basic Books.

Chapter 2

Back to the future
The new psychoanalytic revisionism[1]

My father, who was a family physician, told me this story: A Russian physician (in the days before antibiotics) is called to the bedside of a tailor dying of pneumonia. As he is about to expire, his wife timidly suggests a peasant remedy—blinis with sour cream. The physician, being a pragmatist, figures, "Why not?" They spoon the blinis into the moribund tailor and the physician leaves. The next day, to the physician's astonishment, the tailor is totally recovered. Meticulously, he notes in his diary, "Blinis with sour cream, a specific for pneumonia."

About a week later, he is called to the bedside of a butcher, who is also dying of pneumonia. Referring to his notes, he feeds him the curative blinis with sour cream. With the first mouthful, the butcher's eyes roll back and he expires. The physician amends his diary: "Blinis with sour cream, a specific for pneumonia, *only in tailors!*"

This *reductio ad absurdum* of the scientific-medical model is not so irrelevant to my thesis. I would like to suggest that psychoanalytic theory suffers from a tragic flaw. Like the Russian doctor, it, too, wishes to be "scientific": to define the general principles, the "set of transcendental human universals" to which the specifics of experience must adhere (Bruner, 1990). Psychoanalytic principles, we insist, must apply with equal relevance to the tailor and the butcher. In addition, we wish it to be progressive, to unfold in a linear fashion, always toward greater relevance and clarity. As Habermas put it, "In principle, [there is] an ultimate answer to every emerging scientific question" (Habermas, 1971, p. 32).

If it cannot meet these criteria, we fear that it is merely a craft—not a science—a most unhappy contingency for psychoanalysts who, alas, suffer from a severe case of science envy. We are still laboring under an

10 Unfolding of Interpersonal Psychoanalysis

anachronistic, medicalized version of science bequeathed to us by Freud who never doubted for a moment that psychoanalysis was a natural science and that his famous "Project" was entirely a neuropsychological construct (Habermas, 1971, p. 246).

Parenthetically, this traditional psychoanalytic model of science is of nineteenth-century science now displaced by relativity theory and quantum uncertainty. One need only refer to Stephen Hawking's popular book, *A Brief History of Time*, to realize that pure science is a much more imaginative and playful game than we have been led to believe by medicine's austere Koch's postulates (Hawkings, 1988). It turns out that in pure science, one may invent a theory long before there is *any* substantive data to justify it. Theories in mathematics and physics may come into play long after their invention, when some new and unexpicable (by the old science) data appears. "What if?" is as much the cardinal question of pure science as the traditional, "How does this work?"

So if science is the search for the universal principles implicit in experience, psychoanalysis does not, by my definition, meet the criterion. Rather, psychoanalysis is the search for the unique patternings of experience that characterize each person, as unequivocally as fingerprints. It is true that these singular variations take place within a certain limited number of parameters set by biology: needs for nurturance, contact, sexual drives, separation anxieties, social needs. But, ultimately, psychoanalysis is the examination of a unique life in its social matrix. To quote Habermas again, "[For social sciences] . . . The object of inquiry is not Mankind, but the world in which the historical and social life of man expresses itself" (Habermas, 1971, p. 146).

This cultural immersion is as true of the analyst and his/her referred metapsychology as it is of the patient. Psychoanalysis and its goals are so tied into the culture and its expectations, tacit and spoken, that an Argentinian Kleinian and a British Kleinian are probably doing different things, using the same language to quite different ends. Kurzweil has elaborated this thesis, namely that each country creates the psychoanalysis it needs, although, she says, it does so unconsciously (Kurzweil, 1989). Freud knew that. With his immense antipathy to America, he foretold that psychoanalysis would be subverted to American purposes, discarding his Austrian austerity: the repression of gratification and the submission of instinct to society would give way to self-gratification and an idiotic optimism.

If psychoanalytic meaning will always be perspectivistic, ambiguous, and context-dependent, then not only will the ostensibly same metapsychology be understood and applied differently in different countries synchronically (at the same time), but in the same country over time (diachronically) a given metapsychology will show a decided drift, changing outline and meaning as the culture changes. As I shall suggest, one may track significant changes within decades.

As Marshall McLuhan said, we don't know who discovered water, but we do know it wasn't a fish (McLuhan, 1964). It is very difficult to see what one is immersed in and we, along with our theories, our way of working, our expectations of outcome and our patients, are all immersed in the same sea (Levenson, 1972). I, for one, can remember when males (patients and therapists alike) lived in dread of their "latent homosexuality" overtaking them. Then came the next decade when the "schizophrenogenic" mother, like some manifestation of Durga, ruled supreme. Now, in our current wisdom, the not-good-enough mother is the subject of our inquiries. What are all these but culturally determined shifts in gender perception? Yet, psychoanalysis often tends to see these mirrorings of its own culture as universal scientific verities.[2]

By deeming itself acultural, above culture, traditional psychoanalysis is necessarily also conservative, revisionist and, albeit unwittingly, operating in the service of the status quo. Yet, the history of psychoanalytic ideas is a veritable palimpsest of cultural change and circularity. What are dynamics? Can they be stated as culturally defined? Where are the hysterics of yesteryear? Where were the narcissists of today? (Apparently, hysterics are alive and well in Vienna, where a woman is still expected to scream and jump onto a chair in the presence of a mouse (Kurzweil, 1989, p. 317)). Were Freud's sexual dynamics beyond culture, universal; or did they reflect Victorian mores that did not simply repress sexuality, but were extremely erotic and sadomasochistic while simultaneously positing restraint? Was the dark side (well-documented) of Victorian sexuality a result of repression? Did hysterical symptoms develop as an escape from repression? Or were they pathognomonic of the paradoxical message: Act repelled, then do anything you wish in the privacy of the bedchamber? We laugh at accounts of Victorian ladies blushing and swooning, calling chair legs "limbs": we forget that they blushed because it was believed that women were in a constant state of sexual rut, barely in control, and extremely dangerous to themselves and to susceptible males.

The hysterics Freud saw at Charcot's clinic were not just suffering paralyses, they also threw swoons of the most overt sexual posturings. Sulloway points out that many of Charcot's patients were (presumably without the Master's knowledge) coached in advance by the staff about the requisite manifestations (Sulloway, 1979). He also very cleverly picks up, in the famous painting *cum* lithograph of Charcot's clinic at the Sâlpetrière by A. Brouillet (reprinted in virtually every book on Freud), that the young woman patient erotically swooning in the assistant's arms is replicating the position of a woman in the painting on the back wall of the room (Sulloway, 1979, p. 33). Freud, on his return to Vienna, had no question at all that 18-year-old Dora was—and reasonably ought to have been—sexually aroused by Herr K's sexual advances. So, was hysterical psychopathology a result of sexual repression or was it a complex response to the claims of a particular culture? Is it drive or what is done with drive?

Anyone following the cycles of popular culture as represented in the movies, our mythmaking machinery, can see how the view of sexual woman has shifted from the sweet things of the 1940s and 1950s to the rapacious man-consuming succubi of the 1980s (from the harridan in *Fatal Attraction* to *both* women in *Presumed Innocent*, the exploitative seductress and the sweet wife who coolly frames her husband for a murder she commits). Don't trifle with women is the message! As acknowledgment of female sexuality has surfaced, man's terror of women has kept pace. Are we returning to Dionysian mysteries where men were torn limb from limb by women acolytes? Dare we posit a new "Dionysis Complex"? Will there be renewed pressure for a return to pinioned womanhood? Yes, indeed! Consider the popularity of subsequent movies like *Pretty Woman*, which are gussied-up versions of the Cinderella story.

The shift in theory (*and* in the attention paid the theory) from the paternalistic "Name of the Father" Oedipal thesis of Freud and Anna Freud to the matriarchal *Mütterrecht* of Melanie Klein and her followers, the emerging emphasis on pre-Oedipal experience (that is, experience with mothering) parallels entirely the emergence of women from their role as man's handmaiden (one also notes that the British culture is far more at home with matriarchal leadership than is the teutonic). Psychoanalytic cure, some now believe, lies in restitution of defective nurturance (maternal), rather than in confronting neurotic bad faith (paternal). Presenting complaints have changed from conflict to deficit, from symptoms to difficulties in loving, work, and relatedness. Many of our recent patients might not have been considered in *need* of treatment 30 years ago.

If analysts are immersed in their own culture, if our concepts of treatment and cure are reflections of that culture, then we are all inevitably part of the problem we've set out to cure. We are not standing outside the patient's life, helping him/her to deal with reality. We are struggling with the same issues as the patient. Participant-observation becomes a case of not helping the patient distinguish what is real from what is not real. Rather, it is helping the patient understand and see how immersed he/she and we are in a perception of the world which is defined by our social experience, and the extent to which that perception either facilitates or much constricts the possibilities of—to use Jerome Bruner's term—"negotiating" the world successfully (Bruner, 1986).

There was a period, now 50 years ago, when a very powerful culturally oriented psychoanalysis developed as a consequence of the Nazi-inspired diaspora that brought to the United States many of the European analytic community. Their heady and often acrimonious encounters with American pragmatic psychiatry and psychoanalysis brought into unavoidable focus the cultural presuppositions that inhabited their positions.

Through the intercession of Clara Thompson, an American analyst who had worked with Ferenezi in Budapest, H.S. Sullivan became part of the cultural group of analysts, joining Horney, Fromm, and others who were attempting to synthesize the two cultures. (I would point out that Sullivan scrupulously called his theory Interpersonal *Psychiatry*, not psychoanalysis.)

Sullivan's position is somewhat ambiguous, and he is often considered acultural. Yet in his clinical work (see Kvarnes and Parloff, 1976) he was exquisitely attuned to the nuances of social experience; i.e., he knew that the patient would not be understood without a very clear sense of the context, the texture of the patient's life. If the patient grew up on an army base, Sullivan wanted to know, "Which base? When? What rank did his father hold?" For all Sullivan and Fromm's differences, they shared this social awareness. Fromm, of course, was invested in changing society to allow man to live more humanely. He felt that loneliness was the existential price of freedom. Sullivan was far less Utopian, holding adjustment to whatever the culture was as the necessary price of human socialization. He believed excruciating loneliness to be far more devastating than

14 Unfolding of Interpersonal Psychoanalysis

an over-investment in material goods (the earmark of the "Marketing Personality" of Fromm's jeremiads).

At any rate, that period of cultural awareness seems to have had its day. Freudians, object-relationists, self-psychologists, relationalists, and even some interpersonalists seem to believe that the particulars of human experience are of not much interest except to the extent that they illuminate general principles. The humble context of life, what Bruner called "folk psychology," has become once again "unscientific" (Bruner, 1990). Yet, in truth, as clinicians we often play by ear, *then* secondarily reframe our activity in acceptable formulaic terms. As Friedman not altogether facetiously put it, "Psychotherapy is a relationship interfered with by theory" (Friedman, 1988).

In spite of the current object-relations (especially British) claim that attention is paid to individual experience, most psychoanalytic formulations begin with the mythologized, universalized parents; either as the battle-field for warring instinct, or as defective caretakers, the Bad Parent, to be corrected in therapy by the ministrations of the Good Parent, the you-know-who. Certainly failures of nurturance take place. But I suspect that they are not as total or reflexive as current theory would have us believe. The terms of nurturance are complicated and imbedded in a cultural matrix. So the child is given and not given; gives and does not give. That the parents are the victims of *their* parents is not parti-cularly attended to by psychoanalysts although it is an article of faith for every family therapist. Most parents act badly in good faith. They are doing their best; they are doing what they have been taught to do. Unnurturant mothers had unnurturant mothers and, like the little fleas, on *ad infinitum.*

There is an excellent example of this parent-bashing in Margaret Little's account of her therapy with Winnicott. "He was 'shocked' when I told him how till the age of ten and over I had to 'rest' every afternoon in a darkened room with no toy or book. 'I really *hate* your mother,' he said" (Little, 1985). Come on! That was not at all an unusual program for children. *I* can remember when a rest in a darkened room every afternoon was considered a palliative for what was believed to be children's normally overstimulatable nervous systems.

Where does all this lead? There are several interesting consequences. As William Blake put it, people become what they behold. Their profound, unexamined assumptions about the nature of social reality come from their sociocultural experience and permeate their every belief and action. This must be as true for the analyst as it is for the patient, except that the analyst's training has presumably expanded his/her awareness of what he/she has become as a consequence of experience. Psychoanalysts ought to be experts, not authorities; we have no claim to superior wisdom or lifestyle. We do not cure by example, but by aware participation.

Since the patient's initial indoctrination into the nature of the world occurs very early in the family and persists over a very long period of time, we may assume that many of these assumptions about life are so taken as bedrock reality that it never *occurs* to the patient to see them, let alone question them. There are subsequent immersions in peer culture (usually when the child goes off to school) and, by gradients, in the outside world through direct experience, television, movies, even perhaps the soon-to-be vestigial written word. These larger parameters of experience may be concordant or very discordant with the earlier family experience. Obviously, later and wider circles of sociocultural experience are easier to deal with, since the commitment to belief should be far less imperative. Nevertheless, as social movements strongly attest, people can be very unquestioningly committed at the most extended circles of social, political, and religious community.

Why do people cling so to their worldview? Why are they so hard to change? This is, after all, the *cri de coeur* of psychoanalysts. Psychoanalysis works by examining why psychotherapy and the sweet voice of reason *don't* work; ergo the pre-eminence for psychoanalytic work of the "resistance and transference."

> People cling, with a certain tense franticness [sic], to certain idealizations of life which get them into a great deal of trouble; but the intensity with which they cling indicates that the ass [Balaam's ass]—the deeper, older part of personality—knows the thing isn't true, knows it isn't so.
>
> (Sullivan, 1953)

Interestingly, Sullivan got the story of Balaam's ass backwards! As you remember from the bible story, Balaam's ass saw the angel blocking Balaam's path. Balaam beat the ass three times for balking when Balaam saw nothing amiss. But the ass had stopped because something was there which Balaam could not see. I think the deeply unconscious part of the personality may balk because it senses a danger, a terrible price to moving on, not known to the conscious self.

I think the patient both knows and does not know. The answer is stratified. To repeat, I believe that at the deepest level are those beliefs which are pervasive, unexamined, and axiomatic, not open to question, as absolute in their influence as gravity and where questioning—if it occurs at all—provokes a kind of existential vertigo. Next are those beliefs that might be questioned, are not seen as ineffable, but where questioning them calls forth anxiety *in* the family. This is akin to Sullivan's contagious anxiety. If the family gets frightened by inquiry or behavior, the topic is disowned. The patient learns, as R.D. Laing put it, "To not know what he/she knows." This level is, I suspect, more accessible to analytic inquiry than the deeper level of unquestioned belief, since the anxiety elicited by questioning acts as a signal to the patient of something wrong. At the third level are those beliefs that become conflictual only at the interface of the patient and the outside world, when family primacy is at risk. They may cause relatively little difficulty within the family arena.

As I said, the infant and child must learn to negotiate his/her world, and the social community is the instrument of learning. Perhaps it is even an ethologically developed necessity. Humans are, after all, social animals. Expulsion from the group has been in pre-literate communities and even present in more sophisticated tribal rituals (one need only review the development of the psychoanalysis movement) the direst of threats, a virtual death sentence. Any violation of the canonicity, conscious or unconscious, of the group worldview may, by threatening expulsion, be enough to set into action the mechanisms of defense and denial.

It follows, from what I am postulating, that many neurotic operations are relatively functional in the family milieu, preserving family integrity. They only become nonfunctional in the outside world because they are maladaptive there and because to change would mean severing the vital connection to the family that, for better or worse, is all the patient has.

This leads to a most significant clinical observation. In working with supervisees, I am struck by how much they see themselves in alliance with the patient to work out his/her problems, however conceptualized. They view the patient's anxiety as coming from resistance to awareness. They often do not suspect the extent to which they are the *outsider*, the stranger talking to the patient across what Lyman Wynn called the "rubber fence" of the family (Wynn et al., 1958). Resistance is usually conceived of as resistance to insight, an internal process. I would suggest that resistance is often resistance to the outsider who threatens the integrity of the family worldview.

For example, as a candidate, my first supervisor at the White Institute was Meyer Maskin. Maskin was the Oscar Wilde of White, very clever and aphoristic. I was working with an adolescent boy, whose mother every morning would help him dress, putting on his stockings and shoes while he lay abed. My patient agreed enthusiastically with all my suggestions (increasingly outspoken) that his mother was possessive, infantilizing, inappropriate in her need to baby him (we hadn't yet thought of "narcissistic" as the ultimate clinical epithet), but nothing changed in their morning ritual. Maskin, wreathed in cigarette smoke, listened with his usual air of worldweariness, then drawled, "Say to him, 'God, your mother sounds like an awful Bitch!' and see what happens." So I did. To my astonishment, the patient nearly fell out of his chair. He seemed really shocked and upset—"possessive, infantilizing—okay . . . but, a BITCH!" The next morning he said to his mother, "Mother, I wish you would stop doing that." She looked surprised, said, "Oh. Okay," and never did it again.

I learned, to my absolute amazement, that the patient did not really take literally all the terrible things he was saying about his mother. It was a concession to the stranger. The patient tells us what we should feel about what they are telling us. They are not telling us initially what *they* feel. It is also often true that the parent who is nominally the most damaging is also the one to whom the patient owes the greatest successes in life. The therapist blithely supporting the patient in assessments about how terrible, unnurturing, destructive the parent is fails to see that the patient sees himself/herself (quite accurately) as sharing the same characteristics and will be wary of voluntarily exposing himself/herself to the therapist. Fortunately, the correction usually occurs quite naturally when the therapist develops a "countertransference"; that is, finds himself/herself struggling with a dislike of the patient for the very same traits the therapist so blithely denounced in the parents. "Like parent, like child" is far more than a truism.

I have found it very useful to consider that in working with patients we are trying to extract them from the family system and introduce them to a larger world. In this undertaking, we are first seen as the stranger, the enemy. The world we are trying to introduce them to is *our* world, which, for better or worse, may be over-identified with the culture. We are not

18   Unfolding of Interpersonal Psychoanalysis

especially in this particular cycle of psychoanalysis—very judgmental of our own social enactments. Psychoanalysts are rarely hermits or holy men, or even rebels. One finds more analysts in the Hamptons than in the Himalayas. In truth, the patient has no very good reason to trust our directions.

Our instrument for introducing the patient to our world is interpretation. Interpretations have been divided into interpretations of awareness and of meaning (Gill, 1982). Interpretations of awareness point out sequences of interaction, or recurrent patterns. Presumably they do not attribute value. Interpretations of meaning are always value assertions by the therapist. They represent the way the world looks to him or her; what he/she thinks matters. I wonder if there is any difference, really. They are both participations with the patient, since what the therapist notices or comments on will reflect his/her organization of reality. I would suggest, then, that the therapeutic praxis consists of the therapist interpreting then monitoring his/her interpretation as interaction. The interaction need not be explicit. Just listening involves a continuous participation, inevitably a nonneutral construction of what the patient is talking about. The therapist then attends to the patient's responses: silence, relief, submission, spontaneous memory, resistance. The therapist must understand that his/her response comes out of personal experience—not just generally accepted category of countertransferential anxiety—but out of profound biases, blind spots that emerge, not necessarily from the analyst's personal neurosis, but from the very nature of the work and the social matrix in which it is carried out. If we think of therapy as dealing with universal issues, then even our countertransferential responses must be universalized, at the price of failing to see how much of psychoanalytic interaction is determined by cultural blind spots. Psychoanalysis is not a search for predetermined Truth, but a dialogue of strangers.

In the following clinical material, I wish to emphasize how seriously this dimension of therapy is underestimated. In both cases, I am focusing on those aspects of the therapy relationship that are imbedded in the circumstances of the therapy rather than neurotic difficulties in either therapist or patient. In the first example, a woman in her forties tells a dream: she is at her hairdresser and is extremely embarrassed to find that she cannot tell her Korean hairdresser from the other Korean women present. She is a staunch liberal and recognizes her difficulties as a prejudice; to wit, "they all look alike to me." The second part of the dream finds her in a supermarket. She sees in the food locker two packaged chickens. One looks a bit odd, as if the refrigeration had failed and it was spoiling. She thinks, "I could take it home and re-freeze it, and maybe it would be OK to eat."

Dreams, I suspect, often present the two polarities of an issue. In this case, the issue is individuality. She cannot tell the Koreans apart and who, after all, could tell two plucked and packaged chicken carcasses apart. Of course, the human failure is prejudicial; the chickens, on the other hand, are virtually indistinguishable, except for the beginning spoilage (which I am not focusing on). One failure is human and regrettable; the other, totally dehumanized and irrelevant. It is very much what Portmann said about animal biology; the insides of all birds are the same, it is their outsides which are different (Portmann, 1964).

Why does this woman bother to dream about a rather minor prejudicial failure? Why the chickens in a supermarket (a sterile and impersonal source of food)? Where is the transference? What if I now add that she is gay and living in a lesbian relationship? Immediately it leaps to mind: is the therapist, a man, having a problem with this? Is he the one who is prejudicial, who cannot see the singularity of the patient because of her lifestyle? Is he perhaps leaning over backwards not to be prejudicial, and consequently not finding out enough about the relationship? Is this what she is saying? It sounds likely. Note that her extremely interesting dream cleverly brings into focus a problem that lies more in the circumstances of the therapy than the therapist's idiosyncratic difficulties. Why did she pick a male analyst?

My second example is reported by Mitchell (Mitchell, 1988). The patient, a young woman called "Lucy," reports a dream in which the analyst appears undisguised—the dream is in bright technicolor:

> I am walking along the beach with you and my sisters—you and I are walking together—I take off my clothes and go into the water—you remain on shore—I am frolicking with the fish. I catch a gorgeous blue fish and throw it to you. You catch it deftly. It all seems exquisite and wonderful.

This dream, says Mitchell, "reflects something of the quality of perfect attunement that Lucy, and frequently the analyst, experienced in the transference-countertransference integration at the start of the treatment"

20   Unfolding of Interpersonal Psychoanalysis

(Mitchell, 1988, p. 221). True, the dream reflects the patient's search for perfect unity (see the bond of a shared color). But why does it take this form? Why aren't they paddling off into the sunset together? Or frolicking in the water together? Why doesn't the analyst throw the patient the fish? The nude patient is in the water: the analyst is fully dressed and on the shore. It seems to me worth pointing out that the analyst is not disguised, which I believe to be a tip-off to countertransference; i.e., the patient is seeing the therapist without distortion. It seems to me that the patient is working very hard to make the analyst happy. If this were pointed out, would it make a difference? Would it change the analyst's perspective on the patient's "wish for fusion"? Would it perhaps alert the patient to this kind of servicing earlier in life, perhaps with mother? Would it alert the therapist to something in her own need to perceive the patient/therapist relationship in a particular way?

The perspective has changed from the patient's intrapsychic circumstances to something far more interpersonal. Perhaps the therapist *is* depressed and needy; or, at least, in training and needing a successful outcome to the therapy. But note that the perspective is determined by the therapist's culturally determined attitudes about the appropriate therapist role, defined by the "medical model." She is *The Doctor* and that determines her behavior as much as does her depression.

Should she stand outside the process? Should she be immersed in it? Why doesn't the therapist immediately "see" the inequity in the patient's role in the dream? In a subsequent dream (after supervision?) the patient goes to the therapist's house (home?) to help her (she hears, or senses, the therapist screaming or crying) and finds that somehow she, the patient, is now the one who needs help.

The *mise en scène* shifts to a hospital. Now the therapist is cold, clinical, and in a white coat. Mitchell says, "The illusion of sameness serves as a defense, warding off feelings of depression, emptiness, damage and rejection" (Mitchell, 1988, p. 222). True, but also the therapist has changed. She *has* withdrawn from her countertransference that she defines (as does the supervisor) as a deficit in performance. The patient is freed to work on her own problems and stop "helping" the therapist. Very good. But wouldn't it also be therapeutic for her to see that role as it operated in her family and to credit her attunement to sadness or neediness in the Other? Hasn't she accurately picked up the therapist's new decision to be more "professional," to wear a white coat? Isn't it of some real value for her to appreciate the perspicacity, the in-tuness, of her perceptions of the therapist?

Mitchell continues to develop his thesis: "The illusion of sameness was a narcissistic, counterdepressive defense to be interpreted . . . as a longing for symbiotic union with the mother . . . The mother's eagerness to return to her own fusion with *her* mother . . ." This "twin-ship" thesis is, of course, Kohut's, and "represents a missing developmental experience re-created in the treatment situation, an experience to be encouraged and slowly outgrown" (Mitchell, 1988, p. 222).

We have moved from individual to class, from the specifics of the patient's life to a generic set of statements that apply equally well to *all* patients who are fixated at that particular level of development. So, we are now presumably scientific inasmuch as we have a diagnostic entity, a causative history and a therapy that is restitutive because it emerges from the diagnosis and history. It is not that any of this is wrong or irrelevant. But, for me, it illustrates the difference between an interpersonal and a relational viewpoint. I think that the patient and therapist interaction is based on a real perception they have of each other's needs and operations. The patient is particularly sensitized—because of her personal life experience—to certain kinds of neediness and depression, and responds by throwing the therapist a fishy if well-intended uplifting. I think it registered because the therapist *did* need it. I suspect that in the process of supervision she became more aware of her own neediness and withdrew behind the traditional doctor's role, the white coat of the dream. True, doing that permitted the patient to see her "own" problems more clearly, but at the very considerable price of mystifying her experience with the therapist in a way that recapitulated her earlier life experience. Her perceptions must be sacrificed to the needs of others out of *her* need for a dependable caretaker. The reality of their interaction cannot be minimized as simply the stimulus of a complex fantasy system rooted in the past. Consider that by recapitulating her family role with the therapist, the patient can perpetuate her perception of that family system as normative, the way the world is. The therapist, rather than extracting the patient from a damaging system, becomes part of it; she is no different from the other members. The therapy, like life, becomes predictable and controllable with all the perverse redundant security of any well-functioning neurotic system.

When change takes place, it does not occur via corrective emotional experience. It is a novel emotional experience with the therapist that is *resisted*, causing anxiety, not change. This anxiety, manifested as resistance and transference—in the traditional sequence—is brought into awareness, actualized and analyzed, and *that* leads to change.

The supervisory formulations are all one-person, not two-person, not truly interpersonal. The therapist is left out altogether. The formulations of countertransference are traditional: i.e., to help the therapist get her stuff out of the way of the patient. In contrast, I feel that the patient must come to see her behavior as intersubjective, as functional with another person. The outcome would be to reinforce her respect for her own perceptions; it would release her—not only enabling her to stop doing what she does, but maybe to acknowledge her loyalty and lovingness and to allow her to *meet* the needs of the other person without feeling enmeshed and trapped. It would also allow the therapist to examine the implications of the doctor role and its inherent premise of a sick person and a healer in the room together, and that the therapist's perspectives are as limiting to awareness as the patient's.

Psychoanalysis is a bootstrap operation. We are not lifting the patient out of a hole: we are standing in the same hole. But what we can do is provide a much richer assessment of the context.

> The problem of the psychiatrist is more or less to spread a larger context before the patient: insofar as that succeeds, the patient realizes that, anxiety or not, the present way of life is unsatisfactory and unprofitable in the sense that it is not changing things for the better: whereupon, in spite of anxiety, other things being equal, the self-system can be modified.
>
> (Sullivan, 1953, p. 302)

I believe that patients suffer, not from being wrong, but from not being right enough. This is not to say that the patient is always accurate in his/her perceptions, nor does it intend to support the patient's stand of self-righteousness and injured entitlement. Nevertheless, the patient must recapture a sense of validity, a respect for his/her own perceptions of the world. Since, from an interpersonal viewpoint, the major pathogenic injunction operating on the patient is not to see what is there to be seen because it mobilizes too much anxiety, then simply giving up distortion would throw the baby out with the bathwater.

To summarize: Freud anchored his psychoanalysis in the scientific-medical model of his times. It was not until the diaspora of psychoanalysts to England and the United States that the dislocations in culture fostered the development of a cultural psychoanalysis—one rooted in the particularities of social experience. This psychoanalytic position was so "common sense," so rooted in ordinary experience that it seemed rather too simplistic, too obvious. Clara Thompson, Karen Horney, Erich Fromm (unfortunately not Sullivan) were—dare one say—*readable*, easily comprehensible to any reasonably literate layperson who cared to try—and, of course, many did. But if anyone can understand, can this be science?

In recent years, American culturally oriented psychoanalysts, weary of being disdained and excluded, discovered in British object-relations and American self-psychology their *carte de passage*. It all sounded interpersonal, it dealt with relational concepts, and once again, with simple folk psychology issues like mothering, empathy, and separation, but imbedded in very sophisticated and arcane conceptual systems. Unlike Thompson, Horney, and Fromm, they were not easy to read.

So, what is wrong? From my perspective, what has gone about has come about and we have returned again to a pseudoscientific occupation with generic principles, with an ontology of Man. The idiosyncratic, *obvious*, individual experience gets totally lost, as I've tried to show in the clinical examples. Concepts such as self-object, self-self-object, projective-identification, projective counter-identification, and so forth, to me smack of a dehumanized scientific obscurantism, antipathetic to Bruner's "folk psychology." No one could possibly understand this lexicon without indoctrination, preferably organizational. I suspect that many therapists who identify themselves with these positions use them in a bowdlerized commonsense form.

Reading Bruner, I get the definite impression that another turn of the wheel is in progress. Bruner says, "The child does not enter the life of his or her group as a private and autistic sport of primary processes, but rather as a participant in a larger public process in which public meanings are negotiated" (Bruner, 1990, p. 13). Bruner is interested in how the child, as he elegantly puts it, "enters into meaning" (Bruner, 1990, p. 68). The child's most human predilection is the development of a praxis—a way of being—for his/her world. Language is developed as a tool for social interaction and the self develops along with it. I would think that this means that everyone's world is a little different; that family socialization, peer

24   Unfolding of Interpersonal Psychoanalysis

groups, larger social entities, and culture all converge to create in each person a singularity of experience that makes their self-discovery in analysis a source of excitement and pleasure for analyst and patient. Shouldn't we return to listening with great attention to what patients tell us, what they don't tell us, and how we interact over the telling? This potential dialogue requires an enlightened listener, one who knows something about his/her own assumptions about the meaning of life.

The little Russian doctor may have been a dud as a scientist, but he was squarely in the mainstream of a traditionally Russian way of thought represented by Tolstoy, Dostoevsky, Chekhov, and Russia's greatest cultural theorist, Mikhail Mikhailovich Bakhtin (Clark and Holquist, 1984). As Bakhtin put it, the "sad misunderstanding" of all modern systems of thought, is "that [they believe] truth can only be that sort of truth that is put together out of general moments, that the truth of proposition is precisely what is repeatable and constant in it." To quote Morson (1991) on Bakhtin, "Real life, true historicity and genuine individuality are to be found in what is *left over*—in what Bakhtin called the 'surplus'—after all rules are applied and all generalizations are exhausted." Bakhtin called this the *eventness* of events, the singularity and unpredictability of our lives and our decisions (Morson, 1991, p. 206). "As long as a person is alive, he lives by the fact that he is not yet finalized, that he has not yet uttered his ultimate word" (Morson, 1991, p. 214). Perhaps that is a fitting caveat for those of us who entrust too much to our own particular version of blinis with sour cream.

Notes

1. This paper is a revised version of a talk given to the Institute for Contemporary Psychotherapy in New York City, on April 19, 1991.
2. It is true that trend Civilization and its Discontents saw different cultures would act differently in the repression of instinctual drive (Freud, 1930). But it was the universality of and not the specificity of culture which interested him.

References

Bruner, J. (1986). *Actual Minds, Possible Worlds.* Cambridge, MA: Harvard University Press.

Bruner, J. (1990). *Acts of Meaning.* Cambridge, MA: Harvard University Press, p. 20.

Clark, K. and Holquist, M. (1984). *Mikhail Bakhtin*. Cambridge, MA: Harvard University Press.

Friedman, L. (1988). *The Anatomy of Psychotherapy*. Hillsdale, NJ: The Analytic Press, p. 1.

Freud, S. (1930). Civilization and Its Discontents. In J. Strachey (Ed.), *The Standard Edition of the Complete Psychological Works of Sigmund Freud*. London: Hogarth Press, Vol. XXI, pp. 59–145.

Gill, M. (1982). *Analysis of Transference*. Vol. 1. New York: International Universities Press.

Habermas, J. (1971). *Knowledge and Human Interests*. Boston, MA: Beacon Press.

Hawkings, S. (1988). *A Brief History of Time; From the Big Bang to Black Holes*. New York: Bantam Books.

Kurzweil, E. (1989). *The Freudians: A Comparative Perspective*. New Haven, CT: Yale University Press.

Kvarnes, R. and Parloff, G. (1976). *A Harry Stack Sullivan Case Seminar*. New York: W.W. Norton.

Levenson, E. (1972). *The Fallacy of Understanding*. New York: Basic Books.

Little, M. (1985). Winnicott working in areas where psychotic anxieties predominate. *Free Associations*, 1(3): 23.

Mitchell, S. (1988). *Relational Concepts in Psychoanalysis*. Cambridge, MA: Harvard University Press, p. 221.

McLuhan, M. (1964). *Understanding Media—the Extensions of Man*. New York: McGraw-Hill, p. 65.

Morson, S.G. (1991). Bakhtin and the present moment. *The American Scholar*, 60(2):201–222.

Portmann, A. (1964). *New paths in biology*. In R.N. Anshen (Ed.), *World Perspectives*. New York: Harcourt Brace, p. 69.

Sullivan, H.S. (1953). *The International Theory of Psychiatry*. New York: W. W. Norton, p. 340.

Sulloway, F. (1979). *Freud: Biologist of the Mind*. New York: Basic Books, p. 40.

Wynn, L.C., Ryckoff, I.M., Day, J., and Hirsch, S.I. (1958). Pseudomutuality in the family relationships of schizophrenics. *Psychiatry*, 21:205–220.

Chapter 3

Harry Stack Sullivan

From Interpersonal Psychiatry to Interpersonal Psychoanalysis[1]

We all have our myths of the primal ancestor. Traditional psychoanalysis has Freud: we have H.S. Sullivan. In both cases, a great deal of fancy hermeneutical footwork is necessary to maintain tradition and continuity: to show that—what the founder meant, should have meant, would have meant had he lived—is what we are claiming today. I never met Harry Stack Sullivan; he died in 1949, several years before I entered the William Alanson White Institute. However, I did work intensively and enthusiastically with many of the people who knew him well and were great proponents of his work. So, I suppose that qualifies me as an early disciple, if not a true Apostle. Someone once said—rather sourly—that one gets the disciples one deserves.[2] I don't know whether Sullivan would endorse my particular brand of interpersonalism; but I do believe that what I have to say is an extrapolation of Sullivan's position.

As I pointed out in "The Web and the Spider" (1984), Sullivan made no claim, as did Freud, to being the Lonely Hero, on a quest.[3] Sullivan (to quote myself):

> did not claim to work in heroic isolation. He was, in a very significant sense, a conduit for many other people's ideas. One might claim, with a high degree of paradigmatic consistency, that if Freud was the singular architect of a great psychological edifice, then Sullivan was the processor, or collator, of the immense informational explosion of the thirties and forties.
>
> (Levenson, 1984, p. 175)

I would like, first, to delineate Sullivan's position, then illustrate how his essentially open-ended postulates—which he scrupulously defined as

Interpersonal *Psychiatry—can* be, and were, extended into a contemporary Interpersonal *Psychoanalysis*. *I* really do not believe this was Sullivan's doing per se but rather, was the result of the merging of his American pragmatic psychiatry with European psychoanalysis through the contributions of his colleagues, especially Thompson, Horney, and Fromm.[4] This is not to say that he was uninterested or uninformed about psychoanalysis (he had, after all, urged Clara Thompson to study with Ferenczi in Budapest). But, as I shall elaborate, his vision of therapy differed sharply from the psychoanalytic that is based on the centrality of the concept of transference and countertransference. For all of a certain lip-service to the idea of transference, I would claim that Sullivan's insistence on the centrality of anxiety constrained his use of the therapist/patient relationship to a significant degree.

Sullivan's concepts may be divided loosely into three categories:

1. Anxiety (in the very specific way Sullivan used the concept), including its major instrumentality *the self-system*, and the consequences of anxiety; namely, *selective inattention, dissociation and parataxic distortion.*
2. The nature of the patient/therapist relationship; namely the function of *participant-observation* and *consensual validation* (Havens, 1976).
3. The concept of man, which underlay Sullivan's system. First, the dictum that we are all more simply human than otherwise; that is, more alike than different. Second, Sullivan's rejection of the concept of unique individuality; at least, as an appropriate subject for psychoanalytic inquiry. And third, his vision of psychoanalytic cure, which was not coterminous with social cure. Psychoanalytic cure occurred when the patient's self-image was enriched and without major "parataxes," without distortion. "The patient as known to himself is much the same person as the patient behaving with others" (Sullivan, 1953b). Social cure was another issue. It involved will, agency, the desire to translate what had been learned in therapy to the world of outside relationships:

> The problem of the psychiatrist is more or less to spread a larger context before the patient insofar as that succeeds, the

> patient realizes that, anxiety or not, the present way of life is unsatisfactory and is unprofitable in the sense that it is not changing things for the better; whereupon, in spite of anxiety, other things being equal, the self-system can be modified.
>
> (Sullivan, 1953a, p. 302)

Sullivan's concept of anxiety is the linchpin of his entire system of psychology. "Insofar as you grasp the concept of anxiety as I shall be struggling to lay it out before you, I believe you will be able to follow, with reasonable success, the rest of this system of psychiatry" (Sullivan, 1953a, p. 8). First, it is not what we ordinarily think of as anxiety, but rather an experience of such catastrophic dimensions, so utterly disorganizing, that the patient will do almost anything to avoid it; no "satisfaction" is worth the risk to what he called "security needs." Second, anxiety is interpersonal and contagious. Anxiety occurs in the infant and child because it is being provoked in the necessary Other; and, it is the empathically communicated anxiety of the Other which floods the dependent child. The subject develops an instrumentality for detecting, avoiding, and "inattending" those occasions that might precipitate anxiety. This is, of course, Sullivan's famous *self-system*—*not* synonymous with the self, as self-psychologists conceive it; but rather an early warning system. Anxiety, then, is not caused by repression of forbidden impulse; but by fear of the Other (or, more accurately, fear of the other's fear). Intrapsychic fantasy is more the reflection of interpersonal events than the cause. This vision of interpersonal anxiety is so radically different that, as is often the case with paradigmatic change, it is totally misunderstood or bowdlerized into another version of the "same old thing."

So, anxiety is avoided through the operations of the self-system that identifies and avoids those interpersonal crises that would elicit anxiety, and, in addition, establishes an amnesia, or scotoma, for these occasions —Sullivan's "selective inattention." The patient simply averts his/her *eyes*. In more cataclysmic situations, a total dissociation may take place, without that marginal awareness of "knowing that there is something one is not supposed to know" that is present in selective inattention. This is an extremely important distinction between inattention and dissociation. In the former, the person may avert his/her eyes, but the self-system knows and operates strategically to avoid anxiety. In dissociation, the unawareness is total. The person profoundly does not engage the issue.

Interpersonal praxis, then, works to catch those moments of nodal inattention, to inquire into what is unspoken, and then to speak the unspeakable. To not ask—to not think to ask—is the index of the therapist's anxiety and consequently countertransference. It is true that one may have powerful and discomforting emotions toward patients—anger, boredom, sexual feelings. But, these feelings are accessible, often justified and ultimately workable and useful in therapy. The real sins of countertransference are sins of omission. Damaging countertransferences are those that operate out of awareness. I would emphasize that the purpose of the detailed inquiry is not simply thorough history taking, but probing and provoking the self-system, attempting to find out where out-of-awareness takes place, where anxiety lurks; and, by virtue of what the therapist asks or does not ask, defining the parameters of the therapist's participation.

This concept of interpersonal anxiety remains largely intact and absolutely central to understanding contemporary interpersonal psychoanalysis. It is Sullivan's formulation of the relationship of patient and therapist that has undergone the most change. "Consensual validation" and "participant-observation" both clearly imply a mutuality; not one person (the therapist) observing and correcting the second person (the patient). As Racker put it, "The first distortion of truth in 'the myth of the analytic situation' is that analysis is an interaction between a sick person and a healthy one" (Racker, 1968, p. 132). Yet, for all that, Sullivan clearly left himself out of the equation. It was the patient's reality that was at question and the analyst's role was to help him/her distinguish between what was veridical and what was distortion, "parataxic distortion." The analyst monitored very closely his/her own anxiety level to avoid bouts of selective inattention that would compromise his/her clarity of vision and purpose and provoke excessive anxiety in the patient. But, who the therapist is, was not at issue; the patient qua patient is defined by the assumption that he or she is distorting the therapist. Sullivan had no doubt, whatever, that the patient suffered from "parataxic distortion," and consequently misread and misinterpreted the therapist.

The contemporary preoccupation with the nature of reality (naive reality, social constructivism, pluralism) is not apparent in Sullivan. It seems clear that the praxis of therapy is to bring the patient into line with a consensually validated view of the world. When the patient sees himself as seen by others, the therapy is over. The function of the therapist, then, is to participate with the patient sufficiently to act as a guide through the thickets

30 Unfolding of Interpersonal Psychoanalysis

of distorted experience. One gets the decided impression that Sullivan discouraged patients from getting too interested in him or too curious about who he really was. His famous dictum about erotic transference was unequivocal.[5]

There is, in *Clinical Studies in Psychiatry* an excellent example of Sullivan's way of working, albeit as supervisor (Sullivan, 1956, p. 371–372):

> The first case is then that of a schizoid—a young married woman who is extremely tense, apprehensive, and inarticulate. Her main difficulty, as she describes it, is that she is an inefficient housekeeper who "lazes" most of the day away. She looks on herself as a failure. Treatment in the case has bogged down, after several months and the question is, what techniques can be used to get things moving again?

As it develops, she is the product of an extremely traumatic childhood, deserted by her mother, and eventually abandoned to her maternal grandparents by her father. She was very gifted intellectually, and, despite her disadvantages, went on to a doctorate in economics. She married a fellow-student in the same field and subsequently sank into a morass of domesticity, giving up her career and submitting to a husband who criticized her mercilessly, and boasted openly to her about his sexual conquest of other women. She had two children during the course of this deteriorating marriage and now her husband was threatening divorce.

It must certainly strike us, in our times, as odd that it never occurred to the therapist that this woman was taking an awful beating in the marriage; or, if it did occur to him/her, it was undoubtedly considered an epiphenomon of her masochism. Sullivan focused immediately on the pragmatics of her life's circumstances, working on the premise that to understand someone, one must begin by assuming that he/she makes sense. Why didn't she hire a part-time maid? They could afford it. Then he inquires politely into how, with a doctorate in economics, she wound up being a housewife. He does not attempt to bring her into touch directly with her resentment against her husband. He expects that there will be resistance to accepting that, because of the inherent anxiety provoked in her by challenging her husband. If she upsets him, she upsets herself and her security is dangerously compromised. She is aware of how fragile he is and is terrified that he will, if pressed, take flight.

So, Sullivan goes into what he calls "the middle distance" (Sullivan, 1956, p. 375), circling in very cautiously, allowing her to arrive at her own conclusions. He shows, very strikingly, a respect for the patient's privacy and anxiety that was, I believe, an unexpected clinical hallmark of this often cantankerous and abrasive man. His intent is to get her to see what she has been avoiding seeing, because of the disruptive anxiety inherent in seeing. This is done carefully, circumspectly, allowing her to encounter her anxiety in small increments. It is also of note that he does not trash the husband or mythologize him as The Bad Parent. Sullivan is sensitive to the husband's anxiety as well as the wife's. It is hoped that consensual validation promotes her sharing Sullivan's view of life that is presumably more open and benign than hers. His participation consists largely of an exquisite sensitivity to her anxiety and to her self-protectiveness. There is absolutely no sense that Sullivan is bringing himself—in any personalized way—to bear in the treatment.

What, if anything, is wrong with this? It is entirely consistent with what he said about what he did in therapy. It is not what some of us would do now. The clinical case presented seems far too simple: to wit, Sullivan gets her to see what she has been avoiding in her life. She is then relieved of her symptoms, through his validation of her abused life, and is freed to approach her husband differently, possibly to his relief. The clinical experience I believe most of us have in our therapies is that after this clarification of distortion and mystification in her life, instead of getting better the patient resists the insight, and transfers the mechanism of defense to the therapist. We become part of the disease we had set out to cure. It was Freud's great insight that this resistance and transference, rather than being simply a frustrating obstruction to change, is the sine qua non of psychoanalysis. Indeed, Freud said, "Any line of investigation, no matter what its direction, which recognizes these two facts [resistance and transference] and takes them as the starting point of its work may call itself psychoanalysis, though it arrives at results other than my own" (Freud, 1919). If the patient responds successfully to a benign authoritative interpretation (albeit masked as inquiry), it is psycho-therapy. Psycho-analysis begins where interpretation fails. It is defined, both by its recognition of the essentially antagonistic relationship between the patient's defenses and the helper, and its insistence that the adversarial relationship be made manifest and interpreted in the relationship.

32 Unfolding of Interpersonal Psychoanalysis

We would expect the patient to relate to Sullivan with the same degree of masochistic submission she showed her husband, after an initial "honeymoon" period when there would be wonderful improvement. We would expect that Sullivan would soon begin—despite his scrupulous intent—to feel irritation and contempt for her. "Of course," chortles the Freudian analyst, "You've just proven my point! The interpersonal is subordinate to her intrapsychic conflicts. Therefore, the most solicitous, respectful analyst will come up against the self-perpetuating nature of her masochistic defenses." But, remember that resistance and transference can operate against the Other as well as internally. Perhaps the patient resists Sullivan and incorporates him into her system because she does not believe that he is any different from her husband. Perhaps his help, however carefully framed, is seen by her as obvious and patronizing. Her self-system does not so easily trust Sullivan's intent. Sullivan's commitment to the idea of Self as the sum of interpersonal interactions and his dismissal of an intrapsychic component to personality would make it difficult to conceive of a patient actively resisting awareness, once the anxiety was reduced to a manageable level. But, if she "transfers" to the therapist, if what happens between them becomes a transform of what they are talking about in her life; then, one might expect that she would be exquisitely attuned to the therapist's needs, especially in the realm of self-esteem and potency. The self-system is a master strategist and an opponent of the therapy, by no means limited to the more primitive device of inattention, of looking away. Her self-system actively probes the nature of the therapist, feeling for his anxiety spots, his defenses.

Paradoxically, Sullivan's treatment of the therapist/patient relationship may have been, in some ways, closer to the Freudian view than to present interpersonal psychoanalysis (or, at least, my version of interpersonalism); inasmuch as he attempted to show the patient the distortions inherent in his/her perceptions by a carefully monitored neutrality. Like the Freudians, he apparently felt that transference was resistance and interfered with the therapy. As did the Freudians, he interpreted away from transference, to what he conceived to be the key issues in the patient's life; i.e., the patient is told that the focus on the analyst—particularly, the distortion implicit in that focus—is an avoidance of the patient's true issues. "The solution of the transference, resolution of the transference, which is so important in certain psychotherapeutic problems, has, I think, in my case, *usually preceded the appearance of the transference*" (Kvarnes and Parloff, 1976, p. 216, my italics).

In the meager corpus of Sullivan's clinical cases, it would appear that he attempted to minimize the impact of his particular personality. He pays meticulous attention to "countertransference," but it is only to get it out of the way of the patient. There is no sense that the unique personality of the therapist really matters. Indeed, much of what he tells supervisees to tell patients seem mordant, focused, extremely clever observations about the patient; or about areas the therapist is inattending. The general motif seems to be that therapy depends on the therapist's attunement to the patient's anxiety and you—the supervisee—are not attuned enough. Why this particular patient should be having trouble with this particular therapist does not enter the arena of inquiry. At the risk of offending Sullivanians, I must say that I find the clinical examples disappointing, and in many ways, clever grandstanding at the expense of the therapist (see Kvarnes and Parloff, 1976; Pearce, 1950; Sullivan, 1956).

Both "consensual validation" and "participant-observation" are really oxymorons. The moment one participates, one has lost any absolute claim to clarity. It is axiomatic that no self-referential statement can ever be proven to be right or wrong. All the participant can know—and that with difficulty—is his/her own experience of the interaction. The claim that one can participate and still be a judge of the other person's assessment of reality is questionable. It seems to be that Sullivan's position was paradoxical. Either one claimed to be able to make judgments from a superordinate position; or, one gave up the attempt and simply studied the interaction of two persons engaged over an issue, without either position claiming hegemony. With the cases above (Sullivan, 1956), one might reasonably claim that Sullivan did exactly the former; i.e., made an assessment of her life from a position of greater clarity than she possessed. But one might equally reasonably claim that once Sullivan gave her his assessment, he had entered into an interaction with her which was inevitably beyond his total awareness or grasp; and, which depended, not *just on* what she brought to it, but his own personality and defenses. The cardinal issue might well be, not the truth of Sullivan's observations about her, but their interactional meanings. What is the metacommunication: i.e., the communication about the communication? Is it that Sullivan is telling her something she has "inattended" about her life—that she is disastrously submissive? Or, is it that he is establishing himself as a "Good Daddy,"

34 Unfolding of Interpersonal Psychoanalysis

a male authority who thinks that women should use their brains? This is a paradox very familiar to feminist writers in this field who are sharply attuned to the implication of paternalistic authority, no matter how benign or therapeutic the conscious self-regard of the therapist.

It is extraordinary how arrogating and out of awareness is the assumption, mutual really, that the patient is a "patient"; knows nothing about what is bothering him or her, and, for a successful recovery, needs to be a good patient and "open up" to the therapist; who will then figure out what the problem is.

Sampson presents several cases of patients who appeared to be quite knowledgeable about their own dynamics and even improved considerably after making their own formulations (Sampson, 1991). But psychoanalysis requires a psychodynamic explanation, which Sampson provides. Occum's razor is not in the psychoanalytic armamentarium. Yet, if one examines the case reports, the patients suddenly sounded insightful simply when Sampson asked for their assessments! He reports on a woman who has had three previous analyses; 6 years, 9 years and 3 years respectively. In the course of the therapy, she asks him if he is angry and he says, "No." She experiences this as an absolutely novel event—an analyst who simply answered a straightforward question, instead of the usual sanctimonious and superior, "Why do you ask?"

From this perspective, Sullivan would need to work through his own participation, his own experience with women, with women with this kind of problem, his reasons for treating her (he was the supervisor, not therapist), even his reasons for being a therapist.[6] As Gill put it:

> A major disappointment for me on reading Sullivan is his relative failure as a therapist to attempt to make the unspoken aspects of the interpersonal interaction explicit as a central aim of the therapeutic process. Perhaps to do so would have required a kind of participation which he could not permit himself. It could be that the very factor which enabled him to perceive that man is quintessentially a social animal was the same that restricted the types of interactions which he could interact with others comfortably.
>
> (Gill, 1982)

At this point, we have entered the tarpits of constructivism. What is reality? Who can claim to know it? Why is my reality any better than yours? I believe that Sullivan felt clearly there was an external reality, separate from patient and therapist and possible of consensual validation. It was the function of the therapist to help the patient give up his/her distortions and enter the real world. This world was, itself, a matter of consensual validation; inasmuch as Sullivan seemed to believe that there was a community of people living without major distortions in their world. For Sullivan getting well, being normal, was seeing the world the way it was—which was the way normal people saw it. It was this conservatism, this acceptance of the status quo that offended Erich Fromm and caused him to accuse Sullivan of selling out to Mammon. Sullivan apparently felt that being normal—being able to have intimate relationships, avoiding terrible loneliness—was a greater imperative than eschewing seduction by a marketing culture. About that, Sullivan apparently couldn't have cared less.[7]

I suspect that he worked on the premise that to understand someone, one must specify and respect his/her view of the world; not necessarily agree with it. It is perhaps his greatest legacy that he led us to see even schizophrenic patients as essentially logical, operating sensibly out of their worldview. Certainly he was a social constructivist inasmuch as he believed reality was socially constructed. Perhaps this would leave him closely allied with the self-psychologists who protect and respect the patient's "psychic reality"; which, as I've said before, seems to me respect for the patient's right to his/her own viewpoint even if it is wrong! I am struck by the propensity of self-psychologists to assign equal credibility to their view of the world and the patient's (Levenson, 1985).

This is an issue on which I am very unclear and have, no doubt, waffled mightily, earning the disapproval of committed constructivists who at first welcomed me and then decided that I was a "naive realist" (Hoffmann, 1990). It seems to me that there *is* a reality "out there" which can be mutually validated. Real things happen to patients and can be subject to amnesia or partial screen representations. Discovering these events is important.[8] And yet, how I see what the patient tells me, what I do not think to ask about, what values I implicitly communicate are also important, essentially because the patient dare not, in the course of the therapy, talk about those things which will make me anxious. Challenging someone's view of the world produces an existential vertigo and anxiety. This is as true for the therapist as it is for the patient. To assume that the therapist, because he or she is the therapist, has less potential for anxiety

36 Unfolding of Interpersonal Psychoanalysis

than the patient may be a serious misjudgement. Therapists do tend to be more comfortable about being therapists than patients are about being patients; but, that may be because the therapist is armored and protected by the relative anonymity of the role, and by the careful circumspection of the psychoanalytic frame. Why I am a therapist, why I treat this particular patient must be explored. I was very struck, listening to the early Sullivanians, particularly Fromm-Reichmann, to how little attention was paid to what might actually motivate a therapist to work with such extremely difficult and unrewarding schizophrenic patients. There was, in many cases, a powerful odor of sanctity that I cannot believe was ultimately helpful to the patient.

Who I am is central to the process, far in excess of the usual applications of "countertransference" or blind spots. My total personality is at issue. I suspect that the reason most patients are so resistant to change is that they fear that they will be used for the purposes of the therapist, who in spite of protestations of neutrality, may very well operate with his/her own agenda. That is why the initial detailed inquiry, or free-associative approach activates resistance as anxiety is mobilized. Why should the patient trust the therapist? Because we think we are reliable? The patient is a patient because his/her life has been characterized by a loss of authenticity, by being used by other people for their own ends. The mutual exploration of the interpersonal relationship of patient and therapist works because it develops—over time—a sense of trust and respect for the integrity of the other (this cuts both ways). As the sense of safety increases, then the patient can remember to remember his/her own past and make it explicit in the therapy. The core of the therapeutic praxis may be just this development of a relationship of very considerable subtlety and complexity. The inquiry, the developing narrative, the elaboration of fantasy and dreams, are, I suspect, the context of the relationship: certainly vital to the curative process, but not the curative process itself.

I want to use another example of Sullivan's to reinforce the difference between Sullivan's emphasis on the management of the patient's anxiety, and a more contemporary view of interpersonalism as encompassing the unique personalities and experiences of both participants. This is one of the few dreams that Sullivan presented in detail. His approach to dream analysis is well known and unequivocally stated. Dreams that awoke the patient with an uncanny feeling of dread, he treated as incipient schizophrenic episodes and simply sidestepped. Other dreams, he felt were essentially parataxic communications whose referents could be better grasped by going directly to the source—the day residue (Sullivan, 1953a, p. 343). Why he so adamantly refused to use the rich symbolic content of dreams is not clear, but the following example might be relevant.

Sullivan (he tells us) had at one time a "really marvelous assistant," one with a great talent for working with schizophrenic patients (Sullivan, 1953a, p. 336). This young man "rapidly became not only my left hand, but, I suppose most of my upper left extremity." (Why the *left* hand, one might ask? Usually indispensable helpers become one's *right* hand!) This young man had become of interest to a "bitterly paranoid woman." He wanted to talk to Sullivan about his problems with her, which Sullivan felt was a sign of good judgment. "She seemed to be suffering from his very casual heterosexual life away from her, and I thought that such worries would grow if they were legitimized, and so on." (Whatever "legitimized" meant. Besides, why shouldn't she be upset by "his very casual" sexual infidelities?) "Also," says Sullivan, "I didn't want him upset. He was far too valuable."

His assistant comes to Sullivan with a dream in which he is walking on a very small lush island set in an artificial lake, behind a dam, engaged in conversation with Sullivan. The lake is named Loch Raven, which may, or may not, be significant (it does lend itself to thoughts of "Nevermore"). Then he observes that the area of water between the island and the shore, over which they had stepped easily, was rapidly widening. He awakes in terror, "finding himself leaping out of bed into a pool of moonlight." This is, for Sullivan, the prototypical proto-schizophrenic dream.

Sullivan then does a rather perverse thing: he refuses to interpret the dream for the reader, although he implies that he knows what the dream means but that, for the dreamer to know, would be catastrophic. He did exactly the same thing with his presentation of his own dream, the dream of the spider.[9] Yet, why is it so self-evident that the dream should be side-stepped? Suppose Sullivan had said to his assistant, "It sounds like maybe you feel you're getting rather isolated by our being so involved with each other." This does not raise the apparently interdicted, but obviously present issue of homosexual feelings the assistant may be feeling for Sullivan. Don't forget, he was working on a ward of exclusively young male schizophrenics with a great deal of homosexual undercurrents.[10]

Moreover, by putting it "*our* being so involved with each other," the assistant is relieved of an implication of blame, or that the feelings are

38 Unfolding of Interpersonal Psychoanalysis

totally one-sided. By speaking the unspeakable, might not that have put the assistant's terror somewhat at rest? Might he not then have proceeded to distance himself from the isolating relationship with Sullivan and his implied sacrifice ("besides he was too valuable") to Sullivan's purposes as administrator of the ward? Shouldn't Sullivan—presumably picking up the drift of the dream, even why the dream was told to him—have quietly moved to allow the assistant more private life and more freedom to choose a heterosexual partner, even though he, Sullivan, thought she was "paranoid" and "unsuitable"? In a more general discussion of dreams, he says that, "Insofar as he (the patient) remembers it and communicates it, *he is seeking validation with someone else!*" (Sullivan, 1953a, p. 343, my italics).

Please note that this does not require that he discuss his own sexual proclivities, nor the not entirely selfless motivation that invests him in this young man's talents. But, at this stage of the inquiry, who Sullivan is, why he is interested in this man, what his own sexuality is, how he feels about women—particularly aggressive sexual women, how he feels about domesticity, how interested he is in the success of his experimental ward, who or what he would sacrifice for its success; all these issues and virtually anything else relevant about his personality become germane. Why not engage these issues? I cannot see why what appears to be a deliberate inattention to them is less anxiety-provoking than a direct and comfortable inquiry. It has been my clinical experience that patients do not panic or decompensate because they are forced to face an unpleasant and even horrifying issue. It is simply amazing what you can say to patients, as long as you are telling them the truth. Mystifying patients, not confronting them, is what drives them crazy because they know what they are not supposed to know they know; and they are "inattending" that knowledge because bringing it into awareness would mobilize their anxiety and, far more dangerous, possibly mobilize the anxiety, rage, and retaliation of their therapists who might well not wish their own vulnerabilities exposed. All this—it goes without saying—presumably operates outside the awareness of the well-intentioned and ethical therapist.

I suspect that, as Bateson put it, "The point of the probe is always in the heart of the explorer" (Bateson, 1979). Every metapsychology contains the seeds of an incipient countertransference. There is no avoiding it and it must be taken into account by the epigones of a particular position. I would claim that Sullivan's vision of interpersonal psychiatry was bent and directed by his own security needs, as must be so for everyone, if we are, in truth, all more simply human than otherwise. His fastidious attention to the most marginal manifestations of anxiety and his premise that the patient would get better in a milieu of safety and respect for his/her limits, made it simultaneously possible for him to inattend and minimize the use of more intimate and personal interactions. The dictum is: if the patient cannot bear it, then one must not confront it. What if the analyst cannot bear it?

One great virtue of Sullivan's theory, as I said at the beginning of this chapter, is that it is not an all-inclusive and sacrosanct system. Consequently, one need not exercise the agonized casuistry we usually employ in our field to avoid being anathematized by our colleagues and institutes. A simple extension of his basic concepts—his attention to the basic pragmatics of human interaction—but carrying them farther than Sullivan might have found comfortable, leads us to a version of countertransference now fitting well within a broadly defined rubric of psychoanalysis. The same attention to anxiety remains, but now the amelioration of anxiety does not depend so much on a careful avoidance of "too much" inquiry; as it does on clarification of the interpersonal relationship of patient and therapist—in all its manifestations.

I would emphasize that how far one goes in openly manifesting interpersonal egalitarianism and honesty is a difficult issue, and carries with it the same countertransference traps I spoke of earlier. But, I would insist that an absolute minimum requirement is that the therapist be acutely alert to his/her own presence, with an acceptance of the inevitability that one's own needs, preferences, presumptions, and limitations will come into play. This is not a failure of therapy; it is the very essence of therapy. A perfect analyst—and some of our colleagues strive mightily to achieve that epiphany—would drive the patient crazy.

Sullivan established the paradigm for a truly interpersonal psychoanalysis; an accomplishment of great contemporary relevance for our field. He built his interpersonalism around monitoring interpersonal anxiety rather than unique and idiosyncratic interpersonal interactions. I believe this came as much out of his need to protect his privacy as it did out of a need to protect the patient. It is a simple next step to formatting the interpersonal process to include a much more extensive, and intimate, interpersonal interaction. The psychoanalytic concept of resistance and transference comes into play, not exclusively as a projection of the patient's fantasies, but as

40   Unfolding of Interpersonal Psychoanalysis

a virtual re-enactment of the material under discussion in the relational field of the patient and therapist. Thus, the therapist scrupulously monitors his/her participation—not to get out of the way of the patient's fantasies—but as a transformation of the therapy process.

What is curative about all this? What is the "mutative" experience in psychoanalysis? I think we do not really know. There is certainly the patient tapping into his/her own *poesis*, the capacity for creative imagination (Levenson, 1988). There is—dare we say it—a corrective emotional experience with the therapist. But, most important of all may be the patient learning what the Vedanta says: that the meaning of an event is its consequences. And, consequences are quintessentially interpersonal and intersubjective. Ultimately, the meaning of my experience depends on its impact on you. If my benevolence has evil consequences, regardless of my intent, my act is evil. Ultimately, the legacy of Sullivan's theory may well be that it places, not just the patient, but the analyst, too, squarely in the interpersonal realm of inquiry.

Notes

1. This paper was first presented to the Washington Institute of Psychoanalysis on January 11, 1992 and later published in *Contemporary Psychoanalysis*, 1992, 28:3.
2. See Phyllis Grosskurth for an account of Freud's travails with his disciples (Grosskurth, 1991).
3. There is, of course, ample *evidence* to suggest that Freud, too, had his *antecedents* (Rice, 1991; Sulloway, 1979; Yerushalmi, 1991).
4. See Bromberg for a particularly lucid presentation of these issues in training at The White Institute (Bromberg, 1991).
5. To a woman patient who expressed erotic interest in Sullivan, he informed her that when he developed interest in someone, he wanted it to be *with a real person*! "If you go to have your watch fixed, you don't have to fall in love with the watchmaker. People come to me to have difficulties in living untangled—that is what I do" (Kvarnes and Parloff, 1976, p. 216).
6. One need only read Perry's biography of Sullivan to be aware of some of the personal blind spots and limitations he would bring to working with this particular woman (Perry, 1982).
7. Again, one must read Perry's biography for the story of his short-lived psychoanalysis with Clara Thompson, who was, I suspect, terrified of him. When she objected mildly to his profligate spending of money he did not have for Persian rugs and furniture, he denounced her as "too bourgeois" to work with him—and stamped out (Perry, 1982)!

8. This does not justify assuming that one's favorite event underlies the screen memory. One need only recall all the presumptive "primal scenes" evoked by enthusiastic analysts; or, maybe now, implicate molestations.
9. For an extended gloss on that dream, see Levenson, 1984.
10. There was a good deal of speculation about the homosexual tensions on Sullivan's ward at Sheppard and Enoch Pratt hospital, particularly the apparent homosexual orientation of staff members (Chatelaine, 1981, pp. 445–458).

References

Bateson, G. (1979). *Mind and Nature: A Necessary Unity.* New York: Dutton, p. 87.

Bromberg, P. (1991). Artist and analyst. *Contemporary Psychoanalysis,* 27(2):289–300.

Chatelaine, K. L. (1981). *Harry Stack Sullivan: The Formative Years.* Washington, DC.: University Press of America.

Freud, S. (1919). On the history of the psychoanalytic movement. In J. Strachey (Ed.), *The Standard Edition of the Complete Psychological Works of Sigmund Freud.* London: Hogarth Press, Vol. XIV, pp. 7–66.

Gill, M. (1982). On Sullivan, his life and work. *William Alanson White Newsletter (Winter 1982–83),* 17(1):6.

Grosskurth, P. (1991). *The Secret Ring: Freud's Inner Circle and the Politics Of Psychoanalysis.* Boston, MA: Addison-Wesley.

Havens, L. (1976). *Participant Observation.* New York: Jason Aronson.

Hoffman, I. (1990). In the eye of the beholder. *Contemporary Psychoanalysis,* 26(2):291–298.

Kvarnes, R., and Parloff, G. (1976). *A Harry Stack Sullivan Case Seminar.* New York: W.W. Norton.

Levenson, E. (1984). Harry Stack Sullivan: The web and the spider. *Contemporary Psychoanalysis,* 20(2):174–189.

Levenson, E. (1985). The interpersonal (Sullivanian) model. In A. Rothstein (Ed.), *Models of the Mind and Their Relationship to Clinical Work.* New York: International Universities Press, pp. 49–67.

Levenson, E. (1988). Real frogs in imaginary gardens: Facts and fantasies in psychoanalysis. *Psychoanalytic Inquiry,* 8(4):552–556.

Pearce, J. (1950). *Sullivan's approach in therapy with his comments on particular patients.* Unpublished paper read at meeting of the William Alanson White Society, May 19, 1950.

Perry, H. (1982). *Psychiatrist of America, The Life of Harry Stack Sullivan.* Cambridge, MA: Harvard University Press.

Racker, H. (1968). *Transference and Counter-transference.* New York: International University Press.

Rice, E. (1991). *Freud and Moses: The Long Journey Home.* New York: State University of New York Press.

Sampson, H. (1991). Experience and insight in the resolution of transferences. *Contemporary Psychoanalysis*, 27(2):201–207.

Sullivan, H.S. (1953a). *The Interpersonal Theory of Psychiatry*. New York: W.W. Norton.

Sullivan, H.S. (1953b). *Conceptions of Modern Psychiatry*. New York: W.W. Norton.

Sullivan, H.S. (1956). *Clinical Studies in Psychiatry*. New York: W.W. Norton.

Sulloway, F. (1979). *Freud: Biologist of the Mind*. New York: Basic Books.

Yerushalmi, Y.H. (1991). *Freud's Moses: Judaism Terminable and Interminable*. New Haven, CT: Yale University Press.

Chapter 4

Shoot the messenger

Interpersonal aspects of the analyst's interpretations[1]

Kings who were wont to kill the bearers of ill tidings, knew something that psychoanalysts are just beginning to understand; namely, that the messenger is the message. To quote Crapanzano:

> Where does the messenger stand? He himself is not without desire. He is not without power. He lives in a world charged with value, with loyalties and with animosities. . . . He has to understand the message, to interpret it, translate, contextualize, and elaborate it, and he has to justify all these procedures. He has responsibility! The messenger is not an automation—that fictitious role—in which he is socially cast *per necessitate.*
>
> (Crapanzano, 1992)

For all of Freud's devotion to the classic determinism of the Greek myths, his psychoanalysis was firmly imbedded in the Rabbinic tradition; where infinity of meaning and plurality of interpretation are the cardinal virtues (Handleman, 1982, p. 21). Even now, all contemporary psycho-analytic interpretive systems offer so much latitude and choice (timing, focus, developmental level of interpretation, resistance, transference) that every interpretative offering of our messenger, the therapist, is inevitably a highly overdetermined participation that reveals as much about the therapist as it does about the patient. And, what is even more disconcerting, the patient usually knows it. It is this latter aspect of the issue—the patient's awareness of the therapist's participation—that presents us with the greatest theoretical and clinical discomfort.

44   Unfolding of Interpersonal Psychoanalysis

We all seem to be in general agreement that the therapist reveals himself/herself in the course of interpreting and that the patient does grasp aspects of the therapist's participation. Moreover, we agree, that interpretations—either of intrapsychic content or transference—are also behaviors with the patient; since, as I said, there are almost an infinite number of possible points of observation and whatever the therapist focuses is *pari passe* a choice, and therefore a piece of behavior with the patient. As Wittgenstein put it, words are also deeds. And, since the therapist is reflecting on the patient's content, there will inevitably be a correlation between what is said and what is enacted, leading us to the extra-ordinarily useful observation that *what is talked about will simultaneously be enacted between analyst and patient* (Levenson, 1988). If this be so, the patient's perceptions of the therapist, the transference, cannot be dismissed simply as pure distortion or even as incidentally accurate perceptions on the patient's part put to the service of resistance. We can no longer summarily deal with the patient's version of events so as to proceed with the ostensibly true work of the analysis—the patient's unconscious fantasies. But what then is one to do with the patient's perceptions? How may they be used?

Something odd begins to happen. Analysts become anxious about being anxious and the language of discourse begins to obfuscate the issue—what Jacobs, quoted by Peltz, calls the "phraseology of interpretation" becomes prolix and obscure (Jacobs, 1991). Note Boesky as quoted by Peltz: "Patients experience some behavior of the analyst as it was perceived by the patient in the context of the patient's dynamic need to perceive the behavior in certain ways under the pressure of prevailing conflicts and fantasies about the analyst."[2] I understand this to mean that even if the patient does perceive something about the analyst, that perception may be affectively loaded in an inappropriate way; i.e., the awareness will still be biased by the needs of the patient. But, of course, that judgment is being made by the therapist. And, it underestimates the possibility that the patient may be, in a secondary way, contaminating an accurate first perception for reasons I will explicate later.

So, our problem is, having acknowledged an enactment that involves our participation, we must then decide what to do with it. Responses range from not admitting it but taking it to one's own analyst or supervisor; to taking a corrective stance in the therapy, eliminating the behavior that alerted the patient (e.g., being very careful not to feel angry); to confessing one's participation to the patient thus sweeping it out of the way of the "analytic process"—that is the investigation of the patient's unconsciously motivated distortion; through suspending judgment about the patient's accuracy and accepting the "psychic reality" of the patient as the subject of inquiry. In this last instance, it does not much matter whether the patient is objectively right or wrong. Throughout this entire continuum, the basic traditional paradigm is maintained, albeit considerably bent. Namely, it is assumed that our Hermes, the therapist, is the agent of change for the patient through an explication of the patient's unconscious internal process that is signaled by ego defenses and distortion.

In relinquishing this fond belief, we may be suffering the existential vertigo of therapists who are now asking, "If I am not the arbiter of the patient's reality, what am I? What is it to be an analyst? What defines a patient if the patient may be the arbiter of my experience?" If we accept the patient's reality, are we reduced to a nonjudgmental relativism? Is there a consensually validatable outside reality which escapes the patient?[3] If we must deal with the patient's construction of the real world and our construction of the patient's construction, how can we arrive at truth? All of which lands us squarely in the tarpits of social constructivism.[4]

But constructivism is a red herring. What we are really all talking about is not arriving at a verifiable reality as if that cures the patient, but a change in psychoanalytic praxis, a conceptual shift in our perception of "patient-hood," what it is to be a patient. All of us have been reaching tentatively toward changes in process that seem not only to work empirically, but better fit our intuitive sense of appropriateness (a less arbitrary and authoritarian, more democratized psychoanalysis). Psychoanalysis is not entirely superordinate to culture. As the world changes, so do we, not only in our methods, but in our definitions of illness and cure; and, the paternalistic assumptions (Daddy, or the Doctor, knows best!) of traditional psychoanalysis are fallen out of favor. Indeed, the current matriarchal tendency to view the patient as a deprived and compromised child, with its concomitant infantilization of the patient's operations, may be giving way to a more egalitarian and democratized view of the process and the patient.

As I've said, this is a field where the relationship between cause and consequence—what we do and how the patient responds—is very over-determined and reasonable analysts could not claim any great clarity about what it is they do when what they do does work. So many things are going

46 Unfolding of Interpersonal Psychoanalysis

on at the same time: it is a field of contiguous effects. But psychoanalysts have powerful investments in the status quo. Theoretical and, more important, institutional affiliations define their identities; and, for our peace of mind (and livelihood), change must be conceived of as occuring within the constraints of the canonical model—as improvements, perhaps elaborations, but not as radical departures that might risk being regarded as apostasies. One hopes that all this is changing, but consider the apologetics that have been required of object-relations and self-psychology theorists in order to introduce a radically new therapeutic approach, and still stay within the organizational fold.[5]

As a case in point, consider the concepts of "acting-out" and "enactment." Acting-out was originally defined as a behavioral leak; that is, something that was not talked about was enacted and therefore lost to analysis. What was enacted could not be analyzed. Any behavior on the analyst's part was acting-out, particularly if it occurred out of the therapist's awareness (Freud, 1914). If a behavior were to be deliberately undertaken by the analyst, it skirted the dreaded "corrective emotional experience" of Alexander and French—almost universally decried by analysts although we all suspected that patients did have *de novo* and very useful experiences with us—but with the proviso that it "wasn't psychoanalysis"! (Alexander and French, 1946). When it became inescapable that the analyst's behavior was integral to the process, we began to talk of "parameters" of therapy, or "acting-in": all of which sounded more benign, forgivable, and maybe even somehow useful, not a bad idea at all. One might see how enactment would be the next step, carrying a much lower valence of error. Enactment implies, by definition, a behavioral transform of some fantasy, presumably the patient's. One hopes that the enactment offers a window for interpretation. But what if one extends the concept of enactment to include participation, implying the continuous presence of the therapist and particularly that the therapist is participating, not only out of traditional countertransference or projective-identification or projective-counter-identification, but out of his/her own being, own life experience, then what? One must wonder whether the basic paradigm is being honored more in the breach than not.

In a compendium of articles that go back over 30 years, the essence of my position about analyst participation was clearly limned out, especially in *The Fallacy of Understanding* (Levenson, 1972, 1991b). I make this admittedly immodest declaration to suggest that, with a different paradigm (interpersonalism), aspects of the therapist's presence in the process might be examined without the baggage of a superordinate intrapsychic position. This is not to say that interpersonalism doesn't carry its own baggage and impose its own limitations, or even that it's a better theory. But it might imply that converging, as we are, on clinical phenomona from different vantage points, we may yet proceed onto divergent tracks. In other words, are we all finally converging on the Via Reggia, the "Royal Road to the Unconscious" or are we simply passing at the crossroads? After all, that's where Oedipus got into trouble!

Interpersonal psychoanalysis is, of course, at this late date no more monolithic a theory than any other (Gill, 1983). There are a wide variety of positions subsumed under the rubric, but essential to the position is the belief that all through life, the person is dependent on other people to meet his/her needs for both gratifications and the basic necessities (material and emotional) for survival. The infant and child must learn, to use Bruner's term, to "negotiate" his/her way through life, managing relationships so as to maximize the rewards and minimize serious threats of desertion, neglect, or attack (Bruner, 1990). It may well be that the greater the risks to survival, the more exquisite are the skills developed by the patient for reading the necessary Other's level of anxiety and modulating it—this early warning system is what Sullivan called the "self-system," not at all coterminous with the Self (Sullivan, 1953). The theory allows for a context of social and cultural experience that is channeled through the family. Certain aspects of experience are dimly apperceived by the developing child, but meet with family disapproval and anxiety. Since anxiety in others is contagiously experienced and results in serious disruptions in the relationship, the subject learns to "inattend" the event, to use Sullivan's term; i.e., to avert his/her eyes, to not know what is there to be known. This is quite different from dissociation, wherein the awareness mobilizes so much anxiety that it is driven totally out of the realm of perception. In selective inattention, the person has often a vague sense of knowing there is something he/she does not know; much like remembering vaguely that there is something one has forgotten to do.

Dissociation, on the other hand, surfaces without recognition, only through manifestations of severe anxiety.[6] Perhaps there are similarities to unconscious and preconscious, but the striking difference is that both inattention and dissociation are triggered by anxiety in the other person and motivated by a desire to not fracture necessary relationships. Anxiety

48 Unfolding of Interpersonal Psychoanalysis

then is interpersonal and relational. Not that there are not unconscious fantasies, or a self-perpetuating intrapsychic domain, but that, strictly for the purposes of this very operational theory, they are considered the sequelae of interpersonal experience (Beebe et al., 1992).

The neurotic person, then, has constricted and disavowed aspects of his/her experience that would threaten relationships with significant providers. Perception of the world is riddled with blindspots that are deliberate inattentions and profoundly distressed dissociations. The relationship between historical and contemporary experience, especially between the patient and the therapist, is complex.

Let us consider a patient whose mother manifested a largely dissociated anger through passive-aggressive acts, often an obstructionistic pseudo-stupidity. The patient responded by "tantrumy" behavior so that he was regarded generally as a difficult and sullen child. To validate his rage toward his mother would require that he admit her anger. This constituted a double danger. First, her anger was frightening and threatened him with loss of caretaking; since it is frequently true that the angriest parent is the vital caretaker (the other parent is frequently remote). Second, she was unaware of being angry and, if confronted, would overwhelm him with evidence—which she believed!—that he was wrong, crazy, ungrateful, like his father, and, moreover, such attacks make life not worth living. So, the danger of desertion (withholding of love) is augmented by the fear of her anger and most important, the terrible consequences of her unawareness— an undermining, or mystification of his experience and his sense of reality.

Let us also suppose that the patient entered therapy for sexual impotence. In the course of treatment, he discovers the same helpless rage toward his wife that he experienced with his mother. Is this distortion? Well, one might say the degree of affect is: he is not, after all, realistically as dependent on his wife as he was on his mother. Nor is she his mother. So, when he "works through" his childhood experience, he will deal with her with greater equanimity and she will, correspondingly, become more agreeable. Maybe, maybe not. She may, indeed, be very much like his mother. In that case, he should leave her or discover some way of dealing with her, some empowerment with her, which pressures her to change. Usually, at this point in the therapeutic exploration, an enactment takes pace in the relationship with the therapist. The patient may play out the impasse with the therapist, but reversing roles. The therapist finds himself/herself in the role of the child, impotent in the face of passive-aggressive anger.

Resolution may require that the therapist be able to put his/her money where his/her mouth is; that is, be able to enact with the patient a resolution to a problem that the patient believes is unresolvable.

If the patient were to leave therapy with the traditional insight that he is distorting, carrying over a childhood experience into the present; he may reform, learn to be nice to his presumably deserving wife, and inattend his anger—not necessarily a great psychoanalytic resolution, even if she rewards his acquiescence. If he proceeds to the next step, he will feel angry at his wife. Many ex-patients seem to be frozen in that state of injured entitlement. To take the critical step, to move from blame to responsibility, one must acquire a sense of competence—of what I have called semiotic competence because it implies interpersonal skill; first an enhanced awareness of interpersonal subtleties and, second, an ability to reach out to and influence the other person to change, or to change the other person (Levenson, 1987).

I have constructed the above case scenario to illustrate, in a somewhat stylized way, the interpersonal rationale for neurotic development. How does this carry-over into a therapy? What is the corresponding interpersonal vision of transference/countertransference? If we consider the therapist as a participant-observer—as being his/her own message—the fulcrum of leverage shifts from the therapist or the patient, to the interpersonal field equidistant to them both.

For example, if a woman patient has masochistic fantasies and a masochistic transference, she will very likely call out—at least, in male therapists, and, I suspect, many women therapists—a sadistic counter-transference. Surely we would all agree that she has tapped into something about the therapist's problems with masculinity and power. She is not imagining his responses. If we believe we must get through that to engage her problems with masochism, the therapist may acknowledge her right to her perceptions of the interaction (her "psychic reality"); but then attempt to interpret to her the dynamics of her conflict. Is he not reclaiming control? If you tell the patient she is masochistic, aren't you being sadistic?

There is an old analyst's joke: Who is a sadist? Answer: someone who is kind to a masochist. Perhaps to work successfully with a masochistic person, one cannot do it by exorcising one's own sadomasochism through self-therapy or by appeal to one's own analyst. No analyst can be swept so clean of shortcomings as to satisfy the relentless assessments of the patient. Nor can one admit to the patient that perhaps one sounded

50 Unfolding of Interpersonal Psychoanalysis

a bit harsh but, nevertheless, one's interpretations are worth listening to. Nor can one get away with admitting to feeling sadistic but blaming it on projective-identification—the psychoanalyst's version of "The Debbil made me do it!" That is not validation of the patient, but quite simply blame. What then is left? I suspect one must accept the sadism as one's own, coming out of one's own experience prior to meeting the patient. This does not require a *mea culpa* or a confession of all one's sins: that would be nothing more than a restructuring of the sadomasochistic power struggle.

Paradoxically, the resolution may come from a Zen "letting go." At least in my experience, if the analyst simply owns his/her feelings, quite relentlessly blaming patients will suddenly become generous, allowing the therapist some leeway and personal limitation. Patients are, I believe, genuinely unbound by the therapist's openness to their observations—perhaps even to the extent of introducing the therapist to events outside of his/her awareness. Raging, implacable patients may then suddenly become quite generous toward the therapist's observed shortcomings, if they are not denied or blamed on the patient (projective counter-identification); i.e., if the patient's observations are acknowledged as accurate and valuable participations (not simply accepted as the patient's "psychic reality"). Is it possible that patients do not so much demand you change as that you validate their experience of you? Moreover, taking care of the therapist—forgiving shortcomings and maintaining good faith in a less than perfect situation—may well be an act of transcendence, and an antidote to the deadly, "me-first" self-absorption often promulgated by contemporary psychoanalysis.

However, this requires a certain nondefensiveness on the part of the therapist. If one observes closely, the patient often offers a sharply perceptive observation about people in his/her life, including the therapist—closely followed by a disruptive inappropriate behavior that grabs the analysts's attention and allows the previous interaction to pass unnoticed. The patient reaches for power and validity and then does a belly-up! The hostile submission of the masochistic position is a marvelous compromise solution: it offers power to the authority in a way that renders him/her powerless and, in addition, it eliminates any possibility of real anger from the therapist. Of course, the therapist may become angered at the masochism, but then we usually treat that as the therapist's problem, not as an authentic reaction to the patient as an accurate and threatening observer. To repeat, I believe that patients accept mystification of their experience as the price of survival; and, a great deal of working-through in therapy is required for them to feel safe enough to change their minds.

Let me refer briefly to another rather famous example focused specifically on the issue of the mystification of the transference. Greenson (1976) reports on a male patient who after some time in therapy informs him that he has noted that when he says something Greenson approves of, he is rewarded with a grunt and when he has said something Greenson does not approve of, it is greeted with silence (Greenson, 1976; Levenson, 1981). The patient has adjusted his comments accordingly. Greenson is honestly amazed to see that this is true. The patient has read him quite accurately. So, he validates it, admits to the patient that he is right. But then, he goes on to ask the patient why he felt it necessary to be so submissive. This is consistent with the prevalent mid-position of first validating the patient's observations and then dissecting that clear from the patient's problems. "Why," asks Greenson, "do you find it necessary to put yourself in that submissive role?" Or, alternately, "Why do you find it necessary to treat me as if I were so authoritarian?" That's the problem! What if the patient answered:

> Why shouldn't I? You didn't know what signals you were sending. And, if it's out of your vaunted awareness, I have good reason to assume that if I notice it, or defy you, you would get upset. That wouldn't be so bad, if you knew it. What really scares me is that you would feel reasonable, act reasonable, but it would fester out of your awareness and I would be punished or deprived without chance of validation. My experience would be twisted, mystified, to protect your experience.

Of course, polite patients don't talk like that, although borderlines sometimes do. I am suggesting that the therapist acknowledging, with some amazement, his unaware control and even acknowledging that he didn't think he did things like that is enough! Patients will be quite satisfied with that response and be surprisingly generous about any limitation of the therapist's awareness for which they will not be blamed or held responsible. I have found that if I am angry or upset about something outside of the session or tired or feeling ill, at the first suggestion that the patient is uneasy, it helps to simply admit it. I must say I anticipated being excoriated or to having the patient withdraw sullenly. More often, the patient looked relieved and returned to his/her problems with the usual relish. I must confess I felt slightly miffed that only my very polite patients (the hardest to treat) ever expressed any solicitude.

From this perspective, the patient has certainly become the "interpreter of the analyst's experience," as Hoffman so nicely put it, (Hoffman, 1987, p. 213). If we believe that they must mutually resolve their joint problem, that they are two sides of the same coin, then there is a rationale for admitting that the patient has shown you something you did not see. On the other hand, if one is trying to bring the patient into conscious contact with an intrapsychic problem, it is hard to see what value there is in contaminating the field with one's own problems, except to admit them in order to clear the field for a more objective examination of the patient's distortions.

From my viewpoint there are several distinct advantages to a genuine mutuality. By acknowledging what the patient *sees*, one establishes that one is not too anxious to entertain discussion; i.e., the subject is not taboo. As a simple example, consider the patient who dreams that he is standing in the street in the area of the analyst's office. To his horror, he observes a steamroller backing over an unsuspecting grey-haired man. He awakes to a feeling of foreboding. The analyst inquires about day residues, associations to no great avail. Finally, he suggests mildly, "Do you think it might be me?" Instantly, there is a flood of associations to a forgotten flash of irritation the patient had experienced last session. This is, of course, embarrassingly obvious. But what happened? Did the interpretation bring the patient into touch with dissociated rage? But the dream is so blatantly obvious. It seems more as if in telling me the dream the patient is saying:

> Say, listen, if you'll pick up on this obvious hint that I'm angry at you, then I'll see that you can tolerate it, you're not too strung out by it, and I'll be able to bring it into the open. Moreover, if you're not so threatened that you'd just as soon let it go by, I may be reassured that my anger is not a steamroller, not disastrous; and, what's more, maybe in the future I won't have to back into awareness by letting you make the interpretation.

I would call the anger "inattended" and requiring, not the interpretation of the analyst, but the participation of the analyst, particularly in a respectful inquiry into what might have provoked the angry moment in the previous session.

The implication is that for change to take place, the therapist too must change what he/she is doing. Cure becomes a mutual process, and the patient is not only the interpreter of the analyst's experience, but a collaborator in the therapist's cure. I can imagine what response that statement calls forth! I remember a patient, extremely critical and demanding, who kept raging at me, "Before we're done together I'm going to cure you!" Each time, no matter how hard I gritted my teeth, I was flooded with fury. After all, wasn't I the analyst? Only after I wondered to myself why I had to cure her and what did it mean to cure her that we arrived at a compromise: I wouldn't try to cure her if she'd stop trying to cure me! It eased the course of therapy considerably.

Therapy "fills in," enriches the patient who needs an opportunity, not just to recapture fantasies but to recapture awareness and the disowned self. To do so requires a dialogue with someone who will permit that process to take place, whose anxiety is low enough to allow the patient to reach out, rediscover his/her ability to perceive accurately, to engage another person without fear of destruction. This is different from permitting a "holding milieu" or a safe space to recapture fantasy or even to grow. I repeat, it is impossible to function with any richness and complexity in a world in which one cannot count on one's perceptions. It would be akin to being deaf and blind in a jungle, for that's what life is. Only a total fool would come out of therapy with the notion that everyone can be trusted, everyone is caretaking, that all one needs is to recapture "basic trust." That the analyst is presumably well intentioned is not much solace, since the patient suspects that even the therapist—that paragon of mental health— may well be out of touch with something about him/herself. Trust is a developmentally derived semiotic skill. It is not an epiphany following a good experience in treatment. What is necessary, and hopefully an outcome of the process I am suggesting, is that the patient will be empowered to read the world accurately and to negotiate his/her way with other people to get needs met. It may be, as current theory dictates, that patients are enraged and disappointed in their relationships with others because of infantile distortions and irrational expectations that must be modified. But I suspect their infantilizm and distortion may be the consequence, not the cause of their difficulties. Perhaps they are too demoralized, too endangered, to confront their experience.

54 Unfolding of Interpersonal Psychoanalysis

It is striking how often patients present outrageous, distorted, infantile perceptions of their experience (historical, contemporary or with the therapist) to the therapist, not because they necessarily believe it, but to distract the therapist from the panicky, despairing, dependency that binds them to the necessary others. Therapists, thinking they are in alliance with the patient to reveal parental failures and malfeasances, tend to forget that they are the "outsider" talking to the patient across what Wynn et al. called the "rubber fence" of the family, and that the patient is protecting his/her life from the therapist (Levenson 1991a; Wynn et al., 1958). We hope to establish, and indeed require, a working alliance with the patient; but it is important to remember that the neurotic system and the therapy are in an essentially antagonistic relationship.

In summary: we have moved from interpretation as conveying the canonical truths that set one free to interpretation as behavior. Interpretation becomes a message about the patient, the therapist, and the therapist's relationship with the patient. The therapist has a continuous presence, beginning with his/her own life experience, including why he/she became a therapist, what personal needs it met. That presence necessarily has a substratum of anxiety, from low to very high. Every response is a participation out of the therapist's worldview. I would claim that often the patient is most distorting at the moment of greatest contact with something about the therapist that is making the therapist anxious—at least in the room with the patient.

If one accepts the idea of a continuous interaction—no different than anywhere else in the world—then there will be situations wherein anxiety rises and defensive operations will take place on both sides; denial, distortion, anger, distancing, over-intellectualization, acting-out. With some patients, these take the form of dramatic and impelling exchanges, but such high drama is no more vital to treatment than the interactions that go by very quietly, unnoticed. There are patients who never improve because they are no trouble at all; superficially obliging and willing to do whatever you think they should. Sins of omission are more common and telling, in doing therapy, than sins of commission. This is what Sullivan had in mind when he said, "God keep me from a therapy that goes well!"

In 1968, Racker said that, "The first distortion of truth in the 'myth of the analytic situation' is that analysis is an interaction between a sick person and a healthy one" (Racker, 1968, p. 132). If that be so, and if we believe in a democratization of the therapy process, why don't we just plunge in and interact freely with the patient? There are two reasons; first, it is the safety of restraint that makes the process possible at all. Therapists can function as therapists not because they are necessarily healthier than patients, but because the role protects them. If you don't believe me, ask any analyst's family! Second, one must allow space and time for the patient to discover his/her own resources—to recapture what he/she has always known. Ultimately, the patient does not learn from us how to deal with the world. The patient learns to deal with us in order to deal with the world.

Notes

1. This chapter was first given, in shorter form, at the American Psychoanalytic Association meeting of December 18, 1992 as part of the panel "Interpretive Perspectives on Interaction," and published in *Contemporary Psychoanalysis*, 1993, 29:3, pp. 383–396.
2. Contribution to the American Psychoanalytic Association panel on Interpretive Perspectives on Interaction, meeting December 18, 1992.
3. One need only note the tremendous upsurge of interest in possible infant and childhood molestations, with all its trappings of amnesia, post-traumatic syndrome, abreaction in the transference, and cure through recall.
4. There has been an extensive exploration of this issue in *Psychoanalytic Dialogues* (1991) 1:1.
5. It is a veritable shell game. First one defines a new patient for whom classical psychoanalysis is not suitable. Ergo, variations in technique are permissible. Then one changes the nosology of patients until virtually everyone in therapy fits the new category.
6. Much of the current literature on childhood molestation emphasizes the extreme dissociation caused by the trauma. Multiple personality, borderline character disorder, and other severe disruptions of self-organization result.

References

Alexander, F. and French. T.M. (1946). *Psychoanalytic Therapy: Principles and Applications*. New York: Ronald Press.

Beebe, B., Jaffe, J., and Lachmann, F. (1992). A dyadic systems view of communication. In N. Skolnick and S. Warshaw (Eds.), *Relational Perspectives in Psychoanalysis*. Hillsdale, NJ: The Analytic Press.

Bruner, J. (1990). *Acts of Meaning*. Cambridge, MA: Harvard University Press.

Crapanzano, V. (1992). *Hermes's Dilemma and Hamlet's Desire*. Cambridge, MA: Harvard University Press.

Freud, S. (1914). Remembering, repeating and working through. In J. Strachey (Ed.), *The Standard Edition of the Complete Psychological Works of Sigmund Freud*. London: Hogarth Press, Vol. XXII, pp. 145–156.

56 Unfolding of Interpersonal Psychoanalysis

Gill, M. (1983). The interpersonal paradigm and the degree of the analyst's involvement. *Contemporary Psychoanalysis*, 18(2):200–237.

Greenson, R. (1976). *The Technique and Practice of Psychoanalysis*. New York: International Universities Press.

Handleman, S. (1982). *The Slayers of Moses: The Emergence of Rabbinic Interpretation in Modern Literary Theory*. Albany, NY: State University of New York.

Hoffman, I. (1987). The value of uncertainty. *Contemporary Psychoanalysis*, 23(2):205–215.

Jacobs, T. (1991). *The Use of the Self: Countertransference and communication in the analytic situation*. New York: International Universities Press.

Levenson, E. (1972). *The Fallacy of Understanding*. New York: Basic Books.

Levenson, E. (1981). Language and healing. In S. Slipp (Ed.), *Curative Factors in Dynamic Psychotherapy*. New York: McGraw-Hill.

Levenson, E. (1987). How theory shapes technique: Perspectives on a clinical case. An interpersonal perspective. *Psychoanalytic Inquiry*, 7(2):207–214.

Levenson, E. (1988). The pursuit of the particular. *Contemporary Psychoanalysis*, 24(1):1–16.

Levenson, E. (1991a). Back to the future: The new psychoanalytic revisionism. *Contemporary Psychotherapy Review*, 6(1):27–43.

Levenson, E. (1991b). *The Purloined Self*. New York: Contemporary Psychoanalysis Books.

Racker, H. (1968). *Transference and Counter-transference*. New York: International University Press.

Sullivan, H.S. (1953). *The Interpersonal Theory of Psychiatry*. New York: W.W. Norton.

Wynn, L.C., Ryckoff, I.M. et al. (1958). Pseudomutuality in the family relationships of schizophrenics. *Psychiatry*, 21:205–220.

Chapter 5

A Monopedal version of Interpersonal Psychoanalysis[1]

Appearances really aren't deceiving, you just have to know where to look.

Rabbi Hillel—I think it was—was asked to define the meaning of the Talmud while standing on one leg (not an easy task as one gets older!). "Treat others as you would have them treat you," he said. Can interpersonal psychoanalysis be defined while standing on one leg? Some might say that it would require a prosthetic support. Nevertheless, here goes!

Interpersonal psychoanalysis may be defined as the science of omissions. Note *omission*, not *repression*. Repression denotes an intrapsychic process, a one-person psychology: something within the person's psyche must be *kept down*, out of awareness. Omission is an interpersonal event; something is *left-out* in a discourse between people, a two-person psychology.

This is an absolutely crucial distinction between interpersonal psycho-analysis and virtually all other psychoanalytic psychologies, including so-called relational ones (object-relations, self-psychologies). Although it is true that object-relational and self-psychologies are intersubjective, the emphasis is on restitutive function; i.e., making up for deprivations or, at least, supplying a "holding milieu" in which early deprivation may be regressively experienced and then reconstituted by the patient. They attempt to establish an interpersonal milieu within which an intrapsychic experience can take place. The interpersonal does not do that. It attempts to establish an interpersonal field that may be subjected to direct examina-tion by both participants, and that recapitulates the central problems in the patient's life. This making explicit of what is hidden is the essence of interpersonalism. It is not a restitutive experience; it does not attempt to supply a *better* experience than the patient has had, heretofore, in life. Indeed, interpersonalism expects to fail the patient in the same way as did

58   Unfolding of Interpersonal Psychoanalysis

others in life. We are interested in examining *how* this failure takes place, even with the allegedly sophisticated therapist. One must admit that, in all therapies, the patient ultimately does have a different and better experience with the therapist and that the cure depends on that salutary context. But how we arrive at that goal differs considerably.

To grasp the interpersonal canon, one must understand that *anxiety*, as an interpersonal event, is the core of the concept. That is, anxiety is viewed as primarily an empathically communicated interpersonal experience (Sullivan, 1953). The infant, child, adolescent—on unto old age, requires other people for the satisfaction of basic needs. To be human is to be related: otherwise one dies. I am talking, not just of emotional satisfactions, but also of basic sustenance. Disruptive anxiety, then, occurs if the individual feels threatened (that is, at risk of deprivation), or experiences anxiety emanating from the necessary Others. Anxiety, then, is an interpersonal event and the person develops a mechanism for avoiding anxiety; what Sullivan called the self-system, a conglomeration of defenses, ranging from inattention, avoidance, deep disavowal, and, perhaps most important a series of interpersonal manoeuvres to maintain self-equilibrium and to minimize the appearance of situations that threaten to evoke anxiety. Thus, all the security mechanisms of the patient are directed toward the other person, to prevent the disintegration of the interpersonal relationship. So, in a word, defenses are against *other people*, not against one's own unconscious.

All this exquisitely sensitive interpersonal dynamism is kept out of awareness, inattended; indeed, to operate, it *must* be out of awareness. It is therefore axiomatic that the higher the risk—the higher the level of anxiety—the more likely it is that there will be a scotoma, a hole in the fabric of awareness. And, the function of the therapist is to locate these absences. It is not where Id was there shall Ego be; but where absence was, there shall presence be.

This detailed inquiry, which is nothing more than asking "curiouser and curioser" questions about the patient's reported experience permeates every area of the therapy. I have, elsewhere, described the "algorithm" of psycho-analysis as consisting of three parts; the first is a meticulously defined frame; second a detailed inquiry that is a contextual enrichment of the patient's life experience; and third is a meticulous examination of the patient/therapist relationship (loosely called the transference/countertrans-ference) that emerges seamlessly out of the detailed inquiry, as I shall elaborate later (Levenson, 1982a, p. 118).

The first step, the frame, consists of the establishment of constraints and limits: those arrangements that are made in psychoanalysis about contractual commitments—time, money, frequency, cancellation of sessions, vacations and so forth. There is, however, a subtler aspect of framing that invokes the detailed inquiry; and that has to do with being curious about and *asking* about the detailed circumstances of how this particular patient got to you, and decided to stay with you. Some of the most extra-ordinary blind spots seem to overtake analysts at this particular juncture of the therapy.[2] Moreover, it is vital that one explores with the patient what the anticipated cure would consist of. What does the patient want? Expect? Patients often present with a symptom; depression, sexual difficulties, anxiety, which they presumably want resolved. But the symptom is often a compromise solution, better that something else, something far worse; and the patient resists losing the symptom and—oddly enough—will frequently quit therapy (by no means happily) if the symptom is lifted by some form of active, interventional therapy. Inexperienced therapists are often perplexed when their brilliantly formulated and incisive early assessments of the patient's problems may lead to a precipitous end to the therapy.

Patients, not unlike the rest of us, resent being understood easily. It makes it look all too simple and the patient feels obtuse. The effect, then, of this first stage of inquiry is to make patients understand that their singularity and privacy are respected; that the therapist is not doling out clichés, not gratuitously "understanding" the patient! Do people wish to be understood? They want empathy, sympathy, respect, appreciation, liking—but understood? I think not. I mean that they don't want to be understood before *they* understand what is there to be understood. Moreover, the patient has good reasons not to want to know, not to see what is there to be seen; and it is presumptuous in the extreme to rush in to the rescue. Patients certainly must wish to be heard if they say something to you. Even if your inquiry suggests that you do not understand; they will appreciate that you are listening very carefully and not taking for granted what it is you think you are hearing.

All this is prologue to the detailed inquiry into the patient's presentation. The therapist locates these scotomata by looking for absences, omissions, in the coherence of the patient's narrative. These "black holes" are the repository of anxiety and consequently of those issues and experiences that are being excluded from awareness. These absences may reveal themselves by sudden changes of direction, silences, slips, forgettings, postural cues;

or by indirection, simply the consequence of the therapist inquiring into some event in the patient's life without any clear sense of where the inquiry is going, and without any dynamic formulation in mind. There is a vital distinction between a directed inquiry which is Socratic—its intent is to lead the respondent to some inevitable conclusion—and an undirected inquiry that is deconstructive—one never knows quite what will emerge from it. This, by the way, is extremely simple in concept and very difficult to carry out

To repeat, the function of a detailed inquiry is not to construct a veridical or instrumentally useful narrative about the patient's life, however helpful and organizing that might be, in a psychotherapy sense. It is to *deconstruct* the story, locate the omissions, and investigate them. This, by the way, does not preclude the investigation of dreams, fantasies, or free-associations. It is simply that we believe they are swarming around an absence, rather than emerging from a repression. In listening to a patient's account, we are not trying to make sense of it, not doing what Masud Khan disparagingly called, "getting the patient to tell us his/her truth, so that we can tell them the *Metatruth*"; but trying to locate the issues or affects that are inattended, disowned.

Traditionally, psychoanalysis was based on the idea that people acted in predictable ways, playing out predictable patterns. They were driven by universal forces; and therefore, one could speculate about the larger issues; sexual drives, need for mothering, empathic failure, dependency, fear of separation and loss, or fear of death. It was the age of enlightenment, the age of categorization, and the patient's individual neurosis would be manifest as a member of some such general class of behavior. In other words, we were less interested in the *singularity* of the patient than in his/her experience as representative of a universal class of behaviors. This is, after all, the entire intent of traditional metapsychologies; i.e., to provide a superordinate blanket of explanation for individual behavior.

We do not seem to believe any longer in clear-cut cause and effect and in reliable predictions. In the postmodern world, the failure of explanation, the fallacy of understanding is painfully evident (Ingram, 1994, p.166). People are not totally known to themselves or to others. Perhaps they are not even the same people in different contexts. They may be, as Sullivan contended, the sum of their experience; and there may be, within one person, as many personalities as there are experiential contexts.

From all this emerges the third stage of the interpersonal algorithm, a radical use of transference and countertransference. Since the patient needs the therapist, he/she will monitor, with great solicitude and wariness, any evidence of the therapist's anxiety and will avoid it! If the patient suspects the therapist is seriously threatened by anger, he/she will assiduously side-step it, all without conscious awareness. That is why what Gill called interpretations of awareness work: that is, when the therapist says, "Perhaps you are angry at me," the patient is receiving permission to feel what he/she already feels. As Lacan so neatly put it, "the patient [in therapy] learns what the analyst knows, which is what the patient has always known." Omissions are not total absences. The patient knows on some level that he/she is not supposed to know what he/she knows. The therapist indicates that anger, at least from the patient, is tolerable. Transference may be defined as the patient constructing the relationship with the therapist in such a way as to minimize anxiety in the interpersonal field and inadvertently and inevitably recreating, in the relationship, the very problems under discussion. Countertransference, conversely, is defined as what the therapist does not see, does not think to ask about.

Frequently, therapists talk about angry, erotic, or bored feelings toward a patient as emblematic of countertransference. I really do not think so. Those feelings are in awareness and are useful indices of a legitimate experience with the patient. Boredom is a perfectly appropriate reaction to a patient who is involved in a soliloquy, who is talking to himself about himself. True countertransference is, in my opinion, totally *out* of aware-ness. What is kept out of awareness, in this example, is the therapist's anger, which comes out of a desire to be considered, or acknowledged. This desire upsets the analyst's view of his/her idealized participation as caring or concerned or generous. To be aware of it, to reveal it, might get him/her into trouble with a supervisor; or it might anger the patient who would then quit or denounce the therapist as being "too critical." Patient and therapist collude to not see what is there to be seen. What makes so-called borderline patients so excruciating to work with is that they are exquisitely sensitive to these issues and—unlike the well-behaved neurotic who avoids anxiety—they exacerbate them.

To summarize: interpersonal psychoanalytic therapy consists of a carefully framed detailed inquiry that mobilizes anxiety by looking where one is not supposed to look. The heightened level of anxiety pervades the patient/therapist field, calling out security operations from both participants and, in essence, recapitulating the material under examination. Psycho-analytic cure is an enrichment of perception. The patient is left (as is the

62 Unfolding of Interpersonal Psychoanalysis

therapist) with a much more richly textured sense of his/her life; not at all simpler or clearer. I am suspect of those cures wherein the patient learns what is wrong and gets better—as in "my mother didn't really love me." In real life, relationships, particularly with parents, are far more complex than that. Most parents are loving in some ways and not in others; and, besides, one becomes what one experiences and to disown the parent is to disown oneself, what one has become. It was, in my training days, a truism that one should not be too hasty in joining the patient in his/her parent-bashing, since the patient is usually strongly identified with the parent of whom they are being most vociferously critical, and will hesitate to let you in later on those very qualities in themselves which you both agreed to disapprove of in the parent.

I think real health is to tolerate ambiguity and paradox in oneself and others—patients, therapists, and parents alike. Psychoanalytic change is not, in my opinion, a series of epiphanies, and there is not some Holy Grail of mental health that makes it possible to live happily ever after. It is a lifetime struggle to cope with oneself and self-awareness is only the beginning. Sullivan made a distinction between psychoanalytic treatment and real life. Therapy could provide the patient with insight, a clearer grasp into his/her life. But what the patient then did with that awareness was out of the analyst's purview. Insight did not guarantee change: that requires an additional act of social will.

Notes

1. This was first published in 1995, in the journal, *The Review of Interpersonal Psychoanalysis*, 1(1):1–4.
2. See for a sterling example of just such a blind beginning by a very experienced therapist (Levenson, 1982b, p. 161).

References

Ingram, D. (1994). Poststructuralist interpretation of the psychoanalytic relationship. *Journal of the American Academy of Psychoanalysis*, 2:175–193.
Levenson, E. (1982a). Follow the fox: An inquiry into the vicissitudes of psychoanalytic supervision. *Contemporary Psychoanalysis*, 18(1):1–15.
Levenson, E. (1982b). Playground or playpen. Comments on *The Psychoanalytic Process* by P. Dewald. *Contemporary Psychoanalysis*, 18(3):365–372.
Sullivan, H.S. (1953). *The Interpersonal Theory of Psychiatry*. New York: W.W. Norton.

Chapter 6

And the last shall be first

Some observations on the evolution of interpersonal psychoanalysis[1]

> And the last shall be first and the first last
>
> (Matthew 20:16)

This chapter was first published as a paper in a commemorative issue, which seemed an appropriate place to review some aspects of the evolution of interpersonal psychoanalysis since my first meeting with Ruth Moulton in 1951, when I applied for candidacy to the William Alanson White Institute. It is, of course, a personal and impressionistic version with which surely not everyone will agree.

She had, I knew, a reputation as an "analyst's analyst," especially for women. She was a great favorite of bright, young, educated women— analysts, professional women of all ilk, housewives, other analysts' wives and girlfriends. She was writing extensively about women's problems; to be an interpersonalist was, as I elaborate, *pari passu*, to be a feminist. But potential patients select analysts less for their prominence or reputation and rather more because they see the analyst as a role model: someone they feel had faced and successfully dealt with their kind of problems. She overwhelmingly met these criteria. She was married to an analytic colleague, had handsome and accomplished children from two marriages, wrote and taught extensively, lived a sophisticated, intellectual life. Also, she'd had the courage to leave her candidacy at the New York Psycho-analytic Institute and follow her analyst, Clara Thompson, and Erich Fromm into exile. And as I discovered in my interview with her—and I can't remember how I learned this—she was a great admirer of the modernist and protofeminist, Virginia Woolf. Perhaps it's inconsequential,

64 Unfolding of Interpersonal Psychoanalysis

but she was, like the young Virginia Woolf, serenely beautiful. As one may deduce, I was smitten, and on my acceptance to candidacy went into supervision with her, and somewhat later, with Clara Thompson.

The politics of psychoanalysis and of women's rights were conflated, but this was a decade before Betty Friedan's *The Feminine Mystique* (1963) and the founding of NOW, The National Organization for Women (1966). The series of political battles that led to the founding in 1946 of the William Alanson White Institute were fought over Horney, Thompson, and Fromm's rejection of the Freudian vision of female dynamics, and in a later split over Sullivan's radical theoretical departures (see Moulton, 1968b, on the formation of the White institute.) In place of biological destiny and instinct, they substituted social context and culture. Fromm's Marxist sociology and theological slant emphasized the distorting of human potential by larger socioeconomic issues. Sullivan, an autodidact far more eclectic in his sources, was influenced by the "social psychology"—as he called it—of C.H. Cooley and G.H. Mead at the University of Chicago, the pragmatism of C.S. Peirce, W. James, and J. Dewey, and the linguistic anthropology of his "dear friend" Edward Sapir (Chatelaine, 1981, pp. 196–197).

Both Moulton and Thompson seemed far more "commonsense" oriented than Sullivan and Fromm, the Master Theory Builders (Moulton, 1975). Why were they so modest in their goals? Horney, alone among these brilliant, rebellious women, broke off entirely and developed a personal metapsychology. Clara Thompson remained devoted to Sullivan—really somewhat in awe of him—as was Moulton to a lesser degree. She thought of Sullivan's clinical perceptions as "uncanny" (Moulton, 1982–1983, p. 15). Oddly enough, in those early years at White, Fromm was subjected to considerable more-or-less respectful critiquing, but Sullivan was sacrosanct. I recall as late as 1988, when I presented a paper at the fortieth anniversary meeting of the White Institute that questioned some of Sullivan's positions, some senior people (including my former analyst) were appalled.[2]

Politics reify metapsychologies, turn them into battle cries. Having disavowed instinctual drive, cultural psychoanalysts were left with a very heavy contextual slant. They believed, as the Zen saying goes, that to see the fish one must look at the water. The thrust of their work—and, in spite of her studies with Ferenczi, this would include Thompson's—was pragmatic, demystifying.[3] Moulton did pay a great deal of attention to developmental themes; but again, it seemed to me, she saw the issue as the emergence of the child through her family dynamics into the larger social world with all its dissonant pressures (Moulton, 1970).

Her lucid focus on the actual experience of the patient in the interpersonal matrix seemed to me, at the time, a breath of fresh air. Her assumption was that things went wrong with the patient because things were *done* to the patient, both in the immediate family and in the larger society. These events were obfuscated—or "inattended," to use Sullivan's term—because of contagious anxiety. One does not *see* what is there to see because to see would cause unbearable tensions in the interpersonal matrix. So using a Meyerian-Sullivanian detailed inquiry, one searched for the critical omissions, the blind spots—what would now be called the "gapped narrative." One did not need to predicate drive, dark impulses, evil as a real component of human experience, or masochism as anything more than response to powerlessness. In retrospect, it seems somewhat utopian, Augustinian. What of Dostoyevsky's (1961) lamentation,

> And where did these sages pick up the notion that man must have something they feel is a normal and virtuous set of wishes; what makes them think that man's will must be reasonable and in accordance with his own interests? (p. 110).

I believe that their rejection of the Freudian version of women's sexual dynamics and the pressures of an emergent women's movement conspired to repudiate theory building as a version of political oppression, serving to obfuscate, with theoretical and categorical conclusions, the concrete damage being done to the human and social potential of women (and children and men) in the real world. In this sense, interpersonalism provided a much-needed antidote to the overreaching deterministic generalizations of Freudian theory, but it made it very difficult for interpersonalists to entertain the mysteries of the analytic praxis. The irony was that although the Freudian conclusions may have been doctrinaire and predictable, the *method*, the praxis, was not. Perhaps free-association—the *vis à tergo* of classical psychoanalysis—allowed more play of the imagination, more creative collaboration, more unconscious and intuitive leaps than did the early interpersonalists' meticulous attention to real experience. Free-association, I'm afraid, turns out to be a far more potent and mysterious process than we were led to believe in those early years at White.

In my experiences of supervision, I believe that Thompson, older and more imbedded in classical training than Moulton, had more interest in the associative play, the stream of consciousness.[4] Thompson said to me that she'd given up free-association, not because she didn't find it uniquely valuable, but because most patients couldn't do it—"They just nattered on!" She also told me, with wry regret, that candidates didn't "seem to believe anymore in the unconscious." Moulton was much closer to Sullivan and Fromm-Reichman in her belief that behind the world of fantasy and phantasmagoria was a mystified reality, rendered incomprehensible and chaotic by the patient's unendurable anxiety. The play of imagination was part of the disease, not the cure.

> Intellectually, man recognizes outdated concepts, and rationally accepts new ones, but the hidden influence of childhood impressions, reflecting the childhood of the parent, continue to effect behavior. Their persistence in the unconscious cannot be erased by reason or will . . . *Since intrapsychic structures are not innately predetermined but develop in the process of an individual's interaction with his environment*, it follows that social changes influence the manifestations of conflict characteristic of a given decade.
>
> (Moulton, 1972, p. 196; my italics)

This is clearly true, as far as it goes, and typical of Moulton's lucid take on interpersonal experience. Supervision with her, especially for a neophyte analyst, was extremely helpful. She could focus apparently diffuse data, put it into social context. The therapeutic act was helping the patient to see how unwittingly he or she was participating in a familial and general social matrix and what that contribution cost in terms of constricting personal potentials. Although she did feature transference as an issue, it seemed to me to be in the classical context of resistance. Countertransference, as an egalitarian, ongoing, continuous part of the therapy and as a source of information about the interpersonal transaction, was, I believe— as in Sullivan—less emphasized.

Interpersonal psychoanalysis, or as we also thought of it then, "Cultural" psychoanalysis, represented an authentically radical revolutionary movement that inevitably was heavily politicized by its excommunication. It became necessary to demonize the opposition. I remember supervising my first candidate, who was reporting on a 27-year-old woman who was wont to have her mother soap her down in the bathtub. When I suggested to the candidate that this might be considered erotic behavior, she walked out of supervision in high dudgeon! Stunned by this draconian response to my first efforts at analytic supervision, I sought out—and had some real trouble finding—a senior analyst who would support my position. I might add, I didn't think that sexuality was *all* it was, but I didn't think sexuality should be excluded simply because that's what "they" would think. I hasten to add that I'm talking about an early period at White, when we were still on the barricades, before the current atmosphere of ecumenism that, I trust, makes such zealotry unnecessary.

It seems to me, in retrospect, that in rejecting the image of the Freudian woman, imbedded in her instinctual destiny, we threw out the dark mythic components of the Freudian Unconscious. We opened the windows, blew the dust away, let in fresh air. But, as Rollo May (1991) suggested, myths may have their uses. When we threw out the myths, we threw out the mythopöeisis, losing the quality of free-associative creativity that some of us are attempting to re-establish (Levenson, 1988; Stern, 1997; Wilner, 1999).

Can one imagine psychoanalysis without the Oedipus Complex? Freud's appropriation of the Greek myth was an act of literary genius.[5] Rather than establishing a trope demonstrating the power of libido, instinctual drive— after all, Oedipus didn't even know that Jocasta was his mother—Freud tapped into the immense hold of myths over the popular imagination, rather like dreams, that other manifestation of the flow of consciousness. The Oedipus myth (not complex) is as intertextual as any piece of psycho-analytic data.

Both Moulton and Thompson had a certain "commonsense" (as Moulton referred to Thompson's work) simplicity, very appealing in its lucidity and social justice; but perhaps something was also lost (Moulton, 1975, pp. 218–219). Instinct theory had that mythopoetic richness and darkness absent from the apple-pie clarity of pragmatism. Were our cured patients perhaps better oriented, better able to make their own choices, rather than being well-adjusted—that is, "shrunk"? Still, was some capacity for imagination and play not developed? It seems to me that both axes, pragmatics and poetics, seem vitally complementary; that is, we need to hold in dialectic tension the search for inattended experience and the flow of consciousness (Levenson, 1988a).

The cosmic joke may be that after all the endless disputation about the validity of metapsychologies, it is possible that cure may have more to do with the *process* of self-discovery—not self-awareness—than *what* is discovered (see Gedo, 1999, p. 135, for a discussion of this theme). It may be that, as McLuhan (1964) put it, the medium is the message, or, as more recently, Bollas (1999) has said:

> It provides a new form of pleasure and a new skill, which we might call the playing of the unconscious. Patient and analyst repeatedly abandon themselves to unconscious forms of perception, reception, creativity and communication. . . . Well into a fictional world every bit as dense as a Dostoevsky novel, they are partly-aware beneficiaries of a radical new human skill: intentionally arranged for unconscious communication. . . . Whatever their doubts about such possibilities to begin with, in time both are humbled by the waves of realisation that this work, though mediated by conscious deliberative thought, originates in a place out of sight and out of mind, but forever streaming into consciousness (p. 194).

It wasn't until Tauber and Green's (1959) *Prelogical Experience* that a truly Ferenczian play emerged at White. They presented the idea of the praxis as being a play of consciousness that was, in turn, a mystery. I find it intriguing that Tauber, who was analyzed first by Thompson and then by Fromm, felt that Fromm was the major influence on his life and work. Yet his book was powerfully Ferenczian—one must assume via Thompson —and was the major influence on my thinking, although, since Tauber was my analyst, it took me a while to acknowledge that. Wolstein (Hirsch, 2000) presents Thompson as the major influence on his work, which I find to be *quite* in the tradition of Tauber, who, I know, was his first analyst.[6] We all seemed to be assuming the mantles of our fathers and simultaneously disowning them. Surely that sounds familiar.

It is an error to think of psychoanalytic evolution as a teleological process, as though we were proceeding from insight to insight. Rather, like "working-through" in the analytic praxis, it is a helix: each time the material comes around it is on a wider and more inclusive level. So pragmatics and poetics proceed in an ongoing continuous dialectic. Sometimes one focuses on inquiry and intervention, sometimes one sits back and follows

And the last shall be first   69

the associative flow, and sometimes one stimulates the flow by a more deconstructive inquiry. To quote Bollas (1999):

> Is psychoanalysis a dialogue? A conversation? An intersubjective occasion? Is it a one-body psychology or a two-body psychology? Where is it to be found? There are dialogues. It can be interpersonal. In some respects it is also intersubjective. And of course both participants are always intrapsychics [sic]. Transference always occurs as does countertransference, and they are rather enamored of one another. Every above-named element is present. It is all of those things, but in the end, none of them (p. 14).

The conclusions, the final "insights" of a therapy are always predictable, always the same for every therapy; pre-Oedipal issues of nurturance, issues of Oedipal conflict and power, issues of sexuality, desire, separation anxieties, disorders of the self. Analysts may use somewhat different frames of reference, but as Lacan's gnomic saying would suggest, "At the end of the therapy, the patient knows what the therapist knows which is what the patient has always known" (Wilden, 1972, p. 30). What is different and unique to every patient, and what is ultimately a mystery, is the process of arriving at those obvious truths.

Therein may lie the true contributions of interpersonal psychoanalysis. Sullivan's detailed inquiry—used in a deconstructive rather than an organizing way—turns out to be a powerful facilitator of free-association, to my mind still the primary instrument of the analytic praxis. We have also focused emphasis on free use of the transference-countertransference as a field of subtle and inattended interpersonal transactions, and an enactment of material under discussion, rather than as a resistance to insight. Attention to the deforming affects of social process per se, rather than as subordinate to unconscious drive, and a *sense* of play in the treatment, particularly in the use of countertransferential experience, are also intrinsic to the interpersonal canon.

As Moulton (1968a) so presciently put it,

> The advantages of an autonomous institute lie in its freedom to teach various attitudes and approaches. There is a danger of rejecting too completely the group which rejects you, without being clear about the

nature of the disagreement. Many of our students have been prejudiced against Freud because of the irrational stand that many Freudians have taken. Meanwhile the Freudians have been slowly and maybe unwittingly incorporating into their own teachings many of the basic ideas of our founders without giving due credit. This is the fate of dissenters. They may play an important role in stimulating change, but are never loved by the establishment for upsetting its ways (pp. 8–9).

Alas, metapsychology degrades over time. Either it is captured by a cohort of disciples who burnish the canon until it is comprehensible only to the enlightened, or, in despair, the more clinically oriented practitioners grab on to a few pragmatic, often banalized principles and soldier on. There is a Zen saying that the last thing you learn is the first. Like dancers at the barre, it is vital that analysts return repeatedly to basic principles, relearning and reassessing the basics of their craft. These basics lie in the praxis, not the metapsychologies. For all our vaunted and long-contested differences, like the blind wise men and the elephant, we may well all be grasping different aspects of the same process.

Notes

1. I wish to thank Drs. M. Zaphiropolous, S. Shapiro, and J. Brisman for making source materials available to me. This chapter was first published in 2002 in *Contemporary Psychoanalysis*, 38(2):277–285.
2. I suggested that Sullivan retained a version of drive theory (anxiety) and that he really did not utilize the transference-countertransference field (Levenson, 1984).
3. See Hirsch (2000, p. 187) for Wolstein's report of his supervision experience with Thompson. My experience was very much the same.
4. Thompson was a training analyst at the New York Psychoanalytic Institute. Moulton had yet to begin courses when she resigned, following Thompson out of the New York Psychoanalytic Institute.
5. Freud's only official recognition of his work was the Goethe prize for literature.
6. In his interview with Hirsch, Wolstein makes no mention of his analysis with Tauber.

References

Bollas, C. (1999). *The Mystery of Things*. New York: Routledge.
Chatelaine, K.L. (1981). *Harry Stack Sullivan: The Formative Years*. Washington, DC: University Press of America.

Dostoyevsky, F. (1961). *Notes from the Underground*, trans. A. MacAndrew. New York: Signet Classics.

Gedo, J. (1999). *The Evolution of Psychoanalysis*. New York: Other Press.

Hirsch, I. (2000). Interview with Benjamin Wolstein. *Contemporary Psychoanalysis*, 36:187–232.

Levenson, E. (1984). Harry Stack Sullivan: The web and the spider. *Contemporary Psychoanalysis*, 20:174–189.

Levenson, E. (1988). Real frogs in imaginary gardens: Facts and fantasies in psychoanalysis. *Psychoanalytic Inquiry*, 8:552–556.

May, R. (1991). *The Cry for Myth*. New York: W.W. Norton.

McLuhan, M. (1964). *Understanding Media: The Extension of Man*. New York: McGraw-Hill.

Moulton, R. (1968a). Letter to the editor. *WAW Newsletter*, 3:9.

Moulton, R. (1968b). Origins of the institute. *WAW Newsletter*, 3:8–9.

Moulton, R. (1970). A survey and reevaluation of the concept of penis envy. *Contemporary Psychoanalysis*, 7:84–104.

Moulton, R. (1972). Sexual conflicts of modern women. In E. Witenberg (Ed.), *Interpersonal Explorations in Psychoanalysis*. New York: Basic Books, pp. 196–217.

Moulton, R. (1975). Early papers on women: Horney to Thompson. *American Journal of Psychoanalysis*, 35:207–223.

Moulton, R. (1982–1983). Letter to the editor. *WAW Newsletter*, 17:15.

Stern, D.B. (1997). *Unformulated Experience: From Dissociation to Imagination in Psychoanalysis*. Hillsdale, NJ: The Analytic Press.

Tauber, E.S. and Green, M.R. (1959). *Prelogical Experience: An Inquiry into Dreams and Other Creative Processes*. New York: Basic Books.

Wilden, A. (1972). *System and Structure: Essays in Communication and Exchange*. London: Tavistock.

Wilner, W. (1999). The un-consciousing of awareness in psychoanalytic therapy. *Contemporary Psychoanalysis*, 35:617–628.

Chapter 7

Fifty years of evolving interpersonal psychoanalysis[1]

Interpersonal psychoanalysis, or as we also[2] thought of it in the fifties, "Cultural" psychoanalysis, represented an authentically radical revolutionary movement, which inevitably became heavily politicized by its excommunication. I must point out that it never did consist of one unitary position. Rather, it was an amalgam of very loosely related positions, more allied by their mutual objection to the libido theory—or, more accurately to the mandarins who brooked no opposition to the libido theory—than by any metapsychological coherence. We had Erich Fromm, a Marxist social-psychologist, classically trained, who was much interested in ethics and values; Clara Thompson, who was an amalgam of her classical training, which she never disavowed, and her experience with Ferenczi, who radicalized her; and third, Sullivan, whose roots lay in a very American pragmatic Meyerian psychiatry. This made for strange bedfellows, requiring a considerable degree of intellectual agility from its epigones in an effort to integrate these three quite different theorists. One might say that the White community was born postmodern.

If I had been asked in the fifties for White's preeminent influence, I would have said Fromm; but now, it seems that Sullivan's influence was more long lasting.[3] Probably the greatest influence on me was Ed Tauber—although it took me a while to realize it—who, along with Thompson and Fromm, was a training analyst at the New York Psychoanalytic Institute and had been analyzed first by Thompson and then by Fromm. So he seemed to be a fair amalgam of White experience. Tauber and Green's, *Prelogical Experience* (1959) anticipated a great deal of our current variations in psychoanalytic technique. He was also, not incidentally, my analyst.

50 years of interpersonal psychoanalysis   73

Isolation and apostasy encouraged demonizing the opposition. Freud, I must confess, was not really taught very respectfully in many of the courses. The American Psychoanalytic Association was sort of the Antichrist. I cannot resist repeating an incident I reported on in an earlier article (Levenson, 2002). As a newly minted training analyst, I was supervising, with great trepidation, my first candidate (who was older than I). She was reporting on a 27-year old woman who was wont to have her mother soap her down in the bathtub. When I suggested to the candidate that this might be considered erotic behavior, she stood up and stamped out of supervision in high dudgeon—never to return! Stunned and crushed by this draconian response to my first efforts at analytic supervision, I sought out and had some real trouble finding a senior analyst who would support my position.

I might add, I didn't think that sexuality was all it was, but I didn't think it should be excluded because that's what "they" would think. I hasten to add that I'm talking about an early period at White, when we were still on the barricades, before the current atmosphere of ecumenism that, I trust, makes such zealotry unnecessary—or, at the very least, politically incorrect.

It seems to me, in retrospect, that in our emphasis on the experiential field, we threw out something of the uncanny flow of consciousness that so impressed the Freudians. As Bollas (1999) put it:

> [T]he understandable and inevitable tension between the goal of free association and the wishes of the analyst to understand the material: as free association unbinds meaning—in what Laplanche terms and celebrates as the "anti-hermeneutics" of psychoanalysis—while interpretation creates and binds meaning. No sooner are such understandings established than the workings of the unconscious, evident through free association, break the interpretation into particles of meaning, which constitute a "use of the object," hopefully celebrated by the analyst's unconscious working along similar lines even as such use *disperses* his interpretive creations (p. 70).

Every therapist is aware of the thread of continuity that runs through apparently unrelated themes in a session, the odd way an inadvertent opening remark may become a leitmotif for all that follows, and the unexpected turns the patient's meanderings may take. When we threw out the myths, we threw out the mythopoesis—I will elaborate later on this concept—vitiating the quality of free-associative creativity that

74 Unfolding of Interpersonal Psychoanalysis

some of us, in the interpersonal tradition, have been attempting to restitute (Levenson, 1988; Stern, 1997; Wilner, 1999). In the history of these internecine battles, Greenberg and Mitchell's *Object Relations in Psychoanalytic Theory* (1983) was a seminal moment. It had two great virtues: first, it was a veritable "pony" for many of us, bewildered by the explosion of different theories in a field that, albeit exclusionary, used to involve only one theory and one set of canonical writings to be learned. Greenberg and Mitchell supplied a comprehensible frame of reference, explicating the position of virtually every major development in psychoanalysis. In that sense it was monumental.

Second, their rubric of relationalism signaled the end of the isolation heretofore suffered by interpersonalism, and opened the door to an alliance with British object-relations, largely the middle group, the no-man's land between Anna Freud and Melanie Klein. The civilized British had managed to keep talking to each other, not without some considerable rancor. "Relational" managed conveniently to subsume under its rubric virtually the entire psychoanalysis spectrum outside of the Freudians: i.e., British object-relations (Winnicott, Guntrip, Fairbairn), Kohut, Kernberg, Klein, Hartmann, even Kernberg and Kohut who, it was said, along with Sandler, had opted for a "mixed model" solution. That pretty well covered the landscape and left the Freudians well and truly outflanked, at a time that they were lagging badly, in their own cohort and in the general culture, where the adulation of psychoanalysis was coming to an end. Nevertheless, I do believe that the basic premise—dividing psychoanalysis schismatically into relational and drive theories—was ultimately arbitrary and perhaps misleading, deflecting our attention from the communalities inherent in our inquiry into the mysterious, indeed uncanny, flow of consciousness. This, at a time when advances in neuropsychology have brought consciousness and the nature of mind to the fore.

With the barbarians at the Gates, the American made peace, embraced the heretics it could no longer simply dismiss. This is not to deny that there was a generation of psychoanalysts at the American who also were anxious for change, rankling under the political and metapsychological constraints, and welcoming the opportunity to explore new directions and new alliances. Interpersonalism, which was having its own problems keeping current—Sullivan's limitations were becoming more apparent—was also subsumed under the relational aegis and threatened to become a historical byway to the relational juggernaut.

In 1955—in fact, the year I graduated from the analytic training program—there was a potentially very destructive schism between the physicians and psychologists at White. The Institute barely survived. It wasn't the best of times, nor was it the most honorable. At first, the psychologists were given "equal but different" certificates. Even when that was discontinued, there remained a very uncomfortable feeling that psychologists were being treated as second-class citizens. This prejudice was quite ubiquitous. When the Academy of Psychoanalysis was first formed in 1956, virtually their first decision (much to White's Director at the time, Earl Wittenberg's, distress) was to exclude psychologists.[4]

In the 1960s, three prominent White graduates, Singer, Kalinkowitz, and Ben-Avi started a new postdoctoral psychoanalytic training institute at New York University. This was with full White approbation and participation. It in no way represented a theoretical break, but may have reflected disaffection on the part of psychologist graduates. Among some candidates and graduates at White (including physicians) there was growing discomfort at what they felt to be a partly self-perpetuating isolation from the world analytic community.

Subsequently, the New York University postdoctoral program split into four tracks: classical Freudian, interpersonal, relational, and uncommitted. The relational track later became the home base of Mitchell's political and theoretical interests. Under Mitchell's inspired direction, and with the brilliant and multitalented Manny Ghent as resident Guru (also from White), it became the epicenter of an extremely lively and vital renaissance. Women analysts infused a vital dimension with women's studies and postmodern dialectics. Mitchell never entirely disaffiliated from White; he did continue to supervise and teach there. Greenberg, more rooted at White, was more conciliatory, more interested in a continued colloquy. Mitchell sustained the schism with the American, refusing honorary membership at the same time that Greenberg and I accepted.

There was, of course, a vociferous backlash to this preemptive reshuffling of the field: accusations that they had created a false dichotomy and opened the door to a serious banalization of psychoanalysis (see Gedo, 1999; Richards, 2003). To many, it seemed an usurpation of the individuality of these independent psychologies—and indeed it was.

Merton Gill presciently identified the problem in a paper read at White (Gill, 1983). Gill, who has been perhaps the most unyielding of the Freudian analysts on the committee that in 1942 expelled the early group of interpersonalists from the American for (among other shortcomings) not conforming to the 5 day/couch rule, had been drifting toward an interpersonalism of his own. He and I corresponded over my book, *The Fallacy of Understanding* and he came to White and attended some of our clinic meetings (Levenson, 1972). In 1982, he gave a remarkable talk at White, in defying the bans, an act of no small moral courage. He had reviewed the entire corpus of interpersonal writings, and with his fresh and original intelligence, he saw that there were, as he said, two dichotomies in psychoanalysis:

> I refer to the distinction between two major cleavages in psychoanalytic thought. One cleavage is between the interpersonal paradigm and the drive-discharge paradigm. The other cleavage is between those who believe the analyst inevitably participates in a major way in the analytic situation and those who do not. I came to realize that I had assumed that these two cleavages ran parallel to each other, or at least that those who adhered to the interpersonal paradigm would also ascribe to the analyst a major participation in the analytic situation.
>
> (Gill, 1983, p. 201)

You will note that he accepts the relational/drive dichotomy as legitimate. He goes on to say that variations in the use of the second parameter cut across institutional and metapsychological loyalties and affiliations. He is, in essence, saying that within any psychoanalytic group, there will be marked variations in this second cleavage, which one might consider as a continuum running from analysts who see themselves as the curative event in the patient's life (charismatic or restitutive), to those who see the cure as the analyst curing herself (analysis of countertransference), to those who believe in the analysis of resistance and transference as getting out of the way of the patient's self-curative potential, some self-regulating (intrapsychic) activity on the patient's part.

In 1988, I suggested that the basic dichotomy was not between realms—intrapsychic versus interpersonal—but between *functions* of the mind, imagination, on one hand, and on the other experience, the exquisite skills necessary for negotiating the world (Levenson, 1988). I think that drive theory is an ingenious invention to justify the power of imagination, what the patient makes of experience. Imagination, the true power of the unconscious, is what I believe really impressed Freud, whose cases are replete with his sense of wonder at the capacity of a person living in *fin de siècle* Vienna to harbor a secret life of unexpected phantasmagoria. The conceptualizations of psychodynamics is a description of make-believe, a separate world that Freud felt inhabited the patient and dominated the world of social interactions. In imagination one thinks the unthinkable. It is the realm of the conceivable, not the possible. Incest fantasies may occur not because of instinct—the relentlessness of sexual drive—but because imagination entertains no rational limits.

But analysts are also tremendously impressed by their impact on the patient, to the extent that when the patient's experience with others is extended and demystified, or when transference-countertransference issues are recognized and worked through, the therapy may leap forward. We are impressed by both the power of imagination—the patient's and ours—*and* interpersonal experience, being in the real world. I called these two functions, *poetics* (from the Greek, meaning the capacity for imagination, fantasy) and *pragmatics* (from the Latin pragmaticus, meaning skilled in affairs).[5]

If a man loses his erection in bed with a lover, he is having an intrapsychic response to his own excitement and he is having a particular experience with the other person. To caricature the difference: from the intrapsychic perspective, the question is, what are his fantasies? The interpersonal dimension, secondary for the Freudian, is that he is, indeed, in bed with someone. For the interpersonalist, the question is, who is he in bed with? How are they engaging each other? Does his penis, like Balaam's ass, balk at something he doesn't consciously see?

It would be too discursive for this brief presentation, but current neuropsychological research leads us to consider the mind as operating as a "self-regulating" system, according to the principles of Chaos theory (Gedo, 1999, pp. 183–933, Harris, 2005; Schore, 1994; Siegel, 2001). Essentially, this implies that the mind organizes and works in a nonlinear, nonlogical way. Consequently outcomes are not entirely predictable. As Jonathan Miller put it, "We are the unwitting beneficiaries of a mind that is, in a sense, only partially our own" (Miller, 1995).

I find it extremely helpful to consider psychoanalysis to be a two-tiered process: namely, the pragmatics of interaction with the therapist (inquiry, transference-countertransference, dreams, memories) *and* the transformation of that data as it is processed in a nonlinear fashion by the patient's imagination qua consciousness qua mind. It suggests that what analysts view

78 Unfolding of Interpersonal Psychoanalysis

as their vaunted and politically vital differences may simply reflect where they locate themselves—where they prefer to work—in the participatory continuum. Some therapists prefer to use participation heavily, some dreams and free-associations, and some the nuances of interpersonal participation.

We are also constrained by our patient's proclivities: some people, in treatment, don't dream and don't produce a free-associative flow. Some are brilliant at it. In the Good Old Days, we demanded of psychoanalytic patients that they be imaginative, else they were not "suitable" for our esoteric purposes. Well, we are either humbler or more generous in our current appraisals.

It would explain why the work and the cure are not in some nice clear linear arrangement. Small inputs by the analyst sometimes have astounding results (the famous butterfly effect). Sometimes the opposite occurs, long periods of work seem sterile. In the end, the old medical aphorism applies: the physician ministers and the patient cures.

Marshal McLuhan once said, "If it works, it's obsolete." No one knows better than a psychoanalyst how quickly and seamlessly a useful concept morphs into a resistance to change. Had we been less of a discordant and quarrelsome profession, perhaps we might have focused more on the communalities of praxis, the therapeutic approach, rather than on the divisive and politicized metapsychologies. But no such luck.

Notes

1. This chapter was first presented, in slightly different form, at the Manhattan Institute, New York City, April 1, 2005, and published in 2006 in *Contemporary Psychoanalysis*, 42:4, pp. 557–564.
2. Sullivan had died in 1949, and Fromm was spending much of the year in Mexico, returning to supervise and teach seminars.
3. I was present at that fateful meeting. For a review of the history of the Academy, see Zaphiropoulos (2006).
4. It's odd how often in a presented dichotomy, one term is Latin and the other Greek.
5. See Kirsner's (2000) wonderful book on the internecine struggles of the American.

References

Bollas, C. (1999). *The Mystery of Things.* New York: Routledge.
Gedo, J. (1999). *The Evolution of Psychoanalysis.* New York: Other Press.

50 years of interpersonal psychoanalysis 79

Gill, M. (1983). The interpersonal paradigm and the degree of the analyst's involvement. *Contemporary Psychoanalysis*, 18:200–237.

Greenberg, J. and Mitchell, S. (1983). *Object Relations in Psychoanalytic Theory.* Cambridge, MA: Harvard University Press.

Harris, A. (2005). *Gender as Soft Assembly.* Hillsdale, NJ: The Analytic Press.

Kirsner, D. (2000). *Unfree Associations: Inside Psychoanalytic Institutes.* London: Process Press.

Levenson, E. (1972). *The Fallacy of Understanding.* Hillsdale, NJ: The Analytic Press, 2005.

Levenson, E. (1988). Real frogs in imaginary gardens: Facts and fantasies in psychoanalysis. *Psychoanalytic Inquiry*, 8(4):552–556.

Levenson, E. (2002). And the last shall be first: Some observations on the evolution of interpersonal psychoanalysis. *Contemporary Psychoanalysis*, 38(2):277–285.

Miller, J. (1995). Going unconscious. *New York Review of Books*, XLII: 59–65.

Richards, A. (2003). Psychoanalytic discourse at the turn of our century: A plea for a measure of humility. *Journal of the American Psychoanalytic Association*, 51(suppl):72–125.

Schore, A. (1994). *Affect Regulation and the Origin of the Sell.* Hillsdale, NJ: Erlbaum.

Siegel, D. (2001). Towards an interpersonal neurobiology of the developing mind: Attachment relationships, "mindsight," and neural integration. *Infant Mental Health Journal*, 22(1):67–94.

Stern, D.B. (1997). *Unformulated Experience: From Dissociation to Imagination in Psychoanalysis.* Hillsdale, NJ: The Analytic Press.

Tauber, E.S. and Green M.R. (1959). *Prelogical Experience; An Inquiry into Dreams and Other Creative Processes.* New York: Basic Books.

Wilner, W. (1999). The un-consciousing of awareness in psychoanalytic therapy. *Contemporary Psychoanalysis*, 35(4):617–628.

Zaphiropoulos, M. (2006). I remember it well: Reminiscences on the history of the Academy. *Journal of the American Academy of Psychoanalysis and Psychiatry*, 34(1):13–18.

Part II

Psychoanalytic process

Chapter 8

Standoffs, impasses, and stalemates[1]

One of the prime deconstructive functions of psychoanalysis is to question the assumptions that permeate words (Hamburg, 1989). A standard thesaurus treats standoff, impasse, and stalemate as synonyms, which is what is wrong with thesauruses (or is it thesauri?). These words carry quite different implications, and I would like to suggest that Dr. Friedman is more correct than she knows when she calls her problems with this patient a "stalemate."

To put it succinctly, a standoff is what we had with Russia; i.e., no one dares move first since both participants have equal destructive power. An impasse occurs when no further progress is possible and forward movement stops, as in, say union or budget negotiations. A stalemate is something else. Stalemate is a chess term: when it is no longer possible for the losing player to move without putting his or her King in check, when there are no moves left to the player, then that player has provoked a stalemate, which is a draw. Nobody wins. In other words, provoking a stalemate is a strategy the losing player uses to avoid defeat or "checkmate" (which, by the way, is from the Persian, *shah mat*, the King is dead!). I would say the patient did exactly that—forced a stalemate (*stal mat*), to avoid a more total capitulation.

This, of course, sounds rather bizarre. Am I suggesting that psychoanalysis is adversarial, that it is a game in which one person wins and the other loses? In a manner of speaking, I am. Admittedly this is a bit of hyperbole, but it is intended to counterbalance a current tendency among psychoanalysts to see themselves as helpers, collaboratively and empathically aiding the patient in resolving some problem; in this case, it is this woman's inability to rmour her wish to "marry and have a family after all."

84 Psychoanalytic process

I would suggest that psychoanalysis works by showing the patient how it *doesn't* work when the therapist sets out to help the patient with some problem. The essence of the psychoanalytic method lies in its paradoxical discovery that one can get farther by spotlighting the resistances to change than by trying to figure out how to bypass them. Resistance is the very essence of the psychoanalytic praxis. In Freud's words, we study resistance and resistance manifested as transference. Freud said that he would recognize as psychoanalysis, "any line of investigation, no matter what its direction, which recognizes these two facts resistance and transference" (Freud, 1919). What interpersonal psychoanalysis adds to that formulation is that resistance is not only against awareness of intrapsychic conflict, but is also directed against the therapist. Like Pogo, the famous comic strip possum, said, "We have met the enemy, and They is Us!"

I would claim that people enter therapy because something is not working and they want it to work. They wish to perfect the neurosis, to improve rather than to change and a good part of the opening gambits of psychoanalysis have to do with reframing the patient's initial perception of the problem.

This woman wants finally to get married and have a family. Note how vaguely that is formulated. Why does she want that? She'd think you were mad for even asking. But what is marriage? What does having a family entail? Shouldn't life have options, choices? What does a particular man have to be to interest her? I hear that she wants to fall in love—which for her seems to obviate the need to pay attention to whom she is getting— and then to go on to her *desiratum* of marriage and family. Perhaps the resistance to change is not so irrational, perhaps the patient fears that change will obliterate her core of individual self and tear her from her experiential roots, her family.

In this case, the therapist concurs with her stated goals and sets out to help her. Oddly enough, the patient "resists." Therapists, I believe, should recognize that they are the Stranger, the Outsider invading the private world of the patient, pressing on what Wynn called the "rubber fence" that surrounds each patient (Wynn et al., 1958). Every neurosis has a certain integrity; it is a viable way of living in the patient's world. As someone once said, "Remember, however bad it looks, the patient's way of life is an improvement over something else!" However much the patient idealizes or denounces his/her family, it is worth remembering that the family is the patient's known world, that tribal and community pulls are extremely powerful, and that the patient conceptualizes change in the percepts of the unique subculture of the family.

Sullivan leaned heavily on the concept of "contagious anxiety"; that is, that the person builds a complex network of inattentions and dissociations to avoid mobilizing anxiety and disapproval in the caretakers that would then threaten to overwhelm the child's sense of security and self-esteem. The child learns what not to see, to avoid the experience of disorganizing anxiety. I think it may be equally possible that the child is simply terrified of anathema, of expulsion from the group, if it does not concur with the family illusions. Surely to belong is one of mankind's most ancient and compelling social imperatives; expulsion is tantamount to death. Why then should the patient change if it requires a leap of faith, a belief that the therapist must know the right answers? After all, weren't we all taught as children not to go off with strangers?

So, the function of the therapist is, through a detailed inquiry, to challenge the boundaries of the family narrative. And, by virtue of seeing what is not supposed to be seen, and speaking the unspeakable, the therapist opens the world to the patient. However, this is not enough. To avoid the submission to the therapist as surrogate family, the patient must be free to challenge the therapist, to ask the unaskable about the therapist, to wonder what the therapist does not see or allow to be seen. The questions need not be answered (this is a matter of technique); but if they cannot be asked, then it is because the patient knows the therapist is too anxious to tolerate challenge and the patient is back in the same old bind of denying his/her perceptions to avoid banishment. I am suggesting that a stalemate occurs because the patient invokes a draw to prevent the loss of her King or Queen—depending on her family lines of power. The patient sees change as an unbearable loss of connection to her family and a submission to a new and unknown authority.

The entire presentation, for me, lacks a sense of texture, of what makes this woman's life different from anyone else's. Oliver Sacks, the neurologist, describes A. R. Luria:

> He felt that getting historical details, getting an idea of the full richness of a life and the full consciousness of a life was quite necessary if one were to treat any patient. And he felt, by the same token, that an impersonal case history had to be replaced by a deep and essentially personal biography.
>
> (Sacks, 1990)

86 Psychoanalytic process

Note that, at first, we have no information about the context of her life. What are the parents really like? Who is the mother? Not, how did she fail to be mothering? What are the patient's fantasies of closeness? What will her role be in her idealized "family"? The therapist agrees the first guy is no good and she should get out: the second is deemed terrific. What data are available? How can she be sure? Friedman does not really tell us how the patient sees all these issues, although, later in the presentation, the patient describes Bob as, "opinionated, dictatorial and chauvinistic."

It is all very well for the therapist to talk about intimacy but to whom is she talking? Correspondingly, doesn't the patient wonder who the analyst is, whether the analyst—in this case, a woman—is single and wishes she were married, single and glad of it, divorced, married and happy, married and unhappy, with children, without? Doesn't she think that the therapist's personal experiences and biases will press on her? Might she not apply to the therapist the same sensitive probing about what can be seen and what can be spoken of?

It is now almost commonplace that the effectiveness of interpretations depends, not on the correctness of the interpretation, but on the context in which the interpretation takes place. Even the more orthodox institutes are discovering this hoary interpersonal axiom. In a contemporary German text, which has been a dramatic success in Europe, the authors state that, "Our leitmotif is the conviction that the *analyst's contribution to the therapeutic process* [my italics] should be made the focus of attention . . . the course of therapy depends on the influence exerted by the therapist" (Thomä and Kachele, 1985). Mirabele dictu!

Yet, contrast this with Friedman's statement that, "I did not experience what was happening as a resistance to me or to the treatment situation." Is there a choice? From my particular interpersonal perspective, the therapist is omnipresent and there is no delineation between the therapist, real or imagined, and the "treatment situation"; they are one and the same. When Friedman says, "I didn't pay enough attention to what was transpiring between us," it seems to me she is either talking of traditional transference; i.e., the patient is laying something on her or, self-psychology wherein the therapist suffered a deficit in empathy. What is missing, it seems to me, is an examination of the simple issue that here are two women of different life experiences talking about family and marriage without either one knowing who the other is (not her dynamics, which are universal attributions, abstractions, and therefore impersonal).

If Friedman were Freudian she would meticulously dissociate herself from any goals for the patient. It is not her business whether the patient gets married or not. Why should she be invested in the patient's presumed successes or failures? As an interpersonalist, the same principle applies, but it is more difficult since the therapist should be more present and her real nature must then be taken into account.

What then is the problem with this therapy? Rather than "helping the patient make progress" and thereby provoking an iatrogenic resistance, I think the therapist should have simply been interested in who the patient is and how she saw the world and how the therapist saw herself seeing the patient's world. Friedman did come to this later when, as she said, "I no longer got caught up in the endless repetition of how awful the weekend was ... and returned again and again to a detailed inquiry ... feeling curious and less anxious." However, she did not extend that inquiry to include who the therapist is and how she sees the world. I would emphasize this does not require a cozy mutual confession. It does require that the therapist monitor constantly her own participation and, consequently the extent to which her own anxieties, expectations, and values—conscious and unconscious—impinge on the patient. Strikingly, there is no sense of the therapist being present as a real person.

For example, the patient lies on the couch and tells how in her interaction with Bob, "how awful she is. How could he love her," etc. The therapist sees that she does not feel good enough, pretty enough, because her mother failed to nurture those feelings in her. She goes on to describe the competitive nature of the patient's family upbringing. The therapist does not wonder if or why, *when talking to her*, the patient has to devalue her relationship with Bob. Could her self-effacement be directed toward the therapist as a primary object, because she fears the therapist's response of perhaps envy, or competition? Is she necessarily reassured by the analyst's supportive, empathic historical interpretation?

Mother finally enters the psychodynamic field. But again it is all abstract psychodynamics and not a real intersubjective context in the treatment. She is afraid of surpassing her mother, but she is convinced that if she did, her mother, she says, "would be happy for me." She does not anticipate envy. How about surpassing the therapist? Is the therapist as self-effacing as the mother is presumed to be?

Later, she does express her fear that Friedman would be against the relationship. "We did not get far into understanding this fear at this time."

Why not? "Something was transpiring between us," she says. What? The therapist is looking for a formulation that will set the patient free, the mutative dynamic. But that does not include a true sense of interaction. Why does the patient think that the therapist would sabotage the relationship? It is often considered axiomatic that whatever the patient believes, is a distortion from her past (or, perhaps, as Gill put it that the present core of reality must be separated from the distortion from the past (Gill, 1982)). But if the patient can distort the present, why not the past? Why isn't she equally wrong about her parents? Isn't that a distortion, too, based on Oedipal fantasies or sibling rivalry? What is the patient *right* about? Perhaps more than we care to acknowledge, both in the past and in the present.

Ultimately, the therapist hears her plea for space, for the need for integrity, for time to embrace her own neurosis and to discover its truths, and to not be interpreted away. She dreams that she is a racehorse who is not allowed to run or will be prevented from finishing. "But nothing moved . . . We went round and round on this one," says the therapist. Round and round. But isn't that what racehorses do? Never mind that she can't run or finish. Why need she be in a race at all?

To return to my original etymological hairsplitting: they are not at a standoff, because they are not equally armed or armoured. If that happens we have a therapist as defended as the patient and no therapy takes place. That certainly did not occur in this treatment, which was sensitive and concerned. I do not believe any therapy is simply a negotiation, a shared narrative, a collaborative journey, so impasses are not relevant.

It is indeed a veritable stalemate. The patient provokes a draw to preserve her integrity. Neurotic or not it is who she is, as she so poignantly points out. "This is the only self she had, the only one she knew, how could she give it up?" Ideally one hopes that the therapist, who understands that the patient's redoubt is under attack, does not figure out better ways to breach her defenses, but rather creates a potential space, encouraging the patient to venture forth.

From my perspective, the therapist's sense of participation, although consistent with some analytic perspectives (perhaps-self psychological), does not go far enough. She does not conceptualize herself as really present in her own identity and impacting on the patient out of her own needs and expectations. Without that monitored self-awareness, I think one cannot expect the patient to respond. A relationship of intimacy does not depend on getting over one's fears of intimacy, accepting that they are distortions, allergic responses from the past. Rather, it requires being able to evaluate the Other, to negotiate, to compromise, even to fight. Intimacy is not a state of grace; it is an implementational skill and requires mentors and practice (Levenson, 1981). Were your mother ever so warm and nurturant and caretaking to you, but got walked over or was ungiving and unyielding to her husband, your father, you will still have trouble with marital intimacy. Nurturance is not enough. As William Blake put it, you become what you behold, and what you behold is your family and its peculiar subculture.

To summarize: the therapist's efforts to help the patient mobilize a great deal of resistance. In this case, resistance is seen as a perplexing impediment to therapy, rather than its essential core. It is through resistance, and its manifestation in the relationship with the therapist (loosely defined as transference/countertransference), that the patient begins to grapple with his/her reasons for doggedly persisting in a way of life that clearly does not work well. Neurosis is, I would claim, a very complex solution to very simple problems.

A recognition that the patient defends the neurosis to defend his/her integrity leads the therapist to a detailed inquiry into the texture of the patient's life, past and present, and into the relationship provided by the therapist. I believe the patient resists leaving his/her family and moving into the world held forth by the therapist because it feels like a leap from the frying pan into the fire. And, unless the therapist carefully monitors his/her own participation in the process, it is! Sullivan said, "No one has grave difficulties in living if he has a very good grasp of what is happening to him" (Sullivan, 1956). Without this heightened awareness, psycho-analysis becomes an attempt to influence the patient in ways the therapist thinks will help. And influence is never fully benign even when initiated by the best-intentioned therapist.

I think that this therapy, concerned and helpful, and with evident improvement in the patient could have been much enriched by the therapist being present in a more explicit and self-examining way.

Note

1. This chapter was first published in 1991 in *Contemporary Psychoanalysis* 27(3):511–516.

90 Psychoanalytic process

References

Freud, S. (1919). On the history of the psychoanalytic movement. In J. Strachey (Ed.), *The Standard Edition of the Complete Psychological Works of Sigmund Freud*. London: Hogarth Press, Vol. XXIV, pp. 7–66.

Gill, M. (1982). *Analysis of Transference*. Vol. I. New York: International Universities Press.

Hamburg, P. (1989). Bulimia: Construction of a symptom. *Journal of The American Academy of Psychoanalysis*, 17(1):131–140.

Levenson, E. (1981). The rhetoric of intimacy. *Group*, 5:3–10.

Sacks, O. (1990). Neurology and the soul. *New York Review of Books,* 37(18): 46.

Sullivan, H.S. (1956). *Clinical Studies in Psychiatry*. New York: W.W. Norton.

Thomä, H. and Kachele, H. (1985). *Psychoanalytic Practice; Vol. I. Principles*. Heidelberg and Berlin: Springer Verlag, p. 7, reviewed by L. Wurmser in *Journal of the American Psychoanalytic Association* 38(4):815–820.

Wynn, L.C., Ryckoff, I.M., Day, J. and Hirsch, S.I. (1958). Pseudomutuality in the family relationships of schizophrenics. *Psychiatry*, 21:205–220.

Chapter 9

Mistakes, errors, and oversights[1]

An aprocryphal comment attributed to Sam Goldwyn seems appropriate: I may make mistakes but I am never wrong. It has been a long and bumpy path from Freud's 1914 statement that "Analysis presupposes the consent of the analyzed: the situation of analysis involves a superior and a subordinate" to Racker's statement in 1968 that,

> The first distortion of truth in the "myth of the analytic situation" is that analysis is an interaction between a sick person and a healthy one. The truth is that it is an interaction between two personalities . . . and each of these two personalities—that of the analyst and that of the patient—responds to every event of the analytic situation.
>
> (Racker, 1968)

The most ubiquitous and subversive mistake—the "Basic Fault" of psychoanalytic therapy—is to fail to grasp the implications of this shift, which I will take even farther than Racker ever intended. I will spell out for you some of the implications of the shift, as I see them, and illustrate with clinical material.

Psychoanalysis, based on a nineteenth-century medical model and having its roots in the hypnotic phenomena of submission and suggestion has always carried a thinly masked disdain for the "patient," defined etymologically as "the suffering one." Freud is reported to have said to Ferenczi, "Die Patienten sind ein Gesindel" (patients are a rabble), and in 1932 Ferenczi, in a highly controversial paper, bluntly criticized, to quote Grosskurth, "the superiority or hypocrisy of analysts who acted as though their patients were inferior to them. As a result, they did not really *listen*

92 Psychoanalytic process

to what their patients were telling them, particularly in cases of actual abuse. It ended dramatically with a plea to therapists to allow patients to loosen their tongues: 'You will hear much that is instructive'" (Grosskurth, 1991, p. 210, 213; Ferenczi, 1988, pp. 118, 186). To varying degrees, this devaluation of the patient's experience still operates in contemporary psychoanalysis: even among self-psychologists with their meticulous respect for the patient's "psychic reality."

This long-standing and deeply imbedded tacit denigration of the patient qua patient had a number of profound implications, namely:

1. The belief that the patient presents chaotic or defended material to the therapist who must break through the distortions to arrive at the mutative interpretation. That is, the patient needs his/her life to be explained by the therapist. As Masud Khan ironically put it, "We have the patient tell us his truth so that we may tell him the Metatruth" (Milner, 1969). Our proclivity is to see the therapist as an expert helping the patient "get straight"—a comforting conceit. It allows that as long as the therapist can maintain "neutrality," his/her attention can be focused on the patient's problems and—inevitably—the patient's "distortions." The centrality of the concept of distortion is an inevitable concomitant of reifying the patient. Something must be wrong with the way the patient sees the world: why else would he/she be a patient? And, the therapist must have the answers or why else would one call oneself a therapist? Although this is a very aberrant and irritating concept to some analysts, I would like to suggest that the very concept of "distortion" claims for the analyst a clarity of vision and purpose which is not valid and actually defeats the patient's efforts at self-realization. I would claim that the patient "distorts" as a variety of symbolic representation; that is, as caricature, and that this *reductio ad absurdum* is necessary to make the message palatable to the necessary other person (in this case, the therapist) who is having trouble tolerating it. The patient's defenses against others (not intrapsychically induced anxiety)—what Sullivan called the "self-system"—is designed to probe and monitor the anxiety in the necessary other person in order to avoid provoking anxiety and risking a serious loss of caretaking (Sullivan, 1953). Why wouldn't the patient exercise the same care with the therapist?

2. The belief that the patient qua patient is, by definition, much more anxious than the therapist, which leads the therapist to underestimate

or deny his/her own anxiety and consequently to not grasp the necessity for a well-defined therapeutic frame.

3. The belief that the patient is so self-occupied, anxious, immature, and unperceptive that the patient sees far less about the therapist than the therapist does about the patient. I would claim that patients, even those paradigms of self-absorption, the so-called narcissistic character disorders, are exquisitely attuned to the therapist. But, patients being patients, they have learned not to see what they see (or, at least, not tell you) unless you ask. As Wolstein puts it, "A patient's capacity to perceive the unconscious psychic experience of others, including the psychoanalyst, does not shut down by virtue of taking the socially defined role of patient" (Wolstein, 1992).

4. The belief that the therapist is in possession of a superior explanatory system—the canonical metapsychology—which, once grasped by the patient, will make all clear leads therapists to miss what Bruner called, not at all derisively, "folk psychology" explanations (Bruner, 1990); i.e., simple and obvious explanations which are not even considered because they seem too "naive" and ordinary—too commonplace for specialists.[2]

Am I promulgating therapeutic anarchy? If the therapist has no real claim to superordinate clarity how can he/she help? What, if anything, is left? At this point, it would be useful, to delineate a distinction between *mistakes* and *errors*: the former implying the violation of a definitive rule, the latter implying a fluctuation from a perceived norm.[3] A mistake is unequivocal. There cannot be a "right" mistake; to "mistake" is to take the wrong way. Error, on the other hand, etymologically means "to wander," to stray from the right.[4] Both may be inevitable, but we should try to avoid mistakes; conversely, we should capitalize on errors—use them.

To elaborate, all psychoanalysts have a vision of the idealized psychoanalytic performance. For Freudians, it is neutrality; for self-psychologists, it is empathy; for interpersonalists (at least, of my ilk) it is authenticity in participation. This is their guideline, their white line down the middle of the road. To step off it, is to be in error. Nevertheless, no one believes for a moment that it is possible to hew perfectly to the line. Like every other dynamic system, psychoanalytic therapy is in constant oscillation. So, all psychoanalysts, regardless of their doctrinary convictions, monitor their participation, hoping to catch their deviations from the golden mean.

94 Psychoanalytic process

And, it may well be that it is this intense attention to one's own error that is the common denominator of all psychoanalysis. All psychoanalysts may well be closet interpersonalists since their failure to maintain perfect rectitude—regardless of how intrapsychic the theory—is intersubjective, the consequence of their interaction with the other person, the patient; and, their meticulous attention to these deviations is, like it or not, interpersonal.

There is one very important caveat. In order to be able to observe their lapses from perfect performance, therapists need to feel relatively secure. Therapy is a very anxiety-provoking undertaking—for both participants. The higher one's level of anxiety, the greater one's inattention or dissociation. Without a container for the therapy, the therapist would be overwhelmed, lost in a chaotic "real-life" participation.[5] So, in addition to a doctrinary position, analysts require a carefully contrived and maintained psychoanalytic frame that defines, in advance and somewhat arbitrarily, all those conditions of therapy that may be considered as superordinate to the content: i.e., time, money, place (is one's office in the home?), limited extent of social and personal contact with the patient, gifts, cancellation agreements, the requirement of scrupulous self-report from the patient, the analyst's care about self-revelation.[6] In addition to maintaining these procedural rules, the therapist must consider as part of the preconditions of therapy the circumstances of the referral; i.e., whether the patient comes from one's analyst or ex-analyst, another patient presently in therapy, an ex-patient, one's mother, or (a real consideration in our field, as the clinical example I shall use suggests), one's spouse! Establishing these rigid and arbitrary rules allows the therapist and patient a safe place in which to engage each other. I believe this is as true for interpersonalists as it is for psychoanalysts who promote regression in the sessions. To put it succinctly, the frame (or the rules which define the containment of the psychoanalytic process) allow both participants in the process the safety to make errors, wander from the ideal and then utilize those variations. I believe the analyst needs this protection as much as the patient. Frame prevents Freud's "playground" from becoming a battlefield (Freud, 1914a).

One need not play the arbitrary authority. It seems perfectly reasonable to inform one's patients that these rules are intended to reduce both their discomfort, and to make it possible for the therapist to do the work. In my experience, patients—who are rarely fools—find this a perfectly reassuring

Mistakes, errors, and oversights   95

explanation, without the usual authoritarian cant about how "the patient needs the boundaries."

Mistakes in maintaining an arbitrarily defined frame are easier to catch than errors in interactions within the frame. I am, I repeat, making a somewhat arbitrary semantic distinction. But it helps. Mistakes—lapses— in the frame will occur and these "breaking the rules" incidents are quite useful for quickly alerting the therapist to something out of awareness in his/her own participation. And, failures in maintaining the frame—as contrasted with errors within the praxis of the therapy—as I've said, ought not to be used creatively (analyzed), but interdicted, arbitrarily stopped! When I say this to supervisees and students, they are not infrequently appalled: after all, why should one hand the patient any such arbitrary dictum?

As a simple example, consider the patient who comes chronically 10 to 15 minutes late. Not coming on time is a deviation from the frame and should be, I believe, countermanded arbitrarily. Like most acting-out, it is more easily worked with by first stopping it and then talking about it. Stopping it, I repeat, does not necessitate an imperial ukaze: one can simply ask the patient to desist, please, explaining that "acting-out" keeps material from emerging in the therapy. What is acted-out, we say, is not talked about. If the patient persists, one has, at least, made the point. Not everyone would agree: many therapists find this behavior approachable dynamically, and analyze it (i.e., interpret), while permitting it to continue. We might all agree, however, that it is easy to recognize as a deviation from the rules of the frame and therefore indicative of unanalyzed content. No one would assume that coming late doesn't have meaning. But, it is also not necessarily particularly anxiety-provoking for the analyst. Indeed, the analyst may find the defection restful—a chance to read the mail, use the john, whatever.

But what if the acting-out consists of the patient having anal inter-course without condoms, with a drug-using homosexual prostitute? Would one then analyze it without first stopping it? I doubt it. I think one might have to refuse to work with the patient unless the self-destructive behavior (which is—or certainly ought to be—scaring the therapist) is curtailed. Much the same issues are relevant to serious suicidal threats, sociopathic acts, or impulsive, irreversible life decisions. To summarize, I am saying that deviations in what I would define as the frame are mistakes, wrong, interfere with therapy and should be stopped. An authoritarian frame

96 Psychoanalytic process

begets an egalitarian treatment. Paradox? Why not! Paradox is at the very heart of psychoanalysis (Clancier and Kalmonovitch, 1987; Sainsbury, 1988).

Within the containment of the frame which, I repeat, has to do with the constraints imposed on both participants in the course of therapy, one may delineate errors; but what they are conceived to be will differ, depending on one's theoretical and institutional canons. These errors, I must re-emphasize, are inevitable, since they are motivated by ubiquitous counter-participation, and, compared to frame mistakes, are amenable to a creative usage. One may, without explicitly saying anything, correct them, correct them and alert the patient (who may have already picked up the slippage), "act in" (that is, play it through with the patient), or, retrospectively interpret them. These interpretations may be, as Gill put it, either interpretations of awareness or interpretations of content: i.e., one can either simply point out what is transpiring or one can attribute dynamic purpose to it (Gill, 1982). Once the error is in the therapist's awareness, what one does is almost irrelevant; there will be automatically a shift in one's participation. Real countertransference—the kind that makes trouble—operates out of awareness. As they used to say about the minnie ball in the Civil War, you never hear the one that gets you!

To summarize: within the safety and containment of the frame, one tries one's best to be a perfect analyst—fails of course—and uses one's deviations from the ideal as participatory data defining the interpersonal field of the therapist and patient; and, not incidentally, throwing light on the patient's life outside of the therapy room, since it is axiomatic in psychoanalysis that there is a recursion, a repeating of pattern in the transference and in the material under discussion.[7] What is talked about in therapy is re-enacted (in reality or fantasy, depending on one's theory) in the relationship of the therapist and patient.

It would be relevant, at this point, to define the specifics of the inter-personal position—its "white line"—at least as I perceive and practice it. It is, I suppose, a relatively radical interpersonalism, and I would prefer not to talk for "Interpersonalism" or "Sullivanianism," but rather for my own position. I think of interpersonalism as a pragmatic, operational position. It is a two-person psychology, with the basic unit of human relatedness being the dyad (Ghent 1989). Humanness requires the presence of others—even if they are, in Sullivan's term, "eidetic," or imaginary. Psychoanalysis becomes the study of the patient's efforts, in Bruner's term,

Mistakes, errors, and oversights   97

to "negotiate" the world; to manage to live successfully, within a cultural context, with the other people—including the psychoanalyst—vital to his/her satisfactions and security (Bruner, 1990).

It follows that the proper study of psychoanalysis is the study of the patient's interactions, past and present, in the outside world and in the therapy; both being equally weighted and considered. The field of play is semiotic. All the manifestations of communication—behavior as language, language as behavior, reveries, fantasies, memories, daydreams and night dreams with all their concomitant affects—are all considered interpersonal communications, although they obviously have an internal, intrapsychic structure which distorts and reinterpretes experience. My premise is pragmatic, that intrapsychic structures are "black boxes," not directly observable, and that intrapsychic *constructs* (i.e., the observer's version of what goes on in the head of the subject) are, themselves, interpersonal transactions defined by the values and tacit premises of the observer. Since one is quite simply part of what one observes, and since self-referential observations are, by definition, unprovable; the therapist must suspect that his/her observations of the patient constitute yet another level of participation.[8]

I cannot emphasize too strongly that one's preferred theoretical concepts—aside from their aesthetic appeal as grand unifying theories of human development and neurosis—operate in the praxis of psychoanalysis as filters for what kind of data one will see and what kind of data one will totally miss because the theory does not permit. As Einstein said, the theory dictates the data. A metapsychological theory, no matter how appealing, does not come out of a "scientific" observation of the data, but rather selects and pre-configures the data. Therefore, from my perspective, the heuristic value of a theory is not whether it is right or wrong, but what it permits you to see or not see. The key to doing analysis is not having at hand a good explanatory set. Any student has that. Rather it depends on the therapist's ability—talent really—to elicit data; to see what is there to be seen.

It follows that every psychoanalytic interpretation, every intervention of the therapist, is a dialogue. The therapist reveals himself/herself in the process of inquiring into what goes on in the patient. The therapist's declared metapsychology, what he/she responds to in the session, what is said, how a dream is interpreted, are all messages. Thus, the ultimate issue for interpersonalists is not only what the patient says about his/her

98 Psychoanalytic process

life to the therapist, nor is it only what the therapist says to the patient about the patient's life: but also, what they say about themselves—however inadvertently—to each other. This is nothing more that the old linguistic saw that there is a message and a metamessage (a message about the messenger) in every exchange (Strawson, 1963). If I tell you, "the eagle has landed," you cannot possibly know what I mean unless you know the context (World War II, the Audubon Society, a schizophrenic ward), who is sending the message and who is the presumed receiver. Is that message too exotic? What if I say, "My father did not love me. He never came to my football games." Is that less obscure? Don't we need to know the age, the sex, the social context of the patient and his—or her—father?

From the interpersonal viewpoint, which counts very heavily on a detailed inquiry as contrasted with a free-associative one, failure to get the details, the pragmatic texture, of the patient's report, is the most consistent specific error in technique and derives from the view of the therapist as expert and clarifier. The detailed inquiry is at the heart of the interpersonal method, for as the Cabalists say, God dwells in the details (Levenson, 1988). I believe that the inquiry is a much misunderstood and over-simplified concept. It would seem to suggest that the therapist inquires scrupulously into the details, the pragmatics, of the patient's life in order to provide a blueprint that would permit the patient a more coherent overview of his/her life and why it is maladaptive. From this perspective, the therapist monitors closely his/her own anxiety as much as possible to minimize participatory blind spots, areas about which he/she would not think to ask. This "participant-observation" and "consensual validation" would, on first glance, appear to be pretty much what Sullivan had in mind.[9]

Unfortunately, it tends to send therapists scurrying to "make sense" out of what patients tell them. So, they listen enough to conceptualize an over-view, which they then present to the patient, to help the patient correct distortions and "make sense" of his/her life. But it is what patients don't say which defines those areas of "selective inattention," and, it is what the therapist doesn't ask about, or doesn't notice in what is said that defines countertransference, as I shall elaborate in the clinical example. If philo-sophers ask questions for which there are no answers; psychoanalysts have answers for which, often, there are no questions.

As the therapist probes further into the details of the patient's experience; something rather strange happens. Instead of things getting clearer, the sense of coherence dissipates; and, both participants find themselves disoriented and confused. Anxiety levels go up, on both sides, and then the essential mechanism of any true psychoanalysis, its *vis à tergo* kicks in and we have resistance and transference: that is, the problem under presentation is "transferred" into the relationship with the therapist. As Freud said, "Any line of investigation, no matter what its direction, which recognizes these two facts (resistance and transference) and takes them as a starting point of its work may call itself psychoanalysis, though it arrives at results other than my own" (Freud, 1914b). From my viewpoint, transference and countertransference constitute an actual re-enactment in the relationship, rather than a projection onto the therapist, a viewpoint which descends, through Clara Thompson, directly from Ferenczi (Grosskurth, 1991).

To restate the issue: the error most commonly made in the detailed inquiry is to see it as simply a focused pursuit, by a concerned expert, into events in the patient's life, and to miss its more profoundly psychoanalytic purpose; namely, to focus awareness on what is inattended or dissociated. In the course of illuminating the blind spots, the errors in both the therapist's and the patient's perception of events, anxiety is augmented and a carry-over, a replay, of the significant events in the relationship of the therapist and patient takes place.

I would like to use as an example of the particular shift in perspective involved in an interpersonal view of psychoanalysis, an excerpt of a clinical case presented by Estelle and Morton Shane (Shane and Shane, 1990). It demonstrates particularly the interpersonal concept that countertransference lies in the blindspots of the therapist; i.e., what the therapist does not think to inquire into is a collusion with the patient to not see what is there to be seen. Second, that the transference always constitutes an extraordinary re-enactment of the material under discussion and of the patient's enduring patterns of interaction. The resonance between what the patient is talking about and what is being re-enacted between the therapist and patient is, to my way of thinking, the absolute essence of the psychoanalytic process. And, last, that what is taking place is often so simple that it eludes the analyst who is looking for those elegant complexities dictated by his/her metapsychology.

This is a 38-year-old woman, married 15 years, with two children, deeply unhappy and with absolutely no sexual life with her husband. She has made three previous attempts at psychoanalysis, all failures. Her parents were Holocaust survivors and her father had been notably unsupportive

100 Psychoanalytic process

and uncaring. For many years, she did not see him at all. Her bitterness toward him is unrelenting and she is angry with her mother for remaining with him.

Her marriage started disastrously. Unknown to her, her husband was addicted to cocaine and for five difficult years she had to sustain him through a drug program. He is now drug-free, but she is still very angry, seeing him as infantile and unreliable. She had been in five-time-weekly psychoanalysis for a year and a half at the time of the dream to be presented. Prior to the dream, there is an incident with her mother, in which her mother "hypocritically and dishonestly" criticizes her for having an unclean house, while she, her mother, is, in truth, far messier. This concern with the hypocritical denial of the Other came up in prior therapies and precipitated her leaving one therapist after three sessions, because she felt the therapist had been deceitful.

The patient has made unquestionable improvements. She has developed a close woman friend and sometimes business collaborator, "Cynthia," who appears in the dream. She also, for the first time in years, was able to have sex with her husband, "John," without "disgust" although not with any real erotic pleasure. Prior to the dream, she had a serious contretemps with the therapist about the therapist's recent vacation. She says she was not informed sufficiently in advance: the therapist says notification was explicit and timely. The patient is adamant; she is convinced that the therapist is being "deceitful" in the way of her mother and her previous therapist. The therapist does then what the previous discarded therapist did to elicit her ire; that is, accuses her of misreading the therapist's intent because of her carry-over of her experience, real or presumed, with her mother. However, the therapist does not disallow her feelings. Her "psychic reality" is respected: to wit, I did not do it to you, but since your mother did, I can respect your upset and understand the distortion. The next day she has the following dream:

> I go to Cynthia's house. Cynthia always talks about how clean and neat and organized she is, about how difficult it is for her, so often, to keep housekeepers because her standards are so high. But in the dream Cynthia's house is a complete and disgusting mess. I cannot believe how Cynthia has distorted and lied. There are four of us, Cynthia, Cynthia's husband, another man and myself sitting and talking. Suddenly the two men are rolling on the floor, making sexual noises.

I try to ignore them, but Cynthia asks me if I think they are doing something sexual. I find myself having the unpleasant responsibility of gently confronting Cynthia with the truth: "Well, yes, Cynthia, I think they are having sex" (p. 39).

As background for the dream, Mrs. T's husband is involved in a major project for which she has done freelance work. She now feels overwhelmed by the task and brings in her friend, Cynthia, to help. The therapist focuses on Cynthia's "strange" waffling about working with Mrs. T, and, in the dream, her lie about her housekeeping. Cynthia is revealed to "be out of touch with her own life" (p. 40). The therapist interprets in depth on the transference issue of the presumed unreliability of the helper. Cynthia, it is said, is chosen in the dream to represent the therapist and, ultimately, the patient's mother. But, the therapist does not entertain the possibility that there may well be some communality between her past experience and what is, indeed, happening now! The patient, we are told, "[E]nded the hour describing her distress at discovering that she takes a blueprint from the past, her experience with her mother, and then applies it to her relationship with others in the present" (p. 41). The authors conclude by saying,

[W]e have included this vignette to demonstrate a particular developmental lag in this patient's capacity for reality testing. When made anxious in relation to threatened loss of object and/or selfobject support, Mrs. T displays a shakiness in distinguishing the experience in a dream or a fantasy from that of her realistic and awake perceptions (p. 41).

From my point of view, what are the mistakes? What are the errors? What data are assiduously unreported? What is inattended? As I pointed out in an article called "The Purloined Self," what is hidden in therapy, is often hidden by being left out in the open, so obviously that no one notices (Levenson, 1987).[10] For example, what is the sex of the therapist? We are never told which author of this presumably husband and wife team saw the patient. Astonishingly, the gender never slips in. How can we know what to make of the identification without that? Second, no mention whatever is made of the homosexual encounter of the two men in the dream. It is never mentioned again. The simple manifest message of the dream is ignored; i.e., Cynthia, the archetypal hypocrite, has to keep

102 Psychoanalytic process

it neat. She cannot bear the messy fact that her husband and the other man are really homosexual lovers. The patient's role is to see what is there to be seen, even if no one else wants to see it! Her tone in confronting Cynthia is decidedly ironic ("Well, yes, Cynthia . . .") and implies that she knows that Cynthia knows what she is pretending not to know. How then does the central analytic issue become her lack of trust and "developmental lag in reality testing," when, in the dream, she is the only one seeing (or rather, speaking) the truth, and Cynthia, the self-deluded one, stands in for the therapist?

So, large pieces of overt data are inattended and the questions that would make the unspoken speakable are never asked or even contemplated. The patient is the "patient," developmentally retarded; not a co-observer of the field, perhaps more in touch with something going on than is the therapist. I would consider these issues as errors, occurring within the context of the therapy. What might be a mistake, a violation of the frame and containment of the treatment, is the inattention to the relationship of the two authors. It is of considerable importance to know whether they discussed the treatment during its course; or, whether this exegesis is well after the fact. I don't think the latter is true since Mrs. T is presumably still in treatment. If they are a couple, then might not the dream refer to that? Would not their own tensions, competitions, power relations enter into the therapy? Are we to assume that there is no way the patient might know that? Or know their relationship? I am not suggesting that they should not have collaborated; but to do so without considering that data as part of the frame and a leak in the integrity and isolation of the frame, with the consequent anxiety for the therapist, is a mistake—not an error. To treat the patient as "a patient," that is, not to see what is there to be seen, not to consider oneself a part of the equation in a real way, not to consider that the patient may be seeing something real, is to mystify the patient, to confirm the patient role as deficit-directed and to protect the article collaborators in their own interaction over the paper.

Let us go back and reconsider another aspect of the dream. The patient, one recalls, had an angry and inappropriate response to the therapist's vacation, accusing him (her?) of lying about giving adequate notice. The therapist is perplexed. Consider the prelude of that exchange:

On questioning her, I find to my complete surprise that she had not remembered that we had talked at length, for several months, in fact, about that vacation. I remind her that back in April I had told her I was probably going to be gone the first several weeks in August because she had been trying at that time to schedule her own time away, *attempting to juggle the family's vacation with that of her husband's analyst* (my italics). Her husband's analyst had told him that he planned to go away at the end of August, and I told her that I was going away at the beginning of August. I recall saying aloud to her that we had some discussion *about who should have to miss psychoanalytic times, she or her husband?* (my italics). I then told her that I had subsequently corrected my original projection of several weeks in August, to one week, the first week only (p. 38).

Perhaps, "who shall miss analytic times, she or her husband" could be extended to who shall have hegemony in the two therapies; her therapist or the husband's therapist (gender also unstated). Do the therapists charge for missed time, or insist that patient's take vacations when they do? We are not told. But, certainly one begins to wonder if the two men wrestling on the floor are perhaps the two therapists; and, that if her "forgetting to remember" the presumed arrangements might not be anger at the therapist who leaves her to juggle the arrangements and then revises his plans. After all, if her therapist goes away only 1 week and the other therapist 3 weeks then shouldn't her therapy have priority since the therapist is providing more continuity? Her distortion then masks her anger that she does not seem able to bring to the therapist. Well, that's her problem, one might say. But then why doesn't the therapist inquire into whether her "misperception" of the vacation notice is a displacement from something else? Instead, he (?) argues with her, a clear violation of psychoanalytic technique. Might that not suggest that the patient knows that she is not supposed to notice what is going on, as in the dream? Would the therapist be open to the observation, from the "patient" that he (?) is having his/her own power struggle, his/her own sibling rivalry with the other therapist who, for all we know, may be higher or lower in the pecking order of psychoanalysts? Might not the patient pay a price for that observation?

Someone once said that in pure science, a discovery is greeted with, "Who would have thought?" and in the social sciences it is greeted with, "Now that you mention it!" Now that I mention it, it is of course obvious that the patient picked up something in her interaction with the

104 Psychoanalytic process

therapist and about the therapist. Psychoanalysts, confronted with this observation, agree, saying, "Of course, I see that and it must be acknowledged to the patient so that we can proceed with the real work of the therapy, the patient's distortions."[11] But what if this is the work of the therapy; that is, bringing into the awareness of both participants the patient's careful monitoring of the therapist's anxiety and her avoidance of a potentially disruptive exchange?

To summarize: the cardinal mistake in psychoanalysis is to assume that the patient is sick, distorting, developmentally impaired. The reification of the patient qua patient has the effect of protecting the therapist against his or her own anxiety, fosters a subtle disdain for the patient, and reinforces the assumption that the patient needs the therapist to explain the patient's life, or to rectify failures in relationships in the patient's earlier life. What is left? All psychoanalysts have recognized that successful therapy depends on tapping into the patient's rich inner life, which reflects not just fantasy but an exquisite sensitivity to relational events. I recall one of my early supervisors at the White Institute, Meyer Maskin, telling me, "Remember, the patient is always better at what he or she does than you are." A neurosis is not simply a failure, it is a highly developed and ingenious strategy for survival, and the patient has developed in what Sullivan called the "self-system," a subtle mechanism for monitoring and managing the world (Sullivan, 1953).

Once one understands that, several caveats follow. First, the therapist will provide a powerfully delineating frame as much for his/her security as the patient's. Second, the therapist will not consider it his/her task to make clear to the patient what the patient is saying. Whether through free-association or detailed inquiry, we wish to tap into the patient's disowned richness of both fantasy and awareness. We wish the patient and the therapist to discover, by the end of the therapy, what the patient did not know he/she knew.

But with the above requirements met, there still remains a large field for error, for wandering from ideal technique.[12] The therapist will be alerted to these occasions by signs of anxiety (boredom, fantasies), by acting-in or out by either participant, by his/her failure to inquire into areas which, on second thought, seem obvious; or, through dreams (the patient's or therapist's) or by direct confrontation from the patient. These deviations are the work of therapy—the "working-through"—and should not be considered problematic in themselves.

Perhaps this perspective on psychoanalytic process is disappointing to those who would wish for an instructional manual—say this, do that—or to those who feel that if the metapsychology is applied correctly, a cure is sure to follow (Levenson, 1982). Alas, we all know psychoanalysts who are masters of theory, locker-room experts, who cannot see what is under their noses. I believe that the present trend toward a more egalitarian, symmetrical view of the process is a vast improvement.[13] We are not called "shrinks" for nothing. Perhaps we can promulgate a freer and more expansive view of the process, leaving the patient with a much enriched, idiosyncratic view of the world, and—not inconsequentially—enriching the experience for us.

Notes

1. This chapter was first presented at the Cambridge Hospital Continuing Education conference, Cambridge, MA, June 12, 1992. It was published in 1992 in *Contemporary Psychoanalysis*, 38(4):555–571.
2. See Levenson (1987b) for elaboration of this theme.
3. For an explication of the issues of error and creativity in psychoanalysis see Feiner (1991).
4. This distinction is not usually made (Chused and Raphling, 1992).
5. This is why very good analysts are not immune from difficulties in their own lives.
6. The psychoanalyst in the movie *The Prince of Tides* who sleeps with the twin brother of her suicidal patient, violates virtually every rule of psychoanalytic frame rectitude!
7. It was in the process of writing this chapter that I, for the first time, understood what Lacan, the Magus of Obscurity, had in mind when he said, "If Freud's discovery has any meaning, it is that truth grabs error by the scruff of the neck in the mistake" (Lacan, 1975, p. 265).
8. For a stimulating discussion of self-reference and its relation to paradox and recursion, see Hofstadter (1985).
9. For an explication of Sullivan's concept of participant-observation, see Levenson (1992).
10. "The Purloined Letter" refers to the famous Edgar Allen Poe story.
11. For an extended presentation of this position see Gill (1982).
12. "Ideal technique," one recalls, varies according to theoretical orientation; to wit; neutrality, empathy, authenticity.
13. See Havens for extended discussion of the "democratization of therapy" (1986, pp. 107–108).

References

Bruner, J. (1990). *Acts of Meaning*. Cambridge, MA: Harvard University Press.

Chused, J.F. and Raphling, D.L. (1992). The analyst's mistakes. *Journal of the American Psychoanalytic Association*, 40(1):89–116.

Clancier, A. and Kalmonovitch, J. (1987). *Winnicott and Paradox: From Birth to Creation*. London: Tavistock Publications.

Feiner, A. (1991). The thrill of error: Image and appearance, articulation, union. *Contemporary Psychoanalysis*, 27(4):624–653.

Ferenczi, S. (1988). *The Clinical Diaries of Sandor Ferenczi*. Cambridge, MA: Harvard University Press.

Freud, S. (1914a). Further recommendations in the technique of psychoanalysis. Remembering, repeating and working through. In J. Strachey (Ed.), *The Standard Edition of the Complete Psychological Works of Sigmund Freud*. London: Hogarth Press, Vol. XII, pp. 147–156.

Freud, S. (1914b). On the history of the psychoanalytic movement. In J. Strachey (Ed.), *The Standard Edition of the Complete Psychological Works of Sigmund Freud*. London: Hogarth Press, Vol. XII, pp. 1–66.

Ghent, E. (1989). Credo: The dialectics of one-person and two-person psychologies. *Contemporary Psychoanalysis*, 25(1):169–209.

Gill, M. (1982). *Analysis of Transference. Vol. I: Theory and Technique*. New York: International Universities Press.

Grosskurth, P. (1991). *The Secret Ring*. New York: Addison-Wesley Publishing Co.

Havens, L. (1986). *Making Contact*. Cambridge, MA: Harvard University Press.

Hofstadter, D. (1985). *Metamagical Themes: Questing for the Essence of Mind and Pattern*. New York: Basic Books.

Lacan, J. (1975). *The Seminar of Jacque Lacan: Book I. Freud's Papers on Technique* (J. Forrester, trans.). New York: W.W. Norton.

Levenson, E. (1982). Follow the fox: An inquiry into the vicissitudes of psychoanalytic supervision. *Contemporary Psychoanalysis*, 18(1):1–15. Also in: E. Levenson (1991). *The Purloined Self*. New York: Contemporary Psychoanalysis Books.

Levenson, E. (1987a). The purloined self. *Journal of the American Academy of Psychoanalysis*, 15:487–490. Also in: *The Purloined Self*. New York: Contemporary Psychoanalysis Books.

Levenson, E. (1987b). An interpersonal perspective. *Psychoanalytic Inquiry*, 7(2): 207–214.

Levenson, E. (1988). The pursuit of the particular. *Contemporary Psychoanalysis*, 24(1):1–16. Also in: E. Levenson (1991). *The Purloined Self*. New York: Contemporary Psychoanalysis Books.

Levenson, E. (1992). H.S. Sullivan: From interpersonal psychiatry to interpersonal psychoanalysis. *Contemporary Psychoanalysis*, 28(4):450–466.

Milner, M. (1969). *The Hands of the Living God*. New York: International Universities Press.

Racker, H. (1968). *Transference and Counter-transference.* New York: International Universities Press.

Sainsbury, R.M. (1988). *Paradoxes.* Cambridge: Cambridge University Press.

Shane, E. and S.M. (1990). The opening phase: A developmental perspective. In T.J. and A. Rothstein (Eds.), *On Beginning an Analysis.* Madison, CT: International Universities Press, pp. 27–55.

Strawson, P.F. (1963). On referring. In C. Caton (Ed.), *Philosophy and Ordinary Language.* Urbana, IL: University of Illinois Press.

Sullivan, H.S. (1953). *The Interpersonal Theory of Psychiatry.* New York: W.W. Norton.

Wolstein, B. (1992). Resistance interlocked with countertransferance. *Contemporary Psychoanalysis*, 28(1):172–190.

Chapter 10

Beyond countertransference
Aspects of the analyst's desire[1]

> We think of the key, each in his prison.
> Thinking of the key, each confirms a prison
> (T.S. Eliot, *The Waste Land*)

What is desire? The answer is neither as obvious nor as casual as one might think. Desire has very specific implications and, without understanding them, one cannot begin to grasp the nuances of much of present psychoanalytic debate. To begin with, "desire" is a totally un-American concept. It's not a word we really use much. "What do you desire for lunch?" or, "I desire you madly," sounds rather awkward to Americans. Rather, it's one of those words, like "discourse," or "subtext" one tends to hear used only in postmodernist criticism, feminist writings, or, as I shall elaborate, some European psychoanalytic derivatives.

To understand the concept of desire, as it is used in contemporary theory, one must first understand that desire is not a cognate of, and cannot be used interchangeably with, need, want, drive, or satisfaction. Desire, as a concept, is derived directly from Hegel. I would love to tell you that I've read Hegel's *Phenomenology of Mind* in the original German; or, even in English translation. But alas, pre-medical indoctrination—at least in my day—seemed more directed toward dissecting clams and nematodes than studying nineteenth-century German philosophers. At any rate, my sources are all secondary.[2] Nevertheless, one must attempt to grapple with Hegel's concept; since, to quote Wilden,

> The Hegelian conception of desire is what lies behind or explicates most modern conceptions of intentionality (Brentano, Husserl), of

cathexis (Freud), of project (Heidegger, Sartre) and of goal-seeking (non-mechanistic cybernetics) ... And, of course, as Lacan has pointed out, the words translated as "instinct" or "drive" or "instinctual impulse" (in Freud, "trieb") as well as the concept of pleasure (lust) and wish-fulfillment, can all be subsumed under the general category of desire, which is to be distinguished from instinctual need and from demand.

(Wilden, 1972, p. 65)

It is not, however, an easy concept to grasp. For an unwitting example of just how thoroughly recondite and incomprehensible this issue can be, let me quote Kojève, explicating Hegel:

To desire a desire is to want to substitute oneself for the value desired by that desire ... To desire the desire of an other is thus, in the last analysis, to desire that the value that I am or that I "represent" be the value desired by the other.

(quoted by Wilden, 1972, p. 66)

No wonder Americans, pragmatists to the core, abjure Hegel. Yet for all the almost willful obscurity of this language, Hegel's understanding of the melancholy and existential incompleteness of desire is acquired by French and English analysts along with their mother's milk. Therefore, one must understand what is meant by desire as contrasted with "want." Paraphrasing Saul Bellow's *Henderson, The Rain King*, the archetypal American protagonist cries inchoately, I want! I want! (Bellow, 1959). This very American vision, is, "Give me everything, because everything is possible." Freud, as you know, despised America. He feared that we would subvert his austere psychoanalysis, change it into a cheap fulfillment device —a shift from the tragic implacability of desire to the candy-mountain dreams of gratifying wants. He may not have been so far wrong. Much of the current criticism of American psychoanalysis centers on its failure to recognize socio-biological limitations, and its blandly romantic propensity to act as though everything were psychodynamically determined and thus subject to resolution.

Wants, needs can be met. Desire is another kettle of fish entirely. Desire, as Hegel defined it, is a wish to find one's completion in the being of another—to be totally known to the Other. This is, oddly enough, a thoroughly intersubjective concept. Desire requires another person; and, for reasons I shall elaborate, desire cannot *ever* be fulfilled: it is an a *priori*, a function of being. "Desire is the search for a symbolic repetition of a satisfaction whose completion has become impossible" (Thompson, 1985, p. 43); "We do not desire objects we desire desire itself" (Kojève, 1969, p. 1–30) quoted by Wilden (1972, p. 23); "Genuine desire is an acceptance of incompleteness, whereas neurosis is a vain attempt to keep the delusion of ultimate satisfaction alive, an attempt to achieve ultimate certainty" (Thompson, 1985, p. 186).

So desire is something far more obscure than want. There is a peculiar paradox built into this wish to find completion in the regard of the Other. Who I am, my self or my ego—as I understand it—is a consequence of reflected appraisals of me. It makes me an object in my own perceptions and in the eyes of others (Thompson, 1985, pp. 178–179). This is explicit in Lacan's postulation of his "mirror stage" and is also similar to Sullivan's version of self, in as much as he believed that the deeply ensconced concept of core personality was illusory. Self, from this point of view, is *always* an objectification, and therefore always false. Winnicott's insistence on a "true" and "false" self would seem a false dichotomy since there *is* no true self. Self is merely who I think I am. To have my desire met—that is, to be acknowledged in my total subjectivity—I *must be recognized for what I am not*! That is, I must discover myself to be not who I thought I was in relationship with the other person. Isn't this, after all, the essence of true love?

Unfortunately, this leads to what Hegel called the Master-Slave dialectic. In order to obtain the desired recognition, one must totally absorb the other person to one's purposes. To quote Thompson again, "What he [the Master] wanted was the recognition of the autonomous free agent who would recognize his desire as human, but what he ended up with was merely the servile, pathetic recognition of the slave" (Thompson, 1985, p. 179). And yet the slave has a more authentic sense of being than the Master—the slave knows who he is through his task. The Master is nothing without him. It is the power of the submitter, the masochist, who is as much needed as needy.

What are the implications for the analyst for this very particular conceptualization of desire that takes us beyond countertransference that is merely a particular therapist's idiosyncratic participation with a particular patient, a highly specific consequence of an interaction. But what of analysts more generically? To paraphrase Freud's famous question, what, after all, do analysts *want*? Analysts want to be good analysts, get referrals, buy a country house, have a career, write a book, be esteemed, earn their fees, help patients—but help them to do what? Well, get better—whatever that is.

Ah, but what, if they *desire* anything at all, do analysts desire? By definition, it must be to become the subject of the patient's desire: to find *their* affirmation in the cure of the patient. If the analyst seeks the patient to affirm his/her own meaning—then what? Cure then becomes a version of the Master-Slave dialectic with the patient submitting to the therapist, who Lacan called "the subject-who-is-supposed-to-know" (Wilden, 1972, p. 21).

Why do analysts require such a profound fulfillment from the patient which surgeons, for example, are perfectly comfortable eschewing? Surgeons do not require that they become the subject of the patient's desire. They will settle for removing the offending organ and collecting their fee. Why do analysts desire more?

Analysts, unlike surgeons, are not following a prescribed method with a predictable outcome. If the surgery fails, either it is bad luck or bad technique. Blame is easily assignable. Analysts, on the other hand, are involved in a process that is poorly delineated, and subject to violent disputation among both its supporters and detractors. Even within a single Training Institute, the poor bedeviled student is proselytized by teachers of markedly different persuasions. Moreover, we cannot assure our patients of successful outcomes, even with our most skillful efforts, and— what is worse—even when patients do extremely well, we cannot be sure that their improvement is directly due to our intervention; since over the long time involved, many other intercurrent events take place in the patient's life. And even if their cure could be directly attributed to therapy, we cannot be sure which of the many, many things we did and said made the difference. Psychoanalysis is like magic. One makes multiple and contiguous interventions and hopes for the best. And, to paraphrase the Indian chief in *Little Big Man*, sometimes the magic just doesn't work (Berger, 1964).

Why, one might ask, with all these discouraging ambiguities afoot, does anyone become an analyst? It is, of course, hardly an entirely conscious choice. Analysts are usually people who are continuing a lifetime role. They have often played the Sage, the sane one, the healer, the arbitrator,

112 Psychoanalytic process

or the peacemaker, in their families from a very early age; so, they have a very serious investment in their therapeutic relevance. I recall hearing R.D. Laing talking publicly about his relationship with his mother who was, he said, at times overtly psychotic. At her worst, when she was mute or raving, Laing said that he could enter her room and she would have a perfectly straightforward and sane conversation with him. He said that she never acted in the slightest way bizarre with him. Well, this might well be a bit of hyperbole, but it was, for him, emblematic of his effectiveness with psychotic people. In other words, I am suggesting that being a psychoanalyst is different from other professions in the extent to which it lends itself to the exigencies of desire and the Master-Slave dialectic.

If you doubt this, just look at analysts in their work with those impolite, unpleasant patients, the so-called narcissistic character disorders. They are excoriatingly angry people, never gratified, and they manage to make most analysts feel like idiots. They can call out embarrassingly revealing bursts of countertransference. I wonder why it is that anyone treats them? What's in it for us? God knows they don't meet our needs. But, in spite of the grandiosity of their expectations, they hold out the promise of affirming our desire, of *making us into something wonderful* through our experience with them—through our ability to cure them. I recall one woman who used to say to me, "By the time I'm finished with you, I'll turn you into a great analyst!" Then, it seemed to me a grandiose and irreverent reversal of the procedure. After all, I was supposed to cure her. But wouldn't that turn me into a great analyst? I must have thought so. Otherwise why did I persist in the face of her onslaught of abuse? Although the outcome of therapy was actually rather good, she left, as do many of these patients, with a strong sense of disappointment. She did not become who she was not, and I, alas, never fulfilled her promise of my promise.

On the other hand, what does the patient want? Of course, to get better—to have things work, to be happy, to be able to love, to be loved, perhaps in an unqualified way. Maybe to have the neurosis perfected! What the patient is doing in life is not getting the anticipated results, but perhaps the analyst knows a way, or can provide a mutative experience that will make it work.

What does the patient desire? The patient is not in touch with real desire and its consequences, which are always disappointment. In the terms of Hegel's Master-Slave dialectic, the analyst wishes to be desired, the patient wants to be cured. The patient wishes to fulfill the analyst's desire, but can only offer the angry submission of the slave or resist the process, by the passive-aggressive rebellion of the slave. Since love is not freely given, the Master is not validated. The success of an analysis depends on the ability of the two participants to surmount this bind. Hegel did not believe it was possible. As psychoanalysts, we prefer to believe there is a way out of what he considered an existential impasse.

If desire can never be fulfilled, then what? Here we come to the crucial point. When Elizabeth Zetzel went before the Admissions Committee of the London Psychoanalytic Institute, Ernest Jones told her that, "Whatever you do, don't tell them that you want to help the patient."[3] This advice is not as silly as it sounds—or as it makes the Admissions Committee sound. *The analyst must stop trying to cure the patient*, not out of respect for the patient's need for autonomy, but because cure is in the service of the analyst's own desire and, moreover, is unachievable. The patient must come into touch with desire, which is a lifelong state and must be accepted as existential. No one is ever fully satisfied. If the analyst holds out the promise of being the perfect parent or mate—of knowing the patient—it is a seduction of the patient in the service of the analyst's need to be affirmed by the patient. In psychoanalysis, the therapist succeeds by *failing* the patient. This is absolutely axiomatic, whether one is a classical Freudian, a self-psychologist, or an interpersonalist. In all psychoanalytic therapies, the patient learns to listen to his/her own small voice through a series of incremental disappointments in the analyst and the analysis. Even Kohut, one notes, said that cure results from an adequately maintained understanding, an "echo of empathic resonance," *and* the analyst's occasional failures, optimal frustrations which lead to the building up of self-structure (Kohut, 1984, p. 78).

But failing the patient is a very difficult thing to do or even conceptualize. It sounds mean. Yet when Bion said that one must enter each session "without memory or desire"; it is precisely this need of the therapist to be helpful, to be able to offer an overview—a useful conceptualization of the patient's problems—that he was subverting.[4] To repeat, one must have no interest in curing or helping the patient. This is not doing nothing; it is non-doing. The Tao says, "The sage goes about, doing nothing." It may sound bizarre but it is, I believe, the key to psychoanalytic change. The patient learns two things. First, that resolutions and gratifications are always incomplete. And, second, that it is possible to discover oneself— albeit imperfectly—in the regard of the therapist. I cannot emphasize

114 Psychoanalytic process

enough that this is self-discovery, not reflected appraisals or insights instituted by the therapist.

This is the hardest thing for therapists to learn. *The single most consistently undermining error that analysts make is the effort to do something that works*! This can take the form of a mutative interpretation or a mutative interaction—doing something with the patient that makes a difference. Listen to analysts' work. The patient tells his/her story. Does the analyst think, "What can I say about this?" And does he/she then proceed to supply a metaexplanation, an overview? As Masud Khan said, we ask the patient for his truth so that we may supply him with the metatruth (quoted in Milner, 1969). Or, the therapist thinks, how should I react to this? If I say this, the patient will hear that. If I say that, will the patient hear this? If I do X, will the patient hear me as doing Y? It is not at all uncommon, at clinical presentations, to hear analysts who believe in relational participation, not neutrality, worrying about the nature of their participation; like Hamlet, pondering their choices—afraid of supplying the wrong response or, Heaven forfend, if it is effective, afraid that they have inadvertently provided what I have referred to as the Dreaded Corrective Emotional Experience—one of psychoanalysis's cardinal sins. Behind all this is the fervent wish to make a difference, to do something that will work.

The real issue in an intersubjective field is to present (or at least monitor) one's own experience without the slightest concern about whether it is helpful or not! "Right or wrong," in this context, is only another way of saying "helpful or not." Should I answer a patient who asks me whether I live in the city or the suburbs? If I customarily proceed according to a strictly maintained frame neutrality then I must not answer regardless of how benign the request seems. I may ask why the patient asks, what fantasies he/she has, why now? If I believe more in an intersubjective field, then my emphasis must be not on what response would be most helpful to the patient—would "work"—but rather on what my experience is of being asked. The issue becomes, not what is good for the patient, or even why he/she is asking, but what I am feeling. Do I feel pressured to respond? Do I not want to, for some reason? Or, is this one of those occasions in which I felt like volunteering the information? Is the patient asking because I was 10 minutes late to the session? Was it because of traffic on the road? Should I have left earlier? Did I, this morning, leave later than usual? Did I fantasize that the patient might be angry? Is this patient rigidly on time?

Never on time? Is he/she a forgiving sort? And so on *ad infinitum—well*, not quite *ad infinitum*. One stops at some reasonable point simply because time does not allow. And yet, an entire therapy might be done through an endless examination of this one incident, and its recursions into the lives of both participants. This self-scrutiny does not necessarily require informing the patient, although one might well do so. But it is a rich source of data about the intersubjective field. Again, I must emphasize that I am not suggesting that the correct (in this case, most authentic) response to the patient is curative. I *am* suggesting that it clears the way for the patient to explore his/her own experience. Psychoanalysis is a bit like curling, that ice-bowling sport in which the second player runs ahead of the disc, sweeping the ice, clearing the way.

Is all this nihilism? Am I suggesting one go for training to an Ashram? Basically the idea is that psychoanalysis requires an analyst in touch with desire and enough sense to not try to convert it to want. Does this sound wildly radical? Let me present two quotes, for which I am indebted to Dr. Gerard Chrzanowski. The first is from Freud:

> However much the analyst may be tempted to act as teacher, model and ideal to other people and to make men in his own image, he should not forget that this is not his task in the analytic relationship, and that indeed he will be disloyal to his task if he allows himself to be led on by his inclinations. He will only be repeating one of the mistakes of the parents, when they crushed their child's independence, and he will be replacing one kind of dependence by another.
>
> (Freud, 1940, p. 67)

Or, this quote from Fromm's posthumously published book:

> all this is possible only if the analyst experiences within himself what goes on in the patient and does not approach him cerebrally—if he sees and sees and sees, and thinks as little as is absolutely necessary and, furthermore, if he gives up the illusion that he is "well" and the patient is "sick." . . . The analyst has the patient's genuine confidence only if he permits himself to be vulnerable and does not hide behind the role of a professional man who knows the answers because he is paid for knowing the answers. The fact is that he and the patient are engaged in a common task—the shared understanding of the patient's

116 Psychoanalytic process

experience, and the analyst's response to his experience—not of the patient's "problem;" the patient *has* no problem but *is* a person suffering from his way of being.

(Fromm, 1992, p. 70)

If one abjures helping, what is left? One returns to the Ur tool, the sine qua non of psychoanalysis, free-association or its modern analogue, the detailed inquiry. They both operate as a way of investigating the holes, the inattentions, what is left out in the dialogue. In the Kabbalistic tradition, Rabbi Levi Isaac said that the truth of God lay in the white spaces around the letters, the absences, of which, in the Messianic age, God would reveal the meanings (Ecco, 1984, p. 155). The therapist eschews understanding, looks into the "white spaces;" simply inquires to deconstruct the story. It is interesting how close this comes to recapitulating the premises of hermeneutics that,

events, gestures, things suddenly appear as a strange, inexplicable, intrusive evidence within a context which is too weak to justify their presence. So they reveal that they are there to reveal something else: it is up to the reader to decide what it is.

(Ecco, 1984, p. 157)

In other words, patients, instead of simply talking to us, begin to listen to themselves talking to us, and discover that they are other than they thought they were. This is as close as we get to true desire.

Let us imagine a young woman in her early thirties. She has traveled to the Himalayas to consult a famous Holy Man. At her first meeting, the Guru asks why she came. It is clear he has no particular investment in her being there. He did not ask her to come. Moreover, he has curiosity, perhaps compassion, but no investment whatever in her life, her values or what matters to her. She says, "I am not happy. I think I have a problem with intimacy." "What is intimacy?" asks the guru. "The ability to sustain a close relationship with another person, specifically my boyfriend." "What is a close relationship?" "We should like the same things, feel the same way, he should understand me." "What is it to understand?" asks the Guru, curious. "He is a wonderful person," says the patient. "What is wonderful?" "He is a lawyer, Jewish, his parents are well-to-do, he is attractive, wants what I want." "What is it you want?" "To have children, a nice house." "Where is the house to be? What is it to be a lawyer?" . . . And so forth.

A 36-year-old woman lawyer, consulting with me because she was inexplicably depressed, making much the same presentation as above, said, "I have everything a child could desire." "A child?" would ask the Guru, "What is it to be a child?" The guru is not at all interested in figuring out what's wrong and how to fix it. He is simply curious about the other person and how the world looks to her, since it clearly doesn't look that way to him and he has no real desire to live her life. I suggest that this is highly therapeutic, because the supplicant discovers herself—that is to say, who she is not—in the process of the intentionless inquiry. Her desire begins to emerge through her own voice.

Parenthetically, I have as one of my iconic memories an incident when I was in the army as a medical officer. My Colonel, who was a perfectly nice guy, made an observation about me (the negative implications of which I shall withhold), and it was one of the most formative experiences in my life. I thought, My God, he's right! Of course, as in all these epiphanies, it was what everyone had been trying to get across to me for years. Why did it register this time? I think it was that he really didn't care whether I listened or not. He was not angry, hurt, or offended. He was just telling me something because he felt like saying it and, I think, because he did like me. This is now 46 years later and I still feel grateful. I am convinced it was his lack of intentionality that was critical. My Colonel's desire was invested elsewhere.

Well, let us say that our patient returns dissatisfied from the Himalayas and goes to an analyst. "Why are you here?" he/she asks. "I am unhappy and I cannot establish an intimate relationship." "What happens?" "I start with a boyfriend, feel very close and involved and then after a while, it all falls apart. I begin to find fault, pick fights, and finally he leaves me." "You never leave first?" "No. I think I am afraid of the risk of desertion." "Tell me about your parents." "My mother is very close, but intrusive and provocative. Every time I get together with her we end up fighting. I used to be my father's favorite, but when I became a teenager, we began to fight like mad. Now he is distant and morose." Any psychotherapist, following this exchange, is building a precept, wondering what questions to ask. But a problem with intimacy has been accepted as a given, and an attempt is being made to make sense of it—to put it into historical perspective. The method is that the therapist is gathering data, making

118 Psychoanalytic process

connections, and conceptualizing an overview, a blueprint, based on his/her theoretical canons which will, presumably, provide the patient with a frame of action.

Up to this point, one is engaged in a rational psychotherapy, in the Meyerian or even Sullivanian tradition. Psychoanalysis begins when the inquiry begins to touch on the absences, the scotomata in the narrative, which conceal the patient's areas of anxiety. Instead of getting clearer, the story becomes "deconstructed," breaks down, becomes inconsistent, inexplicable gaps and absences appear.

Where is transference and countertransference? First, the patient, becoming increasingly anxious and revealed, mobilizes against the therapist and works to incorporate the therapist into the defensive system. We become the enemy, not the helper. We become the disease we have set out to cure. Ergo, resistance and transference. Countertransference emerges from the failure of the therapist to maintain his/her own focus, whether defined as neutrality, authenticity, or empathy. In the course of attempting the inquiry, meanings become less and less apparent. The analyst loses his/her own moorings in neutrality as the inquiry blooms. It becomes evident that the analyst participates, brings his/her self to the inquiry, by virtue of what is asked, reveals himself/herself by virtue of the inquiry. The inquirer becomes part of the inquiry. It then becomes evident that the inquiry takes on the pattern of what is being inquired into, that there is an isomorphism between content and inquiry. This, again, does not make things clearer. Clarity is always a parenthesis around events; a stopping of time, a time-out, a breather in the flow of events. If the therapist "interprets" he/she makes things temporarily clear; but the flow stops and the therapist finds himself/herself ahead of the patient, pulling the patient into clarity. If the therapist resists the temptation and simply continues the process of inquiry, he/she finds himself *behind* the patient, following the flow, riding the crest of a wave, and bemused by the shifts and turns which come unplanned and unpredicted. Interpretation is the instrument of understanding and understanding is emblematic of the Master—He Who Must Know. The analyst who is not consuming the patient with his/her own desire will leave the patient room to come into touch with desire, not want.

I want to present a clinical example that I have used before (Levenson, 1988, p. 193–194). This is a young woman who is telling her analyst— with some trepidation—her secret fantasy.

Beyond countertransference | 119

There's a doctor—a Mad Scientist—and his nurse—and he ties me down to do things to me. The fantasy has to do with—something—it has to do with getting bigger breasts . . . The Mad Scientist would do something to give me bigger breasts. I wanted bigger breasts very much. I had to submit to the Mad Scientist like I was his slave and he was my master. I try not to think about this fantasy . . . I don't want to dig into it.

(Levenson, 1988, p. 193)

She proceeds to talk about her Master/Slave feelings, but not really telling the fantasy. The analyst interprets, "You want me to be the Mad Scientist Doctor forcing and hurting you and making changes in you." She denies it. "No," she says, sounding injured, "I want you to use your knowledge and your understanding to change me. I have to reject that. I can't agree with you on that" (Silverman, 1987).

Note that the patient tells (very guardedly) a fantasy. The therapist interprets in terms of his understanding of resistance and transference—to wit, he is the Mad Scientist. That is, she is converting him to the Mad Scientist as a resistance against examining her intrapsychic fantasies. This is a canonical Freudian interpretation. As Gill says, "All resistance manifests itself by way of transference" (Gill, 1982). The projection onto the analyst protects her from hearing the mutative insight interpretation that would confront the meaning of the fantasy, presumably her incestuous and sadomasochistic dynamics. Insight is the goal, transference is a resistance to insight, and interpretation is *away* from the therapist and his alleged participation, and back to her intrapsychic processes. But note that the patient not only rejects his interpretation, but treats him as sadistic by experiencing his intervention as unfair—she is "hurt" by his interpretation. One hopes the therapist maintains his "cool," his neutrality. But one could hardly blame him for a flash of countertransferential irritation; thus enacting the very problem under inquiry. It is my strong belief that the interaction of the therapist and patient always enacts the problem under inquiry. Interpretation qua interpretation fails because it is also always simultaneously a transferential enactment. It is the analysis of this enactment as a reiterative replay of the problem that, I believe, carries the therapeutic leverage.

But what if one were, like the Guru, simply curious about the fantasy? Can we get her to tell us it? What exactly is a Mad Scientist? How mean is the Mad Scientist if he is giving her her heart's dream—big breasts? Why should he want to? How will he do it? Certainly, it is implied, against her will, strapped to some devilish device. Will it hurt? Probably. What is so marvelous about big breasts? Why not just go to a reconstructive surgeon (this was before the insert scandals)? Why must it be done against her will and by a Mad Scientist?

Well, that's the whole point. It is not simply a matter of getting bigger breasts; *she wishes to be the object of the Mad Scientist's desire*! It would be too simple to have inserts installed by a surgeon. The Mad Scientist, in defiance of the laws of God and Nature, out of a consuming passion to be the Creator (which is, after all, what *all* Mad Scientists are about), will give her *real* big breasts, the kind one is born with—not some simulacrum available to any woman with the necessary money and incentive. And, having accomplished that miracle, he will love her, his creature—not because he always wanted a woman with big breasts—but because it is through her devotion that he is realized. True, she will have her desiratum of large breasts, but that is a small triumph compared to her service to her Creator.

The goal of the fantasy is to be desired through her capacity to fulfill the scientist's dream. After all, what greater passion was there than between Professor Frankenstein and his creature? Can one doubt that this woman, in therapy, wishes to do anything to be the perfect patient, redeeming her analyst (of course, she won't). How could he then not love her? What must he do to cure her? He must, unlike the Mad Scientist, fail her. The Mad Scientist becomes the Wizard of Oz, and the patient, resigned to never being the subject of such passion, begins to listen to her own voice.

All this defines, as I see it, the difference between psychoanalysis and psychotherapy—psychoanalysis's favorite conundrum. The latter is pragmatic and goal oriented. One does whatever works to achieve a defined outcome—which is, after all, the therapist's idea of what cure is. Psychoanalysis works differently: it intends to fail the patient's hope for a magical cure, force him/her to fall back on his or her own resources and begin to arrive at his or her own construction of the world. I dread the present trend toward the climactic cure—abreactive amnesia recall, the search for an event that will fulfill life. Even the present ecumenical movement in psychoanalysis reflects this chimeric dream of final understanding, clarity at last. Why must we all agree? Find a common pathway? What's wrong with disagreeing, living in doubt, not knowing whether one is on the right track or not? Psychoanalysis should not be a trade or even a craft. To quote Crapanzano:

> Relationships between individuals, institutions, or disciplines which surrender the agonistic approach to facile affirmations of harmony and accord are in danger of losing the vigor, critical reflection, and creativity that come with the disquieting knowledge that the world may indeed appear differently to those with whom we engage. Even more disquieting is the knowledge that there is no knowledge complete in and of itself, but only a thinking which aspires to a knowing.
>
> (Crapanzano, 1992, p. 154)

Many analysts see a caring, empathic, or "holding milieu" as providing a powerfully restitutive experience for the patient. Am I denigrating the analyst's genuine caring for the patient? Am I promulgating detachment or indifference? It is a really difficult question. We must distinguish caring as a state of being, an a priori instrument of treatment, from caring as an emergent process between two people. Why am I caring? Because I am a caring person? Then you had better not threaten my perception of myself. Am I caring as a prerequisite to curing someone? Then the patient will resist and cause me to fail, for who wishes to be cured by the submission to the ministrations of the other person—no matter how saintly.

Empathy is an equally difficult concept. Surely we must distinguish it from sympathy. I can sympathize with someone else's experience, but I cannot empathize with it unless I can truly feel it, and that, it seems to me, requires that I have had the experience or something very close. Empathy must also be voluntary, spontaneous. An arbitrary position of empathic understanding looks very much like a boundary diffusion—a failure of presence, an absence. What a paradox! To be totally responsive may well be an absence.

Since this is frequently misconstrued, it might be well to quote a caveat:

> A version of psychoanalysis as professional kindness, psychoanalysis reduced to empathy, or to a long process the denouement of which is confirmation that the patient's life was indeed ruined by his parents, was quite foreign to Winnicott.
>
> (Rodman, 1987)

122 Psychoanalytic process

I believe all this is very difficult to grasp and sounds somewhat abstruse and possibly, if you will forgive a pun, "guru-some." Since I am rather used to this happening, let me, as a sort of codicil, predict a dialogue between two persons leaving this meeting:

A—[Wearily] What the hell was he talking about? It sounds like he said that psychoanalysis doesn't work, there is nothing the analyst can do that is right; and that everything we've been taught to do either fosters the patient's submission or mobilizes resistance and is therefore wrong. Desire-shmesire! I never could understand Lacan and anyway what's wrong with wanting to be helpful, even cure patients?

B—I don't think he was saying the psychoanalysis doesn't work; rather, he was saying that psychoanalysis doesn't work in the same way as psycho-therapy that works by providing the patient with a coherent overview, a blueprint for making changes. If the changes work, they reinforce more change. Psychoanalysis works by failing the patient's expectations of a master helper. The patient is thrown back on his/her own resources and discovers, to his/her amazement, that there is a flow of consciousness, a deep river of awareness, which he/she can tap into and use. By eschewing direc-tion, organizing, helping, or offering corrective experiences, the therapist creates a vacuum into which the patient moves, not replacing or destroying the Master by identifying with him/her; but in Wilden's words, making him/her *irrelevant.* "In the end the patient must know what the analyst knows, which is what the patient has always known" (Wilden, 1972, p. 30).

The function of the detailed inquiry or the promotion of free-asso-ciations, dreams, fantasies, is not to accumulate data to make clear to the patient what is the problem as the analyst (he/she who-knows) sees it; but to fragment, deconstruct (to use another trendy term) the patient's story, which always consists of reified narratives which leave no room for novelty. Neurosis, it must be said, is always both anachronistic and clichéd.

Of course, giving up the Master-Slave dialectic means giving up the dream of a magical outcome, an epiphany, an insight or experience which permits one to live happily ever after—mature, related, intimate and loving. As he said, Freud was afraid that psychoanalysis, in America, would be bowdlerized into some facile version of uplift. Americans don't like difficulties: they want comforting answers. Maybe, as Mel Brooks put it, "Life stinks!" and recognizing that is a prerequisite for living successfully.

A—YEH, but then he's been saying for years that we have to get away from the old idea of the analyst as neutral observer. That, first, neutrality is not really possible and second that it cuts out a lot of useful interactional data. But then he goes on—in my mind—to contradict himself by first encouraging an awareness of the interactional field (in which the therapist is an equal participant); and then to claim that the therapist must avoid using the interaction in any deliberately corrective way. That is, he says that to attempt to cure the patient through a superior experience with the analytic helper is what he so archly calls the Dreaded Corrective Emotional Experience—an analytic No-No. I don't get it.

B—Well, I think he's trying to say—admittedly in his usual prolix and confusing fashion—that the analyst's meticulous monitoring of the interaction and his/her own participation is not to perfect the participation in some way that will be therapeutic; but to get the analyst out of the way of the patient's flow of consciousness. The patient's awareness of self is shaped by its interface with the therapist; that is, the security operations of the therapist limit and define the patient as well as the patient's own defenses. The patient flows into the space created by the therapist's ability to define and constrain his/her own security operations, and it is there that the patient expands his/her own self-awareness.

A—[Begrudgingly] Well, I suppose that does help make it clearer. Say, listen, have you been in supervision or therapy with Levenson? You're beginning to sound just like him.

B—Well, we all have our shortcomings.

Notes

1. This chapter was first published in 1994 in *Contemporary Psychoanalysis*, 30(4): 691–706. First presented to the Manhatten Institute for Psychoanalysis February 4, 1994.
2. For the following exegesis of Hegel, I am heavily indebted to several secondary sources; namely, Anthony Wilden (1972), M. Guy Thompson (1985), and Lacan (1975). Presented to the Manhattan Institute for Psychoanalysis February 4, 1994.
3. Told by Zetzel at a panel of the American Psychoanalytic Association. Quoted by L.M. Zabarenko (Zabarenko, 1993).
4. That quote of Bion's is from the opening stanza of T. S. Eliot's *The Waste Land*.

> April is the cruelest month, breeding
> Lilacs out of the dead land, mixing
> memory and desire, stirring dull roots with spring rain.

(Eliot, 1930, p. 69)

References

Bellow, S. (1959). *Henderson, the Rain King:* New York: Viking Penguin.

Berger, T. (1964). *Little Big Man.* New York: Dial Press.

Crapanzano, V. (1992). *Hermes' Dilemma and Hamlet's Desire: On the Epistemology of Interpretation.* Boston, MA: Harvard University Press.

Ecco, U. (1984). *Semiotics and the Philosophy of Language.* Bloomington, IN: Indiana University Press.

Eliot, T.S. (1930). *Collected Poems of T. S. Eliot.* New York: Harcourt, Brace and Co.

Freud, S. (1940). An Outline of Psychoanalysis. In J. Strachey (Ed.), *The Standard Edition of the Complete Psychological Works of Sigmund Freud.* London: Hogarth Press, Vol. XXXIII, pp. 144–208.

Fromm, E. (1992). *The Revision of Psychoanalysis.* Boulder, CO: San Francisco, CA: Oxford: Westview Press.

Gill, M. (1982). On Sullivan, his life and work. *William Alanson White Newsletter (Winter 1982–83),* 27(1):6.

Kohut, H. (Ed.). (1984). *How Does Analysis Cure?* Chicago, IL: University of Chicago Press.

Kojève, A. (1969). *Introduction to the Reading of Hegel.* New York: Basic Books.

Lacan, J. (1975). *The Seminar of Jacque Lacan: Book I, Freud's Papers on Technique* (J. Forrester, trans.). New York: W.W. Norton.

Levenson, E. (1988). The pursuit of the particular. *Contemporary Psychoanalysis,* 24:1–16.

Milner, M. (1969). *The Hands of the Living God: An Account of a Psycho-analytic Treatment.* London: The Hogarth Press.

Rodman, F.R. (1987). *The Spontaneous Gesture: Selected letters of D.W. Winnicott.* Cambridge: Harvard University Press.

Silverman, M. (1987). Clinical material. In S. Pulver (Ed.), How Theories Shape Technique (special issue). *Psychoanalytic Inquiry,* 7(1):147–165.

Thompson, M.G. (1985). *The Death of Desire: A Study in Psychopathology.* New York: New York University Press.

Wilden, A. (1972). *System and Structure: Essays in Communication and Exchange.* London: Tavistock.

Zabarenko, L.M. (1993). Review: John Gedo. *The Biology of Clinical Encounters: Psychoanalysis as a Science of Mind.* In *Psychoanalytic Books: A Quarterly Journal of Reviews*, 4:33–39.

Chapter 11

Aspects of self-revelation and self-disclosure[1]

Gill, in a seminal paper called "The Interpersonal Paradigm and the Degree of the Therapist's Involvement," saw, with his usual lucidity, that there was no clear correlation between analysts' doctrinaire positions and their use of themselves as the therapeutic instrument (Gill, 1983). In other words, the use of both self-revelation and self-disclosure cuts across institutional boundaries.[2] This observation came after his careful review of interpersonal literature, and it gave him "an illuminating and unexpected jolt," since it had been an article of faith among Freudians that interpersonalists all "interacted" with their patients (Gill, 1983, p. 204). What else *was* interpersonalism?

In my efforts to delineate an interpersonal perspective on self-revelation and disclosure, I must reiterate that "being interpersonal" and "getting personal" are not, by any means, synonymous! The essence of the interpersonal position lies in the analyst's *self-awareness*, that is, in an exquisite attention to the nature of his or her participation. As Gill put it, "The emphasis falls on being aware of what one is doing, rather than on what to do" (Gill, 1983, p. 211). For the interpersonalist, every perception of the therapist, every interpretation, every inquiry, every omission of inquiry, comes out of the analyst's own participation in the intersubjective field. This requires that the analyst meticulously monitor his or her reactions, including his or her own spontaneous associations and memories; but how much is revealed to the patient is an entirely different question. Among interpersonalists, there are wide variations, not in the emphasis on awareness, but in the use of the patient-therapist relationship, ranging from quite conservatively nonparticipatory to quite radically interactive.

The title of this chapter is "self-revelation" *and* "self-disclosure," implying some distinction between the two. To *reveal* is to allow to be known what has heretofore been hidden (a passive act). To *expose* is to make public something reprehensible, a crime (we are not dealing with that), and to *disclose* is to act, to make known an occurence that has been under consideration but, for valid reasons, has been kept under wraps. I would like to elaborate that distinction. Self-revelation (unveiling) would refer to those aspects of the therapist that are inadvertently or deliberately permitted to be apprehended by the patient. Self-disclosure would be whatever the therapist deliberately decides to show (or tell) the patient.

As I see it, self-revelation is inevitable. Even if analysts were issued standard orange jump-suits and standard office equipment (the cartoon couch, chair, picture of Freud, and diploma), they would still reveal themselves by their appearance, their mien, their taste in office decoration, their books, their regional accents. This, of course, is obvious. There are, however, less obvious revelations. Traditionally, we tended to view patients as overwhelmed by anxiety, self-absorbed, and so out of touch with the realities of the treatment room that they would fail to notice even blatant changes—for example, a therapist developing a limp or shaving off his beard. These days, with the erstwhile mystique of psychoanalysis considerably depleted, we might entertain a more egalitarian interpersonal concept; namely, that anxiety is a contagious and shared experience. An anxious patient will make for an anxious analyst and vice versa; and an analyst made excessively anxious is, for the ordinary patient, a very dangerous collaborator.

So, patients monitor analysts with exquisite attention to their anxiety, and are alert to any self-revealing clues. Patients who are up for presentation often pick up a change in the tone of the analyst's interventions—interpretations become more elaborate, more doctrinaire. It is, for example, a commonplace in the supervisory experience for the patient to dream of the supervisor, usually getting the gender correct. There are, of course, marked variations in this sensitivity to the analyst. Some extremely obsessional patients do seem blind to the presence of the other, although I suspect this obtuseness may be more strategic than real. So-called narcissistic patients, in contrast, are extremely alert to the therapist's anxiety and—unlike the protective neurotic patient—will not hesitate to excoriate the therapist for his or her shortcomings. Way at the far end of this spectrum are those rare patients who seem uncannily in touch with the therapist—

who tune in on early pregnancies, sicknesses, life changes. There are even those few patients who seem truly prescient, who seem to operate in the realm of Jung's synchronicity, or who seem, in some inexplicable way, to violate the normal world.[3]

The patient may disclose his or her observations to the therapist, or, more likely, may keep them private. These observations may not even be consciously registered by the patient; i.e., they may be kept out of awareness, "selectively inattended," to use Sullivan's term for a preconscious averting of the eyes. Awareness of the analyst's dissociated anger, depression, sexual feelings, or despair may then be revealed in a dream, or in a piece of acting-out.

If self-revelation can be defined as what the patient may see, through a veil darkly, regardless of the therapist's efforts at inscrutability (not neutrality, which I don't believe possible or desirable), then the only issue is whether the therapist confirms or, at least, acknowledges what the patient sees. That may require the therapist's accepting that the patient may have seen something out of the awareness of the one Lacan called, "The-Subject-Who-is-supposed-to-Know" (quoted in Wilden, 1972, p. 21). Here one opens a veritable psychoanalytic can of worms. The continuum of responses, starting on the far right, is:

1. The patient is projecting onto the analyst; any issue of verisimilitude is irrelevant.
2. The patient is partly correct—has picked up something—but is putting it to the service of a distortion out of his or her own intrapsychic dynamics.[4] It is necessary to validate the accuracy of the patient's perceptions in order to clear the way for the investigation of the patient's distortions.
3. We are not particularly concerned about the accuracy of the patient's perceptions. We are interested in the patient's "psychic reality"—how it looks to him or her. This position accepts the reality of the patient without accepting it as veridical, i.e., as reflecting reality as the therapist correctly perceives it.
4. The social constructivist or hermeneutic position is that the patient's narrative is as intrinsically valid as the therapist's; issues of objective or "naive" reality are irrelevant.
5. There is a mutually validatable external reality. Because of the nature of anxiety and defenses, both parties have large areas of unawareness,

128 Psychoanalytic process

scotomata in their perception of the interpersonal field. Awareness is consensually developed between the two participants, not just by focusing previously inattended areas of experience, but also in the examination of multiple perspectivistic interpretations of the meaning of what is observed. As Morris Eagle put it, "For whatever one might say in the theoretical papers about 'stories' and 'constructions,' the fact is that most therapists make a genuine effort to grasp what is really going on and what is the case" (Eagle, 1987, p. 167). This requires that the therapist respect the perceptions of the patient and acknowledges the possibility that the patient may see something the therapist does not. After all, what is countertransference but the therapist's blind spots? If a patient thinks I am angry, and I don't feel it—then what? If I carefully examine my feelings and still don't find anger, what does that signify? It still might be out of my awareness. One does not need to know, to find closure. It is possible to simply sit with it and wait for further clarification.

I don't think that unpleasant feelings about patients are really countertransference. Dislike, boredom, sexual feelings, anger are all, to my mind, usually appropriate responses to something about the patient and are eminently useable in therapy. As they once said about minié balls in the Civil War—you never hear the one that hits you. As Gill pointed out, awareness of countertransference is often retrospective, hindsight (Gill, 1994). Really troublesome countertransference operates well out of awareness. It usually takes some acting-out (on either side) or a dream (again, on either side) to be exposed. Parenthetically, I was taught that any dream the patient had in which I appear undisguised should be considered a statement about my countertransference; i.e., the patient has seen me.

My position, then, on self-revelation is that it is inevitable. It is not an active decision on the part of the therapist. The patient will detect things whether the therapist is meticulously careful about lifting the veil or quite casual. The only question is how much to validate. Thus the issue becomes self-disclosure—an action—in the service of self-revelation—an experience.

I am strongly in agreement with Gill, who was in favor of confirmation at this point; I believe that "making explicit" what is seen is inherent to the psychoanalytic praxis (Gill, 1983, p. 232). It validates the patient's

Self-revelation and self-disclosure   129

sense that his or her perception of the world is worth paying attention to, and that he or she has something to contribute to the therapy. Nothing is worse than a patient who must believe in the omnipotence of the therapist and who has no faith in his or her own ability to accurately read the world. This, unfortunately, is not an uncommon outcome of therapy, when it becomes a rhetorical persuasion and creates true believers—those unfortunate people we see in second and third therapies, who know the incantations, understand their dynamics in every last detail, but are not autonomous enough to change (Levenson, 1978).

Do not equate this version of self-disclosure with a corrective emotional experience or a holding milieu, in which the patient is allowed the experience of being respected because it is "good for him or her." I had in mind a less patronizing process. The therapist cannot use his or her canonical concepts as a roadmap to the territory. We *need* the patient's feedback to make any sense at all of the context. Therapy takes place in the intersubjective field—between the two participants. This does not necessarily imply that *cure* takes place through the transference-countertransference, or that interpersonalists ignore the patient's private experience, real and imagined, past and present. But we do believe that in listening to a patient's report of an experience at age five, how we hear it, what we make of it, will come out of our own experience. There is no unbiased listening. Cure, then, is an emergent and collaborative process of awareness. This may seem perfectly obvious and on the side of the angels. Who would disagree with it? But the literature, to my mind, is littered with examples of total dismissals of patients' experience.

Note that awareness does not presume self-disclosure, which is an entirely different matter and implies an active decision by the therapist to reveal something about him- or herself, or some reaction of the therapist to the patient. This is a problematic process that exists along a continuum, as does self-revelation. Self-disclosure might be utilized either as a general philosophy of therapy or as a specific response to a specific context. As the former, self-disclosure can take place simply through a casualness about frame, as, for example, talking easily about one's weekend, children, vacation; or it can take place more actively, in socializing with patients, going to shows, openings, marriages, parties. As response within a context, one discloses specific reactions one is having toward the patient—i.e., disclosing one's countertransference—but within a generally more constrained frame.

It is more difficult to justify self-disclosure, since it is *not* in response to the patient's input, as is self-revelation; virtually all analysts, as does Gill, counsel discretion, to avoid "wild analysis" (Gill, 1994, pp. 118–119). But, with that caveat, what might legitimately justify self-disclosure as a general philosophy? Perhaps egalitarianism, a feeling that the patient has a right to know the therapist as a person rather than as an icon. What might motivate disclosure as a response to specific context? Obviously, the belief that that kind of interaction is of therapeutic value. But how does one decide? What might motivate inappropriate disclosure? There is a long list: loneliness, reaction to the patient's disdain, a desire to be a role model, to be admired, to be envied. Many of the people we work with are richer and often more social and more successful than we are.

Patients learn the rules, and a general attitude of self-disclosure may be, paradoxically, less problematic than trying to use it intermittently, at the "right time." If you are trying to be inscrutable, patients will understand that this is how the game is played—not that you are necessarily a cold or distant person. If you are trying, in general, to be totally spontaneous and present, they will likely forgive some clumsy or self-absorbed gaffes. Disclosure of specific responses to patients is far trickier. These may be divided into two categories: reactions you think you understand and are imparting to the patient as part of the interactional process; and reactions you are having that perplex you and that you are, so to speak, simply throwing into the hopper, offering them up for the patient's response.

In either case, one must be prepared to work through the patient's reactions to one's self-disclosure. If, Heaven forfend, you *expect* it to work, then I fear you are promulgating that anathema of psychoanalysts, The Dreaded Corrective Emotional Experience—that is, leaning on the patient to change. That wouldn't be so bad if it worked; but, in my experience, these interventions usually work only when one doesn't expect them to— when they are made out of some internal pressure. One must do what one does, and work through the consequences without concern for whether it is "good," "bad," or "countertransferential." One must abdicate correctness, being The-One-Who-Knows.

I would like to use a brief case example to demonstrate some of the intricacies of these issues. This is a man in his early fifties. Details of the therapy are not particularly relevant to my present purposes. Suffice it to say that, in the third year of therapy, he reports a dream that strikes him as "coming out of left field."

He is standing in the vestibule of a private club, talking with the manager. Suddenly a very large apelike man attacks the manager and proceeds to crush him in a bear hug. My patient (who is a smallish man) is horrified and leaps on the attacker's back, trying to pull him off. The giant sweeps him away with a backhand blow. He leaps on him again, and again is thrown backwards across the room. He is not really hurt. All this takes place in total silence. There is no blood or apparent damage to the manager.

Associations? He has none. No day-residue of significance. He is perplexed. I ask, "What is the manager like?" This is a detailed inquiry, somewhat different from free-association in its intent, which is to establish context. The manager is a man about seventy (as is, by odd coincidence, the analyst). What is the name of the club? It is the "Harmonie Club." So, the man who manages the Harmonie Club—who manages to maintain harmony—is under attack by an unknown assailant and defended (ineffectually) by my patient. I ask, "Do you think this might be me?" The patient readily agrees. The intent of this interpretation is not to suggest to him something he doesn't already know, but to indicate that I am prepared to entertain the transferential implications of the dream.

I elaborate: "Perhaps you feel you have to defend me against some part of you that would like to throttle the man who maintains harmony, doesn't let you show anger." In truth, our relationship is unreasonably cordial. I have long wondered at how and why there is so little friction, competition, hard feelings, disapproval between us. I am aware that there is some countertransferential participation in our *entente cordiale.* He hastens to reassure me that he is excessively benign; he knows it, he has trouble showing, or even feeling, any aggression or anger toward me. He would be delighted to oblige me if he could. I say that I thought the dream was his comment on my participation and that he was now playing out the dream by leaping to my defense.

His disarming, inoffensive style has been critical to his remarkably successful career. He is a very intelligent and competent professional, aggressive and driving, who manages to avoid mobilizing any counterattacks, although he deals regularly with very difficult, even predatory people. His relationship with his father was characterized by amiability, affection, and a total lack of the usual adolescent Sturm und Drang; he never hated his father, disdained him—nothing. His mother was very ambitious for him, but also never expressed the slightest disdain or contempt for his father, who was a kindly but not terribly successful man.

132 Psychoanalytic process

He is perfectly delighted to acknowledge all this; but the effect of it is to let me off the hook. As the old psychoanalytic saw goes: remember, the patient is always better at what he or she does than you are. He is a master at deflecting masculine aggression. How could one resent so agreeable a man? I am aware that I have great difficulty disapproving of him for activities that, in another patient, might have elicited more negative feelings. Now, I could consider, through some variant of self-object legerdemain, that this was something he did to me, something he put into me; but I know that I have motives and participations of my own that lend themselves to this seduction.

I told him that I thought he was protecting me against an attack, and, I added, I am aware that I have great trouble feeling any disapproval of him, or mixing it up with him. We then proceeded to discuss it amicably. So, something had gone wrong. The effect of this tentative self-disclosure was, I think, to disarm him, to say to him, "See what a nice guy I am," not, as one might hope, to facilitate his anger. Indeed, the entire process of analyzing the dream might have been an enactment of our collusion. Perhaps he has the fairly transparent dream, leaves it to me to be clever and interpret it as a form of seduction. Why doesn't *he* see its meaning? Why doesn't *he* experience his anger? What would have happened if I had done *nothing* with the dream? Would he have gone on to some other issue? Might it not have led to a more aggressive encounter, with more real feeling? What would have happened if I had offered a more authentic disclosure? What if I had talked about my feelings of competition and envy toward him? On the other hand, perhaps the course I chose was effective. Who knows? The meaning of a psychoanalytic encounter is its outcome. You don't know what you've done till you see what happens!—it sounds like a title for a country-western tune, but it is true.

The therapist stands revealed, in the patient's dream, as the manager of harmony. The therapist confirms this as a self-revelation, refuses to allow the patient to assume sole responsibility—an enactment that, albeit corrective, might well be disarming. The therapist proceeds to a self-disclosure about his difficulties with engaging the patient's aggression, which may have inadvertently served as a further countertransferential blunting of the patient's anger. As I said, I don't believe one can set out to do the thing that works. This leads to what Freud called the sin of therapeutic ambitiousness. The playing-through is the working-through, and it is the meticulous examination of the various perspectivistic viewpoints on the interaction that leads ultimately—and never on a nice, straight line—to change. I think self-awareness is the key. Once the therapist is aware that there is, in their interpersonal field, a *mutual* problem with anger and competition, and once the patient has indicated—through the dream—that he also is aware of it and ready to lock horns, then a working-through the enactment in the patient-therapist relationship will gradually, almost inevitably, and ineffably take place.

Telling patients about countertransference reactions one is having when one feels totally perplexed about them goes a very large step further than self-awareness. Telling patients one's dreams about them and asking for their input is yet an even bolder step (Tauber, 1954). I do think it can be useful. In this latter case, one needs to throw concerns about counter-transference to the winds and simply make one's own experience, as an equally confused coparticipant in the process, available to the patient, asking for the patient's input. As I've said, one might reasonably argue that if one were to discard the concept of countertransference as distorted response to the patient, and the corollary concept that the therapist's job is to sort out what is appropriate and what is distorted, then one might treat one's own participation simply as relevant data. I think it is a laudable idea, but very difficult to carry off. One certainly cannot assume that the therapist, in bringing in this material, has no ulterior motive—is simply contributing his or her data—nor that the patient will have the fortitude to resist the therapist. It is a lot to ask of both participants to meet the demands of such rigorous participation.

I believe we may all agree that therapy only works because of the containment of the frame. Therapy is play; it is not a superior slice of real life. The containment of the frame limits the participation of both parties and thus their anxiety. Psychoanalysts are no better or worse than anyone else; they have no claim to superior emotional maturity, as their mates and children will readily attest. But, like sea captains, they are often far more noble aship than ashore. So, the looser the frame, the more risky the game becomes. The elasticity of the process is limited by the anxiety of the therapist—or one might substitute, the grandiosity of the therapist—but, again, grandiosity tends to be a rather fragile enterprise, with retribution in the air for the debunker.

Ordinarily, one thinks of frame as the preconditions of therapy; i.e., frequency and length of sessions, use of chair or couch, agreements about payment, cancellations, and so forth. There is, however, a component of

134 Psychoanalytic process

framing, frequently underestimated, that deals with the initial circumstances of treatment: how the patient gets to a particular therapist, why therapist and patient agree to work with each other, and what initial understanding they have about the patient's complaints and why they might be amenable to a psychoanalytic approach. Many therapies founder on a failure to clarify this vital opening gambit of treatment (Levenson, 1982). In much clinical material that one hears presented, what is most striking is the inattention to the initial circumstances of therapy. Is the patient a "control" case? How was he or she selected? Who did the screening? How much say did the therapist have in the selection? How badly was the therapist (candidate or not) in need of a patient? How generous was the patient pool? Analytic patients can be rare; training institutes often have to scrape to get patients willing to come five times weekly.

There is a subtext to all this. Remember, both self-revelation and self-disclosure are dimensions of the therapist-patient relationship. It is implied that the therapeutic leverage lies in somehow getting it right. But relationship is only half the treatment story. There are *two* striking therapeutic instrumentalities in therapy: what I have called elsewhere *poetics* and *pragmatics*, i.e., the patient's imagination and the interactional world (Levenson, 1988). One can hardly fail to be impressed by the power of imagination, of the patient's fantasy life, which seems to operate autonomously. It often has a "message-in-the-bottle" quality, as though someone inside the patient is passing secrets out past the censor. On the other hand, one must be equally impressed by the subtlety and complexity of the interpersonal field, of the patient's "self-system," the extremely sophisticated self-equilibrating operations of defense, not against interior fantasies, but *against others*, and the capacity of these defenses to recapitulate, in the relationship with the therapist, the very problems and issues under discussion. What is talked about is simultaneously enacted—an astonishing, and therapeutically very useful, isomorphism.

Analysts have traditionally leaned very heavily on the patient's imagination, and largely viewed the interactional field with the therapist as resistance—to be analyzed and gotten out of the way. Sullivan, by the way, very much held the same view.[5] Increasingly, analysts are viewing the patient-therapist interactional field as the locus of therapy, rather than an interference. This, as I've said, provides the therapist a very powerful therapeutic leverage, albeit a risky one. It provides a chance to see, firsthand, *in vivo*, the problems under inquiry and to use one's participation as collaborative data. But, it also lends itself to proselytizing the patient, curing through a laying on of hands.

In summary, I would consider self-revelation inevitable. I believe if one stands revealed, one should recognize it, admit it, and use the occasion as a source of relevant data. I am much more wary about self-disclosure. I have had some striking successes, but also some disasters. Self-disclosure often seems to be a reparative effort by the analyst after some acting-in on his or her part. It is a device to be used sparingly, and only with patients with whom one has a solid therapeutic alliance. Of course, not everyone would agree with this. Success with this technique may ultimately depend on one's ability to communicate goodwill to the patient without stifling him or her; and this may vary widely with one's style and general aura of benevolence.[6]

I don't really like the idea of cure emerging exclusively from the relationship with the therapist. Ultimately I would like therapy to be energized by the patient's flow of material, and cure to emerge through the patient contacting his or her own riches of imagination and attunement—finding his or her own voice. Largely, I see the relationship with the therapist as defining the field, the playing ground, for that endeavor. I do believe that patients can arrive at startling insights into their own lives that are not a direct consequence of the interaction with the therapist, but could *not* have emerged without the facilitating effect of the therapist's participation.

The Sufis say (with tongue in cheek) that no problem is too difficult for a theoretician. Harry Stack Sullivan once said that clarity is the last thing one experiences before becoming schizophrenic. He also said, "God keep me from a therapy which goes well!" I concur heartily. Ambiguity is the chosen lot of the clinician—our burden and our glory. My convictions tend to shift somewhat with what seemed to work best last. Sometimes I am impressed by the impact of my interventions, sometimes by a sudden and unexpected shift in the direction of the patient's flow of material, or a sudden insight that seems to come from nowhere—certainly not from something I can think of that I did or said.

One must admit, it is all perplexing. How we use ourselves in the psychoanalytic praxis, the clinical implications of participation and enactment, the political ramifications of metapsychological positions, and the relationship of all this to pur *sang* psychoanalysis is in the balance. If, indeed,

136 Psychoanalytic process

psychoanalysis does stand at a crossroad, then what do we do? Perhaps, in the words of the immortal Yogi Berra, "When you come to a crossroad, take it!"

Notes

1. This chapter was first read, in modified form, at the meeting of the Extension Division of the New York Psychoanalytic Society, March 11, 1995. It was published in 1996 in *Contemporary Psychoanalysis* 32(2):237–248.
2. Irwin Hoffman, in his paper "The Patient as the Interpreter of the Analyst's Experience," extended and developed this theme (Hoffman, 1983).
3. I remember an extremely enraged paranoid woman. In the midst of a diatribe, the window behind her blew out in a loud explosion—not shattering, but pulverizing and blowing glass all over the room. I thought for a moment that a bullet had come through the window. She sat there and smiled. I think she felt it was a virtuoso performance, like the soprano whose high note shatters a glass. I never found a reason for it happening.
4. As I once heard a classical analyst say at a meeting, somewhat facetiously, "Sure, we all believe in the interpersonal. It's where the intrapsychic plays itself out."
5. See Gill (1983, p. 332) for a review of interpersonal positions on this point.
6. I remember when Erich Fromm came from Mexico City to supervise us in the early fifties. We would try to apply his confrontational, rather judgmental, approach to patients. It worked for Dr. Fromm to call someone a "marketing personality." On the other hand, when we tried it, we usually lost our patients— no doubt, a failure of stature!

References

Eagle, N.M. (1987). *Recent Developments in Psychoanalysis*. Cambridge, MA: Harvard University Press.

Gill, M. (1983). The interpersonal paradigm and the degree of the therapist's involvement. *Contemporary Psychoanalysis*, 19(2):200–237.

Gill, M. (1994). *Psychoanalysis in Transition: A Personal View*. Hillsdale, NJ: The Analytic Press.

Hoffman, I. (1983). The patient as the interpreter of the analyst's experience. *Contemporary Psychoanalysis*, 19(3):389–422.

Levenson, E. (1978). Psychoanalysis: Cure or persuasion? In E.G. Witenberg (Ed.), *Interpersonal Psychoanalysis: New Directions*. New York: Gardiner Press, pp. 47–63.

Levenson, E. (1982). Playground or playpen. Comments on *The psychoanalytic process* by P. Dewald. *Contemporary Psychoanalysis*, 18(3):365–372.

Levenson, E. (1988). Show and tell: The recursive order of transference. In A. Rothstein (Ed.), *How Does Treatment Help?* Madison, CT: International Universities Press, pp. 135–143.

Tauber, E.S. (1954). Exploring the therapeutic use of counter-transference data. *Psychiatry*, 17:331–336.

Wilden, A. (1972). *System and Structure: Essays in Communication and Exchange.* London: Tavistock.

Chapter 12

Psychoanalytic love and therapeutic despair[1]

I'm grateful for this opportunity to comment on Dr. Poland's excellent paper. However, I must first specify my own position. As an interpersonalist, I believe that, in Gregory Bateson's felicitous phrase, "The point of the probe is always in the heart of the explorer"; namely, that every voyage of discovery leads back to the self (Bateson, 1979, p. 87). Both clinical and theoretical formulations will necessarily and inevitably reflect the unwitting participation of the analyst. Moreover, I believe that therapeutic action lies in the enactment, in the patient-therapist relationship, of the very material under discussion; i.e., their interpersonal field (loosely defined as the transference/countertransference) is a behavioral transform of what is being talked about.

Why and how this could be mutative is not relevant to this discussion (Levenson, 1985; Levenson, 1987). Rather, I wish only to emphasize that I do not consider speculating about the analyst's participation as an *ad hominum* attack, but rather as a vital dimension—always present and ongoing—of the therapeutic action. One's choice of metapsychology (notwithstanding all its political and institutional implications) is, to a considerable extent, determined by personal psychology; and how and when one applies that metapsychology to a particular patient will be grist for the mill. In this sense—as therapeutic praxis—metapsychologically determined interpretations are behavior with the patient.

I would like to address myself to the two clinical examples Poland offers. His first, he describes as an "unhappy clinical moment." Presented with a personal catastrophe in his patient's life, Poland feels, for a moment, totally at a loss in how to respond to her grief. To his everlasting credit, he realizes that both empathy and sympathy are wholly inadequate to the moment, and that all he can do is to give her respectful space to have her own experience, without his interference. He then adds, "[T]he riddle for me during the years since that hour is what it was that I was doing with that patient that she found helpful."

The second case presented is an unusually trying man, the treatment characterized by "years of anguish," and, until relatively recently, frustrating, disappointing work. We are presented with an extensive formulation of his dynamics, particularly his sadomasochism. But, as Poland notes, he starts his clinical presentation with a self-revelation. He thinks, "If you have tears to shed, prepare to shed them now." Not an odd thought, perhaps, but what an odd locution! This is more than an analyst anticipating sadness. In truth, it sounds like an inscription over the Gates of Hell.[2]

Poland conveys his feeling of sadness and loss, his "silent witnessing" of the patient's desolate confrontation with his destructiveness. Yet, it is conceivable that this man's moment of truth is not so much the consequence of the accretion of months of prior formulations as it is Poland's current resigning of any influence. The clinical moment described is one in which the patient is beginning to face and accept what an awful, destructive person he has been. He is, we are told, grieving his losses, which are reported as irrevocable. The analyst is a sad witness. Somehow this sounds to me more like a mea culpa than psychoanalytic insight. Has he really lost everyone who cared about him? Was he really that destructive? Has he lost the analyst's caring? Usually one expects awareness of destructiveness to emerge in the patient incrementally with the growth of self-esteem—with awareness of his or her unrealized potential for decency and love. This man sounds like an anguished shade in Purgatorio (not yet the Inferno, so still subject to contrition) already cast out of human company. "If you have tears to shed, prepare to shed them now" sounds right for his predicament. I believe he has given up on trying to change this difficult man, and that something therapeutic—much as in the first case—is ineffably transpiring.

Poland is aware, in both clinical examples, that he stopped trying to act therapeutically and gave the patient space. In the first case, it was a spontaneous response to the patient's crisis: in the second, he felt he had done his work and is standing back to allow the patient to experience his own desolation. He then constructs a metapsychological extension to explain how this "witnessing" might have worked—since work it did. In the first instance, it is a technical innovation for a certain patient; in the second instance, it becomes, generic, a principle of psychoanalytic therapy.

I would like to suggest that his very attempts at grasping his own participation and formalizing it as clinical technique—that is, a methodology that might be replicated in other patients for similar therapeutic effect—could paradoxically work to his disadvantage. This is not a novel idea, since it has long been common knowledge that atypical interventions seem to work best when they are both spontaneous and contrary to the therapist's sense of appropriate technique—as, for example, getting "inappropriately" angry at a patient. That is, the intervention only works when one thinks it is the *wrong* thing to do. Once it is sanitized, legitimized, sanctified as appropriate technique, it falls flat.

I believe that there is another possible perspective on these cases. Quite possibly, in both cases, Dr. Poland is confronting a moment of therapeutic despair, ordinarily a highly unpopular admission in psychoanalytic circles, since we much prefer to report our successes.

To quote Farber:

> It is a general hazard of the profession that our case reports should be chivalric legends, homiletic exercise, and large annunciations of the small success, we can understand why this should be so ... Like the short short-story in a magazine, episodes in treatment come to be reported as though they were tidy slices of life: compact, over-simplified, and contrived in their denouement.
>
> (Farber, 1958. p. 17)

Nevertheless, we have all had those moments where we simply give up, let go, "open the fist" in the Zen phrase, and to our surprise the patient becomes productive, even seems to move compassionately to rescue us from our morass. I can recall several occasions when a patient, sharply peering at me, noting my expression of hopelessness, suddenly began to work. Perhaps, our "allowing" autonomy is still too controlling; perhaps we must be defeated for the patient to feel autonomous enough to work with us.

Harry Stack Sullivan was wont to say to supervisees, "God keep me from an analysis which goes well." Would it be excessive to suggest that every successful treatment operates, at some point, on the edge of disaster; and, that, at the termination of a good treatment, both we and the patient feel as though we've been to the wars?[3] I first encountered this concept of therapeutic despair in an article by Farber:

When faced with the inevitable despair, which I am suggesting must sooner or later overtake the conscientious therapist, it will not matter how indomitable or inventive may be his efforts to keep going: he cannot hope that his despair will be entirely unnoticed by his patient. To the extent that the therapist becomes "present" for his patient, that patient is capable of pity for his friend's distress.

(Farber, 1958. p. 14)

One might say that psychoanalysis succeeds because it fails; indeed, it begins where psychotherapy ends. Psychoanalysis takes the limitations of instrumental psychotherapy techniques, like persuasion, direction, cognitive re-education, and reformulation, and puts them to its use as resistance and transference. I believe that is what Lacan had in mind in his gnomic comment, "If Freud's discovery has any meaning, it is that—truth grabs error by the scruff of the neck in the mistake" (Lacan, 1975 p. 265). Were this not so, psychoanalysis would be only an elaborate persuasive psychotherapy, selling the patient on one's ideas of change (Levenson 1978).

We are confronted with the possibility that change may take place at those moments when we "let go" out of despair or fatigue, allowing the patient the necessary room to change autonomously; neither to oppose nor to submit to us. If this be so, there is an implicit caveat that if we attempt to master and conceptualize our moments of therapeutic despair—we may lose out. "Non-action" of this sort feels impotent. I cannot help but believe that Poland may be struggling with this same clinical awareness from a different frame of reference. His "witnessing" sounds, on the face of it, more hopeful than my "despair." But look again at the clinical examples— was he proactively allowing space, or was he giving up influence? I do believe that as psychoanalytic praxis (not as manifest theory) he is using the concept of "witnessing" to restitute his lost sense of control qua analyst—an extension of the Cartesian assumption that order and understanding is superordinate to change. I prefer to think that order occurs at the edge of chaos, and change emerges from disorder (Levenson, 1994).

Poland's metaphysical elaborations of his case material stand apart from his clinical theory and praxis; i.e., they are conceptually relevant and, I believe, constitute a thoughtful and creative elaboration of his core theoretical position. He explicates an extension of his central therapeutic concept of holding, to incorporate a more differentiated relatedness, that of "witnessing." His discussion of intersubjectivity, the dialectic between

142 Psychoanalytic process

self and other, intrapsychic and interpersonal, separateness and fusion, his exegesis of Heidegger, Husserl, and Lévinas are all admirably lucid.

But I must say that I wish that he had given a passing nod, a faint genuflection, in the direction of the immense psychoanalytic (not philosophical) literature on intersubjectivity. He talks of the "early union evident in the *locked* (my italics) gaze of mother and infant" without reference to infant studies, most notably Stern, which make manifestly clear that making and breaking eye contact—not locked gaze—starts, at least, at birth and is inherent to the mother-child dyad (Stern, 1977; Stern, 1984). Martin Buber, Harry Stack Sullivan, and the writings of the interpersonalists; e.g., Greenberg, Lionells, Mitchell; and the intersubjectivist Stolorow are entirely centered around the issues he raises (Buber, 1957; Greenberg and Mitchell, 1983; Lionells et al., 1995; Mitchell, 1988; Stolorow et al., 1987, Sullivan, 1953). In our current atmosphere of ecumenism, with the maturing of psychoanalytic metapsychologies, and the secondary elaborations and refinements that entails, it is becoming increasingly evident that there are huge overlaps and that no one position may legitimately claim either total originality or hegemony. The same caveat applies to the psychoanalytic literature, which is, alas, often parochial in its references.

I am most appreciative of Dr. Poland's explication, in detail, of the direction and development of his thinking, beginning with clinical experiences that were neither entirely predictable nor explicable in terms of his then current metapsychology and its concurrent clinical theory; and on to an elaborated theory of witnessing which "actualizes and evidences the patient's growing autonomy." I certainly have no argument with the idea that therapy, much like any other interpersonal intimacy, requires a dialectic of making and breaking contact, of closeness and separation, of engagement and privacy; and, that this alternation might well be experinced by both participants as normative and without anxiety However, I did not think that the clinical examples, as given, exemplify a relatively serene and tranquil "witnessing." They seemed to me to be more despairing, and more discordant and disruptive to the therapist's expectations—and, paradoxically, that may be where their therapeutic efficacy lies. I admire immensely what Poland does as a therapist, his obvious skill and concern, and his sophistication as a theorist. Where we might well disagree are the terms in which we would conceptualize what it is he does when he does what he obviously knows so well how to do.

Notes

1. This chapter first appeared in 2000 in the *Journal of the American Psycho-analytic Association* 48(1).
2. "Through me you pass into the city of woe through me you pass into eternal pain; . . . All hope abandon ye who enter here." Canto III of *The Divine Comedy*, Dante (Dante, 1994).
3. An example of this kind of clinical experience is to be found in Meltzer's report of a wonderful, open and anguishing treatment (Meltzer, 1978).

References

Bateson, G. (1979). *Mind and Nature; A Necessary Unity*. New York: Dutton.

Buber, M. (1957). Distance and Relation. *Psychiatry*, 20:97–104.

Dante (1994). *The Divine Comedy*. Rutland, Vermont: Everyman.

Farber, L.H. (1958). The therapeutic despair. *Psychiatry*, 1(February):7– 20.

Greenberg, J. and Mitchell, S. (1983). *Object Relations in Psychoanalytic Theory*. Cambridge, MA: Harvard University Press.

Lacan, J. (1975). *The Seminar of Jacque Lacan; Book I, Freud's Papers on Technique* (J. Forrester, Trans.). New York: W.W. Norton.

Levenson, E. (1978). Psychoanalysis: cure or persuasion? In E.G. Witenberg (Ed.), *Interpersonal Psychoanalysis: New Directions*. New York: Gardiner Press, pp. 47–63.

Levenson, E. (1985). The interpersonal (Sullivanian model). In A. Rothstein (Ed.), *Models of the Mind and their Relationship to Clinical Work*. New York: International Universities Press, pp. 49–67.

Levenson, E. (1987). How theory shapes technique: Perspectives on a clinical case. An Interpersonal perspective. *Psychoanalytic Inquiry*, 7(2):207–214.

Levenson, E. (1994). The uses of disorder: Chaos theory and psychoanalysis. *Contemporary Psychoanalysis*, 30(1):5–24.

Lionells, M., Fiscalini, J., Mann, C., and Stern, D. (Ed.). (1995). *Handbook of Interpersonal Psychoanalysis*. Hillsdale, NJ: The Analytic Press.

Meltzer, D. (1978). Routine and inspired interpretations. *Contemporary Psychoanalysis*, 14(2):210–224.

Mitchell, S. (1988). *Relational Concepts in Psychoanalysis*. Cambridge, MA: Harvard University Press.

Stern, D. (1977). *The First Relationship*. Cambridge, MA: Harvard University Press.

Stern, D. (1984). *The Interpersonal World of the Infant: A View from Psycho-analysis and Developmental Psychology*. New York: Basic Books.

Stolorow, R.D., Brandchaft, B., and Atwood, G.E. (1987). *Psychoanalytic Treatment: An Intersubjective Approach*. Hillsdale, NJ: The Analytic Press.

Sullivan, H.S. (1953). *The Interpersonal Theory of Psychiatry*. New York: W.W. Norton.

Chapter 13

On seeing what is said

Visual aids to the psychoanalytic process[1]

Ward Just wrote that a good story is like a film scenario, the contours of the action that leave something to the imagination (Just, 2002). Harry Stack Sullivan once said that the last thing that happens to you just before you go crazy is that everything becomes clear! Well, I had an epiphany about a year ago, when it occurred to me that the detailed inquiry, particularly the deconstructed detailed inquiry, is really *visual*, not, as one might reasonably expect, verbal, and that, indeed, the entire psychoanalytic praxis, although annotated in words, actually takes place in a visual-spatial modality. I limn out recent developments in neuroscience that may provide a rationale for this apparent logical inversion. Finally, focusing on visual imagery, I elaborate a primer of psychoanalytic technique that is form—not content—oriented and that I am convinced captures the absolute essence of the psychoanalytic praxis.

It may have been a signal contribution of interpersonal psychoanalysis to posit a disconnect between metapsychology and technique, that is, to suggest that successful therapy may depend more on what one does than what one says about it. I have long claimed that psychoanalysis works as a therapeutic instrument, not because of the correctness of its metapsycholog(ies), but because of its praxis, that is, what we *do* when we are plying our trade, rather than how we then proceed to explain what we have done (Levenson, 1972). It seems likely that the inquiry *is* the therapeutic act; that as Marshall McLuhan put it, the medium *is* indeed the message.

I would now suggest that our praxis is organized more around pictures than words, more around interactions than explanations. The analytic algorithm—the steps we take in doing analysis, regardless of metapsychology

—and the unconscious flow of data itself are both organized along visual-spatial lines. Think of any question, any inquiry one might make of an interaction. It occurs to me that the questions come out of visual images. One attempts to grasp the situation by imaging, or imagining, it. Even our instrument par excellence, free-association (and its corollary, the detailed inquiry), consists more of linked and nested visual-spatial images than coherent language. The patient's free-association is usually, but not always, in visual, pictorial form, as are dreams. The rare exceptions are vivid language memories that are often visualized (e.g., "When I close my eyes, I see a banner with 'never give up' written on it"). Usually, the canonical metapsychology will be introduced by the therapist—"interpreted"—to transfer this visual flow into confirming language, because it was assumed that verbal interpretation was the therapeutic, mutative act. Interpretation, then, puts a verbal parenthesis around the flow of content that, I would claim, is largely visual-spatial in form.

I would say this ultimate privileging of the verbal over the visual is virtually ubiquitous in the history of psychoanalysis. This is not to gainsay that there is a long history of interest in imagery from Freud's use of dream images as symbols to Reyher's "Emergent Uncovering Psychotherapy," which depends almost exclusively on stimulating visual imagery (Reyher, 1963, 1977; Singer and Pope, 1978). The underlying premise remains consistent however: to arrive at deep unconscious fantasy, drive derivatives, which are then contained or mastered by verbal interpretation. I am pursuing a different direction.

When I do therapy, I like to think of myself as a director perusing a script that I must transform into visual images. How is it to be played? What are the nuances? As Edelson (1993) explicates the clinical process to students, "Ask yourself as you listen to the patient: Can you see what they are doing? Hear what they are saying?" (p. 317). Sullivan's detailed inquiry essentially explores different scenarios. In the process, the patient provides a "gapped narrative." What is anxiety-provoking is left out—inattended, dissociated, repressed. The analyst, by *imagining* what might have occurred, unpacks the narrative and simultaneously creates transference and countertransference, because what one decides to pursue, what scenarios are visualized, will obviously depend on one's personal experience, and will be, willy-nilly, a piece of behavior, an enactment. I am positing that the therapist, as participant, could only grasp the patient's narrative by visualizing it.

Therefore, even though the inquiry is carried on linguistically, it is misleading to assume that our goal is to clarify and linguistically order the patient's experience. It may be that the detailed inquiry, or free-association, is not an attempt to clarify and delineate through language, but is a shift from a linguistic to an image-driven pictorial mode of thinking. I suspect that Sullivan, who worked largely with severe obsessional and schizophrenic patients, leaned heavily on verbal formulations to decrease mystification. His patients were chaotic enough, and using visual imagery, especially in dreams, would probably have only added to the confusion. Sullivan (1953) preferred to use what he considered less "parataxic" communications (p. 333). This is what often gives Sullivan that pragmatic essence. Our current patients, however, may require more loosening up than organization. As H. Gardner (1985) put it:

> It made sense to think of an individual as having pictures in his head ... [it] made respectable the idea of an analogue mode of mental representation, a mode capturing certain of the relationships of proximity that can be perceived in the physical world ... [it] called into question current attempts to explain all thought in terms of one kind of computational mechanism—that of serial, digital computer which processes one kind of information ... Imagery should be thought of on its own terms, rather than as a cryptic version of verbal mediation or symbolic manipulation. Perhaps there are two separate and equally valid forms of mental representation (p. 325).

Gardner believed that the rubric of "intelligence" is far too ubiquitous to be really useful. He divided intelligences into different categories: linguistic, musical, logical-mathematical, spatial, bodily, kinesthetic. He claimed that individual cognitive functioning is heavily loaded in one category or the other: that is, people have styles of intelligence, and much confusion results from our traditional prioritizing of verbal skills. He made an elaborate case for the idea that creativity inheres especially in visual-spatial intelligences. About Einstein, for example, Gardner (1983) writes,

> Like Russell, he became mesmerized in first reading Euclid: and it was to the visual and spatial forms, and their correspondence, that Einstein was most strongly drawn: His intuitions were deeply rooted in classical geometry. He had a very visual mind. He thought in terms of images—gedanken experiments carried out in the mind (p. 190).

There are, of course, many other famous examples; for instance, Kekulé's discovery of the benzene rings in a dream, or Darwin's vision of the origin of species as an ever-branching tree. Temple Grandin (1995), a high-functioning autistic person, a self-described Asperger's syndrome, provides a fascinating inside view of what a largely right-brain intelligence must be like. She says, for example, that she cannot grasp an abstract conceptual and linguistic category like "dog." When she thinks "dog," she sees every unique dog she's ever known—great Danes, dachshunds, poodles—each by name. One might say, then, that not only is visual-spatial cognition distinct from verbal, but that creativity seems to be an integral function of the visual-spatial.

I would like to suggest that recent developments in neuroscience now offer a new perspective on this verbal-visual dichotomy; for example, how and why what we are doing clinically may be working for reasons far removed from our metapsychological assumptions. The dream of a neurobiological vindication of psychoanalytic theory goes back to Freud's *Project*, his famous unfinished magnum opus. Freud began this work in 1895, in a state of great excitement. He wrote to Fliess on October 20, 1895,

> [T]he barriers suddenly lifted, the veils dropped, and it was possible to see from the details of neurosis all the way to the very conditioning of consciousness. Everything fell into place, the cogs meshed. And the thing seemed really to be a machine which in a moment would run of itself.
>
> (Freud, 1954, p. 129)

Subsequently, he so lost hope for it that it was not revealed to the world until a full decade after his death (Sulloway, 1979, p. 119). The nineteenth-century neurological concepts that buttressed the *Project* proved insufficient to his theory. But even more significantly, as Sulloway pointed out, Freud's "neuro-anatomical model was defined not so much by the findings of current neurological science as by his previously clinical and abstract metapsychological insights" (p. 121). In other words, Freud went looking for a neurological substrate that would substantiate his metapsychology. In so doing, he violated the precepts of the traditional view of scientific inquiry: that is, one accumulates data and *then* postulates a theory that covers one's observations, fits the current paradigm, and has predictive value.

148 Psychoanalytic process

Yet, in current scientific practice, we pretty much do what Freud did. It often turns out that one has observational data that are not adequately explained by current theory, and must await a new theoretical paradigm, or one has an intriguing theory that does not fit the current facts, and must await new technologies that provide new data. As Gopnick (2002) put it, these days "Everyone accepts that science centers on the hypothetical and the conjectural, the imaginative leap and the subsequent search for a significant test, and the questions turn on just what tests, and just what guesses, count" (p. 88).

Freud's foray into neurology was intended to validate his metapsychology, to establish a neurobiological basis for drive theory. He assumed, I believe incorrectly, that his praxis—his clinical technique—must follow automatically from the application of his metapsychology: it would not require a separate frame of reference. Freud's bifurcation of theory and praxis, and his privileging of theory, has been well documented (Levenson, 2001).[2]

Currently, advanced neuro technologies and changing cultural emphases have led to an immense burgeoning literature in what Schore (1994) calls "socioaffective ontogeny—neurobiology, behavioral neurology, evolutionary biology, sociobiology, social psychology, developmental psychology, developmental psychoanalysis, and infant psychiatry" (p. 64). Surely, this constitutes a far more formidable technological armamentarium than was available to Freud, although he did believe that one day the necessary tools would be there. As Schore describes them, the two outstanding parameters of current neurobiological formulation are brain *plasticity* and functional *symmetry*, the former an entirely novel concept and the latter a revitalization of an old concept.

It has been long considered a truism in neurology that brain architectonics are immutable. One might certainly lose brain cells over a lifetime, but they could neither be replenished nor structurally reorganized. It now would appear that brain cells have entirely unexpected plasticity, the ability to proliferate or decrease according to contextual stimuli, and, most unexpected, the ability to rearrange themselves. This is particularly true of earlier developmental periods, and has led to a notable convergence between current neurological thinking and attachment theory (Ainsworth et al., 1978; Schore, 1994, pp. 373–446). Variations in early mother-child bonding may result in structural changes in the brain that may be either immutable or very difficult to shift.

As for the second parameter, brain symmetry, the idea of the bicameral brain—the notion that the two hemispheres serve different but synergistic purposes—so popular in the forties and fifties has been revitalized. Siegel (1999) elaborates at great length on the hemispheric differences. Language is a left-brain process. In contrast, the right brain operates as a pattern-recognition center:

> The right brain appears to be able to perceive patterns within a holistic framework, noting spatial arrangements that the left is unable to sense. The right brain is able to create the gist or context of experience and the overall meaning of events, more intuitive functions than the sensible, and rather stodgy, left brain can handle alone (p. 197).

Wheeler, Stuss, and Tulving (1997) review neuro-imaging studies that suggest semantic memory (memory for facts) is functionally different from episodic memory (autobiographical memory) (Seigel, 1999, pp. 35–36). Semantic memory is a left-brain function (e.g., memorizing the declaration of Independence). In contrast, right-brain memory encompasses the whole experience—visual, spatial, sensory. As we know phenomenologically, the most vivid memories seem to be set off by sensory cues: visual, olfactory, or auditory. Proust's famous madeleine memory is, of course, the most famous literary example. So, right-brain memory is not only more affectively intense, but seems to arise more spontaneously, less from deliberate recall. As Siegel (1999) puts it,

> [T]he right hemisphere is considered to work as a pattern recognition center, assessing the gestalt and context from a synthetic mode of processing. The left, in contrast, uses logical and analytic processing to construct its detail-based representation of reality. Because of these differences of processing, writers have often summarized the contrast between right and left as that between the intuitive and the rational, between context and text, and between the monosemantic and the polysemantic meaning of words (p. 180).

Schore, another prominent investigator, has extensively explored the relationship between affect and hemispheric laterality.[3] He points out that, developmentally, visual clearly antecedes and is superordinate to verbal. Early language (before age two) is right-hemisphere mediated.

Thus words learned very early, like "good," "bad," and "Mother," are mediated through an entirely different right-brain network than later left-brain language, endowing them with an intense and mysterious affective power—perhaps that is what Sullivan had in mind when he talked of early "uncanny" experience (Schore, 1994, p. 482). The right hemisphere, we are told, reads social and emotional cues from other people (p. 181). "The left hemisphere appears to be inept at reading social or emotional cues from others" (p. 185).

Both Schore and Siegel see psychoanalytic therapy as mediated by right hemisphere to right hemisphere connections. They both believe that this insight can be developed into a contrived technique, what Schore (1997) calls "guided imagery" (pp. 288–290). Right-brain to right-brain imagery may well be, in itself, mutative, but to nail home the experience, to convert it into insight (i.e., to organize this chaotic right-brain visual imagery into a narrative, a coherent story), left-brain input is required. Referring to Gazzaniga's work, Schore uses the term "the interpreter" for the left-brain's use of reason to explain cause-effect relationships (Gazzaniga et al., 1996). The left hemisphere's drive to understand cause-effect relationships is a primary motivation of the narrative pro-cess. Coherent narratives require participation of both the "interpreting left hemisphere and the mentalizing right hemisphere." According to this hypothesis, coherent narratives are created through interhemispheric integration (Siegel, 1999, p. 331). Whether "coherent narratives" have much to do with clinical improvement is another story.

Consistent with this privileged valuation of right-brain, visual/spatial imagery, I would like to advance a set of visual images that I believe are the key to the clinical process. In contrast to interpretations, which are content and theory-dependent, logical and linear, the following visual images are spatial, pattern-dependent, and independent of content.

I have found them extremely helpful both in teaching and in my own work. Practitioners of any craft know, as the Zen saying goes, that the last thing one learns is the first: that is, one maintains one's skills by relentlessly revisiting and relearning the basics. I do believe that they constitute the basic exercises of our profession, and much like a dancer who works daily at the barre, we should constantly refresh our aware-ness of them. I define them as *the square, the plane, the circle*, and *the helix*. You will note that although they are the underpinnings of psychoanalytic technique, they make no direct reference to specific or privileged content: they are equally relevant to *any* metapsychological set.

The square: This very basic concept starts with Freud's "playground," the analytic working space—the square within which one works. It also encompasses Lyman Wynne's wonderful visual concept of "the rubber fence": the fence around every family, no matter how far stretched by the distancing of any member, especially one's patient. It is the square one stands outside of (Wynne et al., 1958). It creates a very powerful reminder that in working with a patient, one is standing on the other side of the family divide, an outsider—a vital caveat when you are listening sympathetically to a disaffected patient complaining about her family. This is particularly relevant these days, with the huge emphasis on empathic relatedness and emotional restitution. It is easy to miss the covert and protected bonds, and disavowed identifications, between the patient and her family. The square also defines the difference between acting-in and acting-out (the former to be analyzed, the latter to be blocked). The delineations of the square set limits that are, significantly, predefined and preestablished, obviating the need to evaluate issues afresh each time they arise: for example, arrangements regarding cancellations, vacations, payment, and issues of self-disclosure and privacy.

One notes that different analysts may define these perimeters differently; they are not writ in stone. Essentially, they establish a line in the sand, a rule of behavior that one may violate if one wishes—but one, at least, will then necessarily be aware of the violation.

The plane: This is the most important and most elusive of the images. When I listen to clinical material, I try to keep in visual reference a horizontal line—a horizon. Above that line, material is organized, made more coherent, abstracted, "understood." Below that line, material is extended, deconstructed, allowed to branch out, without reference to meaning or clarity of purpose. It is of some interest that Alfred Korzybski (1954), the founder of General Semantics, who collaborated one summer with the linguistic anthropologist Sapir and with Sullivan, postulated that the level of abstraction rose and fell with the level of anxiety in *both* participants in a dialogue—certainly a version of Sullivan's "participant-observation." Anxiety, then, increases our desire to abstract, to organize, to move to a higher level of abstraction.

So, when listening to a narrative account, the first impulse of a therapist, even a quite experienced one, is to make sense of it—to go above the line. One listens and then—out of a need to be useful—tries to figure out what it might mean. We do what Masud Khan derided when he said, "The patient tells us his Truth so that we may tell him the Metatruth" (Milner,

152 Psychoanalytic process

1969, p. xxxi). It is very difficult to acquire and sustain the discipline necessary to stay below the horizon, to pressure a deconstructive inquiry. Most neophyte psychoanalysts have done a good deal of psychotherapy before they undertook psychoanalytic training. The very human impulse to help, to clarify, to make sense of what one is hearing that is the essence of *psychotherapy*, becomes, as Freud pointed out, counterproductive therapeutic ambition in *psychoanalysis*.

For example, a woman patient and the therapist have agreed to set a termination date, 6 weeks ahead. They have been mired in what seems to be a rather unimaginative, concrete therapy, limited to pragmatic problem solving. Unexpectedly, she reports with an abashed smile that she's been having a symptom she was ashamed to mention. Besides, she says—in that most famous understatement in psychoanalysis—she "didn't think it was important!" Namely, she was having a strange anal sensation at times during the sessions. For how long, one asks? Months. What did it feel like? She couldn't exactly describe it. One's mind begins to race: anal penetration, childhood abuse, anal-compulsive resistance to interpretation, transference. Is it related to the content of the analyst's interpretations? *What could it mean?* Why did she bring it up now? Should one interpret resistance? Point out that it occurs whenever the therapist says something? Would that be a mistake, another form of unwanted penetration?

If one can resist, say nothing, simply indicate interest, the patient increasingly becomes aware of the strange sensation. If one restrains the impulse to suggest that the feeling appears whenever the therapist has made an interpretation—which, by the way, is not entirely correct—the patient begins to bring in a flow of consciousness heretofore inaccessible to her. She loosens up, begins to hear connections through the session; the much-desired and oft-lamented associative "thin red line" becomes evident. And, one begins to hear the first manifestations of my next axiomatic image.

The circle: I first came across this image in Menninger's book (1958). Menninger described a "correct" direction in the flow of clinical material that, at the time, seemed to me to be arbitrary and pointless. I have since learned better:

> [T]he patient successively goes from the contemporary situation to the analytic situation [i.e., resistance, transference, and countertrans-ference], thence to related aspects of the childhood situation, thence to the reality situation, and on around the circle in the same counter-

clockwise direction. This is the typical, proper and correct sequence. But as successive material tends to move from the depths directly to the present movement, i.e., in what on our diagram is a clockwise direction, something is wrong (p. 151).

It must be said that Menninger, of course, saw resistance as resistance to the impact of a potentially mutative interpretation. In this view, transference is the patient's way of defending against the interpretive impact by displacing the resistance from the interpretation to the analyst. Nevertheless, by defining a direction of flow as the therapeutic cycle, Menninger quite rightly warns against attempting to reverse the flow by going from the narrative to a mutative interpretation, bypassing the transference complex. This would be a violation of my first axiom, going above the horizon to arrive at a higher level of abstraction. It is equally a mistake to try to directly correlate the patient's narrative with her past, for example, "didn't your father do the same sort of thing as your boyfriend?" Correlating the present distress with the past frequently has the unfortunate effect of making the patient feel that the therapist believes her current distress is all displacement and that the cure will consist of giving up "distortions" of the present carried over from the traumatic past. I prefer to believe that a traumatic past evokes a traumatic present.

A patient tells you that she is aware that she is inordinately suspicious of other people's motives. Should we remind her that her mother, vociferously disowned and discredited, was notoriously paranoid, and that she may have unconsciously identified with her? It sounds correct, so why doesn't it register? It seems to be necessary for her to "work through"— to cycle through—the experience of suspiciousness in her mutual relationship with the therapist. In the interpersonal mode, this will necessarily involve examining actual malfeasances on the therapist's part, no matter how well intentioned she might be. Trust in the reliability of others, for the patient, requires not blind faith, but developing an interpersonal skill, the ability to accurately "read" the act of another, and perhaps to develop the generosity to forgive an unwitting failure. This is a long and painstaking process, but most of us might agree that this is the sine qua non of the psychoanalytic praxis, the "working-through."

If a childhood memory comes *after* the working-through in the transference, it is clearly the patient finding historical closure, not inventing a self-serving excuse for her lifetime intransigence. The process automaticly cycles back to the present inquiry. So, the circle or cycle is from the present through the transference-countertransference and then to the past and back to the present. This cycle is hardly novel in concept to most therapists, but it is remarkably easy to forget, and one forgets it at one's peril. To try to cure the patient through arbitrarily connecting her present with her past, or simply empathically appreciating her distress, allowing room for restitutive experience, certainly has some value—the former intellectual insight, the latter an affective corrective emotional experience. I feel, however, it falls short of the creative, undirected results of a successful psychoanalytic encounter. The cycle is something one sees in one's head—it works visually—as a mnemonic, a caution, and as a right-brain reminder of a right-brain to right-brain process.

The helix: This is perhaps the simplest of the visual axioms: it essentially defines the process of working-through. It reminds the therapist that the praxis consists of revisiting the same material, over and over again, but at a higher level of awareness and with a wider grasp of pattern. It is not a linear process, going from point A to a desired endpoint B. It is not an elimination of resistances to the truth that sets us free. One must eschew the Holy Grail of insight, the "Ah-hah, at last I understand" phenomenon. If one thinks of the data of psychoanalysis as right-brain, then it is pattern-defined and overdetermined (that is, subject to a variety of perspectives and interpretations). A picture will not sustain a singular explanation. Otherwise, how would we have a Thematic Apperception Test?

I would like to pull all this together in a somewhat more extended piece of clinical material. I call him Mr. X. He is a handsome, tall man in his late forties. Since childhood, he has had several therapies. He has run the gamut from a supportive, sustaining, motherly therapist to a more traditional Freudian analyst. All have been helpful, but none conclusive.

He comes into therapy because of his inability to sustain an intimate relationship with a woman. He has never been married, has had many relatively brief relationships with women. As is not unusual in these circumstances, he remains long-term friends with many of them after the relationships have ended. He also has many long-term male friends. He comes from a well-to-do family with one sibling, an older sister. He has virtually nothing to do with his family. His father is dead; his mother seems blissfully unaware that he largely doesn't talk to her—she thinks he lives in another part of the country. He is pervasively disappointed in her, feels that she is narcissistic and self-absorbed. He has had two relationships with women that he considered to be profoundly intimate and loving; that is to say, both women adored him without reservation. Both relationships broke up. He became distrustful, felt the women were "manic-depressive," ergo unreliable, and consequently, without wishing to, would betray him, and so he exited first. In both instances, the woman went on to marry someone else. In the first case, she becomes a lifelong friend, totally trusted; and in the second instance, after the woman had married and had a child, he then becomes a trusted third, going everywhere with them, becoming Godfather to their children.

He suspects his father was gay, wonders whether he is, although he has had no actual homosexual experiences, nor even fantasies, nor does he consciously experience sexual desire for a man. Again, the temptation to formulate is powerful, particularly because there is something uncommitted and unrelated about his presence in the therapy. One wonders, does he need the presence of the husband, the strong man who can manage the borderline lover qua mother and protect him against being consumed or rejected? Or does he create an Oedipal third, replaying his secret defiance of his father and possession of his mother? Or does he wish to re-establish the perfect family, with him as the loved child, the cherished innocent? Of course, all these formulations are true, must be true, because nothing one might say could be wrong. Psychoanalytic interpretations a priori fail to meet Popper's (1962) famous test of falsifiability.

Why don't the interpretive sallies work? He appreciates their ingenuity, but they simply slide by. His affect is bland and elusive. When I was foolish enough to attempt formulations, he seemed rather slyly gratified that I was working so hard, but was otherwise not too impressed.

Can one avoid the impasse by following axiom one—simply inquiring further, trying to visualize the scenario? Can one see the three of them *en scene*? How does the husband act? Does he seem bemused, patronizing, genuinely affectionate? Do they seem to have much in common? Is there an underlying homoerotic note? Does the patient look benign, childish; does he flirt with his former lover? In the process of expanding the inquiry, the patient does begin to become aware of incongruities. The analyst is drawn into the mix. He feels disdainful of the patient, notes his competitive feelings (the patient is taller, younger, handsomer, richer), wonders whether he ought to be feeling more protective, concerned—perhaps Mr. X wants only to be loved like a child, or how a child imagines love, without reservation. He notices that he is uncomfortable, that he feels somehow defeated, rendered ineffectual. He notes the pressure he feels to do some-thing, to help—no, not help—to *impress* the patient who seems somehow to be stonewalling the process.

Traditionally, analysts saw transference as resistance to the truth of the interpretation. It is peculiarly interpersonal to see transference as the interactive component of the therapeutic transaction, simply the enactment of whatever the patient and therapist are talking about. We differ among ourselves on how to deal with it. Should one actively explicate and engage what one is experiencing? (Ehrenberg, 1975). Should one simply note it, believing that is enough to shift the trajectory of the interactive field? Whether one engages actively or simply notes one's own flow of consciousness, there is no doubt that the analyst has become part of the problem he has set out to resolve.

Shortly after, the patient visited with his former lover when her husband was away on a business trip. This was not at all a novel occurrence, but this time they had a passionate sexual encounter, which she initiated. The next day, she called her husband and confessed her transgression. He was furious and forbade X ever to see either of them again. My patient feels terrible remorse, that he has lost a cozy family milieu, will never see his Godchild again. Oddly enough, he does not feel betrayed. She contacts him and suggests a secret liaison, which he rejects. She raises the issue of leaving her husband for him, which seems very unlikely for a variety of reasons. He is not sure he wants to have her without the bulwark of the husband. And so it goes.

It is not yet clear how this will resolve. But I think he is now inexorably confronted with dimensions of his participation that were heretofore out of awareness. The equation has certainly shifted. The dye is cast. Interestingly, this pattern of a forbearing husband, hysterical wife, with him as the benign third, has been repeated on several occasions. By permitting the inquiry to extend without interpretive judgment, by attempting to see the scenario, the analyst experiences it, becomes part of it. This participation need not be clearly explicated or eliminated. In this case, it led to some acting-out, ideally to be avoided, but that will, one hopes, lead to historical recall and reassessment.

So, the sequence is—somewhat schematized—first staying below the horizon, avoiding abstractions, clarifying interpretations, trying to see what one is being told, asking questions, extending the narrative. Second, sustaining alertness to the simultaneous interactive field of the patient and therapist, with the therapist monitoring his own stream of consciousness. I suspect, consistent with my view of the Menninger cycle, that this is enough to shift the parameters of the therapy. If I am correct, what one gets next is a historical recall and reassessment. In this case, it consisted of his recalling and telling me about how he would talk with his father about his problems and feelings about girls. His father was always sympathetic and helpful. How helpful? Alas, we hadn't gotten to that before the summer break. Nevertheless, the working-through will be a helical reworking of the data, not really something altogether new, but the same material reassessed on a higher and wider level.

Summary

I have always felt strongly that there is a major discontinuity between psychoanalytic theory and praxis, that Freud bifurcated his theory, privileging the more elegant metapsychology. The subsequent formalization of training and the institutionalizing of the field reinforced this tendency. Obviously, praxis is too amorphous an activity to be subject to proprietary claim. Only metapsychology had sufficient scriptural integrity to sustain a True Church. Subsequently, Sullivan (1953) shifted the emphasis from causality to phenomenology: one might see how anxiety worked, how it was transmitted and defended against—the famous "security operations." Sullivan did have a developmental theory, but I believe his clinical praxis was not so much about what was defended against as it was his exquisite attention to the final common pathway of anxiety, namely, elisions, dissociations, inattention. It was the increasing awareness of these defenses that enriched, fleshed out, the patient's experience of his or her own life. The cure came from recapturing one's being in the world, not the past, real or fancied, although that came along to some degree.

Sullivan used the detailed inquiry to focus blind spots in the patient's self-system. This was quite in opposition to the Freudian free-association, which loosened connections and permitted the emergence of unconscious associative flow. As the interpersonal movement matured, a conflation of free-association and detailed inquiry occurred as it became evident that the inquiry could be used in a deconstructive fashion, and to the same end as free-association—the latter being a very difficult skill to master. Clara Thompson, when I was in supervision with her, told me that she'd given up free-association, not because she didn't believe in it, but because patients couldn't do it—"they just nattered on."

158 Psychoanalytic process

I am suggesting that the detailed inquiry, no less than free-association, is a visual act, not a verbal one. Much like poetry, it uses language in a nonlinear, impressionistic way, to convey imagery.

Chessick (2002) quotes Ezra Pound's definition of poetry, which sounds quite congruent:

1. throwing the object onto the visual imagination,
2. inducing emotional correlations by sound and rhythm and
3. stimulating the associations (intellectual and emotional) that have remained in the subject's consciousness (p. 369).

Current neuroscience supports the concept that therapy is a right-brain to right-brain process, having to do with the transmission of images, patterns. To reiterate my quote from Siegel, "[T]he right hemisphere is considered to work as a pattern recognition center, assessing the gestalt and context from a synthetic [synthesizing] mode of processing." From an interpersonal perspective, the entire transferential-countertransferential field is an amalgam of patterned interactions—behavior, not words—and open to the same imaging as the inquiry. To assign all this a narrative integrity (i.e., to make a good story out of it) may or may not be a prerequisite for therapy. I think it is a crutch. The therapist—and her institute—needs the coherence, the sense of a Tale Well Told. But ask the patient: at the end of a successful therapy, what the patient has to say is usually an embarrassment—a few lame clichés. As Wilden (1972) said, "At the end of a therapy, the patient knows what the therapist knows, which is what the patient has always known" (p. 30). The process has clearly not been dependent on the verbal translation, the understanding.

I am suggesting a set of visual images, visual axioms, that are synergistic with the process, and relieve the therapist of the historical necessity to be clear, to make sense, to tell a good story. In Freud's famous dream, after his father's death and just before his renunciation of the seduction theory, he heard a voice say, "It is requested to close the eyes."[4] Perhaps it is now time to open them.

Notes

1. This paper was presented at the October, 8, 2002 meeting of the clinical Services of the William Alanson White Psychoanalytic Institute and published in 2003 in *Contemporary Psychoanalysis* 39:2, pp. 233–249.

2. See Reisner (1999) for extended discussion of this issue.
3. I am leaning heavily on Siegel's and Schore's books. They are professional collaborators in a study group called "affectionately" the ID-CNS and consisting of Drs. Cozolino, A. Schore, J. Schore, and J. Schuman. Schore uses a Kleinian psychoanalytic frame of reference, as contrasted with Siegel's more interpersonal slant; but they are otherwise quite similar in outlook (Siegel, 1999, p. xiii).
4. See Levenson (1983) for exploration of this theme.

References

Ainsworth, M.D.S., Blehar, M.C. Waters, E., and Wall, S. (1978). *Patterns of Attachment.* Hillsdale, NJ: Lawrence Erlbaum Associates.

Chessick, R.D. (2002). Psychoanalytic peregrinations III: Confusion of tongues, psychoanalyst as translator. *The Journal of the American Academy of Psychoanalysis*, 30:361–382.

Edelson, M. (1993). Telling and enacting stories in psychoanalysis and psychotherapy. In P.B. Neubauer, A.J. Solnit, S. Abrams, and A.S. Dowling (Eds.), *The Psychoanalytic Study of the Child.* New Haven, CT: Yale University Press, pp. 293–325.

Ehrenberg, D. (1975). The intimate edge in therapeutic relatedness. *Contemporary Psychoanalysis*, 11(3):320–331.

Freud, A. (1969). *Difficulties in the Path of Psychoanalysis.* New York: International Universities Press.

Freud, S. (1954). *The Origins of Psychoanalysis: Letters to Wilhelm Fliess, Drafts and Notes. 1887–1902.* New York: Basic Books.

Gardner, H. (1983). *Frames of Mind: The Theory of Multiple Intelligences.* New York: Basic Books.

Gardner, H. (1985). *The Mind's New Science.* New York: Basic Books.

Gazzaniga, M.S., Eliassen, J.C., Ninenson, L., Wesinger, C.M. and Baynes, K.B. (1996). Collaboration between the hemispheres of a callostomy patient: Emerging right hemisphere speech and the left brain interpreter. *Brain*, 119(4):1255–1262.

Gopnick, A. (2002). The porcupine: A pilgrimage to Popper. *The New Yorker*, April 1:88–93.

Grandin, T. (1995). *Thinking in Pictures, and Other Reports from My Life with Autism.* New York: Vintage Books.

Just, W. (2002). *The Weather in Berlin.* Boston, MA: Houghton Mifflin.

Korzybski, A. (1954). *Time Binding: The General Theory.* Lakeville, CT: Institute of General Semantics.

Levenson, E. (1972). *The Fallacy of Understanding.* New York: Basic Books.

Levenson, E. (1983). *The Ambiguity of Change: An Inquiry into the Nature of Psychoanalytic Reality.* New York: Basic Books.

Levenson, E. (2001). Freud's dilemma: On writing Greek and thinking Jewish. *Contemporary Psychoanalysis*, 37(3):375–390.

Menninger, K.A. (1958). *Theory of Psychoanalytic Technique.* New York: Basic Books.

Milner, M. (1969). *The Hands of the Living God.* New York: International Universities Press.

Popper, K.R. (1962). *Conjectures and Refutations.* New York: Basic Books.

Rehyer, J. (1963). Free imagery: An uncovering procedure. *Journal of Clinical Psychology,* 19(4):454–459.

Reyher, J. (1977). Spontaneous visual imagery: Implications for psychoanalysis, psychopathology, and psychotherapy. *Journal of Mental Imagery,* 2(2): 253–274.

Reisner, S. (1999). Freud and psychoanalysis into the twenty-first century. *Journal of the American Psychoanalytic Association,* 47(4):1037–1060.

Schore, A. (1994). *Affect Regulation and the Origin of the Self.* Hillsdale, NJ: Lawrence Erlbaum.

Schore, A.N. (1997). A century after Freud's project: Is a rapprachment between psychoanalysis and neurobiology at hand? *Journal of the American Psychoanalytic Association,* 45(3):807–840.

Siegel, D.J. (1999). *The Developing Mind: Towards a Neurobiology of Interpersonal Experience.* New York: Guilford.

Singer, J.L. and Pope, K.S. (1978). *The Power of Human Imagination.* New York: Plenum Press.

Sullivan, H.S. (1953). *The Interpersonal Theory of Psychiatry.* New York: W.W. Norton.

Sulloway, F. (1979). *Freud: Biologist of the Mind.* New York: Basic Books.

Wilden, A. (1972). *System and Structure: Essays in Communication and Exchange.* London: Tavistock.

Wheeler, M.A., Stuss, D.T., and Tulving, E. (1997). Towards a theory of episodic memory: The frontal lobes and autonoetic consciousness. *Psychological Bulletin,* 121(3):331–354.

Wynne, L.C., Ryckoff., I.M., Day, J. and Hirsch, S.I. (1958). Pseudomutuality in the family relationships of schizophrenics. *Psychiatry,* 21:205–220.

Chapter 14

The enigma of the transference[1]

Psychoanalysis has from its inception been biased toward theory, metapsychology, presumably the font of the mutative therapeutic action. Far less emphasis has been put on the phenomenology of therapeutic action; that is, *how* people change. This valorization of metapsychology is coming increasingly under scrutiny as the erstwhile sharp-edged doctrinaire distinctions between positions blur and attention shifts to an emergent neuropsychological paradigm—to be sure, at this stage of knowledge, more a metaphor than a genuine model (Pulver, 2003). In other words, now that it is less clear that we are right and you are wrong, we are all beginning to wonder what it is we are doing when we do what we all know how to do.

Metapsychology, for all its claim to ontological truth, always reflects the current culture, the social context in which we are all immersed, but of which we are largely unaware. As Gregory Bateson (1979) said, the point of the probe is always in the heart of the explorer (p. 87). The current emphasis on the vicissitudes of early mothering, especially as described in attachment theory, reflects a cultural change, from the patriarchal, Oedipal-oriented (conflict and envy) world in which I both grew up and became an analyst, to a matriarchal, nurturing one in which early mothering and empathy are privileged. One also notes, not inconsequentially, that the demographics of psychoanalysis have shifted from largely male and medical to female and psychological along with a radical shift in the economics. Believe it or not, when I entered the field in the early fifties, psychoanalysis was the second highest-paid medical specialty and we had waiting lists! Clearly this circumstance made for a therapeutic milieu that tolerated more frustration and tempted therapists less to overaggressive interventions.

But does anyone entirely believe that if secure attachment takes place, all subsequent troubles are weathered: Oedipal, family, sibling, peer group, societal, midlife, and old age? Whatever happened to the father? It appears that, although we are ostensibly ecumenically intended, agreeing to disagree amicably, psychoanalysis is still split into what Cooper (2008) calls a "growing plurality of orthodoxies" adamant, entrenched, and highly politicized (p. 235). Yet surely everyone from Freudian to relational therapist is on to something, has grasped some aspect of our proverbial elephant, the nature of mind.

Once thought of as the "Ghost in the Machine," mind and its correlate, consciousness, have become of cardinal interest (Levenson, 2001). We are now in the Age of the Mind, and the nature of consciousness is hotly debated in an obscure, virtually medievalist sectarianism among the "mentalists," the "functionalists," the "materialists," and the "mysterians" (Damasio, 1994). Suffice it to say that the debate centers on whether consciousness is merely an epiphenomenon of the brain—an inevitable outcome of organic complexity—or whether it is of another essence altogether.[2] Consciousness, as Damasio says, is "the last great mystery and may lead us to change our view of the universe we inhabit" (p. 21). What "mind" is remains something of a mystery. As Jonathan Miller (1995) put it, "[W]e are the unwitting beneficiaries of a mind that is, in a sense, only partially our own" (p. 64).

Consequently, I suggest that our current focus be not on competing metapsychologies and their interpretive sets, but on how mind works, how experience is processed and integrated. We must understand the phenomenology of change, how people comprehend their being in the world, and how the analyst's presence and interactions foster flexibility and growth.

Regardless of theoretical positions, most analysts are struck by two oddly autonomous parameters of observation: first, the flow of consciousness as it is evidenced in the patient's narrative—the unconscious associations, the "red line" of coherence that runs through the ramblings of a session—and, second, the transference enactment, the way analyst and patient behave with each other in the course of the inquiry. Clearly, both the interpersonal and the intrapsychic coexist: the relationship between the intersubjective world and the still mysterious internal processes of change must be synthesized. Integrating these two striking aspects of the analytic process has been, for me, consistently the most puzzling and yet rewarding aspect of the therapeutic endeavor.

The patient's flow of consciousness, the intrapsychic, is the classic sine qua non of the analytic process—not necessarily limited to free-association, since the same order is equally evident in a detailed inquiry. As Bollas (1999) put it,

[There is an] understandable and inevitable tension between the goal of free association and the wishes of the analyst to understand the material: as free association unbinds meaning—in what Laplanche terms and celebrates as the "anti-hermeneutics" of psychoanalysis—while interpretation creates and binds meaning. No sooner are such understandings established than the workings of the unconscious, evident through free association, break the interpretation into particles of meaning, which constitute a "use of the Object," hopefully celebrated by the analyst's unconscious working along similar lines even as such use disperses his interpretive creations (p. 70).

The second striking manifestation is, of course, the relationship between the patient and therapist, the uncanny way the two play or enact, or re-enact, the very patterns that are under inquiry. This is, of course, the storied transference, these days considerably loosened from Freud's original constraints, but still clearly central to the process.

Two clinical excerpts are, I think, illuminating. The first illustrates the coherence of the patient's unconscious flow of associations, which seem, at least at first view, to be independent of the therapist's participation. It very much reflects Masud Khan's aphorism that we are the servants of the patient's process (quoted in Milner, 1969, p. xxxi). The second example, also a dream, illustrates less the flow of unconscious associations than the intricate interweaving of content and transference enactments.

The first patient, a 30-year-old man, has a dream about 3 weeks into therapy. He is "with another guy." Perhaps they are reviewing his port-folio. That's all. That's the dream. Who is the guy? He doesn't know. He is thinking of working for a friend of his mother's brother—his famous Uncle Max, the family patriarch, who is wealthy and powerful and helps them all with their problems, financial or personal. Oh yes, there are snakes floating around overhead. Also something like hieroglyphics, bits of information. Any other associations? Other ideas? None. Suddenly he remembers that the dream takes place in his parents' garage, at their country

164 Psychoanalytic process

house. What about the house? His parents own an isolated country house. He often visits there without them. He must enter the house through the garage, which is always left unlocked. He must first reach over a shelf in the dark to find the light switch. Then he must reach deeper into the dusty, cobwebbed space to find the house key. Then he must take the key around to the front of the house and open the main door. Otherwise, he could enter through the garage, go down the stairs from the garage to the cellar—a very spooky place that he has always avoided—and then he can go up the back stairs into the house. He never *ever* goes into the cellar. The garage is scary enough since it is never locked. Every time he opens the door, he expects to be attacked by "a bum or bear or something."

Why doesn't he just leave another key hidden near the front door? It's not clear; he never thought about it. Does his father go through all this when he uses his house? Where were the bits of hieroglyphics? The associations begin to proliferate: to the movie *Indiana Jones and the Temple of Doom*. It seems that entering the garage is like the movie—always hidden rooms, monsters, having to reach through icky bugs and snakes—Indiana Jones's Achilles heel, his phobia. What about snakes? Constrictors . . . not vipers . . . constriction . . . squeezed. He doesn't have a snake phobia, but he hates spiders!

Hieroglyphics come back into play. He has always been interested in archeology, thought it would be a wonderful thing to do. It is his grandfather's and his father's interest. His grandfather would spend weeks meticulously repairing antique vases from his homeland. His father also loved antiquities. When my patient was a child, his grandfather would play with him, breaking a vase, burying the pieces and having him find them, dig them up, and reconstitute the item.

This profuse flow of associations to a very brief dream! Some of the associations were totally spontaneous, others a consequence of my detailed inquiry; all seem to come from some entirely autonomous source. They are, to put it technically, metonymic not metaphoric; that is, they are private associations,[3] whose relevance only the patient knows, as compared with metaphor, which is in the common domain, a story. Certainly I have no idea where it is headed, although I do ask detailed questions that focus on the odd omissions.

One certainly could infer a transferential subtext. The patriarchal Uncle Max who helps everyone, the fascinating game of inquiry and reconstitution (Freud, after all, considered psychoanalysis an archeological process), the coded messages—all point to a view of transference and of the therapy. Is it a game to make the patriarch happy? Does it really engage him? The questions proliferate, but here I want simply to show how this dream has a blatant associative aspect and a much more implied and less self-evident transferential dimension.

The second dream is far more elaborate, richly metaphoric, and chock full of blatantly obvious transferential implications. Indications of an associative flow are sparse. For this 50-year-old woman, it is her first dream in vivid color and occurs one year into therapy. In the dream she is at a conference where she meets Osama Bin Laden. He is her height, has hazel eyes, but something seems to be wrong with his shoulder. He asks if she hates him. She explains that she is Jewish and pro-Israel. She's telling him "straight." He is listening, looking her straight in the eye. Then Bin Laden wants to kiss her. He chews food and then passes it to her lips, as a mother bird or a wild dog would (note the polarities of nurturance—a bird or a carnivore). This, he explains, is "an old Indian custom." He has a virus, and she is thinking of getting him medicine (she doesn't seem concerned about catching some disease from being fed by him).

In contrast to the first dreamer's, her associations are minimal: namely that her mother had visited India twice (without her father). I point out to her the stunningly obvious—that I am her height, have hazel eyes, and, when she started in therapy with me a year earlier, I had just had shoulder surgery and my arm was in a sling for many weeks. (In both Bin Laden's and my case, it was specifically the right shoulder.) This dream is a veritable palimpsest of unconscious process: first, the content, her apparent unawareness of perfectly obvious themes; her presenting me with the themes so that I can prechew them and force feed them back to her—which, of course, I proceed to do by explaining the dream to her. Does she need to be told that her feelings about Osama are ambivalent? That he represents me, the therapist? All he lacks is a name tag!

She has wonderful dreams—at least at that stage of the therapy—that make me feel very insightful and clever, and I usually fall for "interpreting" them to her. If they are so obvious, why doesn't she see them? How can someone so smart be so dumb? It is a prime example of R.D. Laing's (1967) dictum about mystification: the patient learns not to know what the patient knows she knows but is not supposed to know. In this dream, although there are many rich threads of inquiry into her

166 Psychoanalytic process

history, the interactive replay of those themes with me is most instantly obvious.

The two dreams illustrate the polarities in the dialectic between the intrapsychic process of unconscious flow and the interpersonal process of transference enactment. Why don't analysts simply use both parameters of therapy flexibly, moving freely between them? One would think that a therapist could easily be aware of these two clinical parameters. However, they exert a strangely compelling gestalt figure-ground effect; while one is being observed, the other tends to disappear. In each of the clinical cases that phenomenon is so striking that one is tempted to think, "Ah. So that's how it works. That's where the clinical leverage lies!" A surprising amount of deliberate effort is required to move back and forth between inquiry and the awareness of interaction.

Psychoanalytic groups do seem to privilege one or the other as a means of institutional definition; drive, interpersonal, theory, relational theories, all prioritize either flow of consciousness or interaction. It all used to be much simpler. In the Good Old Days of only one psychoanalysis, you either were or were not an analyst: this, of course, was decided by the powers that be—and the White Institute, and its epigones, were not analysts. Simple as that. It was a pragmatic application of Popper's (1963) principle of falsifiability—you can't say what a thing is if you can't say what it isn't. Psychoanalysts defined themselves by declaring who wasn't. The struggle for status, prestige, patients, and candidates invokes a polarization: them-us. The minute you are convinced you are right and that your system is the only Truth—you've established a religion. Current ecumenism allows for multiple versions of psychoanalysis, some of which admittedly may strain the definition of the process. But at least we now talk to each other.

In 1983, Greenberg and Mitchell published their seminal *Object Relations in Psychoanalytic Theory*. By subsuming virtually every psychoanalytic position—other than Freudians—under the rubric of "relational" (including Kleinian, Kohutian, interpersonal, Winnicottian, etc.), they essentially politically outflanked and isolated them and pressured them to participate in an ecumenical movement that may have had as much to do with pragmatics as any genuine substantive synthesis would have.

At about the same time, Merton Gill (1983) presciently identified the problem. Gill, who was perhaps the most unyielding of the Freudian analysts on the committee—that in 1942 expelled the early group of interpersonalists from the American Psychoanalytic Association (for, among other shortcomings, not conforming to the 5-day/couch rule)—had been drifting toward an interpersonalism of his own. He and I corresponded about my book *The Fallacy of Understanding* (1972), and he came to White and attended some of our clinic meetings. In 1982, at White, he gave a remarkable talk defying the then current draconian bans, an act of no small moral courage. He had reviewed the entire corpus of interpersonal writings and, with his fresh and original intelligence, saw that there were, as he said, two dichotomies in psychoanalysis.

He was referring to the distinction between two major cleavages in psychoanalytic thought. One cleavage is between the interpersonal paradigm and the drive-discharge paradigm. The other cleavage is between those who believe the analyst inevitably participates in a major way in the analytic situation and those who do not. I came to realize that I had assumed that these two cleavages ran parallel to each other, or at least that those who adhered to the interpersonal paradigm would also ascribe to the analyst a major participation in the analytic situation (Gill, 1983, p. 201).

Note that Gill accepted the relational-drive dichotomy as valid. He went on to say that variations in the use of the second parameter cut across institutional and metapsychological loyalties and affiliations. He was, in essence, saying that within any psychoanalytic group there will be in this second cleavage marked variations, which one might consider as a continuum of activity, running from analysts who see themselves as the curative event in a patient's life (charismatic or restitutive), to those who see the cure as the analyst curing herself (analysis of countertransference), to those who believe in the analysis of resistance and transference as getting out of the way of the patient's self-curative potential to allow some self-regulating (intrapsychic) activity on the patient's part. The spectrum runs from the mutative effects of the analyst's engagement to emphasis on the unimpeded flow of consciousness.

These are, obviously, different stations on the currently loosely defined and delineated continuum of "transference." The distinctions Gill made may define analysts' doctrinaire and institutional loyalties; but I suspect that when they work most analysts intuitively employ, sometimes even outside their awareness, both sides of the interaction, language and behavior. In that way they can monitor the interpersonal field closely, either to influence it or to get it out of the way of the mutative insight. This attention to the transference may, sometimes inadvertently, be far

168 Psychoanalytic process

more relevant to the cure than the canonical metapsychological considerations.

Transference is, of course, a highly overloaded rubric. Freud's (1905) case study of Dora is considered the emblematic origin of his thinking on transference. That 3-month treatment ended with an abrupt and unanticipated termination. Dora had told Freud at the beginning of the session that she would not continue. Freud continued his inquiry, ignoring her statement. At the end of the session, she said goodbye pleasantly and came no more! Freud's first reaction was hurt—why did she treat me so shabbily? But Freud being Freud, he morphed his disappointment into the concept of resistance and transference.

Erik Erikson (1968) subsequently made much of Freud's complicity in the female repression of the day—that is to say, Dora had good reason to be angry. I would like to take it one step further and suggest that *her response was inevitable no matter what Freud did*! Psychoanalysis begins when even the best-intentioned efforts fail. It is the analysis—not the avoidance—of the failure that defines transference and countertransference and constitutes the major leverage of the process.

Freud (1914a) defined the centrality of transference: "Any line of investigation no matter what its direction, which recognizes these two facts [transference and resistance] and takes them as the starting point of its work may call itself psychoanalysis, though it arrives at results other than my own" (p. 10). And about the same time, Freud (1914b) wrote that the whole structure of psychoanalysis stands apart from metapsychological considerations, which, he said, can be replaced and discarded without damaging the structure.

People resist change, for whatever reason, and that resistance takes the form of an interaction with the therapist *that recapitulates, in action, the very issue under discussion*. Freudians saw this enactment as a resistance to a confrontation with unconscious fantasy, and consequently they interpreted *away* from the transference to get back to the fantasies. Currently, most of us interpret *into* the transference since we view it as a fruitful area of inquiry. We all agree that what happens between the patient and therapist is integral to the cure. We differ on what it is: the elucidation of fantasies projected onto the therapist, or the field of interaction itself.

It is my contention that transference is far more enigmatic, indeed uncanny, than one might suspect. It is not simply a form of resistance to change, as the Freudians would have it, but rather some *mysterious, inherent, correlate of the* inquiry—inherent, insofar as it may be a natural aspect of cognitive process, not an artifact of anxiety or defense.

The two striking phenomenological aspects of the analytic praxis are patients' flow of consciousness and the uncanny tendency of their simultaneous relationship to play out or *mirror* what is being said. Say a patient tells you how hurt he was by his father's criticism when he was a child and then is hurt because you are ending the session 5 minutes early. It may matter less whether you interpret his hurt feeling as a distortion carried over from his childhood or as a real enactment between the two of you that he is overvaluing, even if you wonder why you ended the session too early. The real value may lie in the recognition that *something is being replayed.* Why this should be so requires the elaboration of a number of axioms.

First, all experience (perception) is an interpretation. This is not an issue of philosophic realism. How you experience a bear or, for that matter, a potential lover, depends not just on the immediate circumstances (the bear is blocking your passage on the trail or sunning itself in a zoo enclosure), but on sociocultural experience: that is to say, memory. Perception is 90 percent memory—the "mind's best guess" (Gregory, 1966, p. 2).

Second, all interpretation is selectively biased. Perception is always distorted or constricted; however caused, distortion is the sine qua non of neurosis. But how? There is a range of possibilities: simply the necessity to select from multiple perspectives; the force of unconscious drive; interpersonal anxiety (out of awareness); or being misled by other people, deliberately or unconsciously. Our therapeutic endeavors with our patients are, then, all about omissions—what is left out of awareness—be it by repression, inattention, dissociation, or mystification.

From my point of view, all experience is interpersonally determined. Cognition itself is interpersonal. The interpersonal modus is contagious anxiety. Sullivan (1953) posited that it is the anxiety of the significant other, the necessary caretaker, which frightens the child, causing a wave of "contagious" anxiety that then becomes responsible for the subsequent mechanisms of neurotic denial. This disruptive anxiety creates a cognitive dissonance that is then obscured, by the other, largely through the medium of language. The child is *mystified*; that is, she learns through the pressure of anxiety not to see what is there to be seen. She must learn to "close the eyes." This was the theme of Freud's (1900) dream about this father's death and, not incidentally the Greek meaning of *mystes—to* close the eyes, to not see.

170 Psychoanalytic process

This is not to deny that there is distortion at play in patients' current lives. Nor am I implying that all a patient need do is to see what is there to be seen. Mystification and its concurrent anxiety operate most strongly in early life events, but current events reiterate the earlier patterning. It is not that the patient is wrong about the present, but the affect and, more important, the sense of semiotic confusion and impotence resonate powerfully with earlier experience. The patient is not wrong in perceptions, but the affect and sense of helplessness surely are.

As Peter Fonagy and his colleagues (2002) put it:

> We move away from the model where an early relationship is principally seen as the generator of a template for later relationships. Instead, we argue that early experience no doubt via its impact upon development at both psychological and neuropsychological levels determines the "depth" to which the social environment may be processed. *Suboptimal early experiences of care affect later development by undermining the individual's capacity to process or interpret information concerning mental states that is essential for effective functioning in a stressful social world* (p. 7; italics added).

Axiomatic to my view of therapy is that one cannot *not* interact: one cannot *not* influence. The major instrument of mystification is language; language being not merely speech, but the sum of all its semiotic cues: nonverbal (tonal, prosodic); nuances of irony, sarcasm, humor. The child learns to not know what it knows it knows; that is, she is essentially talked out of her perceptions. But language, unfortunately, is less about communication of information than about deception and control—power. This "anxiety of influence," as every therapist is aware, may keep the patient from accepting insights from the therapist who may well be right but experienced as intrusive (Bloom 1973). So, again from the interpersonal view, resolving neurotic conflict means getting a better grasp of what's going on around you and to you; that is, mastering the semiotic world of experience.

Mystification, then, is the gap between what is said and what is shown: in semiotics, between *langue* and *parole*, speech and language (Levenson, 1983). Mystifications severely limit the possible range of responses, so that neurosis becomes a variety of cliché. According to the old psychoanalytic aphorism, the patient knows only one way of doing something and that doesn't work; or, alternatively, it works too well to allow change! It follows that the major instrument of demystification is the matching of what is said against what is done. The therapist and the patient talk; the talking is an interaction because it is not possible to talk without taking a selective position about the content; and that selective position is a bit of behavior with the patient. Speech *is* behavior: to repeat, one cannot *not* interact. The interpersonal field between patient and therapist is an enactment of what is simultaneously talked about. This correspondence may well be, not some consequence of psychoanalytic inquiry, or stress of the field, *but an intrinsic part of semiotic communication.*

The experience of transferential enactment is often eerie. For example, analysts may find themselves imitating, or mirroring, the behavior of patients. Years ago, I worked with a depressed and self-devaluing young woman. I caught myself, on leaving the office in the evening, imitating her strange gait. In another, more extensive example, I had a vivid experience of this mimetic response. A 60-year-old man is telling me about his childhood, how he felt tortured by his father's teasing, which was always ostensibly playful. He is the younger of two brothers, with an 8-year age gap between them, and he was always being ragged about things he really could not be expected to have grasped at his age. As he tells me about the teasing, he begins to laugh and laugh and—when I say to him that he sounds on the edge of tears—he breaks into sobs, saying how much he loved his father. Two weeks later, in his first session after his return from a ski trip, he turns on me in a rage as he is leaving at the end of the session, and says, "Why were you laughing at me when I first came in?"—staggering me.

After he left, I realized I had started laughing when I came out into the waiting room to greet him. I thought I was glad to see him—but why laughter? And, in truth, as I tried to review it, I had been feeling, very faintly, something akin to ridicule. He was on to something, and I told him so the next session. I still do not entirely understand my reaction.

We tend to think of empathy as affective, as containing the patient's fear of emotional flooding; that is, empathy is the ability of the therapist to grasp the patient's affective experience and to contain it. But what of imitation? I suspect that it is a powerful therapeutic response, an attempt to capture the patient's experience by essentially embodying it. It is quite possible that a patient may, in addition to experiencing the therapist's empathic holding (presumably a requisite for restitution of a developmental

172   Psychoanalytic process

deficit), also experience an opportunity to learn, by imitating the therapist, a theory of mind, or empathy for others: change may be less a matter of containment and restitution than really of new learning.

Here we get into fascinating aspects of current neuropsychological research. The dichotomies between left and right brain are now long familiar and hardly require repetition (Schore, 1994). I would like, however, to spell out some remarkable new findings on what have been called "mirror neurons." There are fascinating developments in the phenomenology of learning and, fueled by new techniques of brain monitoring, in the study of consciousness and mind that collate with current studies in child development and mother-child interaction. Children, we are told, learn first mimetically, imitatively. Tilting one's head, sticking out one's tongue calls out an imitative response from very young infants. As they mature, they imitate, experience the imitation, and then categorize the experience in language.

I have elaborated on the body-mind link and on this very possibility— that learning may be first bodily, first imitative, mimetic, and *then* cerebral (Levenson, 1998). This idea suggests the interesting possibility that psychoanalytic insight may be first experienced and *then* formulated; that the direction of learning may be, not from the head to the body, but quite the opposite—a matter of what is said about what is experienced. According to Rizzolatti and Simigaglia (2008),

> The rigid divide between perceptive, motor, and cognitive processes is to a great extent artificial: not only does perception appear to be embedded in the dynamics of action, becoming much more composite than used to be thought in the past, but the acting brain is also and above all a brain that understands (p. xi).

It is a common clinical experience that interpretations of both meaning and awareness (Gill, 1983) work better *after* enactment. If interpretations precede enactment it doesn't work. At best, one gets intellectual agreement, compliance, from the patient.

Mirror neurons were first reported in 1995 by Iaccomo Rizzolati at the University of Parma (Iacoboni and Mazziotta, 2007; Rizzolatti and Sinigaglia, 2008). Mirror neurons are neurons that fire both when an animal performs and acts and when it observes another animal performing the same act. This mirroring or imitation is felt by some researchers to be the

The enigma of the transference 173

next big thing in neurological discovery, the "great leap forward" in human evolution, the next cognitive revolution, after the Copernican, Darwinian, Freudian, the discovery of DNA and the genetic code. Now the claim, admittedly florid, is made that empathy, language, theory of mind may all depend on this mirroring capacity. Also claimed, but open to a good deal of question, is the finding that autistic children may lack mirror neurons and that this link may account for their inability to empathize—however hyperbolic this may be, it is clear that mirror neurons may open the door to a new understanding of how people learn through interaction, through behavior as well as language (Ramachandran, 2000).

All this certainly advances a conception of psychoanalytic learning qua change as the matching of interpretation to transference. How does this speech-action parallel process translate into therapeutic praxis? I have written elsewhere of the algorithm of therapy (Levenson, 1983). It consists of three components: frame, inquiry, and enactment. The frame is a set of constraints defined outside and before the psychoanalytic interaction. It provides the patient, and, more important (and less frequently noted), the therapist with a sense of safety and containment. It protects both participants from becoming overanxious and limits the risk of mutual out-of-awareness interactions.

The therapist and the patient engage in a verbal inquiry that may be free-associative or a more detailed inquiry. Inevitably this leads, not to greater clarity, but to a deconstructed inquiry: coherence is lost, tangential associative threads emerge. Dreams, leaps of association occur. In pursuit of the inquiry, the enactment I have been explicating takes place.

Menninger and Holzman (1973) called this direction of flow the "therapeutic cycle"; that is, when the process was proceeding correctly, the material cycled from the present; *through the transference*, and then to the history and back to the present. Note that the useful recall of the past only occurs after the resolution (enactment with therapist) of the transference. A therapy that links present difficulties to past experiences is educational but not quite psychoanalytic in scope if it lacks the transition through the patient/therapist enactments.

Summary

I am proposing that the therapeutic power of psychoanalysis does not depend on the primacy of metapsychology or on the presumably mutative interpretations thereof. Metapsychology is ontology; and the claim to knowing—to having a coherent theory of causality and treatment—undermines our appreciation of how little we understand about how people experience change and the underlying neuropsychological processes of change. Sullivan is purported to have said, "God keep me from a clever psychoanalyst!" Truly, humility is the beginning of wisdom.[4]

Observation of the praxis of therapy—what it is that we actually do, the *act* of therapy—illuminates two cardinal aspects of the process: the patient's flow of consciousness and the analyst's vocal and behavioral participation. Very early, Freud saw in that process that patient-therapist interactions obstructed insight and change. What he saw as resistance to insight, with all its ramifications, I now see as enactment, which differs from "acting-out," that anathema of psychoanalysis. Acting-out is a breaking of the frame, when some out-of-awareness material emerges as a disruptive piece of behavior in or outside the therapy room. How we assess enactment varies. I see it as an inherent part of the interaction, necessary to the process and the cure, not as a byproduct of pathological defense.

One might well see this dialectic between speech and action in terms of the long-established neuropsychological paradigm of a right brain-left brain dichotomy. Recently, however, the discovery of "mirror neurons" has suggested that mirroring may be a vital part of relating to another, as vital an *embodied* aspect of empathy and theory of mind as affective empathy—I know you because I feel your feelings. The original distinction between sympathy and empathy is considerably obfuscated in current psychoanalytic discourse. Much of what therapists call empathic response is simply sympathy and solicitude, since the therapist often cannot have a real grasp of the patient's experience. For true empathy, we must have experienced to some significant degree what the patient experiences; mirroring or imitation may serve that purpose, albeit in an adumbrated form. Bodily learning, "embodied cognition," may be an essential part of the therapeutic process. To quote Saporta (2008):

> Cognitive scientists and linguists are coming to a new appreciation of Freud's body ego in their recent emphasis on embodied cognition. This is an appreciation that the experience of the body in motion and the body's encounter with the world structure the way we think and the metaphors and language through which we conceive of ourselves

and the world. *There is evidence that the influence of the body and physical context is not limited to early development but has an ongoing influence on the structure of thinking* (p. 8; italics added).

The distinctions Gill (1983) made still define our doctrinaire and institutional loyalties, But I believe that our "talking cure" may invoke, indeed require, a corresponding behavioral component, not as an issue of psychoanalytic technique (the use of transference), but because it is an inherent aspect of the still mysterious processes of cognition and consciousness. The inquiry (flow of consciousness, detailed inquiry, drift of topics) and the transferential enactment—what is said and what is shown—may not be different points on a therapeutic and theoretical continuum, but, rather, two sides of the same coin.

Notes

1. This chapter was presented as the 11th annual Sydney E. Pulver M.D. lecture at the Psychoanalytic Center of Philadelphia on October 17, 2008. An earlier version was presented at the conference of the American Psychological Association, Division 39, "Knowing, Not Knowing and Sort-of Knowing: Psychoanalysis and the Experience of Uncertainty," New York City, April 9, 2008. This version was published in 2009 in *Contemporary Psychoanalysis* 45(2):163–172.
2. See Chalmers (1996) and Searle (1997) for a discussion of a belief in a fundamentally irreducible consciousness.
3. See Levenson (1991, p. 38) for elaboration of this theme.
4. See Richards (2003) for an eloquent plea for a measure of humility.

References

Bateson, G. (1979). *Mind and Nature; A Necessary Unity*. New York: Dutton.
Bloom, H. (1973). *The Anxiety of Influence*. New York: Oxford University Press.
Bollas, C. (1999). *The Mystery of Things*. New York: Routledge.
Chalmers, D.J. (1996). *The Conscious Mind*. New York: Oxford University Press.
Cooper, A.M. (2008). American psychoanalysis today: A plurality of orthodoxies. *Journal of the American Academy of Psychoanalysis and Dynamic Psychiatry*, 36(3):235–253.
Damasio, A.R. (1994). *Descartes' Error*. New York: Grosset/Putnam.
Erikson, E. (1968). *Identity, Youth and Crisis*. New York: W.W. Norton.
Fonagy, P., Gergely, G., Jurist, E. and Target, M. (2002). *Affect Regulation, Mentalization, and the Development of the Self*. New York: Other Press.

Freud, S. (1900). The Interpretation of Dreams. In J. Strachey (Ed.), *The Standard Edition of the Complete Psychological Works of Sigmund Freud* (Vol. IV). London: Hogarth Press.

Freud, S. (1905). Fragment of an analysis of a case of hysteria. In J. Strachey (Ed.), *The Standard Edition of the Complete Psychological Works of Sigmund Freud* (Vol. IV). London: Hogarth Press.

Freud, S. (1905). Fragment of an analysis of a case of hysteria. In J. Strachey (Ed.), *The Standard Edition of the Complete Psychological Works of Sigmund Freud* (Vol. VII). London: Hogarth Press, pp. 7–123.

Freud, S. (1914a). On the history of the psychoanalytic movement. In J. Strachey (Ed.), *The Standard Edition of the Complete Psychological Works of Sigmund Freud* (Vol. XIV). London: Hogarth Press, 1957, pp. 1–66.

Freud, S. (1914b). On narcissism: An introduction. In J. Strachey (Ed.), *The Standard Edition of the Complete Psychological Works of Sigmund Freud* (Vol. XIV). London: Hogarth Press, 1957, pp. 69–102.

Gill, M. (1983). The interpersonal paradigm and the degree of the analyst's involvement. *Contemporary Psychoanalysis*, 18(2):200–237.

Greenberg, J. and Mitchell, S. (1983). *Object Relations in Psychoanalytic Theory*. Cambridge, MA: Harvard University Press.

Gregory, R.L. (1966). *Eye and the Brain*. Princeton, NJ: Princeton University Press.

Iacoboni, M. and Mazziotta, J.C. (2007). Mirror neuron system: Basic findings and clinical applications. *Annual of Neurology*, 62(3):213.

Laing, R.D. (1967). *The Politics of Experience*. New York: Pantheon Books.

Levenson, E. (1972). *The Fallacy of Understanding*. Hillsdale, NJ: The Analytic Press, 2005.

Levenson, E. (1983). *The Ambiguity of Change: An Inquiry into the Nature of Psychoanalytic Reality*. Hillsdale, NJ: The Analytic Press, 2005.

Levenson, E. (1991). *The Purloined Self*. New York: Contemporary Psychoanalysis Books.

Levenson, E. (1998). Awareness, insight and learning. *Contemporary Psychoanalysis*, 34(2):223–249.

Levenson, E. (2001). The enigma of the unconscious. *Contemporary Psychoanalysis*, 37(2):239–252.

Menninger, K. and Holzman, P. (1973). *Theory of Psychoanalytic Technique*. New York: Basic Books.

Miller, J. (1995). Going unconscious. *New York Review of Books*, 42:59–65.

Milner, M. (1969). *The Hands of the Living God*. New York: International Universities Press.

Popper, K. (1963). *Conjectures and Refutations*. London: Routledge.

Pulver, S. (2003). On the astonishing clinical irrelevance of neuroscience. *Journal of the American Psychoanalytic Association*, 51(3):755–772.

Ramachandran, V.S. (2000). Mirror neurons and imitation learning as the driving force behind "the great leap forward" in human evolution. (www.edge.org/3rd-culture/ramachandran/ramachandran).

Richards, A. (2003). Psychoanalytic discourse at the turn of our century: A plea for a measure of humility. *Journal of the American Psychoanalytic Association*, 51(suppl):72–125.

Rizzolatti, G. and Sinigaglia, C. (2008). *Mirrors in the Brain: How Our Minds Share Actions and Emotions*. London: Oxford University Press.

Saporta, J. (2008). Digitalizing psychoanalysis and psychotherapy. *American Psychoanalyst*, 42(2):1–9.

Schore, A. (1994). *Affect Regulation and the Origin of the Self*. Hillsdale, NJ: Erlbaum.

Searle, J. (1997). Consciousness and the philosophers. *New York Review of Books*, XLIV(4):43–50.

Sullivan, H.S. (1953). *The Interpersonal Theory of Psychiatry*. New York: W.W. Norton.

Chapter 15

Psychoanalysis and the rite of refusal[1]

I'm delighted to have this opportunity to participate in Tony Bass' plan for a series of informal essays on psychoanalytic issues. The essay format allows for a more relaxed and playful—albeit admittedly less disciplined—presentation; and it provides a forum for our examining some of the more perplexing and curious difficulties in the psychoanalytic domain.

You will note that my title is a double entendre—rite/right, ritual or privilege. Why is it so hard to get anyone to change? And, why is change itself so often suspect? If it's too easy, perhaps it's "transference cure" or "flight into health." Ultimately all psychoanalytic therapies are about this conundrum. I am suspicious of any therapist who promulgates a theory, announces that application of that theory produces clinical results directly attributable to the theory—and then, of course, claims that the therapeutic results validate the theory. Ultimately, the irony may be that successful treatment depends less on the application of the therapist's canonical theory than on the therapist's ability to capitalize on its failure. I believe psycho-analysis begins where psychotherapy fails.

Freud's famous cri de coeur might be extended to "What do *patients* want?" Throughout his discovery of resistance, transference, counter-transference, negative therapeutic reaction, the repetition compulsion, and finally the much-contested death instinct, in a long and anguished diminuendo of therapeutic expectations, he became so despairing of the intransigence of his clients that in 1932, Ferenzci reported Freud as having said to him that "patients are a rabble (Gesindel)." Patients, he said, "only serve to provide us with a livelihood and material to learn from. We certainly cannot help them" (Ferenczi, 1988, p. 93).

Increasingly, he came to believe that resistance to therapy was less a consequence of psychodynamics than a profound ontological issue—the death instinct. In "Analysis Terminable and Interminable," just 2 years before his death, he said,

> If we take into consideration the total picture made up of the phenomenon of masochism immanent in so many people, the negative therapeutic reaction and the sense of guilt found in so many neurotics, we shall no longer be able to adhere to the belief that mental events are exclusively governed by the desire for pleasure . . . only by the concurrent or mutually opposing actions of two primal instincts—Eros and the death-instinct . . . can we explain the rich multiplicity of the phenomena of life.
>
> (Freud, 1937)

Post-Freud, analysts continued to struggle with the issue of patient intransigence. Klein, of course, made the death instinct a keystone of her metapsychology. Balint and the British object-relation analysts (Winnicott, Little, and Khan) postulated that inadequate regression in the transference accounted for the failure of treatment of many borderline patients. Masud Khan attributed his failures in treatment with Winnicott to his inability to regress sufficiently. Little attributed her improvements to Winnicott's capacity to tolerate and permit severe regressions, requiring on several occasions, hospitalizations. The astute observer might find in both Khan's and Little's accounts a plethora of other issues in play, most particularly transgressions in maintaining psychoanalytic boundaries and in the exploitative use of the other (Hopkins, 1998; Little, 1985).

H.S. Sullivan is alleged to have said, "God keep me from a therapy that goes well," and correspondingly, "God keep me from a clever psychoanalyst." However one formulates the failure of one's therapeutic intentions: that is, inappropriate timing of interpretations; unexamined countertransference; insufficient regression; "malignant" regression; failures in empathy—or, a position I have espoused, that the patient is having the same old experiences in the enactment of the transference; no matter what the therapist ostensibly asserts, change is not really being offered— we are all in agreement that successful psychoanalysis requires "working-through"; actually a quite enigmatic and poorly understood process, described by Freud as early as 1895 but most elaborated in *Remembering,*

Repeating and Working Through (Freud, 1914). It refers to that extended period in which clinical material is reworked, turned round, examined from different perspectives, dreams and associations are elicited, and transference enactments tracked and explicated. Why should this be necessary, indeed central, to the therapeutic praxis?

Above all, it offers time and breathing space. Perhaps it offers the patient some restitution or a truly de novo experience; or, it allows the therapist a chance to examine the nuances of his/her own participation. I believe that its most important implicit aspect may be that the analyst is not, as Lacan ironically put it, "HE WHO KNOWS" (Wilden, 1972). The patient's participation, it becomes evident, will be necessary for any progress to occur; that is, the therapist *needs* the patient to reciprocally fulfill his/her role This may lead to a time in the working-through when the patient may leap ahead of the therapist, come up with a memory, an idea or a dream that leaves the therapist happily in his wake; in Khan's felicitous phase, becoming the "servant of the patient's process." If the patient works through resistance—not to passively accept the therapist's insights—but to collaborate, to bring his/her own contributions into play, then working-through assumes all the attributes of a creative process— hard work, persistence, confusion, and despair, leavened by flashes of originality and discovery.

Although we might largely agree that change is resisted and that working-through is a necessary component of the praxis, we tend increasingly not to hold the patient responsible. One hardly hears, these days, of the "untreatable" patient, although the concept of character diagnosis, especially psychopathy, is enjoying something of a renaissance. In the days of male-oriented, medically dominated, classical psychoanalysis, patients were screened for analysis. Diagnoses were applied and entire categories deemed "un-analyzable"; as were the patients who failed in treatment, retroactively labeled mistakes in diagnosis. The analyst and his/her process could not be at fault. With the advent of a more matriarchally oriented psychoanalysis, with greater emphasis on developmental issues, analysts, like parents, tend to hold themselves responsible for the failures of the child.

And so, currently, we look to the failures of *our* efforts. As sporting as this might be, I believe it underestimates the contribution the patient makes to the impasse, out of—so to speak—reasons of his/her own. Adam Phillips (2001), in an endearing article based on Melville's mysterious little story "Bartleby the Scrivener" (who would "prefer not to") said,

"Psychotherapists treat a great variety of people who, in a great variety of ways, would 'prefer not to'" (p. 86). I would like to examine some aspects of "refusal" that may be less an issue of personal dynamics; rather more ontological, a consequence of the nature of being.

- *Fear of influence*: It has been said that people come into treatment because their neurosis isn't working and they want it fixed. Wanting change is something else altogether; and wanting to *be* changed even more so. It seems that influence—however well intentioned and whatever its ostensible value—is resisted. There is a Buddhist saying, "If you meet the Buddha on the road, kill him!" Autonomy is defended; for to submit to the power of another is a highly risky and resented proposition. Freud's early hysterics, in the best tradition of Hegel's master/slave dialectic, made a flamboyant display of submitting to the hypnotist. They made it their own, creating a theater of submission. The signal patient of a later time, the obsessional, presents quite another face. Obsessionals do not willingly surrender power to the therapist. They fight to the end; often not changing until after the therapy is ended. I have had the odd experience, and I believe, so have many other psychoanalysts, of having a stagnant therapy suddenly begin to move when I have given up in despair. Obsessional and particularly so-called "difficult" borderline patients will often become quite collaborative once it becomes evident that the therapist is defeated.
- *The fear of helplessness*: A neurosis, it must be remembered, however bad is always better than something else; and, that the patient is far better at what he/she does than you are. To wit, the neurosis, however discomforting, *works* with a high degree of redundancy: it is a "compromise" solution, not only in the Freudian sense of between drive and ego but between individual and society. Neurotic strategies, albeit constricting, are extremely redundant, with highly predictable outcomes. If you are afraid of being unloved and rejected, an interpersonal strategy that alienates everyone is comforting in its predictability.
- *The fear of expulsion*: Surely the oldest and most compelling social anxiety is the fear of expulsion from the group. Deracination, excommunication, in all its forms—family, Church, society—is a powerful incentive to submission to the group—and to refusal of the analyst, the dangerous outsider. Lyman Wynne, the family therapist, promulgated a wonderful visual concept he called "the rubber fence": that

is, the fence around every family, no matter how far stretched by the distancing of any member, especially one's patient—it is nevertheless the containment outside of which one stands (Wynne et al., 1958). The further the patient moves away from her family, the greater the pull back. This very powerful reminder, that in working with a patient, one is standing on the other side of the family divide, an outsider, is a vital caveat when one finds oneself presumably aligned sympathetically with a disaffected patient complaining about her family. In this sense resistance may be as much tribal as individual. These days, with the current valorization of empathic relatedness and emotional restitution, it is easy to miss the covertly protected bonds and disavowed identifications between the patient and her family; and the extent to which a patient will go to protect a damaged, brittle parent.

- *The fear of growing up*: Lévi-Strauss, in a neat little aphorism, called myth a machine for stopping time. A neurosis is equally a machine for stopping time; that is, the patient remains, like Peter Pan, lost but forever young. Sometimes, after a therapeutic advance, a patient will noticeably fall into time; begin to think about aging and change; to dream about death and time passing.[2] Being an adult, after all, has its shortcomings. Even a neurotic childhood has its compensations; namely, the security of the familiar. Moreover, leaving behind one's childhood means giving up revenge. The tattered rags, the stigmata of one's childhood, are both a powerful reproach bearing witness in a way that is hard to relinquish, and a cry for further reparations.

- The joy of blowing things up: Dostoyevsky (1961) in *Notes from the Underground* put the question:

> And what makes you so cocksure, so positive that only the normal and the positive, that is, only what promotes man's welfare, is to his advantage? Can't reason also be wrong about what's an advantage? Why can't man like things other than his wellbeing? Maybe he likes suffering just as much. Maybe suffering is just as much to his advantage as well-being. In fact, man adores suffering. *Passionately*! (p. 117).[CP1]

Maybe people just like to make trouble, to blow things up. Can there be passion without danger? Georges Bataille, in *Death and Sensuality*, added a further refinement, saying, "Erotic excitement resides in the risk of death." He hastened to add, "not death itself" (Benjamin, 1988, p. 64). To underestimate this all-too-human impulse to blow it all up, to make a mess, may be to fail to grasp an aspect of everything from passion to addiction. Note the spate of prominent politicians (male) who have demolished their careers through reckless indulgences that seem inexplicable by current Augustinian (evil is the absence of good) psychodynamic formulations. One clearly hears echoes of Freud's more Manichean death instinct, his recognition of the dark and irrational aspects of human desire.

In summation, psychoanalytic praxis is all about refusal and working-through. Resistance opens the doorway to the vaunted working-through; the process that converts dross into gold, our defeat into our triumph. However, it is important to bear in mind that resistance to change is not unique to analytic patients; nor is it entirely a consequence of neurotic difficulties; but is, for the variety of reasons I postulated (and probably others I've missed), implicit to the human state or, at least, the social state.

It might seem that what I am postulating is merely an extension of the resistance/transference model. I do believe it goes considerably further, in a way that I have found immensely helpful to my own work and in supervising. The analysts' dictum has always been "What can I do or say that would promote change?" I am suggesting a perspectivistic shift to "Why is the patient unable or unwilling to use my efforts?" We are, after all, often the court of last resort. Patients have been exposed, in their lifetimes, to many people who tried to influence them (for better or worse). They "preferred not to." Why that should be so is our enterprise.

I do believe, *pace* Freud, that psychoanalysis remains the most effective instrument for real growth in patients.[3] Since *The Fallacy of Understanding* in 1972, I have pursued the notion that the power of psychoanalysis lies, not in its highly contested, competitive explanatory systems, but in the very process of communication (Levenson, 1972).[4] I believe that our analytic communality—if we truly have one—must be procedural. Our effectiveness may have less to do with the application of our metapsychologies than our capacity to confront and to endure the highly overdetermined nexus of resistances to our best intentions.

Notes

1. This chapter was first published in 2012 in *Psychoanalytic Dialogues*, 32(1):2–6.

2. The affect in these dreams of death and dying is often remarkably bland, even accepting. They are not dreams of panic and despair, which leads me to believe they may be premonitory of positive change.
3. Perhaps Freud's treatments were simply not long enough! Many therapies were a short few months or several summers in a row.
4. See Gedo (1999, p. 135) for an explication of this theme.

References

Benjamin, J. (1988). *The Bonds of Love*. New York: Pantheon.

Dostoyevsky, F. (1961). *Notes from the Underground*. New York: Signet.

Ferenczi, S. (Ed.). (1988). *The Clinical Diaries of Sandor Ferenzci*. Cambridge, MA: Harvard University Press.

Freud, S. (1914). Remembering, repeating and working through. In J. Strachey (Ed.), *The Standard Edition of the Complete Psychological Works of Sigmund Freud*. London: Hogarth Press, Vol XII, pp. 145–156.

Freud, S. (1937). Analysis terminable and interminable. In J. Strachey (Ed.), *The Standard Edition of the Complete Psychological Works of Sigmund Freud*. London: Hogarth Press, Vol. XXIII, pp. 211–253.

Gedo, J. (1999). *The Evolution of Psychoanalysis: Theory and Perspectives*. New York: Other Press.

Hopkins, L.B. (1998). D.W. Winnicott's analysis of Masud Khan: A preliminary study of failures of object usage. *Contemporary Psychoanalysis*, 34(1):5–47.

Levenson, E. (1972). *The Fallacy of Understanding*. New York: Basic Books.

Little, M. (1985). Winnicott working in areas where psychotic anxieties predominate. *Free Associations*, 1(3):23.

Phillips, A. (2001). On preferring not to: The aesthetics of defiance. In J. Petrucelli and C. Stuart (Eds.), *Hungers and Compulsions*. Northvale, NJ: Aronson, pp. 81–94.

Wilden, A. (1972). *System and Structure: Essays in Communication and Exchange*. London: Tavistock.

Wynne, L.C., Ryckoff, I.M., Day, J., and Hirsch, S.I. (1958). Pseudo-mutuality in the family relationships of schizophrenics. *Psychiatry*, 21:205–220.

Part III

The philosophy of psychoanalytic theory and practice

Chapter 16

The uses of disorder
Chaos theory and psychoanalysis[1]

Psychoanalysis is haunted by a peculiar dilemma. For all of the immense effort that has been invested in metapsychological theories, and for all the subsequent, and often acrimonious disputations about their comparative values, there remains considerable doubt about the relevance of those theories to the practice of psychoanalytic psychotherapy. Anna Freud, in 1969 said, "[Theory] . . . has become the bugbear of the clinically oriented analyst who feels wholly divorced from it"; a skepticism still shared by many practitioners of the craft, who genuflect in the direction of their institutional canons—and then do whatever they think works (A. Freud, 1969, p. 386). Astute clinicians have always understood that they were, in Masud Khan's felicitous phrase, "the servants of the patient's process."[2] That is, therapy proceeded by our tapping into, and melding with, a mysterious flow, a conflux, which defies the linear explanations provided by metapsychologies that explain everything and understand nothing. To paraphrase Calasso (1994), myth brings repetition and soon the skeleton of the system emerges. The Sufis were wont to say, somewhat sarcastically, "No problem is too difficult for a theoretician." If this were really so, then any polished theoretician would be *ipso facto* an accomplished clinician; and that is clearly not the case. Talking knowledgeably about something is not at all the same as doing it.

I would like to explore, in greater detail, aspects of the therapeutic process which, I believe, operate in some realm not accessible to our ordinary linear concepts of cause and effect and not subject to our usual perceptions of time and space; e.g., intrapsychic/interpersonal, fantasy/reality, even present/past. I shall use several clinical examples to illustrate my point and offer some speculations as to its nature and uses.

188 Psychoanalytic theory and practice

To begin with, every psychoanalytic position consists of a metapsychology and a theory of therapy. The term, metapsychology, was introduced by Freud in his letters to Fleiss. It was an attempt to establish a grand psychology which would be equivalent to a metaphysics, or a philosophy.[3] Metapsychologies are essentially ontologies—Freudian, Object-relations, Self, Sullivanian, Kleinian—all present both a theory of human development and a philosophy of life (from Freud's "leiben and arbeiten" to Sullivan's examined life); i.e., what matters, how life should be lived. Gerson refers to Wrightsman as,

> [H]euristically identifying three categories of developmental theories: 1) early formation theories which stress the first few years of life; 2) stage theories which focus on the tasks germane to each stage of development; and 3) dialectical approaches, which chart a timeless struggle between fundamental polarities in personality structure.
>
> (Gerson, 1993; Wrightsman, 1988)

These developmental theories are explicitly tied to corresponding theories of pathogenesis and treatment.

Regardless of what analysts actually do in the seclusion of their offices —the praxis of therapy—the theory of therapy must appear to follow from the metapsychology, or there would be no political basis for the oppositional camps all claiming hegemony. A metapsychology without a claim to superior therapeutic relevance would be simply an intellectual curiosity. So, therapeutic efficacy is purported to follow the proper application of the metapsychology, either by propitious interpretation (which requires canonical correctness); or through an enactment in the transference—or some combination of the two (Meissner, 1991). If the theory is correct, then the way of conceptualizing clinical practice must work; otherwise we are wrong and they are right, and, after all, our very self-esteem and legitimacy lies in our clinical efficacy. Still, in spite of claims to theoretical coherence, and to superior clinical outcomes (totally unsubstantiated) one is left with the sneaking feeling that each metapsychology grasps only one aspect of experience, is perspectivistically constrained. Yet, how can one be eclectic, use them all, when they presumably do not share a clinical method or even a common concept of pathogenesis and cure?

The significant point is that metapsychologies are not Truths but simply worldviews, particular perspectives on experience held by particular therapists. They are not wrong, but they are not right, either. Nothing a metapsychology claims *can* be wrong and for anything a metapsychology says, the opposite position is equally true and valid.[4] This is why psycho-analysis fails to meet Popper's famous "falsifiability" requirement; that is, to be proven true, a thesis must be accessible to being proven untrue (Popper, 1962). It is not really an issue of truth: metapsychologies are adopted by therapists because there is a certain aesthetic "fit"—it *feels* right; and that fit depends on the personality of the therapist and his/her particular cultural context.[5] Fromm used to say, "In Mexico, everyone is a Catholic including the Protestants." In New York, a Kleinian may bear more resemblance to a New York Freudian than to an Argentinean Kleinian. Remember how Klein was for many years considered—in this country, if not in England—to be promulgating some bizarre fantasy about early childhood. Now, as cultural premises have changed, Klein's phantasmagorial constructions are quite comfortably entertained in this country, even by those who cannot endorse them.

Consider the context of object-relations and Self psychology. These are pre-Oedipal, two-person psychologies which see the patient as suffering from maternal deficits, being fixated as early developmental levels and requiring some restitutive function in the therapy. Freudian theory emphasizes a later developmental stage, the entrance of the Father, a three-person psychology, more agonistic and competitive, and with an outcome that emphasizes responsibility for one's one fantasies and participation. Sullivan is more concerned with stage-specific tasks, but essentially deals with the nuances of anxiety and interpersonal communication throughout life and tends to include all-important persons in the patient's life, including the vital chums of pre-adolescence and adolescence. Existential psychoanalysis deals with the big problems—life, meaning, death.

As the culture changes, a particular theory seems to fit *for the relevant age group.* So now, in a feminist-aware culture, Winnicott, Klein, and Kohut seem right, and, dare we say, politically correct. Indeed, one might quite successfully predict the popularity of a particular school of psychoanalytic thought by following other cultural indices of change; for example, the movies. Afficianados of the cinema would certainly recognize the changes over time in movie heroines, from the clinging dependent woman, to the helpmate who instead of cowering in the corner hits the villain over the head or shoots him in the heart with the approved FBI two-handed pistol hold, onto the present spate of malevolent sexual *fata*

190 Psychoanalytic theory and practice

morganas who lead dumb, trusting men to their deaths. "Cherchez la femme" as the detectives were wont to say. See where women stand and you will see where theory is going.[6]

Unfortunately matriarchy is not altogether benevolent, nor has it ever been.[7] The ancient, pre-olympian, matriarchal gods were nurturant but also terrifying, and modernity may still harbor the ancient myths. As men (and women) become more frightened of unleashed pre-Oedipal mother, we may see a return of both patriarchy and the concept of character—a patriarchal concept as opposed to personality (Levenson, 1993). I am not suggesting that this constitutes a step forward or back, since I do not believe that the process of change is straightforward; I am saying only that changes in metapsychological position will reflect the shifts in general culture. What seems patently "right" to us is right only because it resonates with what we already believe to be true.

So, I am saying the metapsychologies are worldviews, not absolute truths, that different perspectives at different times will appeal to analysts of different ages, sexes, orientations and culture. However, they will tend to see their choices, less as an aesthetic preference, than as a superordinate Truth, to be defended to the death. I believe that every position is correct, but insufficient. For every statement of canonical doctrine, the exact opposite is equally true in some other context. Where are we left? I would say that, regardless of doctrinal conviction, all good therapists circle through the entire gamut of human possibilities because the praxis—the very nature of therapy—insists. If the therapist resists, likely the patient will insist. Every metapsychology starts as an organizing principle and winds up as a countertransference! No sensible analyst sticks entirely to his canons, although to teach or write one must promote a viewpoint, or risk sounding "chaotic"—which, I shall suggest, may not be such a bad thing after all.

One of the great ironies of psychoanalysis is that therapists don't necessarily do in therapy what they advise in supervision. It is often illuminating to talk to one's colleagues and compare the experience of analysands and supervisees with the very same person. The austere and confronting supervisor may be a kindly, even seductive analyst; and the generous and benevolent supervisor may reveal, in the privacy of the therapeutic session, a not inconsiderable degree of intolerance and authoritarianism.

A metapsychology, therefore, is a way of stepping into the stream, it is not the stream. It is the way the therapist brings himself/herself to the encounter. Then the psychoanalytic process, a mysterious and fascinating flow, takes over. I have written about this before, but I feel I am just grasping the edge of some process that can only be dimly apperceived (Levenson, 1983). It has two major manifestations. First, there is the astonishing flow of consciousness—to use James's famous phrase—from the patient. There is a thread of continuity and purposefulness in what, at first inquiry, may seem like inchoate ramblings. Often, a continuous theme emerges from this flow of material. As every analyst learns, this is "free-association," the instrument, *par excellence*, of traditional psychoanalysis. Moreover, there is a continuity in the flow—over time—from session to session (not necessarily readily apparent to the therapist), but sometimes running well ahead of the therapist. There may be sudden changes in direction, the emergence of new themes, or return of themes long absent from the sessions. The patient may introduce topics before the therapist begins to think about them. For example, supervisees not infrequently report their surprise that a patient takes up at the very next session what the supervisee discovered in the prior supervisory session—providing some supervisors with an unwarranted reputation for prescience. Free-association is only one way of engaging the flow: a detailed inquiry may have the same effect, if it is not pragmatically oriented. That is, if the therapist uses the inquiry to loosely deconstruct the material, rather than accumulate data for a focused interpretation, one may discover the same spontaneous and unpredictable outflow of material from the patient (Levenson, 1986). I must emphasize that this is not, in any way, a coherent linear process with issues getting clearer and more focused as the flow expands. Any great clarity that emerges at this point is imposed arbitrarily by the desperate therapist trying to keep on top of what feels to be a runaway process.

Second, there is the absolutely overwhelming sense of iteration within a given session. By that I mean that the same patterning is played out, with harmonic variations, throughout the session from the opening gambit—as the patient walks through the door—through accounts of current events, historical references, dreams, associations on into the relationship between the therapist and patient, the transference *and* last but not least the often unwitting participation of the therapist—the countertransference. Looking back over a session, it is often possible to see—if one is looking for it—a most remarkable coherence of patterning, from the smallest event to the most panoramic overview. I would say that this coherence is powerfully present even in sessions when we cannot see it, but often, retrospective

192 Psychoanalytic theory and practice

looking for it can prove suddenly illuminating. In other words, this is not a rare occurrence limited to wonderful psychoanalytic sessions but the quotidian essence of therapy. Moreover, any brief excerpt of the session, say 5 minutes, contains in implicate order the entire session. That is, one can follow the flow of material over the entire session; or one could limit oneself to the brief excerpt and explicate that to cover the same material as the more extended session overview. Virtuoso clinical teachers have been known to extrapolate the entire therapy, past to future, from 5 or 10 minutes of a single session.

So, along the dimension of vertical time (from session to session) and across the dimension of horizontal time (within a given session) there is a remarkable reiteration of theme, both in what is said and what is done. It is all of a piece. And, as this seamless coherence emerges in the therapy it comes to inhabit not only the therapist qua therapist, but the therapist's life outside of his or her analytic role. I must re-emphasize that this strange phenomenon is not usually accompanied by a flash of insight. It is not a case of, "Ah-hah, now I understand what it all means." Rather, it is a matter of recognizing that there is a striking coherence underlying the apparent chaos; *even* if one is *not* at all clear what it means. Let me give you two clinical examples, one simple, the other more elaborate.

This is a man in his forties, an expansive rather self-congratulatory person who thinks of himself as a ladies' man. He brings the therapist, a quite attractive woman about his age, a long, rambling dream that virtually fills the entire session. The dream begins at the Metropolitan museum, which is entirely filled with his paintings! She leaves the session feeling overwhelmed. He calls her 2 days later, gets her voice mail and the tape says, "If this is an emergency—push 2." So he does and gets through to her immediately. He then begins a vague and discursive discussion of something not remotely an emergency. She is annoyed, but thinking she may be missing something, she listens politely for a while and then offers him an extra session that he enthusiastically takes and during which he has nothing particular of interest to say—which is often the way of extra sessions.

I don't wish to go into details or explore dynamics. I simply want to illustrate how every interaction I've presented is on exactly the same theme—namely, his having to fill all the possible space with himself. Never mind why! I can hear everyone's thoughts—"Why does he do that? What does it mean? How can it be presented to him or enacted with him *in order to make a difference?*" Certainly one can come up with a variety of rational explanations of what this might all mean—his grandiosity, boundary diffusion problems, and so forth. I would prefer to focus on the phenom-enon of reiteration, not the specific dynamics of this case.

My second example is a woman in her late sixties whom I have been seeing on a once-weekly basis with a presenting complaint of inability to really enjoy her life, which is substantively pretty good. As in the famous quote from St. Luke, for her, "The salt has lost its savor." Partly, I present her to suggest that this remarkable coherence is not exclusive to intensive psychoanalytic therapy but occurs in even a low-frequency treatment. If one does not hear it, then perhaps one is too busy making sense of the data.

She begins a session, about a year into the treatment, by entering the room cordially and telling me a dream.

> She is in some "lovely" place with other people. She is bringing a "lovely" tray of food she has prepared for "Martha" her mentor/teacher in college. Martha says she has to leave. My patient is severely disappointed. "Martha won't eat the lovely meal I've prepared for her." All the people leave. She is left entirely alone, feeling deserted and very forlorn.

Associations? None! Detailed inquiry into Martha established her role as mentor in college. Hasn't seen her since. Is she alive? She doesn't know. The place, the food, offer no insights. It is like pulling teeth. For some reason, I have an association. It felt to me like she might be dealing with the death of someone. "Oh yes," she says, "The anniversary of my mother's death is tomorrow." Then, "Oh, my mother's name was Martha, too." She then associates to a repeated childhood occurrence when she would not eat her breakfast. She had been several months premature and has always been very small and thin. At any rate, she would be told she'd have to sit at the table until she finished her breakfast. Mother, father, siblings would leave and she would sit there, unyielding. Finally the servant, an amiable Irish woman, would dump the breakfast and promise not to tell. She denies ever having had an eating disorder but she is very thin.

I am feeling rather good about myself. Extracting associations to the dream from her was very difficult. My association seemed to open the door to her connecting the dream with her mother and then to a childhood time with an eating event that seemed extremely relevant. Certainly, we were talking about feeding, being fed, and refusing to be fed. About 10 minutes later, as the session is about to end, she tells me, quite cheerfully, she is going to have to stop treatment—she'll come one more time—she can't afford it any longer; one has to make choices, after all; and, besides she's leaving next week for a 2-week trip to Europe! This trip was never mentioned before. As you can imagine, I was flabbergasted. She leaves. I think it over and begin to laugh. Hoist on my own petard! Her leaving was a hilarious re-enactment of the session. All the trouble I went to cooking up those formulations and *she won't eat*! The metaphor (literally, to carry over) is her refusal to eat what has been prepared for her or the other person's refusal to eat what she has lovingly prepared. It is a symmetrical presentation—viewed from both sides—of what might be called an orality problem or an issue of power and control.

It is a classical instance of acting-out (or acting-in). What is not analyzed will be enacted. Her final move broke the frame of the therapy, but my failure to notice and respond to her very irritating refusal to participate in examining the dream was, I believe, my countertransference. I should really have stopped at that point and focused on her not telling me the two blatantly obvious clues to the dream (the date of her mother's death and the shared name). I should also have examined my own experience. Why was I so jovial about it—"Ho, ho, that's something that you forgot to tell me. Your mother had the same name." For some reason, it all seemed to me terribly funny. I felt neither frustrated nor disappointed; nor, in the language of her dream, "deserted and forlorn"—one might well ask why not.

She returned for her last session. She sits down and says, "I have another dream." I said, "What's the point of talking about your dream if you're stopping. Why bring in a dream?" Then I reviewed the session with her, the sequences and connections. I also told her my experience—that I'd been left with my tongue hanging out.[8] My experience was like her experience in the dream. Since I felt under the sword, I did attempt a more formal explication of the issues involved and suggested to her that that's what her presenting complaint was about; namely, that she cannot be fed or feed happily; that her low grade depression and dissatisfaction has to do with her inability to sup fully, and so forth. The time came for her to leave and, in truth, I was feeling totally comfortable. I felt I'd done my job, at least given it my best shot. She said, "I'd like to see you again in 2 weeks when

I return." I said, "Do you want to call me when you come back?" She wanted to make an appointment now and so we kept her old hour and the therapy continued.[9]

There are, of course, many other considerations. Perhaps if I'd listened to the new dream, she would have arrived at an insight without my pushing. On the other hand, I wasn't about to cook another meal for such an ingrate. Dynamics may refer to orality, depression, power, autonomy—you name it. As you can see, once the field is delineated, virtually all metapsychological formulations apply perfectly, even if they are contradictory or exclusive. Any analyst, of any canonical bent, listening to this presentation, could come up with an explanatory set, a different way of engaging the issue, and, a critique that includes my countertransference, what I missed and how I might have better done it. But, and it is a very big but, one must *hear* the melody with all its variations; and there is a great deal of question, in my mind, whether it is one's coherent explanation of the melody, or one's recognition of it and of one's own participation in it which makes the difference.

I do not mean to suggest that this brief interaction resolved the patient's problem—that after it, she was collaborative and animated. She may very well quit therapy next week. Clinical vignettes, in the literature, tend toward that marvelous clarity: she did this, I said that *and then* she improved remarkably—to wit, I identified the issue, applied my theory and, voila! Regrettably, this has not often been my experience. Rather, I find I become embroiled in a series of these interactions, never clearly leading anywhere (although I can't help wishing they would) and often abruptly changing direction and content. When improvement occurs in a patient, it may creep in almost before one notices it, or it may be sudden and dramatic. It may even take place after the therapy is over. But what impels the change is never entirely clear to me; and it hardly ever seems to proceed in a clear-cut fashion from something I've said or done. I do not mean to imply that I have done nothing or that, Heaven forbid, my patients do not improve. I am merely suggesting that the relationship between cause and effect is very complicated and that small efforts may produce immense changes and immense efforts, small or even negative effects. If the primary therapeutic activity is facilitating this flow, then too much understanding, too much effort at linear clarifying of the process, will block its appearance. If the process is rolling along, so to speak, with the therapist traveling on the crest of the wave; then, I suspect, small interventions—interpretive or

196 Psychoanalytic theory and practice

enactments—may make a tremendous difference. It is a bit like trying to push a car with its brakes on and pushing one that is already rolling.

I presented this material to show how powerful and coercive this ineluctable process is. Never mind for the moment, what it all means. How does it happen? How does a patient come in with a dream, treat the dream like the dream, associate to the dream like the dream, react to me like the dream, call out a counter-response like the dream and have, in an overview of her life, a problem that the dream illustrates—all within one session! If we get interested in the meanings, how our metapsychologies explain the data, we miss the miracle that it takes place at all. We become like those dreadful tourists who think everything looks like home—the Taj Mahal is like the mosque on 97th street: Istanbul looks just like Prospect Park.

Assuming that you will agree with me that something interesting is going on, what does it have to do with treatment? Is it the *vis à tergo* of treatment? If patients don't get better because of the mutative impact of our metapsychologies, then we must suspect that improvement comes out of the patient's process. As in the physician's classic admonition, we do not heal—the patient heals himself/herself; we only assist. I do believe that it is indeed the case and, were one to accept that, it may be seen that our differences in approach, our institutional and political camps, are less substantive than we believe. The implication would be that this process, this flow, carries the therapist out of his own position and ultimately into every conceivable perspective of engagement with the patient. When our metapsychologies become reified (when we hear everything the same way) and thus countertransferential, the patient acts out or dreams or does something to awaken us to the need for a shift in our mode of interaction. If the therapist will not permit, one of two things happen: either the therapy fails and becomes an indoctrination; or the patient finds other people in his/her world to play surrogate analyst, splits the transference and—if we're lucky—works it out outside of our bailiwick and awareness. I believe this happens far more frequently than we recognize. Most analyses have surrogate analysts lurking somewhere on the fringe, providing a symmetry to the process. If we are the mother, there may be out there a father; and, of course, the reverse is also true. Clara Thompson told me, in my supervision with her, to always look for my döppleganger, the Other, out there somewhere who could effectively sabotage or complete the therapy for me.

If one were to consider this process as essential to therapy, how does it work? The most obvious possibility is that its mode of action is through expanded awareness, both in the therapist and in the patient; who not only sees much more about his/her being in the world, but also learns to trust his/her own perceptions, to accord them relevance, and to follow where they lead. This may be what cure is. As Sullivan said, if you have a good grasp of what's happening you don't get into too much psychological difficulty (it can however, constitute a considerable social disadvantage).

A second possibility might be that attention to this phenomenon leads to a changed enactment between patient and therapist—a adumbrated version of the Dreaded Corrective Emotional Experience (Alexander and French, 1946). That might entail a holding milieu; a restoration of empathy and warmth; a chance to deal with problems of competition and envy, hostility and rage; a chance to learn new ways of coping with real events by coming up against another person who cannot be totally intimidated into playing the patient's reciprocal role; or perhaps by seeing the therapist successfully deal with an interaction that the patient had always felt was unresolvable—in this sense a variety of parallel process or mirroring. You will note that I have ranged over the metapsychological spectrum and some of these explanations are mutually exclusive. But the explanation might not matter if the process is taking place.

A third possibility is that its effectiveness has something to do with the nature of language. Again, eschewing the esoterics of semiotics, one might simply say that maybe patients never believe anything that is said.[10] Maybe *nobody* believes anything that is said. Allow me to clarify this apparently paranoid position. Communication always involves a spoken message and a piece of behavior, a nonverbal metacommunication that is in phase with the spoken message and is a message about the message. These two dimensions of communication are usually seamless in adults, but can be strikingly apparent in children. When one talks to a child, he or she monitors very closely what goes with the speech—facial expressions, actions, body posture. That is how they learn about teasing, irony, sarcasm; modes in which there is a marked discrepancy between words and deeds. When Auntie leans over and gushes "Kiss your dear Auntie" and the child recoils, it is reading the metacommunication, the hovering overly-close presentation, the rigid smile and the glittering eyes. Dogs are actually pretty good too at sniffing out, so to speak, bogus affability and responding accordingly.

Language, it has been said, is our instrument for controlling our inter-actions with others; and to maintain autonomy, the listener must match the speech against the nonverbal cues. It may be that patients are constantly measuring the correlation of what is said about their past, their present, their dreams and fantasies and what you *do* with them in the explication of those formulations. They observe what is done with what is said. So, my patient is interested to hear what I have to say about the dream, but what *I* do when she does to me what they did to her and what she did and does to them—this may be of the essence. So, one might say the patient is matching speech against experience, making patterns and looking for a correlation. Since it is often too dangerous to consciously recognize the integrated message because it threatens loss of the necessary caretaker, this extensive search for correlation often goes on out of awareness, preconsciously or in Sullivan's term, "inattended" (Sullivan, 1953).

None of these explanations, however, touch on the intrinsic mystery of the process. They are far too pragmatic and, as far as I can ascertain, do not deal with the remarkable thematic iteration. A far more esoteric explanation of why this process might be crucial would lead us into the magic forest of Chaos theory, with its fractals, strange attractors, mathematical recursions (as in Mandelbrot equations), and computer logic.[11]

It may seem terribly fanciful to refer to an abstruse mathematical theory for psychoanalytic explanation, but there are certain aspects of Chaos theory that provide a paradigmatic basis for understanding some of the odd phenomena I have been attempting to describe. In brief, Chaos theory describes the behavior of nonlinear dynamic systems. Complex systems do not proceed methodically from A to Z. At some point in the expected progression, something goes awry and disorder occurs. If this disorder or "noise" is minor it is often disregarded. If it is major, the entire system goes awry. The example most often used is weather reporting that, beyond a day or so, is totally unreliable because of the large number of unpredictable factors, "noise," entering the calculations. From turbulence in fluid dynamics, to unpredictable shifts in medical epidemiology, to aberrant heart rhythms, chaos occurs in large nonlinear systems in unexpected ways. The genius of Chaos theory was to invert the order of interest and to focus on the disorder, rather than considering it as simply an interference with the prevailing orderly development. The mathematics of chaos was, of course, almost unbelievably recondite and consequently of interest to hardly anyone—until the development of the home computer. With even a simple Macintosh, it became possible to readily convert the numbers to pictures, to create what is called "phase space." Each position of the total system in time could be represented by a dot, and over time, these dots created consistent patterns of great coherence and beauty. In other words, when viewed pictorially, chaos had a great hidden order; most strikingly, it created consistent patterns, fractals, which appeared on different scales at the same time. From micro-scale to the most macro-scale, these patterns were the same, yet, as in snowflakes, minor variations could cause unique changes. All snowflakes look the same and yet, all snowflakes, examined through a glass, are different. As Hofstadter put it, "[T]here is an infinite regress of detail, a never-ending nesting of pattern within pattern" (Hofstadter, 1985, p. 384).

Chaos theory has been applied to virtually every nonlinear system from the weather to brain physiology and psychology (Bütz, 1992; Mandell, 1985).[12] Investigators in artificial intelligence have begun to apply the formalisms of Chaos theory and to consider it as a paradigm for actual mental functioning. To quote Gleick,

> Their fractal structure offered the kind of infinitely self-referential quality that seems central to the mind's ability to bloom with ideas, decisions, emotions, and all the other artifacts of consciousness. With or without chaos, serious cognitive scientists can no longer model the mind as a static structure. They recognize a hierarchy of scales, from neuron upward, providing an opportunity for the interplay of microscale and macroscale so characteristic of fluid turbulence and other complex dynamical processes (1987, p. 299).

Suffice it to say, that from this viewpoint, the process defines its own terms for change. In other words, one keeps expanding the field and at some point it overloads and shifts. The nature and prerequisites for the shift are never entirely clear; but, as I said, small inputs can have major consequences.

In Chaos theory, they say that the butterfly flapping its wings in China may change the weather in New York (Gleick, 1987, pp. 20–23). Silly? Well a goose defecating into a pond in Beijing, where its excreta is eaten by a hog, *does* cause the influenza we see every following winter in New York. That's why it is called swine influenza.

For an engagingly trivial instance of our "butterfly effect," I've always been astonished by how wonderfully helpful patients often find totally banal remarks from the therapist; as, "I never promised you a rose garden," or, "Rome wasn't built in a day." One hears these funny reports from therapists who ask a patient, after 9 years of treatment, what was it that seemed to make the difference and are told that, "Well, about 3 years into the treatment you said, 'Don't wish your life away'." What ever became of all the painfully elaborated wonderful insights?

So minor or oblique interactions can have major and unpredictable consequences and the therapist, instead of striving for effect, need only attend to the process. That is to say, perhaps the therapist need only stick to his/her last, follow the flow and disavow any intentions of curing or helping the patient. After a certain amount of chaos, change may abruptly appear. And, as we have all observed, it does not necessarily follow from any of our lapidary interpretations. Often it is precipitated by some casual outside occurrence. Consider the therapist who, without much success, has been trying to bring a patient into touch with her dissociated anger. As she leaves the session, crossing the street, a truck driver yells, "Hey lady, what are you so mad about?"—and she has an epiphany!

The therapeutic method, according to this premise, is deceptively simple; one need only stick closely to the free-associative or detailed inquiry process. That is, rather than reaching for mutative interpretations or interactions, one eschews the overview, the Big Picture, and sticks to expanding details, exploring the context of every event reported by the patient or occurring in the relationship between patient and therapist. The therapist must suspend understanding and pursue the details, the "particulars." The "output" of each inquiry is fed back in and becomes the "input" of the next inquiry—precisely the process used in computer modeling of fractals (Spruiell, 1993, p. 21). If one can accept the discipline of not knowing, an expanding sense of reiterating pattern begins to emerge, to disappear and re-emerge and the feeling of being carried along by a powerful subsurface process, as I described it earlier, takes hold.

Is this therapeutic? It feels so but I really can't know if any of this is truly relevant or just playing with metaphors. We don't know much about the essence of mind and perhaps as Hofstadter says, "Making variations on a theme is really the crux of creativity" (Hofstadter, 1985, p. 233). Also, it seems so dramatically similar to the holographic model of mentation offered by Pribram, who was intrigued by similar phenomena of scaling and the iteration of part and whole (Pribram, 1971). Again, I am making a delineation between a description of the process of transformational elaborations that is, I believe, the absolute core of therapy and the problem of why it works, which is considerably more obscure. I can only say that, in reading about Chaos theory, I had the same shock of recognition reported by mathematicians and other scientists—that is, that the appearance of reiterative themes extending over and over in every scale, making a landscape of recognizable behavior, seemed to suggest a fractal component to psychoanalytic data; much as in fractal built up coastlines where every level of macro- and micro-magnification shows the same configuration.[13]

But psychoanalysts abhor unclarity. In psychoanalysis, as in any other historically rooted process, one might say—facetiously, of course since this is a now a discredited notion—that ontogeny recapitulates phylogeny; that is, every poor candidate must recapitulate the history of the field in his or her personal gestation. We teach it that way—first Freud and then everything since. We would not dare to say, "Let's start with what we do now. Forget the past." Nor am I even faintly suggesting that we should. But historicity has its drawbacks. Look at the present retrograde fascination with the idea that early traumatic experience accounts for much of adult psychopathology. It is of course given the usual rhetorical twist, or, as they say these days, "spin." First one says, "Oh no, that's only true of people with post-traumatic syndrome—people to whom something terrible was really done." What are the symptoms of post-traumatic syndrome? Virtually every manifestation we used to think defined anxiety neurosis. Ergo, a very large proportion of our patients may be reclassified and the search for the forgotten trauma becomes paramount.[14]

Why is that so appealing? Because like Strachey's mutative interpretation, it promises to return us to the lost paradise of analytic clarity which never was (Strachey, 1934). Well, you can take the analyst away from the source of the belief in mutative interpretation, but it's a good deal more difficult to take the belief out of the analyst. I suspect that, buried deep in every therapist, is a dogged atavistic wish, if not belief, that if we can only *grasp* the patient, understand his/her problems and communicate clearly, he or she will get better and we will know what it is we do when we do what we do.[15]

To summarize:

1. Every therapist must have a metapsychology, even if it is unacknowledged, because a metapsychology is nothing more than an institutionally endorsed worldview, and it is not possible to be without a personal perspective.

2. No metapsychology is sufficient in itself. Every metapsychology excludes or minimizes the truths of the others. For every truth of a metapsychology, the opposite is equally true. As Handelman pointed out, psychoanalysis belongs more to the Rabbinical tradition than Freud's beloved Greek one. Aristotle's rule of the excluded middle, that a thing must either be A or not-A does not apply. Things can be true and not true simultaneously (Handleman, 1982). If psychoanalysts wish to be truly scientific, then they must accept confusion, impasse, dissent, competing paradigms, imperfect understanding—ironically, all the accoutrements of contemporary science. It would be immensely facilitating if analysts did not act as though their position marked a clear advance on the road to therapeutic perfection. No one else believes any longer in a view of science as building a tower to the Heavens.[16]

3. All good therapists must ultimately desert their canonical viewpoints and cover the field, following where the patient leads.

4. Therapy proceeds through the interaction of the patient and therapist. Interactions need not be directly focused on the analyst. When patients talk about their lives, they are talking *to you* about their lives and that constitutes an interaction and a relationship. By not reifying the patient's productions as a manifestation of one's particular metapsychology, but, rather, by pursuing the idiosyncratic detail—that which makes the patient's experience uniquely his/her own—one extends the field of awareness and the recurrent, resonating, iterative pattern begins to emerge.

5. Thus the therapist facilitates, and becomes part of, a process that is very difficult to grasp, but whose manifestations appear in the coherence of the patient's flow of consciousness which is an internal process and the extraordinary thematic consistency which appears in the therapist/patient relationship which is an external interactional dimension of the field, as I tried to demonstrate in the clinical examples. Anyone can easily explain what happened in the case extracts I offered. Of course, all the explanations will not be the same. But I cannot believe that the explanation is the process. Why does it take the form it does? Why is there such remarkable coherence and thematic consistency? Why does all the material of a session seem to be harmonic variations on a theme? Perhaps one need not know, but it seems to me we could be in danger of confusing the map of our premises with the territory of the patient's mental realm.

6. I've offered a number of possible explanatory sets, somewhat in the way of a coda. One need not understand something to experience it. I suspect, that in our contesting over metapsychologies, we are missing the point; and that shifting our attention to the mysteries of the process may be infinitely more rewarding than being theoretically correct, and may offer the key to a more effective, albeit disordered, therapeutic intervention.

Notes

1. This chapter first appeared in 1994 in *Contemporary Psychoanalysis*, 30(1):5–24.
2. Quoted in Milner, 1969, p. xxxi.
3. See Laplanche and Pontalis for Freud's development of the concept (Laplanche and Pontalis, 1973).
4. Analysts have hauled up the principle of complementarity to explain this incompatibility. But as Eagle points out, in physics it is two explanations for the same phenomenon; while in psychoanalysis it is two explanations for two entirely different emergent sets of data—a totally different issue (Eagle, 1987).
5. See Weinberg (1993) for the peculiar aesthetics of theory-making in pure science.
6. See review essay by Robert Benton (1993) on feminist critiques of women in the movies.
7. One must remember that The Goddess dwelt in *patriarchal* societies. There is no convincing evidence that matriarchal cultures ever existed.
8. The choice of oral imagery is not out of awareness. This was a method I picked up from Milton Erickson's crypto-hypnotic technique. It serves the same purpose—but far better, in my view—then formally interpreting her refusing my offering of food (Zeig, 1982 p. 122).
9. I do not, by the way, charge for vacations as long as I have notice. So I would not have given her any difficulty about going away.
10. For a review of semiotic possibilities in psychoanalysis I refer you to (Levenson, 1983).
11. If you'd like to bite into that magic mushroom, I'd recommend Hofstadter's playful book (Hofstadter, 1985) and Glcick's magisterial overview of Chaos theory (Gleick, 1987).
12. In the process of revising this article for publication, I came across Spruiell's article that expands, with far better detail and lucidity that I can muster, the essence of Chaos theory. What is lacking is a sense of the clinical application of the theory other than as an "Inspirational Metaphor" (Spruiell, 1993).
13. In 1976, in a paper on holography and psychoanalytic memory, I made much the same observation. In a hologram, the smallest fragment of the plate when projected shows the same picture as the intact plate. There is no fragmentation,

204 Psychoanalytic theory and practice

only detail is lost (Levenson, 1976). Or, see Spruiell's fascinating and barely believable description of topological play with a pizza that demonstrates much the same strange irregularities (Spruiell, 1993, p. 24).

14. See Loftus for a review of memories of molestation (Loftus, 1993).
15. There is a particularly eloquent Lacanian presentation of the pitfalls of goal-directed activity in Thompson (1985).
16. For a review of contemporary mind science, see Gardner (1985).

References

Alexander, F. and French, T.M. (1946). *Psychoanalytic Therapy: Principles and Applications*. New York: Ronald Press.

Benton, R. (1993). Femmes Fatales. *Psychoanalytic Books: A Quarterly Journal of Review*, 4:370–373.

Bütz, M.R. (1992). The fractal nature of the development of the self. *Psychological Reports*, 71(3 Supplement):1043–1063.

Calasso, R. (1994). *The Marriage of Cadmus and Harmony*. New York: Vintage: Reprint edition (p. 136).

Eagle, N.M. (1987). *Recent Developments in Psychoanalysis*. Cambridge, MA: Harvard University Press.

Freud, A. (1969). *Difficulties in the Path of Psychoanalysis*. New York: International Universities Press.

Gardner, H. (1985). *The Mind's New Science*. New York: Basic Books.

Gerson, M.J. (1993). Sullivan's self-in-development: Family context and patterning. *Contemporary Psychoanalysis*, 29(2):197–217.

Gleick, J. (1987). *Chaos: Making a New Science*. New York: Viking Press.

Handleman, S. (1982). *The Slayers of Moses: The Emergence of Rabbinic Interpretation in Modern Literary Theory*. Albany, NY: State University of New York.

Hofstadter, D. (1985). *Metamagical Themes: Questing for the Essence of Mind and Pattern*. New York: Basic Books.

Laplanche, J. and Pontalis, J.B. (1973). *The Language of Psychoanalysis* (D. Nicholson-Smith, Trans.). New York: W.W. Norton.

Levenson, E. (1976). A holographic model of psychoanalytic change. *Contemporary Psychoanalysis*, 12(1):1–20.

Levenson, E.A. (1983). *The Ambiguity of Change: An Inquiry into the Nature of Psychoanalytic Reality*. New York: Basic Books.

Levenson, E.A. (1988). The pursuit of the particular. *Contemporary Psychoanalysis*, 24(1):1–16.

Levenson, E.A. (1993). Character, personality and the politics of change. In J. Fiscalini and A. Grey, (Eds.), *Narcissism and the Interpersonal Self*. New York: Columbia University Press, pp. 130–43.

Loftus, E.F. (1993). The reality of repressed memories. *American Psychologist*, 48(5):518–537.

Mandell, A. J. (1985). From molecular biological simplification to more realistic central nervous system dynamics: An opinion. In J. O. Cavenar (Ed.), *Psychiatry: Psychobiological Foundations of Clinical Psychiatry*. New York: Lippincott.

Meissner, W.W. (1991). *What Is Effective in Psychoanalytic Therapy*. Northvale, NJ: Jacob Aronson.

Milner, M. (1969). *The Hands of the Living God*. New York: International Universities Press.

Popper, K.R. (1962). *Conjectures and Refutations*. New York: Basic Books.

Pribram, K. (1971). *Languages of the Brain*. Englewood Cliffs, NJ: Prentice-Hall.

Spruiell, V. (1993). Deterministic chaos and the sciences of complexity: Psychoanalysis in the midst of a general scientific revolution. *Journal of the American Psychoanalytic Association*, 41(1):3–44.

Strachey, J. (1934). The nature of the therapeutic action of psychoanalysis. *Journal of the American Psychoanalytic Association*, 2:567–594.

Sullivan, H.S. (1953). *The Interpersonal Theory of Psychiatry*. New York: W.W. Norton.

Thompson, M.G. (1985). *The Death of Desire: A Study in Psychopathology*. New York: New York University Press.

Weinberg, S. (1993). *Dreams of a Final Theory*. New York: Pantheon Books.

Wrightsman, L.S. (1988). *Personality Development in Adulthood*. Newbury Park, CA: Sage Publications.

Zeig, K.J. (Ed.) (1982). *Ericksonian Approaches to Hypnosis and Psychotherapy*. New York: Brunner/Mazel.

Chapter 17

The politics of interpretation[1]

There is a cautionary Sufi tale that captures the essence of this presentation.

> A conventionally minded dervish . . . is walking alongside a lake when he hears someone singing a dervish incantation. But he has the sequences all wrong. Since dervish incantations, properly invoked, could have magical effects, he felt he should correct the singer who seemed to be on a small island in the middle of the lake. So, he hired a rowboat, went to the island where he found a hermit, in a reed hut. The hermit was very grateful for the corrections. The dervish returned to his boat and as he is crossing the water, he hears the hermit loudly singing—and making the same mistake. The dervish thought sadly of the perversity of mankind and continued to row towards the shore. Suddenly, he saw a strange sight. The hermit was running across the water, calling out in despair, "Wait, wait, I have forgotten the proper order!"
>
> (Shah, 1970)

This tale, typically Sufi in not taking itself too seriously, illustrates how the disciple may be devoted to a lifetime study of correct rituals, in the hope of achieving miracles, whereas the simple (in Sufi terms, the "idiot") hermit achieves a miracle without even knowing he has, without being interested in the achievement, and without losing his sincere and humble conviction that he doesn't know anything worth knowing.

How did "getting the rituals (read 'interpretations') right" take on such power in psychoanalysis? Since the earliest days of psychoanalysis, there has been a huge gap between theory—metapsychology—and the practice of psychoanalysis. Of course, this discrepancy is true of any activity that involves a skill. There is always a gap between practicing an activity and talking about it, as any skier, tennis player, or violinist can attest. Theory is usually complex and elaborate, whereas the rules of activity are often simple, deceptively so, and must be learned over and over again, each time "grasped" at a different level of comprehension. "Ah, so *that's* what is meant by . . ." As the Zen people put it, the last thing you learn is the first! This kind of understanding, almost proprioceptive in its body sense, is obviously quite different from theoretical comprehension.

As the dislocation between praxis and theory widens, the metapsychological elaborations become overwhelming. We are currently deluged with fancies of postmodernism, deconstruction, perspectivistic narrative, social constructivism, hermeneutics, hard science, hermeneutic science. Derrida, Gadamer, Habermas, Grünbaum, Ricoeur, Eco—all names from hermeneutics, philosophy of science, semiotics—are the current pundits of theory. And yet, a very large percentage of practicing psychoanalysts couldn't care less about it all. As early as 1969, Anna Freud said that theory "has become the bugbear of the clinically oriented analyst who feels wholly divorced from it" (A. Freud, 1969, p. 49). In 1972, Masud Khan said that "psychoanalysis is facing a crisis from within . . . there is an irrefutable disparity between its theories and its clinical practices" (Kahn, 1972 p. 383). Analysts tend to "wing it" in therapy, and then to use metapsychology as a private language, a guild identification that locates them, authenticates them with their colleagues, and makes it possible to get published by their guild journals, which—at least until recently—operated with a political selectivity that *Pravda* might have envied.[2]

So-called clinical theory, as contrasted to praxis (a distinction similar to Ehrenberg's "clinical theory and theory of therapeutic action") is really the application of metapsychology through interpretation (Ehrenberg, 1992). Its therapeutic validity is taken largely on faith. So, interpretation is an explanation that is supposed to have instrumental impact; it is supposed to work, and it is supposed to work because it is correct. If one thinks that I am beating a dead horse (I shall elaborate later, using some clinical examples), there remains, among some analysts, a very powerful residual faith in the power of interpretation. "It is a truism to say that interpretations are the stuff of clinical psychoanalysis. In general, all the standard tools of clinical psychoanalysis work by providing explanations of things not previously understood" (Brook, 1995); or "Psychoanalysis

208 Psychoanalytic theory and practice

can be characterized as a search of the unknown, as the revealing and interpreting of unknown, unconscious implications" (Bouchard, 1995).[3] Implicit is this belief that the analyst must be, as Lacan ironically put it, "The Subject-Who-Knows." So, the analyst listens and then formulates his or her understanding, with the hope that a "better"—"better" as "truer" or, in a more current hermeneutic variant, as more coherent—narrative will make a difference. I once heard Hannah Segal, at a panel on which I participated, report on a schizophrenic boy she cured—overnight—with one deep Kleinian interpretation! Why should pointing something out to someone make a difference—even if it were true? Why should it work in the analytic chambers when we all know, from personal experience, that it doesn't work in real life? This faith in interpretation qua epiphany has been called the "Rumpelstiltskin fallacy." Rumpelstiltskin was, you will remember, the evil dwarf who threatened to disrupt the wedding unless his name be discovered. When it was, he exploded (I suppose, these days, he'd have "deconstructed"). There are more contemporary versions of the Rumpelstiltskin fallacy, as I shall elaborate later. But, to my mind, any effort to invoke a sudden epiphany misses the essence of psychoanalytic inquiry, namely, the exploration of the remarkably tenacious resistance of neurotic systems to being changed, and their capacity to transmogrify the therapist from being part of the cure to being part of the problem—in a word, the old standby, the sine qua non of psychoanalysis, resistance and transference.

In Freud's seminal *Studies on Hysteria* (1895), the word "interpretation" does not yet appear. Indeed, it did not appear until 1911. Even then, Freud's use of "deutung" translates more accurately as "explanation" than as "interpretation" (Laplanche and Pontalis, 1973, pp. 227–228). How did emphasis come to shift from Freud's earliest, necessarily naive interest in praxis to metapsychology? I would claim that Freud started with an interest in the phenomenology of consciousness as it emerged from his work with hysteria and hypnosis. Metapsychology developed out of his need to explain unconsciousness—how hypnosis worked, and why a similar process of unawareness should occur in neurosis—and finally became reified and entrenched as an issue of social and political cohesiveness. It was also a scientific imperative. If one wishes to be "scientific," patients must be understood to be operating in classifiable and therefore predictable ways, because science does not deal with singularities (at least, not in Freud's time). Analysts continue to defend these particular metapsychologies, because these loci of theory suit their Zeitgeist—they "feel" right—and because they have organizational and political implications.

Anyone who believes that we have left behind the bad old days of cutthroat political battling for a more ecumenical and benign convocation is missing the boat. The same rancorous disputes still go on; but the power is far more masked under the guise of "agreeing to disagree" about metapsychological issues. The issue of clinical relevance is now muted. We have decided to be "postmodern" about it all. Why should I assume that my take on the clinical field is better or more skilled than your take? Postmodernism makes for a strangely numbing kind of ecumenism. It reminds me of a refreshingly retro *New Yorker* cartoon. Saint Peter is looking down on this very upset guy who clearly isn't getting in. Saint Peter says, "I'm sorry. You picked the wrong religion and that's that!"

The historical relationship between hypnosis and consciousness warrants some slight elaboration. The history of hypnotism began with Mesmer in the eighteenth century.[4] Mesmer achieved his results through what he called "animal magnetism." (This is not a reference, as in my time, to Clark Gable's charms, but to "animus"—spirit—a postulated magnetic fluid not unlike Newton's "ether" or, for that matter, Reich's orgone energy.) His subjects were an extremely talented group of women hysterics, the usual flamboyant bunch of groupies who, in a later manifestation, were to entertain Charcot's distinguished visitors.[5]

Mesmer fell into disrepute in his medical community because of his theatricality and charlatanism, and in 1778, following an erotic response (to which he succumbed) from an aptly named Ms. Paradis, he was obliged to flee Vienna for Paris, pursued by her irate Daddy, sword in hand. Once again, his antics became the subject of scandal. In 1785, a commission, which included Lavoisier, the founder of modern chemistry, our very own Ben Franklin, and Dr. Guillotin (who, like Freud, eventually had his head handed to him by his own invention) dismissed "animal magnetism" and attributed Mesmer's effects to imagination, the placebo effect, rather than to an invisible magnetic fluid. Still, animal magnetism continued to thrive in salons all over Europe. But by 1840, James Braid, an English physician, observed that subjects could be somnambulatized or mesmerized simply by staring fixedly at an object. This he attributed to "nervous sleep," which he named "hypnotism," thus dealing a death blow to the pseudoscientific animal magnetism theory and to mesmerism and somnambulism.

Unfortunately, his fascination with phrenology led to *his* disrepute. More respectable contemporaries of Braid—Benjamin Carpenter and Thomas Laycock—saw that Braid's "hypnosis" really threw light on what was then called the "reflex" functions of the brain; that is, those functions that operate out of conscious awareness. Cerebral functioning was considered to be entirely conscious. Only spinal cord function was reflexive, that is, out of consciousness. To quote Marshall Hall, a prominent neurophysiologist of the time, "The cerebrum is the organ of the mind. All its functions . . . imply consciousness." "Unconscious mind" was deemed to be an oxymoron. Carpenter's radical concept was to call for unconscious cerebration, "reflexive" mentation—a very radical concept for its time.

So there had been more than a century of interest in hypnotic phenomena before Freud's time. Moreover, in Vienna and Paris, during the 10 years prior to his *Studies on Hysteria*, a number of Freud's contemporaries were treating hysterical patients with hypnosis, including the highly competitive schools of Janet, Bernheim, and Charcot.[6] Indeed, Freud made the German translation of two of Bernheim's books and consulted with him briefly. Freud, as we all know, studied more extensively with Charcot in Paris, in the mid-1880s. Charcot was working with hypnosis in the treatment of hysterics, who he considered to be suffering a hysterical "diathesis," that is, a constitutional weakness or predisposition to a specific disease.

It was at Charcot's Sâlpetrière clinic that Freud, as he later reported in his autobiography, "received the profoundest impression of the possibility that there could be powerful mental processes which *nevertheless remained hidden from the consciousness* of men" (quoted in Sulloway, 1979, p. 32). So, there had been a long tradition of interest in hysteria and hypnosis as an index of unconscious mentation, and Freud's interest at that time was more in *how* experience could be kept out of awareness than in *what* was being excluded.[7] As Sulloway points out, Freud emphasizes in his autobiography that from the beginning he used hypnosis "in another manner" than simply making therapeutic suggestions to his patients. He intended patients to recall the precise circumstances of the onset of their symptoms. This was a technique he acknowledged learning from Breuer's work with Anna O. Still, as in the case of Emmy von N, the excluded content seems often rather innocuous—rats, worms, small dogs, pulled teeth—but, admittedly, with a few real horrors. The capacity of events to provoke dissociative phenomena was attributed to the hysterical diathesis, not to the inherent symbolic meaning of the event. That came later.

On rereading the *Studies on Hysteria*, Freud's fascination with the phenomenon of unconscious mentation becomes evident: how patients, under hypnosis, could remember events that were out of conscious awareness, and how the content of hypnotic sessions was "forgotten" when awake, but could be recalled, with continuity intact, in the next hypnotic session. His therapeutic technique, along with the ubiquitous massages (what *was* he doing?), consisted of re-establishing the lost connections between events and symptoms, an abreactive flushing-out, a high colonic, of the unconscious mind, by either hypnotically erasing or minimizing traumatic experiences. But the traumatic events seemed insufficient to the symptom. By early 1896, Freud had decided that neurosis was caused by actual seductions perpetrated by adults or older children. The next year, in his famous letter to Fliess, he recanted, introducing the hypothesis that memories of apparent childhood seduction were actually fantasies that had been repressed (Freud, 1954, p. 215ff). If the event is determined to be insufficient to account for the psychic distress, then there must be an internal drive mechanism—hence the Oedipus Complex and libido theory.

Freud's theory of repression was quite different from his earlier theory of dissociation and was entirely consistent with his neurology, as manifest in his *Project for a Scientific Psychology* (1895), his magnum opus. Higher functions suppressed and smoothed out lower functions. For example, if the cerebral cortex is injured, cerebellar functions break through and a tremor is the consequence. Repression requires a paradigm of unconscious drive; that is, the patient is defending herself against her own impulses. If a young girl is seduced, the problem is not primarily the seducer, but the awakening of her forbidden impulses. Parenthetically, dissociation, which requires a more holistic concept of brain functioning, is returning renewed. In this view, data must be processed in many different locations at the same time; the metaphor is more horizontal than vertical. Dissociation requires a psychology of self, of deficits in experience, of some version of object-relations. Bromberg, in a contemporary statement, characterizes mind as a "configuration of discontinuous, shifting states of consciousness with varying degrees of access to perception and cognition" (Bromberg, 1996, p. 58). Something must be split off, disowned—not a threatening impulse but a disavowed self. Integration is the desideratum, not repression. From this perspective, multiple personality becomes the emblematic disorder of the splitting hysteric, rather than hysterical paralysis and amnesia, the

212 Psychoanalytic theory and practice

disorder of Freud's repressing patients, and traumatic experience—particularly early sexual abuse—becomes the emblematic stressor.

In spite of Freud's efforts to establish a topology of the unconscious, we really don't have the foggiest notion of how anything is kept out of consciousness, or of what consciousness is. As Jonathan Miller put it, "We are the unwitting beneficiaries of a mind that is, in a sense, only partially our own" (Miller, 1995). However, what is terribly important to understand is that we all *do* uncritically accept the Freudian idea that keeping things out of awareness is a source of neurotic difficulty. We think of awareness as the superior state. We do not think of reflexiveness or unconsciousness as possibly advantageous, or that, perhaps, consciousness interferes with, or is not accessible for, certain necessary mentations. Remember the cautionary tale of the centipede who tripped over his feet when he began to think about how he managed to walk. Consciousness may be merely self-consiousness, a bubble of awareness in a matrix of human interaction, which largely operates well out of awareness (and necessarily so) and may be more an effort and artifact than not. Chomsky's concept of an unconscious grammar is a good example of a complex mentation totally denied consciousness. As Michael Polanyi put it, "We can know more than we can tell and we can tell nothing without relying on our awareness of things we may not be able to tell" (Polanyi, 1958).

My central thesis is that this "reflexive" mentation (not really unconscious, not repressed or disassociated, but designed to operate out of awareness) is at the seat of human interaction. Perhaps, as Hayek suggests, we should refer to these processes as "'super-conscious' because they govern the conscious processes without appearing in them" (Hayek, 1978, p. 45).[8] Sullivan's concept of the "self-system" approaches this position. Sullivan defined the self-system as all the security operations by which a person defends himself against anxiety. This implies an attuned and sophisticated strategic system designed, not to keep unacceptable *impulses* out of awareness, but to negotiate with others to get needs met. For Sullivan, the organizing force is the avoidance of anxiety—Sullivan's version of a "drive theory." Why not extend the self-system to include the entire range of interpersonal experience, most of which operates out of awareness, not, as in in Sullivan's term, "inattended" out of anxiety, but simply not so constructed as to operate best while under scrutiny.

In Freud's claim for psychoanalysis as an empirical science, the interpretation was both the instrument of therapy and the proof of the metapsychology. If the interpretation worked, it was because the theory was correct; if it was resisted, it was because it was correct; thus the analysis of resistance and transference was, as I said, intended to re-establish its mutative impact. As analysts' faith in the power of the mutative interpretation faded and, under the onslaught of Grünbaum's (1977) and Popper's (1962) critiques, we relinquished our dreams of proving ours to be an empirical science—what some wag called our "physics envy"—hermeneutics was advanced as the new paradigm.

So the first strategic shift was to relinquish claims to scientific status altogether. Psychoanalysis, it was claimed by Schafer, Gill, and Klein (leaning heavily on Ricoeur and Rorty) is a *hermeneutic* enterprise, which by its very nature, implies different criteria of validation. Hermeneutics, one notes, is named after Hermes, the messenger of the Greek gods. Hermes brought the word of the gods, usually of Apollo, to the Oracle at Delphi, who managed to make it more or less intelligible to humankind, but always with an ambiguity that left a choice of decisions to the supplicant, sometimes—not unlike psychoanalysis—with disastrous results. King Philip of Macedon lost his crown and his life when he opted for a too optimistic version of the Delphic utterance. Interpretation did not make everything clearer; it offered the supplicant yet another level of possible meaning.

In its earliest, medieval usage, hermeneutics was the instrument of the Church, and its function was to reveal to Christian followers the multiple meanings of the canonical (from Greek, the "rule," the "Law") writings. The focus was on the discovery of textual meanings. To quote Umberto Eco (better known for his three absolutely unreadable novels than for his wonderfully lucid writings in semiotics), *"Non nova sed noveno*—new things but the same things—increasingly retold in a new way" (Eco, 1990, p. 150). There is a serious catch, though: the authority legitimizes the canonical inter-pretation. But how can the authority legitimize the interpretation when the authority is legitimized *by* the interpretation? This paradox, which, as I said before, is inherent in Freud's concept of interpretation as empirical science, is known in hermeneutic circles as—the "hermeneutic circle"! Eco states:

> The rules for good interpretation were provided by the gatekeepers of the orthodoxy; and the gatekeepers of the orthodoxy were the winners (in terms of political and cultural power) of the struggle to impose their own interpretations.
>
> (Eco, 1990, p. 151)

There is in this, for psychoanalysts of a certain age, a ring of mournful familiarity. To quote a classic example of this level of canonical authority: "Dr. S' interventions were guided by his understanding of his patient's lifelong problems, problems which were currently active as determinants of her behavior." Voila! There is no doubt entertained about what the patient's problems are or about the therapist's authority to define them. The task is to make the canonical interpretation "mutative," to get it to work, and that requires timing and the analysis of resistance to the interpretations, which takes the form of transference.

In the twentieth century, first Dilthey, then Heidegger and his student Gadamer, shifted emphasis away from the discovery of canonical truth to the creation of an emergent truth, a mutually arrived-at truth. "Language is the place where things come authentically to begin" (Eco, 1990, p. 154). This second level of hermeneutics is what psychoanalysts (such as Spence, Schafer, Stern) are currently referring to when they use the word. The therapist and patient mutually create a "good" story: one of many possible combinations and permutations of the data. The story works, not because it is the only truth, or because it is plausible, but because it is *their* truth, their emergent truth.[9]

Unfortunately, this level of hermeneutics led straight into the tarpits of social constructivism and relativism. What then is reality? (Eagle, 1987; Strenger, 1991). Is it just a social consensus? The problem arises out of the need to demonstrate how and why hermeneutic constructions should work therapeutically if, indeed, one story is as good as the next, which is patently not so. Psychoanalytic interpretations remain inevitably canonical and political. Even in the presumably intersubjective mutuality of the Gadamer version, can we really for a moment believe that the analyst and patient are arriving at a consensually developed *mutual* narrative? The analyst is not only bringing to the exchange his or her experience, but also, and inevitably, a set of prefigurations about what matters—and what *better* matter—in human affairs, as far as the analyst's career, income, and affiliations are concerned. The analyst is still the authority, but one allowing the patient a larger menu of interpretive possibilities from which to choose. It would appear that each effort psychoanalysis made to legitimize interpretation only further compounded its difficulties.

The next conceptual shift was the recognition that transference might be seen as an *enactment*, a behavior with the patient. This opened a way out of the dilemma for traditional analysts (interpersonal analysts had been claiming this since the forties). Then one might think of the curative element as *behavioral*, something happening between the two, rather than as interpretive. Ergo, the patient comes into therapy with a version of his or her experience that is not working. The patient wants the neurosis perfected—wants it to work. There is some variety of inquiry—free-associative, narrative, or a Sullivanian detailed inquiry. The analyst intervenes, asks questions, asks for elaboration, asks for fantasies. In this process, the analyst inevitably and inexorably participates. Even the most parsimonious request for "what does that bring to mind?" reveals the therapist, who must choose when to ask even that presumably neutral inquiry. Inquiry begets interaction, which begets enactment. Inquiry and interpretation are both enactments. What the therapist chooses to ask about, notice, or entirely miss is not a matter of accident or of the therapist's training or personality. It is an interaction determined by their inter-subjective field. What is said is relevant only inasmuch as it reveals the therapist in interaction. Whatever narrative they construct, it will also be a relationship. To go hermeneutics one step further, we become not so much interested in the mutually constructed good story as in what it tells us about the two authors in interaction.

If one is prepared to concede that transference is an enactment, rather than a distortion projected on the therapist, the next problem is how might *that* work? Should the analyst, following a variant of the classical dictate of neutrality, use his or her meticulous monitoring of the enactment to minimize it, to get it out of the way of the patient's internal flow? Or should the analyst utilize it as a curative interaction, a therapeutic "acting-in"?[10] The latter veers close to being a sophisticated version of the Dreaded Corrective Emotional Experience, which doesn't necessarily invalidate it, but puts a considerable load on the therapist to "do the right thing."

Both these approaches seem preeminently useful. There is no question that when the therapist identifies his or her own blind spot or unwitting participation, the therapy moves forward. There are relatively uncompli-cated occasions in which the therapist identifies the pull of the patient to replicate a familiar impasse and can point it out, in the traditional way, as resistance and transference—what Gill (1982) called interpretations of awareness of resistance and transference. Nor can one doubt that active interactions and authentic encounters between therapist and patient may be dramatically useful. But I think this still falls short of an analytic interaction.

216 Psychoanalytic theory and practice

"Using one's own participation" should not, I believe, be treated as coterminous with using one's countertransference (Ehrenberg, 1992). From this perspective, the therapist is operating out of his or her marginal perceptions of feelings in reaction to the patient. Feelings are deemed superordinate to patterns of interaction. Note Ehrenberg's definition of countertransference: "I define *countertransference disclosure* as involving the analyst's revelation of his or her feelings in *interaction* with the patient, or in relationship to the patient, at a particular time" (Ehrenberg, 1995, p. 213). These are presented to the patient without qualification. The intent is not to demonstrate the extreme tenacity of the patient's system in maintaining somehow a *repetition* of his or her previous patterns of experience, but, rather, to invoke a de novo experience that, it is hoped, will prove to be mutative. If it is not, a failure to respond may be treated as resistance. One's reactions are revealed to the patient with the intent of promoting change. It is not a gratuitous or danger-free act, and a great deal of discrimination must be exercised. One might postulate a judgment-free, open contribution of the analyst's feelings as they enter awareness, including the use of one's dreams, however poorly understood; but it would take a very high degree of grandiosity or complacency to assume that one is always correct, or that "working-through" the patient's response will always be possible or salutary. In this ostensible use of oneself, the therapist plays another version of Lacan's Subject-Who-Knows—who knows not only *what* to say, but also *how* to act. The analyst's intent is still to have a mutative impact, to effect a change in the patient. It is still canonical but, if you will forgive a double entendre, it is a loose cannon!

Clearly, the therapist's participation is conceived of as more authentic than the patient's, and is motivated by the therapist's belief in the efficacy of such intervention. The injunction to the therapist is to "use the countertransference." But this is, in itself, a bit out of date, rather like Sullivan's "participant-observation" in which the therapist could observe his or her participation and then step out of it to interpret. The interpretations were presumably informed by the participation. We now tend to believe that no such delineation is possible. One cannot step out of the interaction, and whatever one says will be an extension of the interpersonal field, not a dispassionate observation of it.

Moreover, an analyst who believes himself or herself to be in touch with his or her own countertransference is, I believe, missing the true nature of the beast. The therapist's affective response to the patient, no matter how

The politics of interpretation 217

intuitive or brilliant, is not per se countertransference. *Real* countertransference operates well out of awareness and requires a collaborative effort of patient and therapist to bring it into awareness, through dreams, slips, dissociated affects, and so on.

A patient presents this dream. He comes to my office. I show him that I've redecorated. I now have two rooms, one smaller than the other. There are blue walls. Each room has a huge Jacuzzi, empty of water. In the larger room, the analytic appurtenances—couch and chairs—are crowded over in the corner. He is leaving. He has two bags. He puts them down for a moment to stop and say something to me, and one bag is snatched up by someone. He does not see by whom. He runs toward the elevator and the cleaning woman points out the direction in which the thief has fled. He is upset because the bag contained money, and besides, it was his favorite black-leather bag.

I will accept any dream in which I appear undisguised as a clear statement of my unrecognized countertransference. The patient is seeing me more clearly than I am seeing myself. No analyst listening to this dream would doubt that it is also a dream of negative transference. The patient feels he has been to a spa (with empty Jacuzzis!), not an analysis, and, to boot, he has been cheated, and it has cost him money. There is, with this man, a very powerfully seductive, benevolent interaction that makes it difficult for either of us to express anger or disapproval. The sentiment of the dream is far from his conscious experience. I cannot resist adding that the second room probably refers to my private bathroom, entered from my office. He has urgency problems and, not infrequently during the session, has to urinate. He is the only patient I do not send out to the waiting-room bathroom.

I do not wish to explore this dream in great length, only to illustrate what is a rather typical experience for me—namely, that rather than making those strikingly mutative interventions referred to earlier, I frequently find myself catching on, somewhat after the fact, to aspects of our interaction that ought to have been shamefully obvious to me, were it not for my own out-of-awareness participation. It then becomes apparent to me how his life experience, my life experience, and our interactional field all converge to create a powerful transformational field. Mea culpa! But I'd feel worse about it if I didn't think it was both a normative and necessary experience in psychoanalysis.

In the storybooks of my childhood, there was a fabled bird called the "Gooney-bird." It could only fly backwards, so it had a great view of where

218 Psychoanalytic theory and practice

it had been, but not of where it was going. I think of countertransference similarly. After it has all been worked through (over a considerable period of time), when I look back it seems so patently obvious that I am ashamed to present the material to colleagues. If one could grasp immediately what is going on, respond spontaneously to the patient, and then limn out the dynamics, it would certainly be an epiphany, but closer to a religious experience than a therapeutic one. The patient would then be cured by an omniscient therapist, not, as psychoanalysis requires, *failed* by one, so that the patient might mobilize his or her own creative resources to help the floundering therapist.[11] It is what H.S. Sullivan had in mind when he said, "God keep me from a clever psychoanalyst!"

So, we have gone from interpretation as the transmission of canonical truth, to interpretation as an emergent, mutually constructed narrative, to interpretation as an enactment with the patient. Indeed, words are also deeds, as Wittgenstein said. I believe that there is yet one step further to go. I said, in 1972, that the interaction between therapist and patient becomes a transform of the content under examination; that is, the patterning of the transference-countertransference is simultaneously the same as what the patient is discussing.

This resonance, this metaphoric carrying-over of pattern is, I believe, the key to the therapeutic action. Patients, as we know, will enter the room, say something casually, and proceed with the topic at hand. That off-hand opening remark is often a leitmotif for the entire session. Whether one uses free-association, narrative, or detailed inquiry, throughout the duration of the session, and from session to session, there will be a coherent patterning. If one interrupts this flow to press for associations or to ask for details, one sees the same remarkable unfolding take place, the same themes emerging vertically, so to speak, from the horizontal flow. From Freud's fascination with free-association to James's flow of consciousness, and even Sullivan's detailed inquiry, we are aware of the extraordinary intrinsic cohesiveness of psychoanalytic productions. This reiterative patterning, this resonance of theme, runs through the patient's productions, the enactment in the patient-therapist field, and flows out to the therapist's life and even the sociocultural matrix in which both are imbedded. It is all of a piece.

Let me use another example of a transference dream to illustrate this recursion of pattern. When I enter the waiting room, the patient, a very bland and polite man, is talking on a cellular phone. He looks up, but

The politics of interpretation 219

oddly—for him, at least—continues to talk. He walks into my office still attached to his phone, stands there, finishes the call, and then apologizes. It all seemed odd and out of character for him. We proceed with the session, in which he relates two dreams. We spend a considerable time on the first, which seems to bear clearly on his current problem. Indeed, it powerfully substantiates a hypothesis I had about it. (I am avoiding any greater detail, so as not to get too discursive.) Toward the end of the session, he suddenly remembers a second dream he had had.

> I am on the telephone making a business call. Seated opposite me is a nude woman, obviously sexually soliciting me. I wave to her, "Wait, I have to finish this call." I look up and see, off in the corner, my father standing there. He doesn't seem threatening or spooky [his father is dead].

Needless to say, all his gestures—where the woman is seated, where his father is standing—exactly match the dimensions of my office. The acting-in of his telephone call emphasizes that this dream is transferential. The metaphoric patterning applies to his life, his therapy, his history with his family, my life, and my interaction with him, which has been, alas, somewhat seductive. You will note both patients accuse me of the same fault, of which I was, at best, marginally aware. Arnold Rothstein (1995) has recently noted that engaging the reluctant patient (an oxymoron in the good old days when there were more patients than analysts and one had to prove to the analyst one's worthiness) requires some initial seductiveness–the trick is to know when to stop!

Lionel Trilling (1951) called psychoanalysis the "science of tropes," that is, figures of speech. Metaphor, according to Vico, is the "most luminous and therefore the most necessary and frequent" of tropes, and lies at the base of modern linguistic theory (Eco, 1984). Psychoanalysts are always searching for metaphoric carry-over. Correlating the patient's present with past fantasies or past experience, or correlating a dream with current content, is intrinsically a metaphoric act, literally a "carrying-over" of meaning. As I indicated earlier, I believe that this same metaphoric resonance or carrying-over of patterns—both universal and, at the same time, highly idiosyncratic—occurs simultaneously in the interactional field of the patient and therapist, in what is loosely labeled "the transference/countertransference."

220   Psychoanalytic theory and practice

I have always found this strange cohesiveness, this unconscious mentation, the most mysterious and potentially therapeutic aspect of the psychoanalytic praxis. I am endlessly astonished by the extent to which my participation resonates to the patient's presentation and to my own life experience. Such a powerful organizing factor cannot be insignificant. Hofstadter said that "the more different manifestations you observe of one phenomenon, the more deeply you understand that phenomenon, and therefore the more clearly you can see the vein of sameness running through these different things" (Hofstadter, 1985). It is possible that increased awareness of this patterning is the key to therapy. This is not the same thing as a mutually derived narrative, because metaphoric carry-over allows for innumerable narratives. That is, one can construct a variety of stories around the same metaphor, and the value of the narrative may be less in the narrative per se than in its being a container for the ubiquitous metaphor. For example, Kafka's *Metamorphosis* has been translated as a parable of social alienation, Oedipal dynamics, and Christianity.

Bronowski said that "every act of imagination is the discovery of likenesses between two things which were thought unlike" (Bronowski, 1996). I don't know why an act of imagination should make for change, but as this patterning becomes more detailed and more in focus, patients do seem to shift. Possibly awareness is in itself mutative; more likely, awareness stimulates small incremental changes in participation, so much so that the therapist may get the feeling of riding a process, being carried along by some flow. Small inputs may indeed cause large shifts, according to the famous "butterfly effect" of Chaos theory. We are imbedded in this web of syncretic events, and the relationship between what I do and how the patient responds is almost always nonlinear and necessarily obscure.

To a very considerable extent, it avoids the ubiquitous problem of therapeutic ambitiousness—the need to cure the patient. With the shortage of patients, the harassment of third-party payers, and the pro-drug, politically reactionary forces abroad (never mind changing your life, take a pill!), analysts have their backs to the wall. The temptation to push is immense; the consequence is using a psychoanalytic language as a rhetoric, a persuasion to change (Levenson, 1978). Note that the therapist is not trying to perfect or purify his or her participation, but to bring it into awareness, not to have a mutative response to the patient but, as far as is possible, to have a fully elucidated one. Think of all the patients who bring us lively dreams, as though they were stool samples, for our edification—God knows, not for theirs. We want the patient to tap into his or her own resources, to enjoy imagination, and to free the therapist to take part in the process without having to be on top of it all or feeling deficient if he or she doesn't know what's transpiring.

We are, as Masud Khan so nicely put it, servants of the patient's process. But we are simultaneously—all of us—immersed in a larger human process that has to do with metaphor, pattern-making. Whether these patterns are inherent in the world or of our own construction has been argued since Plato, and is not relevant to this presentation. Although I am not much interested in music, and something of a mathematical idiot to boot, I do have a very strong sense that the psychoanalytic process is not so different from those two very related processes.[12] The attuned analyst will certainly hear—to use the image of another Old, Dead, White, Greek Male, Pythagoras, and his "music of the spheres"—melodies and harmonies in the course of a session and from session to session.

Emphasis on content interpretation, with its concomitant insistence on a magisterial, neutral interpreter, and a noninteractive field, has certainly biased clinical assumptions, and a change is long overdue. But the illusion that psychoanalysis is a "hermeneutical science" is not much of an improvement, because the analyst, arriving at joint "narratives," can be just as biased and doctrinaire as his or her predecessors. Something new is required. Psychoanalysis taps into a much deeper and more pervasive process, not limited to psychotherapy or psychopathology per se, but to the centrality of metaphor, a peculiarly human way of organizing experience and perceiving reality. We superimpose our canons on this deep structure; but we'd do well, as Count Alfred Korzybski warned us, not to confuse our maps with the mysterious terra incognita of the mind.

Notes

1. This chapter was first presented at a meeting of Free-association in collaboration with the California School of Professional Psychology, May 10, 1996. It also appeared in 1996 in *Contemporary Psychoanalysis*, 34(2):239–249.
2. Reading the bibliographies was as reliable an index of who was in and who was out as were the Kremlin May-Day photographs.
3. Both these quotes are from the same issue of the *International Journal of Psycho-Analysis.*

222 Psychoanalytic theory and practice

4. I am extracting heavily from Jonathan Miller's article "Going Unconscious" in the *New York Review of Books* (Miller, 1995).
5. Charcot's subjects were coached in detail by his assistants as to the proper manifestations—presumably without the Master's knowledge.
6. There were 801 publications on hypnosis between 1888 and 1893. Two years later, an additional 400 were added (Sulloway, 1979, p. 48).
7. Freud was still primarily a neurologist and, as his later unfinished magnum opus, *Project for a Scientific Psychology* (started in 1892) attests, his interest in the neurological basis of unconscious mentation continued unabated throughout his lifetime (Freud, 1895).
8. See Mahoney (1991) for explication of deep and surface structures.
9. See Strenger (1991) for an overview of hermeneutics in psychoanalysis and Stern (1991) for an exegesis of Gadamer and psychoanalysis.
10. See Gill (1983) and Fiscalini (1994) for a review of interpersonal variations. See Boesky (1992) for a more classical variant, Jacobs (1986) and Ehrenberg (1992) for more radical variants.
11. A point developed at length by M.G. Thompson (1985).
12. See Douglas Hofstadter for several fascinating books on this topic (Hofstadter, 1985, 1995; Hofstadter and Dennet, 1981).

References

Boesky, D. (1992). Review of the use of the self. Countertransference in the analytic situation. *International Journal of Psycho-Analysis*, 73:370–372.

Bouchard, M.-A. (1995). The specificity of hermeneutics in psychoanalysis: Leaps on the path from construction to recollection. *International Journal of Psycho-Analysis*, 76:533–546.

Bromberg, P. (1996). Hysteria, dissociation and cure: Emmy von N. revisited. *Psychoanalytic Dialogues*, 6:65–71.

Bronowski, J. (1996). The creative process. *Scientific American*, 1996(3):5–11.

Brook, A. (1995). Explanations in the hermeneutic science. *International Journal of Psycho-Analysis*, 76:519–532.

Eagle, N.M. (1987). *Recent Developments in Psychoanalysis*. Cambridge, MA: Harvard University Press.

Eco, U. (1984). *Semiotics and the Philosophy of Language*. Bloomington, IN: Indiana University Press.

Eco, U. (1990). *The Limits of Interpretation*. Bloomington, IN: Indiana University Press.

Ehrenberg, D. (1992). *The Intimate Edge: Extending the Reach of Psychoanalytic Interaction*. New York: W.W. Norton.

Ehrenberg, D. (1995). Self-disclosure: Therapeutic tool or indulgence? *Contemporary Psychoanalysis*, 31:213–228.

Fiscalini, J. (1994). The uniquely interpersonal and the interpersonally unique. *Contemporary Psychoanalysis*, 30:114–134.

Freud, A. (1969). *Difficulties in the Path of Psychoanalysis*. New York: International Universities Press.

Freud, S. (1895). Project for a scientific psychology. In J. Strachey (Ed.), *The Standard Edition of the Complete Psychological Works of Sigmund Freud*, London: Hogarth Press, Vol. I, pp. 294–397.

Freud, S. (1925). Autobiography. In J. Strachey (Ed.), *The Standard Edition of the Complete Psychological Works of Sigmund Freud*. London: Hogarth Press, Vol. XX pp.7–76.

Freud, S. (1954). *The Origins of Psychoanalysis: Letters to Wiehelm Fleiss, Drafts and Notes. 1887–1902*. New York: Basic Books.

Gill, M. (1982). *Analysis of Transference. Vol. 1: Theory and Technique*. New York: International Universities Press.

Gill, M. (1983). The interpersonal paradigm and the degree of the analyst's involvement. *Contemporary Psychoanalysis*, 18:200–237.

Grünbaum, A. (1977). How scientific is psychoanalysis? In R. Stern, L. Horowitz, and J. Lynes (Eds.), *Science and Psychotherapy*. New York: Haven Press, pp. 219–254.

Hayek, F.A. (1978). *New Studies in Philosophy, Politics, Economics, and the History of Ideas*. Chicago, IL: University of Chicago Press.

Hofstadter, D. (1985). *Metamagical Themes: Questing for the Essence of Mind and Pattern*. New York: Basic Books.

Hofstadter, D. (1995). *Fluid Concepts and Creative Analogies*. New York: Basic Books.

Hofstadter, D. and Dennet, D. (1981). *The Mind's I: Fantasies and Reflections on Self and Soul*. New York: Basic Books.

Jacobs, T. (1986). On countertransference enactments. *Journal of the American Psychoanalytic Association*, 34:289–308.

Kahn, M. (Ed.). (1972). *Exorcism of the Intrusive Ego-alien Factors in the Analytic Situation and Process*. New York: Science House.

Laplanche, J. and Pontalis, J.B. (1973). *The Language of Psychoanalysis* (trans. D. Nicholson-Smith). New York: W.W. Norton.

Levenson, E. (1978). Psychoanalysis. Cure or persuasion? In E.G. Witenberg (Ed.), *Interpersonal Psychoanalysis: New Directions*. New York: Gardiner Press, pp. 47–63.

Mahoney, M.J. (1991). *Human Change Processes: The Scientific Foundations of Psychotherapy*. New York: Basic Books.

Miller, J. (1995). Going unconscious. *New York Review of Books*, April 20, 1995:59–65.

Polanyi, M. (1958). *Personal Knowledge: Towards a Post-critical Philosophy*. Chicago, IL: University of Chicago Press.

Popper, K.R. (1962). *Conjectures and Refutations*. New York: Basic Books.

Rothstein, A. (1995). *Psychoanalytic Technique and the Creation of the Analytic Patient*. New York: International Universities Press.

Shah, I. (1970). *Tales of the Dervishes*. New York: E.P. Dutton.

Stern, D.B. (1991). A philosophy for the embedded analyst: Gadamer's hermeneutics and the social paradigm of psychoanalysis. *Contemporary Psychoanalysis*, 27:51–80.

Strenger, C. (1991). *Between Hermeneutics and Science: An Essay on the Epistemology of Psychoanalysis*. Madison, WI: International Universities Press.

Sulloway, F. (1979). *Freud. Biologist of the Mind*. New York: Basic Books.

Thompson, M.G. (1985). *The Death of Desire. A Study in Psychopathology*. New York: New York University Press.

Trilling, L. (1951). Freud and Literature. In *The Liberal Imagination*. New York: Viking Press, p. 53.

Chapter 18

Awareness, insight, and learning[1]

There is a fusty academic joke that goes like this: René Descartes is ordering tea in a restaurant. The waitress says, "Sir, would you like lemon or milk with your tea?" Descartes reflects, and says, "Mmm, I think not"—and disappears! The joke may well be relevant. We are approaching a swing away from rationalism with its hegemony of the mind—its "I think, therefore I am," and its "where id was there shall ego be."

I find the concepts of mind and consciousness, and their relationship to each other, quite confusing. From the spate of literature on the topic, I surmise I am not entirely alone (Chalmers, 1995, 1996; Dennett, 1991; Ellenberger, 1970; Horgan, 1996; Meltzoff and Gopnick, 1993; Searle, 1997). I believe that psychoanalytic cure has remained implicitly equated with "mindfulness," consciousness, in spite of Freud's (1923) effort to resolve the dilemma by anchoring the ego in the domains of both consciousness and unconsciousness. It is important to remember that Descartes wrote 200 years before Freud. It was not until 1840, only 55 years before Freud, that the concept of *unconscious* mentation was introduced by Laycock and Carpenter. Prior to Carpenter, cerebral functioning was considered to be entirely conscious. Only spinal cord functioning was reflexive, that is, out of consciousness. Hall, a prominent neurophysiologist of the time, believed that "the cerebrum is the organ of the mind. All its functions . . . imply consciousness" (see Miller, 1995, p. 63). Unconscious mind was deemed to be an oxymoron.[2] In 1996, David Chalmers, attempting to bridge the gap, postulated "phenomenal" mind, which is conscious, and "psychological" mind, in which it does not matter whether a mental state is conscious or not (p. 11).

226 Psychoanalytic theory and practice

Yet, for all that Freudian mind, psychological mind, may be unconscious, Freudian *cure* appears to be conscious and mindful; it involves replacing irrational bodily processes with consciousness. Implicitly, this premise persists even in Sullivan's much later resolution of interpersonal mystification; the assumption is that we are defined by intellect and language, and cured by our capacity for conscious awareness. To quote Crowley (1984), "Sullivan clearly saw unconscious thoughts and feelings as unformulated experience to be remedied by the analytic process of putting what is unformulated into words understandable by another person."

There are, of course, much later versions of cure through direct experience, "through identification, transmuting intemalizations or some other means not mediated by insight" (Eagle, 1987, p. 225). Yet even when we no longer require that the patient understand the process, we still expect that the therapist's interventions—implicit or explicitly defined—will be directed by his or her conscious awareness. Donnel Stern (1996) writes that even

> while the patient's feeling of being understood becomes more important in the developmental model, the content of that understanding remains predictable to the analyst, just as it was in the interpretive model. Theory, that is, still allows the therapist to know the truth (p. 277).

But it may well be that the mind is not master, but is formed and molded by the body; that the unconscious is not a cauldron of irrationality, needing to be tamed; and that our psychoanalytic desideratum, understanding, is neither entirely verbal nor intellectual, but more a limited reflection on an ineffable felt experience. Understanding may be a sort of afterthought, an idea that has radical implications for our concepts of insight and change. If you will forgive a pun, perhaps we have been putting Descartes before the horse.

To make such an impassioned claim for body over mind may sound like an odd kind of Luddite position these days, when the computer Deep Blue defeats Garry Kasparov at chess (with a lot of human coaching), and a little gadget trundles about on Mars photographing rocks. Of course, only Kasparov *felt* anything. Triumph or exhilaration or fear—corporeal experience, affect—remained beyond the grasp or the necessity of the machines. But consider a new trend in electronics, the Tamagotchi; those of you with children may be familiar with it. It is a computer toy baby that doesn't look human, but cries, wets itself, needs to be fed and changed—several times throughout the night—and *dies* if you don't take care of it. You wake up in the morning and your baby is dead—and it doesn't come back, as in video games. Kids are having Tamagotchi-induced depressions. It seems like the revenge of the soma over artificial intelligence: the body strikes back!

For those who prefer a more professional and less flippant example, consider Adam Phillips's exegesis of Winnicott's article "Mind and Its Relation to the Psyche-Soma" (Phillips, 1995, p. 99; Winnicott, 1949). Winnicott says that if early development has been satisfactory, "the mind does not exist as an entity in the individual's scheme of things. . . [I]t is a false entity and a false localization." According to Winnicott's eccentric article and Phillips's brilliant gloss, the mind is developed to fill in and compensate for any experienced failures in the seamless mother-child connection. Were it perfect, there would be no need for mind. The greater the failure of empathic connection, the greater the tyranny of mind. This is not so different from Lacan's version of Freud's grandson's "fort-da!" wherein the word "here-gone!" is substituted for the absence of the mother (Freud, 1920, pp. 8–11; Lacan, 1977, p. 163). The intellectual process, language itself, fills a physical absence. It is no longer an issue of the mind being superordinate to the body. "I think, therefore I am" becomes "I am, therefore I think."

Presumably, we are all past demonizing the Freudian position; nevertheless, from the traditional frame of reference, the unconscious remains the repository of forbidden bodily impulse. Andre Green (1995) said, "I *cannot* conceive of the unconscious differently from Freud's view, that is of *not* being rooted in sexuality and destructiveness."[3] But at best, it is certainly not the repository of unconscious wisdom as, say, Fromm saw it, or, as I indicate later, as it is held to be in some contemporary views.

As I have said before, in spite of Freud's efforts to establish a topology of the unconscious, we really don't have the foggiest notion how anything is kept in or out of consciousness, or what consciousness really is (Levenson, 1996). Moreover, what we are conscious of appears to be a relatively small part of what we know. As Miller (1995) put it, "we are the unwitting beneficiaries of a mind that is, in a sense, only partially our own" (p. 65). What is vital is that we all uncritically accept the Freudian idea that keeping things out of awareness is a source of neurotic difficulty.

228   Psychoanalytic theory and practice

Because we consider awareness as the superior state, we do not think of reflexiveness or unconsciousness as possibly advantageous—that perhaps consciousness interferes with, or is not accessible for, certain necessary mentations.

Remember the cautionary tale of the centipede who tripped over his feet when he began to think about how he managed to walk. Consciousness may be merely self-consciousness, a bubble of awareness in a matrix of human interaction that largely operates well out of awareness, and does so necessarily. Chomsky's concept of an unconscious grammar is a good example of a complex mentation totally denied consciousness. As Polanyi (1958) put it, "We can know more than we can tell and we can tell nothing without relying on our awareness of things we may not be able to tell." Perhaps, as Hayek (1978) suggests, we should refer to these processes as "super-conscious because they govern the conscious processes without appearing in them."[4] Sullivan's concept of the "self-system" approaches this position. Sullivan defined the self-system as all the security operations by which a person defends himself or herself against anxiety. This implies an attuned and sophisticated strategic system designed, not to keep unacceptable *impulses* out of awareness, but to negotiate with others to get needs met. For Sullivan, the organizing force was the avoidance of anxiety— Sullivan's version of a "drive theory." Why not extend the self-system to include the entire range of interpersonal experience, most of which operates out of awareness, not, as in Sullivan's term, "inattended" out of anxiety, but simply so constructed as not to operate best while under scrutiny?

How does anyone learn anything? It may not be so much a matter of making the unconscious conscious as of tapping into an unconscious flow that is not, in the ordinary sense, intellectual or even linguistic, but oddly enough corporeal—bodily. As I said, we tend to think of intelligence and intellectual activity as conscious, as in linguistic and mathematical skills. To be smart, we believe, is to be able to discourse intelligently about a topic—say, the patient's problems. But learning may be a more somatic experience then we realize. Anyone who has been out-skied by her 9-year-old, who has no idea what she is doing but does it better than we ever shall, knows what I'm talking about.

Howard Gardner (1983) has made a distinction between different kinds of intelligence: linguistic, musical, logical-mathematical, spatial, bodily, kinesthetic. It is certainly self-evident that great dancers, musicians, artists, athletes are often extremely pedestrian in other areas.

It is Gardner's category of bodily kinesthetic intelligence that is most relevant to my presentation.

> A description of use of the body as a form of intelligence may at first jar. There has been a radical disjunction in our recent cultural tradition between the activities of reasoning on the one hand, and the activity of the manifestly physical part of our nature, as epitomized by our bodies, on the other. This divorce between the "mental" and the "physical" has not infrequently been coupled with a notion that what we do with our bodies is somehow less privileged, less special, than those problem-solving routines carried out chiefly through the use of language, logic, or some other relatively abstract system (pp. 207–208).

Gardner calls on the interesting analogies between various skills drawn by Sir Frederic Bartlett (1985), a British psychologist. Gardner writes,

> Bartlett goes beyond the sheer analysis of bodily skill in his intriguing claim that much of what we ordinarily call thinking—routine as well as innovative—partakes of the same principles that have been uncovered in overtly physical manifestations of skill (p. 209).

Much the same point has been made by neuropsychologists who suggest that rather than the body being the dumb servant of the mind, one might consider that cerebration functions to refine and direct motor behavior, which has the primary responsibility for adaptation and survival.

There are extensive infant studies that support or reflect the view that infants learn by imitation, virtually from birth (Meltzoff and Gopnick, 1993; Stem, 1984). In a word, it is agreed that the *mimetic* function—learning by imitation—seems to develop much earlier than the *semantic.* Winnicott (as I indicated), Kohut, Lacan, and Sullivan have all made similar observations. As Damasio (1994) put it,

> The body, as represented in the brain, may constitute the indispensable frame of reference for the neural processes that we experience as the mind, that our very organism rather than some absolute external reality is used as the ground reference for the construction of the ever-present sense of subjectivity that is part and parcel of our experiences; that our most refined thoughts and best actions, our greatest joys and deepest sorrows, use the body as a yardstick (p. xvi).

230 Psychoanalytic theory and practice

The relevance for therapy may well be that the signal function of the transference-countertransference enactment, which presently so engages us all, is to supply the corporeal equivalent, the experiential component, to the discourse. The interactional field of the therapist and patient obviously involves not only language, or even language qua behavior, but also a subtle and intricate choreography of affect, expression, semiotic cues—all physical. It is possible that patients resist interpretations, not because of negativism or anxiety, but because no one learns *anything* by being told. When interpretation works, I believe it is because it is reflecting on a felt experience. Perhaps that is why interpretations only seem to work if they are mediated through the transference, where what is talked about is being simultaneously experienced. Let me emphasize that by "experienced" I do not mean a corrective or de novo emotional experience—something different and inherently curative—but a striking correspondence between language and behavior.

As a brief clinical example, here is the dream of a 50-year-old woman.

Jeffry Dahmer, the notorious cannibalistic serial killer, has captured her. She is pretending to collaborate in order to avoid becoming a victim, being killed and eaten. She is in a panic. She gets to a telephone, calls 911, begs for help. She is terrified that she will not be believed (that she is a captive? that she is not his accomplice?). As she tells me the dream, she is feeling more and more anxious, on the edge of panic. She doesn't know why. I suggest that perhaps I'm Dahmer, because she is feeling so anxious in telling me the dream. There are no associations. Nothing happens. We go on to other topics.

About 10 minutes later, she is telling me about a telephone call from her aged and widowed mother, who lives alone in another state. In the patient's early years, her mother had been so fiercely possessive (consuming?) of her that when she tried to go to a college away from home, her mother resisted her leaving so viciously that my patient was briefly hospitalized for a near psychotic depression. Now mother is being assessed for slipped-disc surgery. Her doctor says it is arthritis, not a slipped disk. "Nothing much can be done for me," her mother reports dolefully. She is, she says, facing a future of immobilization. As my patient reports it, "Mother—who has a great sense of humor—says to her doctors, 'Does Dr. Kevorkian have an 800 number?' Everyone laughs heartily." Later in the telephone conversation with her daughter, the mother repeats the Kevorkian remark. My patient then looks at me with a positively beatific expression and says, "Of course! Poor mother, she is *so* worried about her health and trying *so* hard to be brave and funny." Irresistibly leaping to the attack, I say, "it sounds like mother is threatening you with suicide. Besides," I say, "arthritis *is* treatable and certainly has a better prognosis than disc surgery for an eighty-five-year-old woman with heart disease." She looks immensely relieved and says, "*Thank* you for saying that. I feel *so* much better!"

Suddenly I think, so that's the transference aspect of the dream. Jeffry Dahmer—a.k.a. Levenson—will be responsible for all the horrid ideas. She is just going along to stay alive. She calls the police to show that she is not an accomplice. Jeffry made her do it. She would not, on her own, think of dining on mother. Nor is she to be identified with her cannibalistic mother.

I point out to her how I jumped in, couldn't resist when she sounded so cloyingly benign. I attack mother, she remains the good daughter, albeit mother is a real pain. One might say that I merely succeeded in demonstrating my countertransferential hostility to her mother, and that she is just going along with me to avoid being murdered; but even that interpretation would have opened the door to further inquiry. Of course, I might simply have asked her about the repeated references to Kevorkian, or might even have said nothing. The outcome would have been much the same. The only difference is whether I am enacting by leaping into Dahmer's role or by refusing to leap in. It is merely a question of commission or omission. Jeffry Dahmer remains a wonderful trope for all sorts of formulations, from oral incorporation and oral sadism, as in Klein or Freud, to less flamboyant interpersonal explanations

It is of interest that in the next session, she quite spontaneously went to the topic of her deep sense of destructiveness. Once, earlier in treatment, she had said that she could never have had a child, because she was convinced she would have done something horrible to it. When I had tried to get her to elaborate, she became upset and refused to continue the theme. She is a very ethical, kind, caretaking person, long-suffering with friends, pets, lover. This time around, we took it up more seriously. The Dahmer in her emerged *after* the dénouement of the enactment between us. As I see it, her fantasies of destructiveness emerge after the enactment and are not so much mutative as simply epiphenomenal—the smoke from the muzzle of the gun, not the bullet. It is also true that I did a good deal of exposition on our interaction, supplying formulations, interpreting the

232 Psychoanalytic theory and practice

process. But I do not believe that this is the mutative event. It is, rather, after the fact, a way of talking about our mutual experience that remains far more overdetermined and multidimensional than my interpretations— that is, it is a digital explanation of an analogic event. Virtually every metapsychological posture emerges over the course of the working-through. Indeed, that is what constitutes working-through. From my view, what matters is not the metapsychology of one's choice, but the simultaneous enactment of the dream, and possibly—though I am not convinced of the inevitability—that this interplay enter conscious awareness.

All this occurred shortly before our summer break. A few weeks later, she flew into a tremendous rage at her lover. The next day, she suddenly thought, "my God, I miss Levenson!" There followed a much-clarified memory of her feelings after her father's sudden cardiac death when she was 16. There was, for the first time, a real sense of mourning. She said that over the rest of the month she had increasingly felt how smarmy her niceness was. Such gratifying follow-up is not my usual lot. I believe it was an artifact of the vacation. Had I been around, I expect that the resolution would have been far more obscured and layered with resistance.

One notes that although there appear to be real advances in the therapy, they are more kaleidoscopic than linear. Something is happening, but what we are observing seem only burps of awareness in an ongoing and subterranean interactional field. Perhaps we have gone from Freud's archeology to something more akin to spelunking—entering the cave of the unconscious, finding the dark river, and riding its flow to wherever we emerge, if we *do* emerge.

The brochure for the section of the symposium (The Nature of Self-Understanding) at which I originally presented this stated, "To know oneself better could be defined as the goal of psychoanalysis." I disagree with this Cartesian impulse. I would say that to live better, more richly, more intensely—to *be* ourselves—is indeed the goal of analysis. But what does that have to do with understanding? Twenty-five years ago, I titled a book *The Fallacy of Understanding*. At least I'm consistent. I still believe that understanding is no more relevant to psychoanalysis than it is to learning any other skill—that is to say, not much. Although that may seem an extreme remark, it is true. The Cartesian fallacy dies hard. In a recent panel discussion with a colleague, he used the example of learning to ride a bicycle. First, he said, you get the instructions, and then you translate them into action. This sounds reasonable, but is patently incorrect. What you do

Awareness, insight, and learning   233

is to grab the bike from behind, swear that you will hold on forever, and then let go when the kid gets up a head of steam. Voila! One has created a bicyclist.

I believe that the central inquiry for psychoanalysis increasingly will be, not how one gets better, but how anyone learns anything. It is a striking paradox known to anyone who has ever practiced a physical skill, from sports to games to craft to arts, that there is a huge and ineffable gap between the intellectual formulation of an activity and doing it. We all know "locker-room experts" who can "talk a good game" and are inept players. But no degree of library research or detailed and specific instruction will equip one to perform competently—as any skier, dancer, or potter will affirm. In order to experience first hand the elusive phenomenology of learning, all psychoanalysts would do well to be passionately involved in some kind of physical skill: golf, pottery, archery, music, anything. Doing therapy, or for that matter, being a patient, is not all that different.

I would claim that if we are all doing something in common in our practice of psychoanalysis, it clearly lies *not* in our theoretical congruence, but must be something ineffable in our praxis. I would also claim that our activity has little to do with our metapsychological canons, but actually taps into the same unconscious learning process that these other activities do. The essence of psychoanalysis lies not in the hotly debated metapsychologies, but in the phenomenology of learning: in the elusive, perhaps ineffable, relationship between learning and consciousness, consciousness and awareness, instruction and comprehension.

How do instruction and rules "sink in"? Catching on, "getting it" is an extremely obscure process. It requires translating from a formal set of rules to an experiential grasp. All of us have had that experience, the "ah-hah" phenomenon. "So that's what it feels like" has a very indirect relationship to "this is how to do it." But once one has the feeling, the instructions seem suddenly to have acquired a new clarity. We have acquired "insight." All this is so evident that it's a bit embarrassing to talk about it. It is not without reason that we have been called The Apostles of the Obvious. As psychoanalysts, we know that everyone misses the obvious, and that the obvious is not always so obvious. More often than not it is "purloined," left in full view to be not seen (Levenson, 1991). Instruction is not a series of increasingly sophisticated statements, but the same simple rules repeated over and over, yet each time understood on an entirely different level. Note the Zen saying that the last thing you learn is the first.

234 Psychoanalytic theory and practice

I have the very distinct impression that what trainees need is not a catechism that teaches the relation of the institute's beloved canons to treatment, but a way of experiencing the analytic process as not so different from the learning of any other skill. There is some common denominator of learning that is prelanguage, almost proprioceptive; perhaps rather than teaching, we should be establishing the preconditions for learning. We should be paying more attention to *how* we learn, rather than what we learn.

Psychoanalysis is subject to a dialectical rhythm. Every advance is initially productive, turns in to a doctrine, and ends as a cliché and a countertransference. Then the next cycle of reversal begins. Intrasychic and interpersonal exist on just such a dialectic wheel. I believe that, after an intense involvement with transferential enactments and their ramifications—and just as traditional psychoanalysts are discovering the interpersonal—many interpersonalists are experiencing a resurgence of interest in the patient's intrapsychic processes. And by intrapsychic I do not mean what is *in* the unconscious—the libido theory—but *how* unconscious mentation works.

To end on an appropriately millennial note, I gather that many cryogenic institutes are no longer freezing entire bodies for later resurrection, but only the heads. Whether this is an economy or a technological necessity I do not know, but it certainly does define their priorities. Let us suppose that in the year 2460, I am defrosted and revived with my head attached to a new and doubtlessly superior cloned body. Will the new body dictate a new mind? Will it still be me? My precious self resurrected? (Or selves? if you prefer the new modish multiple personalities).

"I think not," he said, and disappeared!

Notes

1. The chapter first appeared in 1998 in *Contemporary Psychoanalysis*, 34(2): 239–249.
2. See Jonathan Miller (1995) for extensive discussion of this theme.
3. Why the double negative? Talmudic scholars, as Dr. B. Wolstein informed me, will remember the "Do not do unto others as you would not have them do unto you" of Rabbi Hillel.
4. See Mahoney (1991) for explication of deep and surface structures.

References

Bartlett, F. (1985). *Thinking.* New York: Basic Books.

Chalmers, D.J. (1995). The puzzle of conscious experience. *Scientific American*, 273(6):80–86.

Chalmers, D.J. (1996). *The Conscious Mind.* New York: Oxford University Press.

Crowley, R. (1984). Book review. *American Journal of Orthopsychiatry*, 54(1).

Damasio, A.R. (1994). *Descartes' Error.* New York: Grosset/Putnam.

Dennett, D.C. (1991). *Consciousness Explained.* Boston, MA: Little, Brown and Co.

Eagle, N.M. (1987). *Recent Developments in Psychoanalysis.* Cambridge, MA: Harvard University Press.

Ellenberger, H. (1970). *The Discovery of the Unconscious.* New York: Basic Books.

Freud, S. (1920). Beyond the pleasure principle. In J. Strachey (Ed.), *The Standard Edition of the Complete Psychological Works of Sigmund Freud* (Vol. XVIII). London: Hogarth Press, pp. 7–64.

Freud, S. (1923). The ego and the id. In J. Strachey (Ed.), *The Standard Edition of the Complete Psychological Works of Sigmund Freud* (Vol. XIX). London: Hogarth Press, pp. 3–66.

Gardner, H. (1983). *Frames of Mind: The Theory of Multiple Intelligences.* New York: Basic Books.

Green, A. (1995). Has sexuality anything to do with psychoanalysis? *International Journal of Psycho-Analysis*, 76(3):871–883.

Hayek, F.A. (1978). *New Studies in Philosophy, Politics, Economics, and the History of Ideas.* Chicago, IL: University of Chicago Press.

Horgan, J. (1996). Why Freud isn't dead. *Scientific American*, 275(6):106–111.

Lacan, J. (1977). *Écrits: A selection.* New York: W.W. Norton.

Levenson, E. (1991). *The Purloined Self.* New York: Contemporary Psychoanalysis Books.

Levenson, E. (1996). The politics of interpretation. *Contemporary Psychoanalysis*, 32(4):631–648.

Mahoney, M.J. (1991). *Human Change Processes: The Scientific Foundations of Psychotherapy.* New York: Basic Books.

Meltzoff, A. and Gopnick, A. (Eds.) (1993). *Understanding Other Minds.* Oxford: Oxford University Press.

Miller, J. (1995). Going unconscious. *New York Review of Books*, April 20, pp. 59–65.

Phillips, A. (1995). *Terrors and Experts.* Cambridge, MA: Harvard University Press.

Polanyi, M. (1958). *Personal Knowledge: Towards a Postcritical Philosophy.* Chicago, IL: University of Chicago Press.

Searle, J. (1997). Consciousness and the philosophers. *New York Review of Books*, 44(4):43–50.

Stern, D. (1984). *The Interpersonal World of the Infant: A View from Psycho-analysis and Developmental Psychology*. New York: Basic Books.

Stern, D. (1996). The social construction of therapeutic action. *Psychoanalytic Inquiry*, 16(2):265–293.

Winnicott, D.W. (1949). Mind and its relation to the psyche-soma. In *Collected Papers: Through Pediatrics to Psychoanalysis*. London: Tavistock Publications.

Chapter 19

The enigma of the unconscious[1]

Marshall McLuhan said, "We don't know who discovered water, but we do know it wasn't a fish." That's the side of psychoanalysis I wish to consider—not the analyst in pursuit of immutable, timeless Truth, but the analyst immersed in his or her world and changed by it. The consequence may be, not that we will do therapy differently, but that we might conceptualize what we do differently, and perhaps even become aware of doing things that heretofore operated entirely outside of our awareness.

Psychoanalysts, it has been said, suffer from "physics envy." We would dearly like to be scientific, to promulgate timeless principles and truths. We have never been happy with the idea that our vaunted theoretical insights reflect larger sociocultural shifts that are part of what Kuhn (1962) called the paradigm of the times. In Zen, they say to see the fish one must look at the water. We are not sui generis, but are carried along by the river of change, and that change is clearly in the direction of a new interest in the nature of consciousness, an interest far more ubiquitous than that of psychoanalysis alone. As McGinn (1999a) put it, "I believe myself that the new interest in consciousness represents the next big phase in human thought about the natural world, as large as the determination to understand the physical world that gathered force in the seventeenth century" (p. 46).

For psychoanalysts, the twentieth century began with Freud's construct of the "dynamic" unconscious and ended with the emergence of a radically different concept, the "enabling" unconscious of contemporary cognitive science. This is part of a more pervasive paradigmatic shift that encompasses, not just "The Unconscious," but changing perceptions of consciousness itself, with its roots in the mind-brain dichotomy—the very relationship of thought to its organic substratum, the brain. Consciousness, previously dismissed as the "ghost in the machine," a discredited Cartesian hangover, is re-emerging as the central issue of twenty-first century philosophy. Metapsychology, our favorite conceit, our search for clarity of motivation and causality—I suspect equally a Cartesian anachronism— is being replaced by a new interest in the far more chaotic issue of the phenomenology of mind and its application to the praxis of therapy. We, it would appear, have been putting Descartes before the horse!

The nature of consciousness is hotly debated in a virtually medievalist sectarianism among the mentalists, the functionalists, the materialists, and the mysterians (Damasio, 1994). Suffice it to say that the debate centers on whether consciousness is merely an epiphenomenon of the brain—an inevitable outcome of organic complexity—or whether it is of another essence altogether. (See Chalmers, 1996, and Searle, 1997, for discussion of a belief in a fundamentally irreducible consciousness.) Consciousness, as Damasio says, is "the last great mystery and may lead us to change our view of the universe we inhabit" (p. 21).

So I may be talking at one and the same time about a centurial and a millennial paradigmatic shift. I suggested, in 1972, that our scientific paradigm (more pervasive and compelling than a metaphor) mirrored our significant technology: for example, Freud mirrored the energic system of steam-powered machines of his time; Sullivan, the nexus of communication systems; more recently, what I called "organismic" concepts had taken hold (Levenson, 1972). It is no great leap to suggest that with the explosive burgeoning of computer technology, we shall soon have machines that can duplicate mental complexity. Will they then think? And, if they think, will they experience consciousness? This is, of course, one of the central debates in "artificial intelligence." At any rate, they'll change the way *we* think. As I elaborate later, I believe that computers may portend a new paradigmatic shift to something resembling the "hyperspace" concept of computer technology, radically changing the way we conceptualize the psychoanalytic process.

Psychoanalysis is in great flux. Psychoanalysts are becoming more interested in less traditional treatment parameters. But there is a certain conceptual lag. We are still arguing metapsychologies, explanatory meta-phors, when the time for that may well be past. Certainly, by now we must admit that for all our debates about the hegemony of our particular position over all others, we are very likely all doing pretty much the same thing,

The enigma of the unconscious 239

sharing the same praxis, albeit using different explanatory sets. Rather than the hoary Platonic-Cartesian conceit that to know is to effect, "I think therefore I can," the present question may be how does anyone learn anything from anybody? The issue for us may be to try to grasp the phenomenology of what it is we do when we do what we know how to do. In other words, we may all be involved in a therapeutic process that is only remotely represented by our metapsychologies.

I believe we are moving beyond our doctrinaire debates about interpretive sets—Oedipal, pre-Oedipal, self, Freudian, relational, interpersonal, object-relational—which have mired our inquiries in the tarpits of dogma. Implicit in all these explanatory sets is the idea that insight is superordinate to change, what has been called the "Rumplestiltskin Fallacy." Rumplestiltskin, as you will recall, was the evil dwarf in the fairy tale who blew up—deconstructed, if you will—when his name was known. Ergo, naming—the mutative interpretation—leads to change. As I elaborate later, what we say or do (much the same thing) has no linear connection to what ensues as a consequence. We are involved, as Wittgenstein said, in a confusion of causes and reasons (Heaton, 2000, p. 52). If we might agree, however, that we are all tapping into a creative, cohesive, albeit largely out-of-awareness process that takes place between analyst and patient, which we try to facilitate by monitoring and clarifying our own participation—regardless of whether we make our awareness openly manifest in the psychoanalytic exchange—then we are all doing a thoroughly contemporary psychoanalysis. We do not cure; we do our work and cure happens. We may *spend* the next millennium happily figuring out how that might happen.

The confusion begins with the way we use the term "consciousness," inasmuch as we equate it with "awareness" or with "mind." *We do not consider the feasibility of unconscious consciousness.* Words used casually as synonyms are often from different etymological roots, and carry, however faintly, powerfully divergent conceptual sets from the distant past. (For a detailed elaboration of the difference between authenticity and sincerity see Levenson, 1974.) "Consciousness" comes from a Latin root, *con siere*, "to know with," *to be capable of complex response to the environment.* Awareness comes from an old English root meaning "to turn toward." I would claim that consciousness is not identical with self-awareness or self-consciousness. One may have complex intersubjective experiences without reflecting on them. Our reflective conflation of

240   Psychoanalytic theory and practice

awareness and consciousness is largely vestigial, a heritage of Freud's first topographical model (unconscious, preconscious, conscious), which is bracketed together consciousness and perception (Laplanche and Pontalis, 1973, pp. 84–85). Of course, later developments in ego psychology posited "conflict-free spheres," and contemporary Freudian theory recognizes the dilemma.

Nevertheless, this spatial metaphor has haunted psychoanalysis ever since. We cannot help but think of "conscious," "unconscious," "inter-personal," and "intrapsychic" as realms, spaces to be filled with content. Again, Wittgenstein:

> We search through a problem "space" and insight is our reward for perseverence. The search metaphor has many of the attributes of searching in physical space so it is pictured as occurring in a conceptual space or a mental one—one searches one's mind!
>
> (Heaton, 2000, p. 18)

Compare Freud's (1895) conflating of awareness and consciousness with William James's (1890) description of the "stream of consciousness":

> Our normal waking consciousness, rational consciousness, as we call it, is but one special kind of consciousness, whilst all about it, parted from it by the flimsiest of screens, there lie potential forms of consciousness entirely different: We may go through life without suspecting their existence; but apply the requisite stimulus, and at a touch they are there in all their completeness ... No account of the universe in its totality can be final which leaves these other forms of consciousness quite disregarded. How to regard them is the question— for they are so discontinuous with ordinary consciousness. Yet they may determine attitudes though they cannot furnish formulas, and open a region though they fail to give a map (pp. 224–290).

Consider further the concepts of another contemporary and familiar of Freud, the eminent neurologist Hughlings Jackson. Jackson referred to the "dreamy state," an uncoupling of consciousness, a dissociation, which takes place in certain forms of "jacksonian" epilepsy. He describes a doctor who, about to examine a patient, feels a seizure coming on. "Coming to" some time later, he finds that he has examined the patient, made the diagnosis, discussed it with the patient's family, collected his fee, and sent the patient to a hospital bed. No one had noticed anything odd or off in his behavior. (See Meares, 1999, for detailed discussion of Jackson's relevance to psychoanalytic thinking.) This is not the retrograde amnesia of grand mal epilepsy, since he was having the seizure during his appropriate performance. Clearly he was, in some sense, fully conscious, albeit insensate. I do not believe this can be considered as dissociation, a psychological mechanism, because amnesia is an intrinsic part of the syndrome, representing focal brain activity.

It is of note that in the extensive current literature on mind-brain and consciousness, only McGinn and Dorpat explicitly refer to an unconscious dimension of consciousness (Bargh and Chatrand, 1999; Chalmers, 1995, 1996; Dennett, 1991; Dorpat and Miller, 1992; Ellenberger, 1970; Horgan, 1996; Meltzoff and Gopnick, 1993; Searle, 1997; Stone, 1997). "Consciousness," McGinn (1999b) says, "has a hidden structure, a secret underside, a covert essence" (p. 140). It seems to me extraordinary that such a facile assumption—that sentience, awareness, and consciousness are cognates—is so widely held.

Before I try to get into all that in detail, let me give you a clinical example, to demonstrate the way data operates for me. I will then try to parse out the theoretical implications of this way of viewing the psychoanalytic praxis. As my clinical material suggests, sometimes awareness comes from the patient's productions, sometimes from the therapist's. One has the odd sense of being carried along by a powerful flow, a river, sometimes above the surface, sometimes beneath it, sometimes through rapids, sometimes tranquilly, but never is the experience entirely of one's own construction. When change does come, is it because of an insight, an awareness of one's own participation, a change in one's participation, or, perhaps, an unconscious working-through in which one's conscious perception is only the tip?

This is a brief and, ultimately, probably an unsatisfying clinical example, because it illustrates no nice, clear linear progression from data to theory to treatment. This young man, a concert violinist, dreams that he has been given two tickets to a concert. One is a brownie, the other is a mulberry tart. He meets a bachelor uncle who asks him how to find a "Westchester whore" (is this a play on "tart"?). Then he is back in his mother's apartment. A big black man jumps out, nude, from a steamy closet, a gay man whom he knows. He does not feel particularly threatened.

242 Psychoanalytic theory and practice

I ask him about homosexual anxieties. Yes—he is worried that he might secretly have homosexual desires, but he has had no experiences, is aware of no interest in men; indeed, he is aroused by women (he is engaged). I ask about "mulberry" tart—he'd never heard of one. His grandfather, who lived in Westchester, had a mulberry tree in his yard. They would collect berries in a basket and eat them (mulberries are large and whitish). In his first session in therapy, he'd unexpectedly burst into tears when mentioning his grandfather. He'd loved him immensely and had grieved over his death several years ago. Had grandfather ever molested him? No, but sometimes they slept in the same bed.

You will note that nothing gets clearer, but there is a kind of "hypertext" jump—hypertext being the little hand on your computer which portends a leap to another link in hyperspace—from one topic to another: from past, to present, to dreams, to fantasies, to transference (to therapist as homosexual attacker or loving grandfather), to "tarts-whores," to "closets-gays"—a number of antitheses and puns. Brownies are brown and mulberries are white, old country-American? I live in Westchester. More-over, I had just recently learned how mulberry bushes came to Westchester (an abortive silk industry). If you credit a cultural unconscious, how about "around and around the mulberry bush" (which is an ancient tune about the plague).

Why should this discursive inquiry make any therapeutic difference? Where and how do these bits of information coalesce? What we define as conscious discourse is clearly only a small part of a pervasive Jamesian stream of consciousness that encompasses, not just the data of the analysis, but a continuous, ongoing, seamless, interaction-enactment that weaves in and out of awareness. I came across this wonderfully illustrative quote from Hadas (1999).

In "The Structure of the *Orlando Furioso*," . . . Calvino evokes what he perceives as "Ariosto's creative method . . . this expansion from within, with episodes proliferating from other episodes, generating new symme-tries and contrasts . . . this poem with its polycentric, synchronic structure, whose episodes spiral off in every direction, continually intersecting with and bifurcating from each other." This description, written in 1974 may look in 1999 as if it anticipates hypertext, the polycentric, synchronic world of the Web (p. 139).

As I have said, reformulating all this requires a radical shift in our concept of the unconscious. I would claim that Freud started with a naive

The enigma of the unconscious 243

(i.e., unformulated) interest in the phenomenology of consciousness as it emerged from his work with hysteria and hypnosis (Levenson, 1996). It was at Charcot's Sâlpetrière clinic that Freud discovered, as he later reported in his autobiography, that "I received the profoundest impression of the possibility that there could be powerful mental processes which *nevertheless remained hidden from the consciousness* of men" (Freud, 1925, p. 17).

On rereading the *Studies on Hysteria* (Freud *and* Breuer, 1895), Freud's earliest fascination with this phenomenon of unconscious mentation is evident: how patients, under hypnosis, could remember events that were out of conscious awareness, and how the content of hypnotic sessions was "forgotten" when awake, but could be recalled with intact continuity in the next hypnotic session. Freud surmised that unconscious mentation was mentation pushed under or out of consciousness. This view was a correlate of his contemporaneous neurology.

Freud's famous *Project for a Scientific Psychology* reflected what we currently call the Papez-Maclean theory of brain evolution (Hampden-Turner, 1981), which was, in the late 1800s, dependent on Hughling Jackson's (1884) concept of functional levels in the brain, according to which there is a stratification of neurological functioning. Each layer represses and smoothes out the layer below it. For example, it was a neurological truism that the cortex smoothed out the functions of the cerebellum: if the cortex was destroyed, the cerebellum "emerged" and the patient developed a typical cerebellar intention tremor. Thus the cortex was seen as repressing the more primitive parts of the brain. It was thence a small step to attributing to the cortex a repressive psychological function, keeping out of awareness objectionable, anxiety-laden material.

In spite of Freud's efforts to establish a topology of the unconscious, we really don't have the foggiest notion of how anything is kept in or out of consciousness. As Jonathan Miller (1995) put it, "we are the unwitting beneficiaries of a mind that is, in a sense, only partially our own." What is terribly important to understand is that we all do uncritically accept the premise that bringing things into awareness is the *vis à tergo* of therapy. As Miller put it, comparing the Freudian Unconscious to what he called the "enabling unconscious,"

> In psychoanalytic theory, the Unconscious exercises an almost exclusively withholding function, actively denying its mental contents

244 Psychoanalytic theory and practice

their *access* to awareness. Through the agency of repression, which Freud identified as Society's censorious representative in the psyche, the individual is relieved of thoughts which might, if consciously experienced, compromise wholehearted cooperation in social life (p. 651).

We are shifting to a more holistic concept of brain functioning. The unconscious, many of us now believe, is where most everything happens. Consciousness becomes an epiphenomenon, a bubble of awareness. For Freud, content was pushed *down*, kept out of awareness.[2] For so-called cognitive scientists, consciousness—in its common usage—is simply a selective awareness of unconscious functioning, pulled *up* into awareness. It is true that things may be kept out of consciousness via "selective inattention" or, more strongly, repression. But both activities require, as Sartre (1956) pointed out, an elaborate unconscious perception and a strategy to prevent emergence *into* awareness—not, one notes, to repress *out* of awareness. I do appreciate that this is a considerable oversimplification, but I am trying to delineate a paradigmatic distinction.

Cognitive science is the scientific discipline that studies conceptual systems. Founded in the 1970s, it has, according to Lakoff and Johnson (1999), made "startling discoveries." To quote, "most thought is unconscious, not in the Freudian sense of being repressed, but in the sense that it operates beneath the level of cognitive awareness, inaccessible to consciousness and operating too quickly to be focused on" (p. 10). Most of what goes on is unconscious, designed and intended to remain out of awareness, and is complexly cognitive. I must repeat, thinking and traditional consciousnesses are not necessarily coeval.

Remember the cautionary tale of the centipede who tripped over his feet when he began to think about how he managed to walk that way. Chomsky's concept of an unconscious grammar is another example of a complex mentation not only operating totally out of awareness, but not accessible to awareness. As Polanyi (1958) put it,

We can know more than we can tell and we can tell nothing without relying on our awareness of things we may not be able to tell. Perhaps, as Hayek (1978) suggests, we should refer to these processes as "superconscious" because they govern the conscious processes without appearing in them.

The enigma of the unconscious 245

Analysts do tend to think of awareness as the superior state; that is, we do not think of reflexivity or unconsciousness as possibly advantageous—that perhaps awareness or self-consciousness interferes with or is not accessible for certain necessary mentations, and not just presumably "conflict-free" ones.

We really do not know how consciousness works, how it *thinks*. We do not have a satisfactory theory of mind. We do not understand how we proceed from our own experience to formulation of that experience, how we grasp and understand the Other's experience, and how our communications of what we believe we know influence the Other. We do know, by inference, that it does not follow the excluded middle principle (a thing is or is not) of Aristotelian logic. It would seem, if anything, to be closer to the paradoxical thinking of the Talmud, wherein a thing might both be and not be simultaneously. Conscious thinking follows the rules of Greek logic—deduction, categorizing, inferring—our Western cultural heritage. In contrast, unconscious thinking seems closer to the free-ranging hypertext sense of mishnah, where words and concepts are pursued to their most unexpected implications. As Handelman (1982) puts it:

> There is, then, no ultimate outside point of view. The text continues to develop each time it is studied, with each new interpretation, for the interpretation is an uncovering of what was latent in the text, and thus only an extension of it: the text is a self-regenerating process (p. 49).

It suggests the "mishnah-ish" conclusion that both free-association and Sullivan's detailed inquiry (used, not to get the facts straight, but in a deconstructive, disorganizing way) are not so much entrées into the unconscious, as the unconscious talking.[3] Freud, it would appear, wrote Greek but thought Jewish. How do we listen and organize what we hear?

Cavell (1993), the in-house philosopher of the American Psychoanalytic Association, has pointed out that Freud's "Unconscious" does not do justice to the subtlety of so-called unconscious process. Primary process is presumed to be responsible for such semiotically complex activities as joking and punning and for very sophisticated decisions about what and when to censor (p. 174). Clearly, neither Freud nor Sullivan's (1953) concepts of a "self-system" and "security operations" make sense without a cognitively sophisticated unconscious in touch with its surround, nor does

Melanie Klein's concept of projective-identification, which requires a subtle and mysterious attunement to the unconscious of the Other. Schore (1994), a neuropsychologist and a subtle integrator of psychoanalytic concepts and neurological substrates, talks of Klein's "projective-identification" as a communication of the right brains of both participants in an exchange that utilizes primitive nonverbal affective cues. How, then, is it possible that projective-identification involves such elaborate interactions and conceptualizations? If therapists resonate to the patient's unconscious, it is clearly in no simple way.

I believe that the central inquiry for psychoanalysis increasingly will be, not how one gets better, but how anyone learns anything. It is a striking paradox, known to anyone who has ever practiced a physical skill, that there is a huge and ineffable gap between the intellectual formulation of an activity and doing it. We all know "locker-room experts" who can "talk a good game" and are inept players. But no degree of library research or detailed and specific instruction will equip one to perform. In order to experience first hand the elusive phenomenology of learning, all psychoanalysts would do well to be passionately involved in learning another skill.

How, for example, do instruction and rules "sink in"? Catching on, "getting it," is an extremely obscure process. It requires translating from a formal set of rules to an experiential grasp. All of us have had that experience, the "ah-hah" phenomenon. "So that's what it feels like" has a very indirect relationship to "this is how to do it." But once one has the feeling, the instruction seems suddenly to have acquired a new clarity. We have acquired "insight." All this is so evident that it's a bit embarrassing to talk about it. It is not for nothing that we have been called "The Apostles of the Obvious." Instruction is not a series of increasingly sophisticated statements, but the same simple rules repeated over and over, yet each time understood on an entirely different level; note the Zen saying that the last thing you learn is the first—perhaps that's why I'm reassessing the potency of free-association.

I would claim that, if we are all doing something in common in our practice of psychoanalysis, it clearly does not lie in our theoretical congruence, but must be something ineffable in our praxis. I would also claim that our activity has little to do with our metapsychological canons, but actually taps into the same unconscious learning process as do other activities. The essence of psychoanalytic praxis does not lie in the hotly

The enigma of the unconscious   247

debated and increasingly convergent and irrelevant metapsychologies, but in the elusive phenomenology of learning—and, I might add, listening. For we have very little sense of how we delineate and distinguish what it is we are hearing.[4]

I have the very distinct impression that what trainees need is not a catechism that teaches the relation of the institute's beloved canons to treatment, but a way of experiencing the analytic process as being not so very different from the learning of any other skill. There is some common denominator of learning that is prelanguage, almost proprioceptive; perhaps, rather than teaching, we should be establishing the preconditions for learning. We should be paying more attention to *how* we learn, rather than *what* we learn.

Why then do patients get better? It is not so clear. Wouldn't it be lovely if we could attribute it to our mutative interpretations? Our empathic engagements? Our superior metapsychological understanding? Our controlled regressions? Of course, we do attribute cure to these interventions, but that is largely canonical warfare. No one needs to be reminded that the debate over psychoanalysis's "scientific" status hangs on just that point. I believe that we cannot convincingly demonstrate a linear, causal connection between anything we do and the outcome.

Obviously, others disagree.

> When I suggest to a patient that he is burdened by irrational guilt feelings, I can see whether his mood improves; or when a patient and I conclude that she no longer needs to be afraid of being more sexually potent than her mother, we can see whether she will begin to have orgasms during intercourse: The circumstances under which psychoanalysts can make predictions may be poorly controlled and definite empirical evidence for a psychoanalytic proposition may be very difficult to obtain, but hypotheses testing via prediction is possible in psychoanalysis. Therefore psychoanalysis is a science.
>
> (Renik, 1988, p. 492)

But Renik must certainly agree that the same interpretation made earlier or later or in a different context might not have worked. This is the vaunted "timing." But who knows when or why? If the time was ripe, did the patient already know what Renik was about to say? Was the interpretation a closure, a parenthesis, an enactment, permission? Was the patient's

248 Psychoanalytic theory and practice

response a flight into health, conforming, submission to a sexual transference, an act of genuine autonomy? All of the above.

This is the hoariest debate in psychoanalysis. We cannot specify the "mutative" variables because we may not use the outcome to validate our interpretive assumptions. Just because something "works," we may not assume it worked for the reasons we think it worked. The out-of-awareness dimensions of any intersubjective exchange are immense. Psychoanalytic praxis is a lot like magic, which depends on contiguous effects. One does a series of things in a certain order. Sometimes the magic works, sometimes it doesn't. Certainly, when the magic works, it is more a matter of the interpretation being the in-awareness component of an entire field of interaction and comprehension.

I think we cure people by tapping into and participating in a largely unconscious—with bubbles of awareness—process. I think that brain is individual but mind is a field phenomenon, a network, a web. To paraphrase Winnicott's famous "there is no such thing as a baby"—implying that the mother-child dyad is the indivisible unit—I would say that there is no such thing as a mind. It takes others to extend that network and the extension may be, in itself, restorative. Perhaps the issue is not insight but learning, which involves issues of memory. Does this networking of data first facilitate short-term memory and then long-term memory? Memory prefigures learning, which prefigures change.

I understand that all this may be very annoying. Everyone wants an algorithm for therapy, wants to feel that he or she has a conception of how psychopathology develops, and a theory of therapy that applies that concept to the treatment room and results in cure. In contrast, what I am offering seems chaotic; but only if one feels one must be in control, know how therapy works, know where the patient is going, know why change takes place. If one can accept that one is tapping into and riding, like a wave, an ineffable process—part conscious, part unconscious, part between people, part autonomous, part rational conceptualizing, and part a mysterious act of mutual creation—then one might wish to augment and facilitate the process without needing to grasp it firmly. As Wilner (1999) put it, "The seeming paradox of unconscious experience is that one cannot be conscious of it without losing the qualitative character of unconsciousness itself—its emergent flow" (p. 621). I would like to suggest that the act, the praxis of psychoanalysis—the inquiry, association, dreams, fantasies, and the reiteration of those themes in the behavioral field of patient and

The enigma of the unconscious 249

therapist, in the office and as it extends into their private worlds—is the cure! The medium may indeed be the message.

Psychoanalysis is subject to a dialectical rhythm. Every advance is initially productive, turns into a doctrine, and ends as a cliché and a countertransference. Then the next cycle of reversal begins. Intrapsychic and interpersonal exist on just such a dialectic wheel. I believe that after an intense involvement with transferential enactments and their ramifications—and just as traditional psychoanalysts are discovering the interpersonal—many interpersonalists are experiencing a resurgence of interest in the patient's intrapsychic processes. And, by intrapsychic I do not mean what is *in* the unconscious—for example, the libido theory—but *how* unconscious mentation works.

Because our goal is to effect change in our patients, it behooves us to attend to how people learn and change, the relationship of what is said to what is done, of experience to conceptualization of experience. Otherwise, we shall be left behind, like magicians, muttering our incantations and wondering why the magic does not work.

Notes

1. This chapter was first read on November 4, 2000, in slightly different form, to the Suffolk Institute for Psychotherapy and Psychoanalysis. It was also published in 2001 in *Contemporary Psychoanalysis*, 37(2):339–249.
2. It is true, as Solms (1997) points out, that by 1910 Freud had decided that mental functions are inherently unconscious, but he was talking about the machinery of repression: still, what enters consciousness is what ego defenses permit to emerge.
3. See Handelman (1982) for discussion of the Greek and Rabbinical roots of Freud's theorizing. See Rosen (2000) for links between the Internet and the Talmud.
4. It would be going too far afield to elaborate, but briefly, it very probably has to do with metaphor making, the ability to distinguish similarities and difference (States, 1998).

References

Bargh, J.A. and Chatrand, T.L. (1999). The unbearable automaticity of being. *American Psychologist*, 54(7):462–479.

Cavell, M. (1993). *The Psychoanalytic Mind: From Freud to Philosophy.* Cambridge, MA: Harvard University Press.

250 Psychoanalytic theory and practice

Chalmers, D.J. (1995). The puzzle of conscious experience. *Scientific American*, 273: 80–86.

Chalmers, D.J. (1996). *The Conscious Mind*. New York: Oxford University Press.

Damasio, A.R. (1994). *Descartes' Error*. New York: Grosset/Putnam.

Dennett, D.C. (1991). *Consciousness Explained*. Boston, MA: Little, Brown and Co.

Dorpat, T. and Miller, M. (1992). *Clinical Interpretation and the Analysis of Meaning*. Hillsdale, NJ: The Analytic Press.

Ellenberger, H. (1970). *The Discovery of the Unconscious*. New York: Basic Books.

Freud, S. (1925). An autobiographical study. In J. Strachey (Ed.), *The Standard Edition of the Complete Psychological Works of Sigmund Freud*. London: Hogarth Press, Vol. XX, pp. 7–74.

Freud, S. and Breuer, J. (1895). Studies on Hysteria. In J. Strachey (Ed.), *The Standard Edition of the Complete Psychological Works of Sigmund Freud*. London: Hogarth Press, Vol. II, pp. 1–309.

Hadas, R. (1999). A great writer's everyday workshop. *The American Scholar*, 68:137–140.

Hampden-Turner, C. (1981). *Maps of the Mind*. New York: Collier.

Handelman, S. (1982). *The Slayers of Moses: The Emergence of Rabbinic Interpretation in Modern Literary Theory*. Albany, NY: State University of New York.

Hayek, F.A. (1978). *New Studies in Philosophy, Politics, Economics, and the History of Ideas*. Chicago, IL: University of Chicago Press.

Heaton, J.M. (2000). *Wittgenstein and Psychoanalysis*. New York: Totem Books.

Horgan, J. (1996). Why Freud isn't dead. *Scientific American*, 275:106–111.

Jackson, H. (Ed.) (1884). *Evolution and Dissociation in the Nervous System*. New York: Basic Books, 1958.

James, W. (1890). *The Principles of Psychology*. New York: Dover Publications, 1950.

Kuhn, T. (1962). *The Structure of Scientific Revolutions*. Chicago, IL: University of Chicago Press.

Lakoff, G. and Johnson, M. (1999). *Philosophy in the Flesh: The Embodied Mind and Its Challenge to Western Thought*. New York: Basic Books.

Laplanche, J. and Pontalis, J.B. (1973). *The Language of Psycho-analysis* (trans. D. Nicholson-Smith). New York: W.W. Norton.

Levenson, E. (1972). *The Fallacy of Understanding*. New York: Basic Books:

Levenson, E. (1974). Changing concepts of intimacy. *Contemporary Psychoanalysis*, 10(3):359–369.

Levenson, E. (1996). The politics of interpretation. *Contemporary Psychoanalysis*, 32(4):631– 648.

McGinn, C. (1999a). Can we ever understand consciousness? *New York Review of Books*, 46:44–48.

McGinn, C. (1999b). *The Mysterious Flame*. New York: Basic Books.

Meares, R. (1999). The contributions of Hughlings Jackson to an understanding of dissociation. *American Journal of Psychiatry*, 156(12):1850–1855.

Meltzoff, A. and Gopnick, A. (Eds.) (1993). *Understanding Other Minds*. Oxford: Oxford University Press.

Miller, J. (1995). Going unconscious. *New York Review of Books*, 42:59–65.

Polanyi, M. (1958). *Personal Knowledge: Towards a Postcritical Philosophy*. Chicago, IL: University of Chicago Press.

Renik, O. (1988). The analyst's subjectivity and the analyst's objectivity: *International Journal of Psycho-Analysis*, 79:487–497.

Rosen, J. (2000). *The Talmud and the Internet: A Journey between Worlds*. New York: Farrer, Straus and Giroux.

Sartre, J.P. (1956). *Being and Nothingness*. New York: Philosophical Library.

Schore, A. (1994). *Affect Regulation and the Origin of the Sell*. Hillsdale, NJ: Lawrence Erlbaum.

Searle, J. (1997). Consciousness and the philosophers. *The New York Review of Books*, 44:43–50.

Solms, M. (1997). What is consciousness? *Journal of the American Psychoanalytic Association*, 45(3):681–778.

States, B.O. (1998). Of paradoxes and tautologies. *The American Scholar*, 67:51–66.

Stone, A.A. (1997). Where will psychoanalysis survive? *Harvard Magazine*, January–February:33–39.

Sullivan, H.S. (1953). *Conceptions of Modern Psychiatry*. New York: W.W. Norton.

Wilner, W. (1999). The un-consciousing of awareness in psychoanalytic therapy. *Contemporary Psychoanalysis*, 35(4):617–628.

Chapter 20

Freud's dilemma
On writing Greek and thinking Jewish[1]

It seems appropriate to begin with a quote from Roberta Held Weiss's 1985 paper "In Praise of Actuality," which is very much in the spirit of my presentation.

> [T]he truth we look for in psychoanalysis is not to be found while searching for historical events or causes, nor in recreating, restoring or repairing the past. Neither would I locate it in a hermeneutic exegesis, a coherent and logical narrative. Instead I would search for it in our patients' struggle to give shape and meaning to their experience, in their efforts, however fragmented, incoherent, desultory, erratic or formless these efforts may be. Psychoanalytic truth, I will maintain, emerges in the analysis of the immediate analytic experience, in the observation and analysis of the participation. That is, it is in a reflection on its own process, in a self-consciousness of the emerging experience between the analyst and the patient, continually being redefined, that psychoanalytic truth is found (p. 2371).

The major appeal of White, for me in the early 1950s, was not Sullivan per se, but the White Institute's slant toward cultural relativism and its accent on social context. Those were heady times. The South Pacific had been discovered, and there was a great burgeoning of enthusiasm for cultural anthropology and the perspectivism it engendered. To the best of my recollection, many of us were not primarily as invested in Sullivan in the 1950s as in Fromm, Mead, Benedict, Buber, Sapir, Whorf, Korzybski. Sullivan seemed more relevant for his outreach to linguistics, sociology, and ethnology than for his metapsychology, which was regrettably couched in very abstruse language. Of our two major theorists, Fromm, being a Marxist, had the clearest sense of the patient defined and directed by social and cultural forces. Sullivan was far more interested in microsubjectivity, in the patient's capacity to sustain relationships, to identify contagious anxiety, and to survive adolescence without becoming schizophrenic. Nevertheless, his concept of participant observation clearly viewed the therapist as immersed in the interpersonal field. We all agreed, as the Zen saying goes, that "to see the fish, one must look at the water."

Belief in the importance of social context is about all we held in common. After our fall from analytic grace in the thirties—that is, after the schism with the American—there was established a shifting and uneasy alliance of strange bedfellows: Fromm, Sullivan, Silverberg, Rado, Freud (taught somewhat in the breach), and Ferenczi (taught by Clara Thompson). Horney was first included, then dissociated herself as a result of her conflicts with Fromm. Seduced by the rubric of "cultural psychoanalysis," it took us a while to catch on to how truly incompatible these people were. Like the apprentice swordsman who spends the first few years of training carrying water and dodging blows, we became adept at managing mutually exclusive or contradictory concepts. White candidates necessarily came to be either masters of perspectivism, or, in despair, embraced a simple hysterical dissociation, fastened on one position, and became acolytes. And so, alas, the White Institute came to have its Frommians, its Sullivanians, its Ferenczians, and even quite a few closet-Freudians.

I believe that this training in fancy footwork sensitized me to the huge and persistent schism in psychoanalytic thinking between those who believe in one underlying Truth and those who hold to multiple perspectives. At our increasingly ecumenical interinstitute meetings, I often have the sinking feeling that many of the Freudians—in spite of all their best intentions—au *fond*, still believe that there is a correct meaning, a mutative Truth, to be arrived at by the analyst, who Lacan referred to derisively as "He-Who-Must-Know" (Wilden, 1972). One hears rather plaintive queries: "But how do you know it's going in the *right direction*?" or, "Don't you have to have some idea of where the material is leading, *where it will come out*?" How, they ask, can one follow a road when the road is forming under one's feet?

This split between those who believe in one Truth and the Many is as old and enduring as philosophy itself. The predominant Greek tradition— Plato, Aristotle, and on to Descartes—gave us Western "science," with its

254 Psychoanalytic theory and practice

disciplines of classification and logic, deduction, and induction that have served us so well. As Isaiah Berlin (1998) put it:

> I should like to suggest that the central core of the intellectual tradition of the West has, since Plato (or it may be Pythagoras) rested on three unquestioned dogmas:
>
> 1. that to all genuine questions there is one true answer and one only, all others being deviations from the truth and therefore false . . .
> 2. that the true answers to such questions are, in principle, knowable.
> 3. That these true answers cannot clash with each other, for one true proposition cannot be incompatible with another; that together these answers must form a harmonious whole (p. 555).

This is the famous Aristotelian principle of the excluded middle: a thing either is or is not.

In contrast to this majority position were the Sophists and the Skeptics, who believed in no absolutes, particularly not absolute Truth. To my surprise, it turns out that they were really the outreaches of a Middle Eastern position that Handelman (1982) calls the Rabbinic.

> As we will discover, the infinity of meaning and plurality of interpretation are as much the cardinal virtues, even divine imperatives, for Rabbinic thought as they are the cardinal sins for Greek thought. The movement of Rabbinic interpretation is not from one opposing sphere to another, from the sensible to the nonsensible, but rather "from sense to sense" a movement into the text, not out of it (p. 21).

I also discovered that "The history of philosophy, then, is ultimately an argument between Jews and Greeks." Matthew Arnold, in the nineteenth century, said that "The essential creative dialectic of Western culture [is] an argument between the Hebrew and the Hellene" (p. 170). Handelman calls on Heiddeger, Derrida, et al. to substantiate this contention. She cites Derrida, for example, who asks, "Are we Jews? Are we Greeks? We live in the difference between the Jew and the Greek, which is perhaps the unity of what we call history" (p. 170).

Now all this was news to me. How did Hebraic and Greek become the critical antithesis? I had always considered the Judeo-Christian tradition an historical continuity. Apparently this is not so. Initially, the Jews and Christians split over the proper interpretation of the Text, the Old Testament. For the Christians, the Word became literally flesh, incarnate, God's Truth. The Rabbinic tradition held, as I *shall* elaborate, to the idea of multiple meanings. For the Rabbis, interpretation, not incarnation, was the divine act. So we have a Greco-Christian (not Judeo-Christian) heritage and a Rabbinic, which are in diametrical opposition.

It also first came to my awareness, in reading *The Slayers of Moses*, that Freud himself, and certain current philosophers, notably Derrida and Lacan, have considered psychoanalysis to be in the exegetical tradition of midrash; that is, what Zornberg (1995) calls "a kind of listening for the metamessages of the text" (p. xii). God, it was said, gave to Moses a Text, not a finished, independent, self-sufficient one, but one open to interpretation. I had this epiphany! Like Monsieur Jourdain, in Molière's *Le Bourgeois Gentilhomme*, who discovered, to his delight, that all his life he had been talking prose without knowing it. Well, I'd been practicing midrash without knowing it. Like Freud, as I shall elaborate, I either never knew or unconsciously denied any familiarity with this tradition.

Freud, one might say, wrote Greek and thought Jewish. Sharing this shortcoming with the Master, I became intrigued by the dialectical split between Greek classicism and Jewish Rabbinical thought which has haunted psychoanalysis, including our interpersonal versions, to the very present.[2] I would also suggest that our cultural devotion to the Greco-Christian tradition is beginning to fade. What Derrida called "White Mythology" is beginning to lose its hegemony, infiltrated by other paradigms of thought (Handelman, 1982, p. 16).

This internal split had perpetuated a long-acknowledged but unresolved schism between metapsychology and praxis, between Freud the theoretician and Freud the clinician.[3] Since psychoanalytic institutes are founded on theoretical premises, we need to establish our intellectual hegemony; that is, establish that our metapsychology (a developmental theory and ontology) is more comprehensive, more correct, and more *therapeutic* than yours. Were it not, why come to our institute? Why work our way? We do all spend an awful lot of time trying to correlate our theoretical teachings—our canon—with our clinical praxis. But the correlation between what one learns in classes and what one learns in one's own therapy and in supervision is, to put it kindly, obscure. No less a figure than Anna Freud (1969) said that theory "has become the bugbear of the clinically oriented analyst who feels wholly divorced from it" (p. 49).

Since *The Fallacy of Understanding* in 1972, I've been interested in the way pervasive, unexamined paradigms structure their contemporaneous modes of thinking. I believe that all these positions are not competing visions of the Truth, but contextually defined and largely out-of-awareness perspectivistic vistas. I said then that I thought Freud shared a mechanical (stream engine) paradigm with forces and powers in opposition; Sullivan an informational paradigm; and post-Sullivanians an organismic paradigm. I would like to bring this up to date. I believe we are shifting paradigms again, in this computer age, to another model based on the concept of hyperspace, which, interestingly enough, begins to converge with aspects of intertextual Rabbinic thought. Thus Freud's original retreat from his heritage comes home to roost—it is indeed the return of the repressed.

I shall elaborate this shift with some clinical material and then explore implications for our views of the clinical praxis itself. My ultimate thesis— and it has always been my ultimate thesis—is that, in this postmodern world, we have gone beyond the classical idea of the "mutative" interpretation, in my view a vestigial bit of Cartesianism. I think we *must* jettison the idea that psychoanalysis works because of our interpretations or interventions. Rather, we must examine and sharpen our awareness of the praxis, what it is we do when we do what we know how to do, but alas do not know how to satisfactorily explain. In this respect, we are no different than practitioners of any other craft.

I have a very strong sense that psychoanalysis cures not so much by the Truths it discovers as by the method it uses to arrive at them. As Roberta Held Weiss (1985) put it:

> We might then conclude that the only psychoanalytic truth we can know is that of the nature of the *inquiry* itself, that we have no transcendental view point outside of our own activity in, and experience of, the analysis itself . . . [Analysis] is the process of discovering itself (p. 241).

As you may know, I have had a long interest in the detailed inquiry. It is what defined me as a Sullivanian. But in what Harold Bloom (1975) would call a "misprision" of Sullivan's technique—that is, a deliberate

Freud's dilemma 257

misreading that is the jumping-off point for one's own ideas—rather than use the inquiry exclusively to focus on inattended data, to sharpen the focus I used the inquiry deconstructively, to "unpack" the text. That is, I simply followed the data wherever it led. I consider this defines me as both post-Sullivanian and crypto-Freudian. I do not consider Sullivan truly analytic, because he had little interest in either a free-flowing inquiry or in transference-countertransference, which I would consider the enactment component of the inquiry. He once said, in response to a query, that he scotched transference before it could take place. He saw it as getting in the way of his efforts at demystification of the patient's experience. It seems to me that Sullivan was a pragmatist, that he did pursue an underlying truth, a singular reality obfuscated by anxiety.

Clara Thompson, Fromm-Reichman, and Fromm were, I think, more interested in the free-associative process, having come from classical psychoanalytic backgrounds. Clara Thompson told me that she gave up free-association with some regret, largely because no one seemed able to do it. Mostly, she said, they "just nattered on." Sullivan, of course, came from the tradition of Adolph Meyer's pragmatic psychotherapy. His only direct experience of psychoanalytic treatment was a very brief sortie with Clara. But that's another story altogether!

So, Sullivan's detailed inquiry becomes, in this misprision, an analogue of free-association, a deconstruction, a way of forcing the flow. When I asked "Whatever happened to the cat?" I was not so interested in the fate of the poor cat as I was in the inattended relationships in the family—the way they dealt with the cat's absence (Levenson, 1989). It is taken as a given that by questioning, the therapist is inevitably participating—no matter how unstructured the inquiry might be. Transference and counter-transference emerge seamlessly from the inquiry. Mirabile dictu, the detailed inquiry becomes midrash.

In a wonderful book, *Reading Freud's Readings* (Gilman et al., 1994), Freud's library and his annotations are explored. I hope you will bear with me as I explicate some details of Freud's relationship to Judaism, findings I found fascinating. Freud studied with Theodor Gomperz, Vienna's foremost classical scholar (ironically, a Jew). He became quite friendly with Gomperz and eventually treated both his wife and his son. He also studied with the philosopher Brentano, who believed in the application of the methods of natural science to philosophy and psychology (p. 233). Found among Freud's very extensive classical readings was an annotated

258 Psychoanalytic theory and practice

copy of Jacob Burckhardt's influential *The History of Greek Civilization.* His library also suggests considerable familiarity with the *Oedipus* of Sophocles. Freud could read classical Greek, indeed debated nuances of translation with the author Arnold Zweig (p. 24).

Yet at the same time, Freud wrote to A.A. Roback, an American who had sent him one of his own books, with a dedication written in Hebrew,

> It may interest you to hear that my father did come from an Chassidic background . . . My education was so un-Jewish that today I cannot even read your inscription, which is evidently written in Hebrew. In later life, I often regretted this lack in my education.
>
> (Rizzuto, 1998, p. 30)

Rizzuto says that this is a surprising claim from a man who taught himself Spanish at the age of 15, who had a solid grounding in the Hebrew language in his childhood, and who remained lifetime friends with his childhood Hebrew teacher, Samuel Hammerschlag, and in fact wrote his obituary (pp. 31, 142). Yet, paradoxically, Freud showed no reluctance to acknowledge his Jewishness. In his private conversations, and in his famous treatise on humor, his jokes, stories, and homilies were comfortably Jewish. In a letter to Rank, he bemoaned Jung's inherent limitations in grasping their "Jewish science" (Freud, 1960, p. 163).

Rizzuto tells us that Freud's famously beleaguered father, Jakob, had his tattered Philippson Bible, which had been in his possession since 1848, rebound in leather and gave it to Sigmund on his thirty-fifth birthday, with a hand-written inscription in Hebrew, which Freud presumably could not translate (p. xx). In passing over his eight living children, he repeated the behavior of his namesake, Jacob the Patriarch, selecting Joseph over his other children (p. 57). Rizzuto makes a fascinating case that the acquisitions in Freud's antiquity collection, which was started shortly after his father's death in 1896, replicates the illustrations in the Philippson Bible, which was a radical text written in both German and Hebrew and heavily illustrated with woodcuts, a violation of orthodox prohibitions against graven images. Rizzuto suggests that Jakob, rather than being the conservative Chassid Freud indicated, was a member of the Jewish enlightenment, the Haskala (pp. 42, 33). So perhaps the acorn did not fall as far from the tree as Freud, the Lonely Hero, would have had us believe.

For obvious reasons, Freud would not have been eager to align himself, at least publicly, with Jewish culture. The blatant anti-Semitism of *fin de siècle* Vienna is not new news. It was only in 1848 that Jews had been accorded full political and civil rights, and the right to travel freely in the Austro-Hungarian Empire (p. 33). We all know of the incident in which Freud's father, Jakob, cowered when his hat was knocked off in a Vienna street by a bully, forever branding young Sigmund's memory. According to Freud's son, Freud later charged a group of street bullies in Vienna, waving his cane and forcing them to give way.

Nevertheless, the rabidity of the anti-Semitism and the extent of its application still surprise in a culture that simultaneously, if not applauded, at least permitted Jewish achievements. Rather than the familiar view of anti-Semitism as religious prejudice—that is, the Jews are big-nosed, greedy people who crucified the True Lord and fostered the Protocols of the Elders of Zion—Jews were characterized in the contemporaneous scientific literature as "sexually addicted, feminized, inbred, neurasthenic, frequently criminal." Or, another quote, "In fin de siècle Vienna, the criminality of the Jew was a major factor in understanding the Jew's sexuality" (Gilman et al., 1994, p. 48). The virulence of the anti-Semitism was not so much based on sociological or religious grounds as on genetics —irrevocable, immutable biological destiny. Certainly that was a far profounder denunciation, and it makes Freud's promotion of sexual libido as a life force appear to be an even more courageous act.[4]

Freud's ambivalence about his Jewishness came out most clearly in his long, agonistic relationship to Moses. In 1914, he wrote an article on the Moses of Michelangelo, withdrew it from publication, did not acknowledge authorship until 1924, and published it 3 years later. In 1939, the year he died in England, he wrote his will and finished the text of *Moses and Monotheism*, his last work, a rather wild take on the Bible story (Freud, 1939). There were two Moses and two Gods. Freud's Moses, as you know, was not Jewish, did not speak Hebrew, and, as Freud attested in a letter to the writer Arnold Zweig, "was an anti-Semite" (Gay, 1988, p. 605). Moses gave to the Jews—an inconsequential tribe of Semites with a vengeful primitive God called "Yahweh"—the religion of his model, the Pharaoh Akhenaten who introduced monotheism to Egypt.

Well, as Yogi Berra said, "When you come to a crossroads, take it!" Freud bifurcated metapsychology and praxis, in a manner totally consistent with his own dichotomized cultural tradition. His metapsychology was

260 Psychoanalytic theory and practice

literary, classic Greek, Apollonian—reason in control of impulses. His praxis was pure midrash, talmudic. In other words, Freud simultaneously developed a metatheory of neurosis *and* a perspective on the praxis, the act of therapy—what actually takes place in the interactional field of patient and therapist, including transference and countertransference, used in the most contemporary inclusive sense. By 1905, in the famous "Dora" case, Freud had already developed a quite sharp sense of transference and countertransference; but, since politics, social prejudice, and the need for a coherent binding theory gave priority to metapsychology, to explanation over praxis, Freud decided to give praxis second billing.

I would like to suggest two related developments that are changing the ground-rules. First is our immersion in the postmodern age, with its emphasis on the relativity of values and the politics of culture. Second is a changing paradigm. What is emerging is a computer-based model, predicated on hyperspace and hyperlinks (that little hand on your computer-screen that opens endless networks of connections).

Both the postmodern sensibility and the Internet converge in a most interesting way with the Rabbinic tradition. In a fascinating little book, *The Talmud and the Internet*, Rosen (2000) elaborates the similarity between the Internet "Web," with its hyperlinks going off in all directions, and the Talmud. I have adumbrated this long quote from Rosen:

> Consider a page of Talmud. There are a few lines of Mishnah . . . about a broad range of legalistic questions stemming from the Bible, but ranging into a host of other matters as well. Underneath these few lines begins the Gemarah, the conversation *later* Rabbis had about the conversation *earlier* Rabbis had in the Mishnah. Both the Mishnah and the Gemarah evolved orally over so many hundreds of years that, even in a few lines of text, Rabbis who lived generations apart participate and give the appearance of speaking directly to each other. The text includes, not only legal disputes, but fabulous stories, snippets of history and anthropology and biblical interpretations. Running in a slender strip down the inside of the page is the commentary of Rashi, the medieval exegete . . . Rising up on the other side of the Mishnah and Gemarah are the Tosefists, Rashi's descendants and disciples who comment on Rashi's work . . . The page is also cross-referenced to other passages of the Talmud, to various medieval codes of Jewish law (that of Maimonides, for example), and to the . . . great sixteenth century codification of Jewish law by Joseph Caro. And one should add to this

mix the student himself, who participates in a conversation that began over two thousand years ago (p. 101).

Where and how do these bits of information coalesce? What we define as conscious discourse is clearly only a small part of a pervasive Jamesian stream of consciousness that encompasses, not just the data of the analysis, but a continuous, ongoing, seamless, interaction-enactment that weaves in and out of awareness. Free-association is not exclusively a tapping into an intrapsychic reservoir, but also a relationship with another person, one who tries to listen without agenda or purpose. The extraordinary singularity of this event creates an interpersonal space, a vacuum that the patient fills, moving into it, with the therapist slightly behind the process, following it. Rather than dragging the patient through analysis, the therapist rides the process. Isn't this why Freud's earliest clinical cases seem so fresh? When Freud did not know what he was looking for, the entire enterprise seemed livelier.

Let me extend that observation to a clinical vignette. This is a 56-year-old man in his fifth year of therapy. He is a successful lawyer. He enters therapy with a long-term history of inability to sustain a relationship with a woman. He has had three marriages and innumerable affairs—all of which run the same course. He starts out with a terrific bang—great interest, madly in love. The relationship goes about 3 months, maybe 6 months, and suddenly—sometimes brutally—it is all over. He is just not interested any more. In spite of the abrupt termination, he manages to stay friendly with most of his former girlfriends, some for years. He seems to be a very attractive, related man, quite likeable. Largely, the women cannot bring themselves to hate him.

In therapy, he is friendly, polite; rather than being compliant he "renders unto Caesar what is Caesar's." He comes from a family of extremely Confucian principles. Everyone is courteous, supportive, caring—never a fight, never an adolescent crisis. His parents, particularly his mother, are enigmatic: really perfect parents, not clearly "as if" or inauthentic. Rather they are authentically not there, if that's possible. Perhaps with his father there is more of a sense of mutual affection and regard. He is, of course, a Good Patient, an exemplar of Sullivan's apothegm, "God keep me from a good patient."

Shortly into therapy, he has a dream of being a circus performer in an equestrian act. As the horse canters around the ring, he leaps on its back, does a somersault, and leaps off, to the applause of the audience. Certainly

262 Psychoanalytic theory and practice

this reflects his sense of life as a circus performance, his relationships with women, and, of course, hints at what might well happen in the therapy. Although I expected he might quit suddenly at any time, rather than pursue the dynamics of the sudden-death relationships or his exhibitionist display—which, I suspect, might have inadvertently deteriorated into an attack on his character—I tried to focus his experience at the time of the sudden shift in his feelings—to become aware of inattended thoughts.

The first to emerge were concentration camp fantasies. These were more inattended than repressed. Whenever he was feeling good, the thought would intrude—"you could be in a concentration camp." Over time, these fantasies came to include the Essex tragedy: "you could be in the bottom of a lifeboat, starving and cannibalizing your comrades."[5] Then gradually he became aware of extremely critical perceptions of his girlfriend. Having considered himself heretofore an easy-going and tolerant person, he now began to recognize an unforgiving, relentless sense of rectitude, of how people should behave, "do their jobs": this in spite of several past episodes in his life, which had been somewhat sociopathic. The process was more a matter of focusing attention than of formulating dynamics, of attempting to understand why he had such fantasies. I did make occasional interpretive sorties, but never with much success.

In the fourth year of treatment, I heard the Shoeshine Story. Before each session [sic!]—when he had time—he was accustomed to have his shoes shined at an establishment in my building. Suddenly, as he sat in the elevated shoeshine chair, his throne, he became aware of a flash impulse to kick the bootblack as he bent to his task. This introduced a major shift. He began a series of Nazi fantasies, changing sides, from victim to victimizer. Then, he began to reappraise a number of episodes of childhood sadism. These were not new, several had been mentioned before, but they took on a more powerful emotional valence. Heretofore, he had seemed rather amused by the recollections.

More recently, he dreamt that he is walking with his current girlfriend (now of several years duration) on a cement path through a nature preserve. It gets swampier and the path begins to disappear. He sees snakes all around in the swamp. Coming at right angles to their path is an old lady with a staff (not a crutch). She calls out, "She won't make it!" He says to his girlfriend, "Turn around, we have to go back." As she turns her back—he is now behind her—an immense anaconda leaps from the swamp and engulfs her. He awakes in horror.

I found the mythic implications interesting. The python was the symbol of the matriarchal Gods who preceded the Olympians. The Oracle at Delphi was known as the "pythoness." She had belonged to the Dreaded Mothers before Apollo defeated them and Delphi became his shrine. All the great houses of archaic Greece had, in the basement, a python that was fed and worshiped.[6] It would appear that a snake is not always a penis.

Please note that the assault on his girlfriend happens after the path disappears and he has become frightened and has turned back. The minute she turns her back, she is attacked. He relates this to his sense of going after people at any sign of weakness. Is the woman sacrificed to the threat? Does her turning back spare him? What then is the danger: his rage, his sadomasochistic impulses, the usual phallic-castration imagery? Is the snake his Daddy? The therapist? Himself? His first dream in therapy was of a huge black man, peeing on the ceiling, his urine splattering down on him.

There are the usual transference-countertransference implications. He has become more critical, more testing of me, yet more identified with me. I like him, he works earnestly, as you see dreams interestingly. Still, there is always the feeling that he could be pseudocompliantly preparing for me the same "sudden-death" fate suffered by his girlfriends.

None of this working-through is truly new to him. Rather, in the Sullivanian sense, it is "inattended." One could make any number of doctrinaire dynamic formulations, but they were evident and predictable from the beginning. What seems to have helped is the indoctrination into a free-associative technique, an awareness of inattended data. The dynamic remains the same; the experience of the details seems to matter. History, current events, dreams, transference, and countertransference all are intertextually related. But I very definitely had the feeling that the transference interaction was not, to this point, powering the therapy; rather, it was his unconscious flow of data. After all, where were these dreams coming from? Who dreams the dream? The dynamic explanations that could have been anticipated near the beginning of the treatment and are clearly present now don't seem to do it.

As we are drawing to a close, I am still disturbed by a lack of closure. I do not understand how this perfectly amiable family caused his problems. I say to him that it worries me that since he was such a good son and works so hard to be a good patient he could get married and suddenly discover it was not for him, but for the other's approval—that in his relationship with me and, I suspect, in the recounting of the family, he hides behind a mask of congeniality. Could it have been that amiable?

He then gives me a psychoanalytic catechism, drawn from previous therapies, about his Oedipus Complex and his losing his mother's exclusive attention when Daddy returned from the war. I point this out as a resistance, as a way of transferring it all into some abstract realm.

He then tells me a series of incidents I had not heard before. Once when his mother reached forward to adjust the car radio his father slapped her hand away—"not hard, of course, just a little love-tap!" He told how, when he visited his son's new law office with his wife, he took the chair behind the desk, an act of *droit du seigneur*, how he never let his son drive him anywhere, and how his mother never dared to drive all through the marriage.

Now, in a way, this is compliance. I asked and he provides! Nevertheless, it opens a door. We have compliance as resistance, interpretation of awareness of resistance, and then some further data that is compliant, and therefore probably useless.

But something interesting happens. He is giving me one of his bright, compliant explanations, one-upping what I had just said. I feel irritated and I suddenly have the fantasy of saying to him, with a Nazi accent, "Vee are not interested in your opinions. Do as you are told!" So I told him the fantasy. He roared with laughter. Now this use of countertransference is not de novo. But I am sure that if I had done it earlier, he would not have thought it was funny at all! The use of one's participation cannot be used as technique. It has to come when it comes. I am participating in his fantasy. Is this projective-identification? Am I admitting my own Nazi proclivities?[7] It is certainly my reaction to his defeating me with his complacent and very intelligent performance. Certainly, countertransference has been actualized. The working-through seems to reside in this midrashic process.

Why should this deconstruction work? After more than 50 years toiling in the fields of psychoanalysis, I think I know how to do it, but I *don't* know why or how it works. We can see how the Aristotelian system would function. It makes the process clearer by bringing the inattended into awareness, and by supplying an explanatory set that collates private experience, general principles (a very Aristotelian device, deriving the abstract from the specific), and pathogenesis. In contrast, what does the Rabbinical method supply?—multiple explanations, unclarity, open-ended inquiry. It is not hard to see why one might prefer the Aristotelian approach. Again Handelman:

The creative force of Midrash depends on stubborn particularization. Furthermore there is never any one single interpretation to which all understandings of the text aims, but a continuous production of multiple meanings . . . conflicting interpretations are set side by side with no concern for reconciling them. There is no hierarchical scheme in Midrash; no interpretation has more authority than any other (p. 75).

I believe that this dichotomy delineates a clear difference between psychotherapy and psychoanalysis. Psychotherapy is organizing. Rather than plumbing for the singular, moving the inquiry downward, it reaches upward for the abstraction, the generalization, for patterns that the patient can grasp and use, that indeed every patient can use. There are no psychotherapeutic truths that are not ubiquitous. Psychoanalysis, in contrast, does not reach for understanding, for the overview. There is no superordinate interpretation. Psychoanalysis attempts to pursue the singularity of the patient's experience, wherever it might lead. I like to think that creativity always requires an unnatural act, something that goes against the grain of common sense. For psychoanalysts, it is resisting the temptation to make sense of what one hears.

Why should this be therapeutic? First, the patient is given space, a playground to discover his or her own flow of consciousness. Simultaneously, we are tapping into the powerful interactional field between the therapist and the patient, which we may either minimize or actualize, depending on our theories. These are the hotly disputed two axes of the intrapsychic and the interpersonal but they are not "spaces" or "places." The dichotomy is more apparent than real. We polarize these positions because of what Wittgenstein called a "spatial fallacy":

We search through a problem "space" and insight is our reward for perseverance. The search metaphor has many of the attributes of searching in physical space, so it is pictured as occurring in a conceptual space or a mental one—one searches one's mind!

(Heaton, 2000, p. 18)

In 1988, in a paper called "Real Frogs in Imaginary Gardens," I identified the intrapsychic with poetics (from the Greek *poesis*, meaning to make, the capacity for imagination, fantasy, magic) and the interpersonal with *pragmatics* (from the Latin *pramaticus*, skilled in affairs). So, one has two different mental functions, not spaces. Nevertheless, the familiar spatial metaphor is tempting. Where, on the other hand, is hyperspace? Nowhere. Not a very appetizing alternative.

I understand that all this may seem disruptive. One would dearly prefer to have a clear conception of how psychopathology develops, and a theory of therapy that applies that concept to the treatment and results in a measurable and predictable cure. If one can accept that one is tapping into and riding, like a wave, an ineffable process—part conscious, part unconscious, part between people, part autonomous, part rational conceptualizing, and part a mysterious act of mutual creation—then one might augment and facilitate the process without needing to conceptualize it clearly. I think that brain is individual, but mind is a field phenomenon, a network, and a web. To paraphrase Winnicott's famous "there is no such thing as a baby"—implying that the mother-child dyad is the indivisible unit—I would say that there is no such thing as a mind. It takes others to extend that network and the extension may be, in itself, restorative.[8]

Really this is no less than what Freud said. I would like to suggest that the act, the praxis of psychoanalysis—the inquiry, association, dreams, fantasies, and the reiteration of those themes in the behavioral field of patient and therapist, in the office, and as it extends into both their private worlds—is the cure! It might be that the cure lies, not in a corrective or restitutive experience, nor in the acquisition of mutative insight, but in the experience per se. Marshall McLuhan (1964) may have been right: the medium may, indeed, be the message (p. 7).

Let me summarize this rather discursive presentation. I am saying that we are undergoing a major sea change. We are moving away from the rationalism that began with Plato and reached its apogee with Descartes. It may turn out that the praxis of psychoanalysis—not its theory of therapy —lies closer to the Rabbinic or hypertext model than we have suspected. It is only with a shifting paradigm that it now begins to seem reasonable, and more importantly, *respectable*, that these other perspectives may have more relevance than our traditional Greco-Christian heritage allowed. Pride of interpretation may give way to a genuine curiosity about how this process works, how we tap into the curative process.

So, is this midrash or mishmash? I ran across this gnomic Keirkegaard quote in Handelman (1982). "He who is willing to work gives birth to his own father" (p. 179). Following Bloom's literary theory of "misprision," I think it means that one returns to one's roots and recreates them in one's own image. Surely this was true of Freud's (1960) return to Moses and his elaborate recasting of the story—"the man and what I *wanted to make of him*" (p. 98). It is, I believe, a legitimate and necessary exercise. Psychoanalytic positions need to be fluid. If one clings too tightly to one position, in the end one is betrayed. Highly invested psychoanalytic insights degenerate into clichés, their proponents into self-referential caricatures, like character actors stuck in playing the same roles their entire careers. We lose the textual fluidity and open-endedness that, as I've tried to demonstrate, is the essence of our work.

Notes

1. This chapter was first read, in slightly different form, on May 11, 2001, as the Roberta Held Weiss Memorial Lecture at the William Alanson White Institute. It was also published in 2001 in *Contemporary Psychoanalysis*, 37(3):375–390.
2. It is of note that the language used widely as a lingua franca in the Roman Empire in Jerusalem at the time of Christ—and, of course, the language of the New Testament—was not Latin, but Greek.
3. This is not news: The dichotomy of the two Freuds has been well documented. See Reisner (1999, p. 1045).
4. See the chapter on Freud and the Sexologists in Gilman et al. (1994).
5. The Essex Tragedy was the source of Melville's *Moby Dick*. It entailed stoving by a whale, shipwreck, and a long sea voyage in which cannibalism occurred.
6. Remember that it was at the shrine of the Mothers at Colonus that the blinded Oedipus ends his life, gives himself over.
7. Having been the US Army psychiatrist for the Nazi prisoners at Spandau, I certainly had a long-standing fascination with them.
8. Donnel Stern (1997) explores the ramifications of unformulated and creative experience.

References

Berlin, I. (1998). *The Proper Study of Mankind*. New York: Farrar, Straus and Giroux.

Bloom, H. (1975). *A Map of Misreading*. New York: Oxford University Press.

Freud, A. (1969). *Difficulties in the Path of Psychoanalysis*. New York: International Universities Press.

Freud, E.L. (Ed.) (1960). *The Letters of Sigmund Freud and Arnold Zweig* (trans. E. and W. Robson-Scott). New York: Harcourt, Brace & World.

Freud, S. (1939). Moses and Monotheism: Three Essays. In J. Strachey (Ed.), *The Standard Edition of the Compléte Psychological Works of Sigmund Freud* (Vol. XXIII). London: Hogarth Press, pp. 3–137.

268 Psychoanalytic theory and practice

Gay, P. (1988). *Freud: A Life for Our Time.* New York: W.W. Norton.

Gilman, S.L., Birmele, J., Geller, J., and Greenberg, V.D. (1994). *Reading Freud's Readings.* New York: New York University Press.

Handelman, S. (1982). *The Slayers of Moses: The Emergence of Rabbinic Interpretation in Modern Literary Theory.* Albany, NY: State University of New York.

Heaton, J.M. (2000). *Wittgenstein and Psychoanalysis.* New York: Totem Books.

Held Weiss, R. (1985). In praise of actuality. *Contemporary Psychoanalysis,* 21(2):237–253.

Levenson, E. (1972). *The Fallacy of Understanding.* New York: Basic Books.

Levenson, E. (1988). Real frogs in imaginary gardens: Facts and fantasies in psychoanalysis: *Psychoanalytic Inquiry,* 8(4):552–556.

Levenson, E. (1989). Whatever happened to the cat? Interpersonal perspectives on the self. *Contemporary Psychoanalysis,* 25(4):537–553.

McLuhan, M. (1964). *Understanding Media: The Extensions of Man.* New York: McGraw-Hill.

Reisner, S. (1999). Freud and psychoanalysis into the twenty-first century. *Journal of the American Psychoanalytic Association,* 47(4):1037–1060.

Rizzuto, A.M. (1998). *Why Did Freud Reject God? A Psychodynamic Interpretation.* New Haven, CT: Yale University Press.

Rosen, J. (2000). *The Talmud and the Internet: A Journey Between Worlds:* New York: Farrar, Straus & Giroux:

Stern, D.B. (1997). *Unformulated Experience: From Dissociation to Imagination in Psychoanalysis.* Hillsdale, NJ: The Analytic Press.

Wilden, A. (1972). *System and Structure: Essays in Communication and Exchange.* London: Tavistock.

Zornberg, A.G. (1995). *The Beginning of Desire: Reflections on Genesis.* New York: Doubleday.

Chapter 21

Creativity, genius, and divine madness[1]

According to the Whorf-Sapir hypothesis, each culture develops the vocabulary it needs. If one wishes to talk about snow, talk with an Eskimo—he has 50 words for it. If one wishes to explore the subtler tonalities of lust, love, passion, madness, and ecstasy, talk with a Greek, preferably an ancient one—the Greeks had a word for it! Plato, speaking for Socrates in The Phaedrus, identified creativity with a "Divine Madness" (mania) (Galdstone 1968, Levenson 1968). Both the Greek word "ecstasy" and its Latin cognate, "rapture," refer to being carried out of oneself, out of one's ordinary being. Plato made abundantly clear that this divine madness was distinct from craziness or insanity, for which the Greeks had a sufficiency of other words. There is no real correlation between creativity and mental illness. But there is a distinct correlation between creativity and its raptures. It is not a big stretch from this connection to the consideration of creativity through chemistry—the use of psychotropic drugs to "blow one's mind." So creativity, divine madness, and drug use have a long, albeit equivocal, history of association.

Tradition requires that one round up the usual suspects—De Quincy, Goya, Bosch, Baudelaire, Rimbaud, Verlaine, and the legion of alcoholic writers, painters, and musicians. Even Sigmund Freud had a notorious connection to cocaine, and perhaps even owed some of his productivity to its use. Sherlock Holmes (and Conan Doyle) used both morphine and cocaine, depending on his moods. In the 1960s, madness and addiction became chic, virtual prerequisites for creativity. Remember Timothy Leary and R.D. Laing (1967) and his "laingeurs"—"If I could drive you out of your wretched mind, if I could tell you, I would let you know" (p. 138).

Fortunately, we are now past that romantic nonsense. The gurus went out of their minds—literally—and madness, we concluded, was a piteous state of disarray, not a prelude to creativity. But perhaps we've thrown out the baby with the bhang. There was, in all of that a glimmer of truth, a critical assessment of the culture, the context in which we were all immersed. We saw aberrancy as having a quality of social "outsiderness," as containing, however distorted, a certain radical awareness.

For all the long list of drug-addicted artists, the relationship between creativity and the disruption of the senses remains obscure. To be sure, there are creative people with no interest in drugs, and addicts with no talent or creativity. Moreover, while there were painters whose productivity depended on drugs, there were others who were destroyed by drugs. What about those artists who used morphine and its derivatives, which are not so much mood-altering as normalcy maintaining? Whether drug use increases or destroys creativity remains a moot question; most of the commentaries seem more homiletic than scientific. Nevertheless, there does seem to be a high incidence of drug use among artists. Why should this be so?

While I have little personal experience with the treatment of addictions, and while what I am about to say may smack of bourgeois romanticism, nevertheless I would suggest that what addicts and creative people (not just artists) have in common is a penchant for risk-taking, for living on the edge of possibility. In this sense addiction and creativity may share a common characterological denominator, rather than a causal relationship.

I first ran across this idea in Bateson's (1972) theory of alcoholism. It does not seem to be an idea prevalent in the addiction literature (see the exceptions of Ehrenberg, Phillips, and Brisman in Hungers and Compulsions, 2001). It is to be found more implicitly stated in Rank (1945), Becker (1963), Fromm (1973, 1992), May (1950), and the existential analysts, that is, those theorists with a sustained interest in the issue of social defiance, risk-taking, outsiderness—even, dare we say, a death instinct, a drive to self-destruction.

Perhaps as Freud prophesied would happen in America (which he heartily detested), his dark and existential theory has been bowdlerized into an uplift program. We Americans consider cure to be living happily in one's assigned role, loving oneself, the mate and kiddies, and possibly even the job (in that order, of course). "Have a good day!" we say to each other in the elevator on the way to our offices. Mental health is conflated with happiness.

Mavericks are socially dangerous people; they threaten the status quo. And so, as cultures are wont to do, aberrancy is dealt with by either trivializing it, making it normal and harmless (body-piercing teenagers), or extruding it, banishing it to a disowned and discredited subculture. The culture of addiction binds the outcasts together, gives them a sense of community, and makes it much harder to break away. Alcoholics Anonymous uses the first part of this coherence very effectively. But, AA says, one never stops being an alcoholic and one never outlives the need for the therapeutic community. Alcoholism becomes another country.

In contrast, some of us would agree that socially aberrant behavior is our own dark and disowned side, and that to understand it, and certainly to treat it, we must own it. A neurosis, it must be remembered, however bad, is always better than something else. It is a compromise solution, not only in the Freudian sense of between drive and ego, but also between individual and society. To treat addicts, I believe we must ask what function—disowned in our own experience—does the addiction serve? What is left when the addiction is disavowed? Does one live happily ever after? I would like to elaborate on this idea, and suggest some of the consequences of this perspective.

It is very difficult to categorize addiction. Traditionally, the addict is defined as a person who requires a substance to feel normal. This may be true of opium and morphine users, but not always of coke and crack users. Even many long-standing coke addicts may take it for the kick, not to recapture normality. What about mood-enhancing drugs and hallucinogens? What about overeating, food addiction, anorexia? What about people addicted to risk—adrenaline junkies? What about the new category of sexual addictions (McDougall 1995)?

What, for example, is sexual addiction? How is an addiction different from a compulsion? Addictions are ordinarily considered to be a variety of compulsion (Dodes 1996, McDougall 1985). But are they? If I have to step on every crack to avoid having an anxiety attack, we can agree that's not addiction—that's compulsion. If a man repeatedly has unprotected sex with prostitutes, that's sexual addiction. But if a man wishes to have sex several times a day with his wife and never goes outside the home for sex, and she reluctantly goes along with it only because he gets so upset if she doesn't—is that compulsion or addiction? If he becomes agitated if refused, is that withdrawal symptoms or pique? Might we not just consider him a glutton, a hostile user? Why?

I believe that addiction always carries with it a connotation of risk, and that risk invokes passion. Can there be passion without danger? Georges Bataille, in Death and Sensuality, says, "Erotic excitement resides in the risk of death—not death itself" (quoted in Benjamin 1988, p. 64). I would postulate that compulsion is a ritualistic act to avoid danger and anxiety, whereas addiction is a ritualized act of courting danger.

In Stanley Kubrick's 1999 movie, *Eyes Wide Shut*, the wife has a soliloquy about a passing stranger, a naval officer she sees in the airport. The uptight, not entirely heterosexual husband listens in horror and awe at this terrible female manifestation. Can one separate the passion from the addictive impulse? We are fascinated by the connotation of danger and destruction—the moth and the flame, the "Blue Angel" motif.

Even in those addictions that sustain feelings of normalcy, the risk is there. It is illegal to buy and to use; there are medical dangers of overdose, needle-invoked infections, the eroticism of the needle itself, and what Mark and Faude (1997) called the excitement of "the hunt for cocaine." There are the expenses that may require illegal activity. Note the recent fascinating book by the Barthelme brothers Frederick and Steven, both university professors, on their passion for casino gambling, and the resulting lust for virtual self-destruction it entailed (Barthelme and Barthelme, 1999). Not only do they acknowledge losing several hundred thousand dollars, but also they were indicted (and later acquitted) on charges related to card counting and bribery. I am saying that risk in addiction is not an epiphenomenon, but a primary motive for the act.

It has been claimed that adolescents start addictive behavior because they can't believe they can become addicted. But I do not believe that is the entire truth: risk is part of it. Why, otherwise, is it so astonishingly difficult to get people to heed all the cautionary tales about addiction risk? After a blizzard of warnings, people will nevertheless smoke, try drugs, and have unprotected sex. There was only a brief period of time in our society when sex was presumed safe (wrongly it turns out), free of terrible dangers such as disease and pregnancy. But wasn't everyone becoming bored? So pleasure replaced passion, and violence replaced sex as the passionate activity. Now one sees deliberately entertained risk re-entering the culture, such as in extreme sports and in outer-limit trips for executives. People seem to be enjoying frightening themselves. Inupiats, in Alaska, have returned to hunting whales from long boats instead of getting drunk. What's going on? Why are people in the best-fed, most cosseted society in history taking unwarranted risks?

Besides our difficulty in delineating a class of addictions that comfortably embraces all its members, it has never been possible to make dynamic profiling predictive. All psychodynamic predictions are post facto: we see the consequences, and then we speculate on the antecedents. One simply cannot predict the development of a particular symptom from a particular constellation of experience. Family dynamics do not specify and do not predict. Years ago, there was a joke about Jewish mothers and alcoholism. To wit, Jewish men have exactly the same family dynamics as alcoholics. So how come there are so few Jewish alcoholics? The answer is, their mothers wouldn't let them! If they wanted to be self-destructive they had to eat themselves to death. (I am "happy" to say that Jews are now totally integrated and have plenty of alcoholics.)

There must be some other predictive factor, and that something may be partly biological, a genetically inherent fault; but ultimately, regardless of endowment or dynamics, addiction is an existential decision. Consider the 95 percent heroin addiction rate among soldiers in Vietnam, which largely fell away on their return to the States. Consider the people who, safely detoxified, return 6 months later to their addictions.

If the antecedents of addiction are not so self-evident, neither are those of talent, genius, and creativity. There is always a marginality, a recklessness, a destructive and edgy component in any real creativity. Picasso once said of another painter that he was "merely a genius." Inherent talent is not enough, nor is skill; as an example, a genius like Salvador Dali was ultimately not a great artist. Some quality of marginality, some willingness to hang out on a limb, even to risk one's sanity is necessary. Leonard Bernstein said, "If you're going to teeter on a shaky ladder, do it from the highest rung." It is what distinguishes an illustrator from an artist, a corps de ballet dancer from a principal, an artist from a Sunday painter.

Creativity also has a strongly addictive quality. It is often not pleasurable, but must be done in order to feel normal, what Isak Dinesen called "the doom of genius—the individual's powerlessness in the face of his own powers" (quoted in Rorem 1967). Ned Rorem, the composer, wrote poignantly in his diary, "The compulsion to compose was with me, until the age of twenty-eight, as intense as the compulsion to drink—and I was helpless before both: music flower out of my body like a sweet but slightly sick liquid" (Rorem 1967, p. 129). I do not think that it would be possible to sustain the tremendous effort and concentration required for productive, creative work without a powerful addictive element.

There is a dialectic between risk-taking and safety, dependency and isolation, separation and fusion, rootedness, belonging and aloneness—all psychoanalytic dichotomies. In this sense, addiction is a perfect analogue of the sadomasochistic relationship, with its alternation of desire and rejection, fulfillment and loss. Addiction may be the compromise solution between the dependency wish, and its opposite, the desire for freedom with all its dangers, passions, and risks. Therapy often reveals the addict sans addiction as a flat and passionless person.

Treatment of addicts requires our recognizing that their return to "normalcy" may seem more boring than they can bear. Is it possible that addiction is the desire of the addicted? Does treatment require that the need for passion and risk be taken into account, not as neurosis but as a legitimate need—not just for addicts, but for everyone? Binswanger (1958), the existential analyst, wrote in *The Case of Ellen West* that addiction is "not only a somatically conditioned need but at the same time the need for filling up the existential emptiness or craving" (p. 346).

From the story of the expulsion from the Garden of Eden to the present, there is this thread of the human fascination with risk, passion, and deliberate loss. Need therapy be a variety of "shrinking"? Should people change, get rid of what's wrong with them, grow up, "get a life"? Or might it be possible to take one's aberrancies and carry them forward, develop them, move into them in a way that permits them to become a part of oneself and a useful element?

I believe we have attenuated two great central themes in psychoanalysis that might bear on this issue: first, the social contract of psychoanalytic therapy; and second, its tragic view of life. What has become of "cultural" psychoanalysis, the great revolution of the 1950s and 1960s? Psychoanalysis has become a child of its time and reflects the loss of this theme in contemporary culture. Psychoanalysis has become safety bound, and mental health a commodity. In the headier days of Fromm, Horney, Thompson, Marcuse, Brown, analysts were supposed to stand, like artists, at least partly outside of their culture and to be critical of its compromises, not least of which is our easy, rather flaccid, sense of good and evil, of infinite possibilities. With the possible exception of Kohut, we seem to have lost the tragic view of man so prevalent in psychoanalysis's earlier years (1984).

Creativity, genius, and divine madness 275

It seems plausible to me that the neglected communality between addiction and creativity is passionate risk-taking that has been largely disowned by our culture and relegated to outsiders. We are pleased to watch and enjoy it on television. Consider our vicarious fascination with the Mafia. From *The Godfather* movies to the television series "The Sopranos," Mafia killers (on the latter show in psychoanalytic treatment—a wonderful irony) combine terrifying murderous behavior and the most banal, stupefying bourgeois aspirations. Let them take the risks; we stay home! As I've suggested, this may be changing, and risk-taking qua passionate activity is beginning to enter the culture.

To treat addiction exclusively as pathology, to seek the psychodynamics that motivate and specify both addiction and creativity, is to miss its existential implications. The analyst's risk-taking—and this may mean, not bungee-jumping, but risking one's income or political career by not pandering to patients, third-party payers, or one's own colleagues—may be a vital ingredient of an authentic therapy. The William Alanson White Psychoanalytic Institute was founded on rebellion and risk. It was no small thing to walk out of the American Psychoanalytic Association, to go one's own way, and it was no small thing for my generation to follow the dissenters into the wilderness. The leaders of the White institute were audacious and defiant, pushing the limits of the cultural envelope. As the physicist Pauli put it, sometimes wrong, sometimes excessive, but never not wrong enough!

As Dostoyevsky wrote in *Notes from the Underground* (1961):

[A] man, always and everywhere, prefers to act in the way he feels like acting and not in the way his reason and interest tell him, for it is very possible for a man to feel like acting against his interests and, in some instances, I say that he positively wants to act that way— but that's my personal opinion ... All man actually needs is independent will, at all costs and whatever the consequences (p. 110) ... And what makes you so cocksure, so positive that only the normal and the positive, that is, only what promotes man's welfare, is to his advantage? Can't reason also be wrong about what's an advantage? Why can't man like things other than his well-being? Maybe he likes suffering just as much. Maybe suffering is just as much to his advantage as well-being. In fact, man adores suffering. Passionately! (p. 117).

Note

1. This chapter first appeared as a chapter in the book *Hungers and Compulsions*, edited by Petrucelli and Stuart, in 2001.

References

Barthelme, F. and Barthelme, S. (1999). *Double Down*. New York: Houghton Mifflin.

Bateson, G. (1972). *Steps to an Ecology of Mind*. New York: Ballantine Books.

Becker, H.S. (1963). *Outsiders: Studies on the Sociology of Deviance*. New York: Free Press.

Benjamin, J. (1988). *The Bonds of Love*. New York: Pantheon Books.

Binswanger, L. (1958). *The Case of Ellen West. In Existence*, R. May, E. Angel, and H. Ellenberger (Eds.). New York: Basic Books, pp. 237–362.

Dodes, L.M. (1996). Compulsion and addiction. *Journal of the American Psychoanalytic Association*, 44:815–856.

Dostoyevsky, F. (1961). *Notes from the Underground* (trans. A. MacAndrew). New York: Signet Classics.

Fromm, E. (1973). *The Anatomy of Human Destructiveness*. New York: Holt, Rinehart & Winston.

Fromm, E. (1992). *The Revision of Psychoanalysis*. Boulder, CO: Westview.

Galdstone, I. (1968). Psychiatry and the maverick. In J. Masserman (Ed.), *The Dynamics of Dissent*.York: Grune & Stratton, pp. 1–17.

Kohut, H., Ed. A. Goldberg. (1984). *How Does Analysis Cure?* Chicago, IL: University of Chicago Press.

Laing, R.D. (1967). *The Politics of Experience*. New York: Pantheon.

Levenson, E. (1968). Discussion of psychiatry and the maverick. In J. Masserman (Ed.), *Psychodynamics of Dissent*. New York: Grune & Stratton, pp. 18–20.

Levenson, E. (2001). Creativity, genius and divine madness. In J. Petrucelli and K. Stuart (Ed.), *Hungers and Compulsions: The Psychodynamic Treatment of Eating Disorders and Addictions*. New Jersey: Jason Aronson, pp. 233–244.

Mark, D. and Faude, J. (1997). *Psychotherapy of Cocaine Addiction*. New York: Jason Aronson.

May, R. (1950). *The Meaning of Anxiety*. New York: Ronald Press.

McDougall, J. (1985). *Theaters of the Mind*. New York: Basic Books.

McDougall, J. (1995). *The Many Faces of Eros: A Psychoanalytic Exploration of Human Sexuality*. New York: W.W. Norton.

Petrucelli, J. and Stuart, K. (Eds.) (2001). *Hungers and Compulsions: The Psychodynamic Treatment of Eating Disorders and Addictions*. New York: Jason Aronson

Rank, O. (1945). *Will Therapy and Truth and Reality*. New York: Alfred A. Knopf.

Rorem, N. (1967). *The New York Diary*. New York: George Braziller.

Shapiro, T. (1979). *Clinical Psycholinguistics*. New York: Plenum Press.

Chapter 22

Oh what a blow that phantom gave me

Observations on the rise of virtual desire[1]

This is a quote from Cervante's masterwork, *Don Quixote*, once standard college reading, known now to a new generation of theater audience as the singing *Man of La Mancha*, "Oh what a blow that phantom gave me."[2] It is, of course, Quixote's comment, after one of his many catastrophic misadventures, when he'd been—once again—knocked off his faithful nag, Rocinante. When Sancho Panza reminds him that it was a windmill, not a giant, that unseated him, he says stiffly, that, of course, he knew that—Frestón, the magician, had changed the giant back into a windmill to confuse poor, simple-minded Sancho. It is a wonderful line, emblematic of Cervantes' continuous interplay of reality and fantasy, which is not just textual: *Don Quixote* is, actually, a book about a book in two parts. In the first book, a fictionalized Cervantes disavows his authorship. In the second book, written 10 years later, Don Quixote and Sancho Panza are recognized as heroes of the first book, which was by then in wide circulation. Critics have almost universally agreed that Cervantes' clever scrambling of reality and fantasy made *Don Quixote* the fount of all subsequent inquiries into the relationship between fantasy and reality—that is to say, all fiction, and, for psychoanalysts, all of life.

It is my contention that we are presently living in a time that, unlike the Don's, does not so much confuse two distinct categories—reality and fantasy—as conflate them, blur the boundary between the two. After all, all reality is constructed, as we have known since Plato. However, that is not to say that reality is, per se, all in the mind. A windmill is a windmill, even if the Don didn't think so. We agree that there is a consensual reality out there, even if our interpretations of it may differ. But it is not directly apprehended; it is mediated through the mind.

278 Psychoanalytic theory and practice

There is a long science fiction history of what philosophers call the "brain in the vat" hypothesis. It proposes an isolated brain, kept alive in a sea of nourishing fluid, and provided with elaborate informational input. How would the brain know it was not attached to a corporeal body? It would dream a life. *Donovan's Brain*, written in 1942, was an early novel based on this mind-body dichotomy (Siodmak, 1942). More contemporary audiences are surely familiar with the *Matrix* movie series that postulates the same idea—a brain that doesn't know it has no body—ergo, virtual reality. Or, for yet another ingenious variation, consider the iconic novel, *Snow Crash*, for the concept of a virtual world on the Web, with "avatars" for purchase. These avatars—which could be as handsome, beautiful, rich, accomplished as one's wallet permits—live one's alternate life, on line, in a virtual, cyberspace world of cafes and bars and adventure (Stephenson, 1992).

These stories reflect a world in which both reality and fantasy are in and of the mind—an interpretation. Under enabling cultural circumstances, fantasy, which is easily accessible, perfectible, and requires almost no personal commitment, may insidiously become preferable to reality. As has been said of masturbation, its great advantage is that one needn't brush one's teeth. But even the effort of sustained imagination required to have a sexual fantasy becomes tiresome. The distinction between the veridical reality of the world out there and the virtual world of pre-packaged fantasy provided first by cinema, and then TV, and now the computer, begins to erode, surely not to disappear entirely, but to seem less relevant.

If Marshall McLuhan was correct in his dictum that the medium is the message, then the Internet has led us one step past the medium of television and through the Looking Glass into the strange new world of the hyperreal. One can see how this might lead to a diminution of true desire, since desire, a manifestation of the real world, is imperfect, frustrating (as I shall elaborate later), and ultimately, if we are to believe Hegel, beyond attainment. In the land of the Lotus-eaters, virtual reality—an oxymoron if ever there was one—comes to rule triumphant.

Quixote, in retrospect, begins to seem less quixotic. He may have been deluded; his brain, as Cervantes says, "dried out" by reading too many of the chivalric romances popular in the sixteenth century. Still, he was an exemplar of true passion; devoted to his private vision, willing to be battered or killed in the process, and perfectly aware that in the end, like his chivalric heroes who would never attain the Holy Grail, he too would die unfulfilled in his quest. Maybe that's why Freud loved him:

> Sigmund Freud, ... would confess to his fiancée Martha Bernays that he was frittering away much of the summer of 1883 by concentrating more on Don Quixote "than on brain anatomy." Freud's efforts to become a neurologist were thwarted by an increasing curiosity about psychopathological issues, and his recollection of this generative period has a distinctly quixotic ring "we were all noble Knights passing through the world caught in a dream" ... "As a young student, the desire to read the immortal Quijote in the Spanish original led me to learn, without teachers, the beautiful Castilian language."
>
> (Finch and Allen, 1999, p. 771)

Freud, that summer, also corresponded extensively with his friend from adolescence, Eduard Silberstein, in Spanish, using as pen names, Cervantes' talking dogs, Cipíon and Berganza. Parenthetically, it is truly astonishing that Freud, who learned classic Greek to read Sophocles, Castilian Spanish to read Cervantes, and had a standard Jewish upbringing, claimed that he could not translate the Hebrew inscription in the Bible his father gave him (Rizzuto, 1998).

Well, what has become of desire? Let us consider for a moment the traditional perversion or, if you will, paraphilia, of voyeurism/exhibitionism. The whole point of voyeurism or exhibitionism used to be that it was an aggressive invasion of the Other's privacy—a visual rape—unsolicited, and moreover dangerous, since it was a decidedly criminal act. Where is the risk, the offence, the perverse excitement of electronic voyeurism? How perverse can it be if it is sanctioned by the media, and by the people being observed? There are currently a large number of Internet sites where one can watch women living in a communal house bare their anatomy or sex lives. For those with a more literary bent, there are individual sites—confessional blogs—where one may bare one's soul, rather than one's dainties. There is certainly erotic stimulation, but where then is the desire?

It is with some pedagogic embarrassment that I find I must turn to the burgeoning references in the mass media; but unfortunately, one can hardly detect cultural trends and changes from reading the professional literature,

280   Psychoanalytic theory and practice

which tends to exist in a loftier parallel universe. Pop culture is where one sniffs change; and awareness of change is the instrumentality of the analyst. There is ample data now accruing about loss of desire, the substitution of fantasy for reality, and of pornography and masturbation co-opting interpersonal sexuality.

For example, in the *New York Times*, a recent article by Staples claims that adolescents are becoming less connected to the world, more cut off from relationships. Oddly, now that one can, on the Internet, interact with many more persons, are we, perhaps, becoming simultaneously more connected and less related? Quoting Staples, "People who communicated with disembodied strangers online found the experience empty and emotionally frustrating, but were nevertheless seduced by the novelty of the new medium." Moreover, low-quality relationships developed in virtual reality tended to replace relationships in the real world (Staples, 2004). Like the old dictum that "Bad money drives out good," fantasy sex appears to drive out real. This may sound lurid or exaggerated, but, in clinical practice, I believe one does see more couples who have lost interest in sex, or who are limiting their erotic activity to infrequent and desultory mutual or solitary masturbation. How can we explain the immense popularity of Viagra and its kindred drugs? Either things are getting worse or they were always worse than we knew.

New York Magazine devoted a large part of the October 20, 2003 issue to the substitution of porn for reality. Amsden, in an piece entitled, "Not tonight, Honey, I'm logging on," claims that there is a downward continuum from the mildly participant act of couples watching porn together on TV to the far more solitary act of watching porn and masturbating to the laptop (Amsden, 2003, pp. 30–35). Presumably, the imperfect real person cannot compare with the perfection of the virtual image. Or, as Naomi Wolf, in an article in the same issue, puts it, "Today, real naked women are just bad porn" (Wolf, 2003, p. 37).

The Internet may be more insidious than TV, in as much as TV porn was at least a social experience if watched with others. For TV porn, a certain degree of commitment is necessary. One must either pay for a porn channel, or go to the store and rent, or buy, a tape. And it is often watched with other people. Internet porn is far more accessible and ubiquitous. It feels more forbidden, particularly since it may evoke a sense of rebellion. It is often watched, in defiance of company policy, on office computers. For pre-adolescents and adolescents, the Internet is not as much subject to parental scrutiny as is the television. If this were merely an issue of sloth, of making lazy choices, it wouldn't be so bad. But it gets worse and the implications are far more insidious.

To explore these implications from a more academically respectable and intellectual perspective—French, of course—Jean Baudrillard quotes a famous story by Borges that describes a map grown so extensive and detailed that it overlays every detail of the territory it represents. The territory disappears and is replaced by what Baudrillard calls a "simulacrum." A simulacrum is distinguished from a copy by the absence of any original. When the map becomes the territory, "something has disappeared: the sovereign difference between one and the other, that constituted the charm of abstraction." It becomes a matter "of substituting the signs of the real for the real." A simulacrum, then, is a copy of an original that no longer exists: "a generation by models of a real without origin or reality: a hyperreal" (Baudrillard, 1944, pp. 1–2). The terrible irony is that the simulacrum does not merely replace reality—reality becomes a poor simulation.

So, put simply, the virtual reality provided by the Internet overcomes and finally obliterates real experience; no longer "true" and "false" selves, but a simulacrum of self. One need only note the odd proliferation of "mocumentaries" where real people and actors playing roles seamlessly interact. And, I would claim, obliteration of reality leads to the death of desire. According to Wilden, "The Hegelian conception of desire is what lies behind or explicates most modern conceptions of intentionality (Brentano, Husserl), of cathexis (Freud), of project (Heidegger, Sartre), and of goal seeking (nonmechanistic cybernetics)" (Wilden, 1972, p. 65). Lacan was, as are most current views of Hegel, heavily influenced by Kojève's Heideggerian-Marxist interpretation. In the Hegelian usage, it is the acknowledgment of the unbridgeable gap between reality and fantasy that begets passion and desire. As Guy Thompson put it in his book *The Death of Desire*, "Desire is the search for a symbolic repetition of a satisfaction whose completion has become impossible" (Thompson, 1985, p. 43). Substitute "whose completion no longer exists" for "impossible" and the linkage to a simulacrum is complete.

A new pair of Manolo Blahniks (a $500 women's shoe, as we have all learned—if we didn't already know—from *Sex and the City*) can engender real passion, especially if the purchase requires sacrifice—say, no lunch for a month.[3] But that is lust, not yet desire:

282 Psychoanalytic theory and practice

Desire is human only if one desires, not the body, but the Desire of the other, if he wants to be "desired" or "loved", or rather "recognized" in his human value: in his reality as a human individual. Desire directed towards a natural object is human only to the extent that it is "mediated" by the Desire of another directed towards the same object: it is human to desire what others desire because they desire it.

(Kojève, 1969)

Is it lust for the shoe, but desire for the regard of the other shoe wearers? Is it desire or compulsion if one cannot—like Imelda Marcus—ever have enough shoes? Oh well, Hegel said, "only one man ever understood me—and he didn't understand me" (Enright 1983, p. 331).

What relevance, then, does all this have for patient change? Freud loathed America. "Analysis," he said, "fits the American as a white shirt the raven" (quoted in Grosskurth, 1991, p. 159). Well, maybe it loses something in translation. But Freud did fear that we would reduce his austere psychoanalysis to a cheery, sentimental uplift, all about happiness and getting rich, endeavors he might have envied, but did not particularly admire. Happiness becomes not a byproduct of experience, but a desideratum.

Pace Freud, patients do wish to be happy, and we do not wish to deny them. But, to paraphrase the Cat in the *Cat in the Hat*: it is really great to be happy, you just have to know how. The search for happiness has unwitting consequences. The current movement toward a therapy based on restitution is at risk of restituting a fantasy. In object-relations theory, maternal caretaking and its restitution in therapy was to provide a solid basis for dealing with the exigencies of the real world through incremental disappointments in ideal nurturance. These would be optimum frustrations. This can, and for many therapists has, segued over to a therapy that strives to provide for the patient a mutative ideal maternal experience. Desire, which has its dark side, has been bowdlerized into satisfaction.

When I first entered the field in the Good Old Days of the early 1950s, patients were screened very rigorously for psychoanalysis. There were long waiting lists, and patients had to demonstrate—to the analyst's satisfaction—that they were worthy; motivated, prepared to undergo a four to five times a week, very demanding process. One felt honored to be chosen for the pilgrimage.[4] Obviously, the subtext was redolent of stoicism and hard work. In a word, real desire was required. Now, changing concepts of suitability, goals, the shift from a patriarchal to matriarchal vision of psychoanalytic praxis, and—let's face it–diminished societal enthusiasm for psychoanalysis has made it a far looser, more permeable category.

Admittedly, my emphasis on desire and its vicissitudes could descend into sounding like Polonius giving portentous advice to patients about the tragic nature of life. But one must also acknowledge that psychoanalysis floats in a cultural matrix:

> What we tend to think of as eternal verities are, in reality, time and place-bound. We, our patients, their complaints, our very concepts of treatment and cure are all manifestations of the particular epoch in which we live, and ultimately of each other. We are as imbedded in our time and place as bugs in amber.
>
> (Levenson, 1972, p. 7)

There is an old aphorism: that says that no one really comes into therapy to change. The neurosis is not working and the patient wants it to work, wants to be happy without the disruptions of change. But the road to change may well be more arduous. As Robert Frost put it, "The way around is through"; that is to say, getting patients to move *into* their neuroses, not to evade them; to own and use their anxiety, even their depression. One can suffer anxiety about being anxious, and depression about not being happy. What is a reasonable degree of anxiety in current New York City? When is it nuts to be hypochondriacal? Are "healthy" people less anxious, more stable, or simply less imaginative? Is it, perhaps, as Hemingway once said, that courage is simply a constriction of imagination.

At any rate, patients do not leave therapy having attained what they came for. As Wilden put it, "therapy is over when the patient knows what the therapist knows, which is what the patient has always known" (Wilden, 1972, p. 30). Patients come to realize that the gap between fantasy and reality, the effort required in coming to terms with shortfalls, the effort to love what is not-me and imperfect, engenders true desire.

Virtual reality begets virtual therapies, which focus more on reducing distress then enriching life. Lubell (2004) reports on an elaborate virtual therapy supplied at considerable cost by a company called Virtually Better, utilizing 3-D imaging software. The patient wears a helmet with screens producing a stereoscopic view—very much like a flight trainer. Patients are desensitized by confronting them with the virtual reality version of their

284 Psychoanalytic theory and practice

terrors. Certainly this must provide a more vivid experience than the usual desensitization processes that require looking at pictures of spiders or sitting in airport terminals.

However, what is the relationship between desensitization and desire? I recall a patient who suffered from a disabling snake phobia. He grew up in a missionary family in India. They had a "house" cobra living in their back yard that was considered sacred by the house servants, who fed it bowls of milk. He does not remember ever being afraid. He subsequently moved to New York and developed so virulent a snake phobia that coming upon a picture of a snake would precipitate a panic attack. Surely, there's more of interest in this story than a simple desensitization would yield. Or, consider a woman who enters therapy terrified to leave her house, disabled by severe agoraphobia, and ends losing both her agoraphobia *and* her deadly marriage?

Don Quixote is, as I have said, the embodiment of pure desire, which does seem, from all I've said, to be a very lofty goal indeed. Personally, I am somewhat put off by Don Quixote's fanaticism. I much prefer Sancho Panza, of whom Don Quixote says, "He doubts everything and he believes everything." He is the Everyman who sees through Don Quixote's grandiose chivalric fantasies and still follows him. In spite of terrible discomforts, he remains loyal—not inconsiderably out of greed. Don Quixote has promised him an island all his own to govern—a truly lucrative appointment in the days of the Spanish Main—and he is willing to risk the possibility that he might be following a lunatic. Don Quixote lives in pure faith: Sancho is rent by doubt. But it is he who gives Quixote his verisimilitude, keeps him from being merely a madman, a caricature.[5] Torn between avarice, doubt, admiration, and love, Sancho Panza soldiers on, one foot in a fantasy world, the other in reality. Can we do less?

Notes

1. This chapter first appeared as a chapter in the book longing: *Psychoanalytic Musings on Desire*, edited by Jean Petrucelli, 2007.
2. "Oh what a blow . . ." The quotation is from the title of Edmund Carpenter's 1974 book of the same title, which is a variation of the Cervantes text from Part I, Chapter XVII: "I am losing much blood from the wound that phantom gave me . . ."
3. I was delighted to see that the cover of this book has a stiletto heel shoe sitting on the couch and that Dr. Halsted's chapter touches on the same fetishistic

mystery. One also notes that the stiletto heel of the shoe is firmly bedded on the couch. This shoe is not taking it lying down!
4. There is a wonderful audiotape in the W.A. White archives, of Otto Will's efforts to get H.S. Sullivan to take him on as an analysand.
5. Kafka went even further, postulating that Don Quixote was Sancho Panza's invention, his fantasy.

References

Amsden, D. (2003). Not tonight, Honey: I'm logging on. *New York Magazine*, October 20:30–35.

Baudrillard, J. (1944). *Simulacra and Simulation*. Ann Arbor, MI: University of Michigan Press.

Enright, D.J. (1983). *The Oxford Book of Death*. New York: Oxford University Press.

Finch, P. and Allen, J.A. (1999). Don Quijote across the centuries. In D.D.A. Wilson (Ed.), *Don Quijote*. New York, W.W. Norton, pp. 767–773.

Grosskurth, P. (1991). *The Secret Ring*. New York: Addison-Wesley.

Kojève, A. (1969). *Introduction to the Reading of Hegel*. New York: Basic Books.

Levenson, E. (1972). *The Fallacy of Understanding: An Inquiry into the Changing Structure of Psychoanalysis*. New York: Basic Books.

Levenson, E. (2007). Oh what a blow that phantom gave me. In J. Petrucelli (Ed.), *Longing: Psychoanalytic Musings on Desire*. London: Karnac Books, pp. 89–98.

Lubell, S. (2004). On the therapist's couch: A jolt of virtual reality. *New York Times*, February 19.

Rizzuto, A.M. (1998). *Why Did Freud Reject God? A Psychodynamic Interpretation*. New Haven, CT: Yale University Press.

Siodmak, C. (1942). *Donovan's Brain*. Mill Valley, CA: Pulpless.com

Staples, B. (2004). What adolescents miss when they grow up in cyberspace. *New York Times*, A14. May 29.

Stephenson, N. (1992). *Snow Crash*. New York: Bantam.

Thompson, G.M. (1985). *The Death of Desire: A Study in Psychopathology*. New York: University Press.

Wilden, A. (1972). *System and Structure: Essays in Communication and Exchange*. London: Tavistock.

Wolf, N. (2003). The porn myth. *New York Magazine*, October 20.

Chapter 23

Deeper, wider: some comments on the Gill/Bromberg correspondence[1]

The letters compose an interesting historical and theoretical exchange (1979–1983). It strikes me that, rather than converging on the issue, they were passing in the night. Gill, a very informed Freud scholar, was moving away from his doctrinaire position, shifting his percepts of transference from a containment to a more fluid and vital interaction but still valiantly making an effort to integrate the classic and interpersonal position. Bromberg was moving in an entirely different direction. Gill remained rooted in the linked concepts of repression/regression: Bromberg fostered the concept of dissociation. They were talking across a paradigmatic gap.

When the editors (Tony Bass) approached me about a commentary on this historical exchange of letters (1979–1984 and obviously incomplete) between Merton Gill and Philip M. Bromberg, they suggested two parameters: my own experiences with Gill, during those early years of rapprochement, and my comments on the exchange per se.

Unfortunately, my recollections of Merton Gill are somewhat fragmented. There is not, to my knowledge, a record of his contacts with White; and I must depend on the analyst's nemesis, memory, for my own experiences with him. Gill, who had been the most sympathetic of the Freudian analysts on the committee of the American Psychoanalytic Association that in 1952 refused admittance to the early group of Interpersonalists—for, among other presumably substantive shortcomings, not conforming to the 5 day/couch rule—had been drifting toward an interpersonalism of his own. He came to White and attended some of our clinic meetings. I don't remember the date, but it was during my tenure as director of the Clinical Services, so it was sometime in the late seventies. Apparently he had read my book, *The Fallacy of Understanding*, and wanted to meet me (Levenson, 1972). Darlene Ehrenberg and I took him to lunch and, much as did Bromberg, found him to be a most intellectually curious and stimulating person. He was interested in the White Institute in all its ramifications, theoretical and sociopolitical.

As Gill explored the potential of a more interpersonal approach, he became labeled at the American, often derisively, as the "Interpersonalist." Perhaps he was feeling somewhat alienated among his erstwhile colleagues as he intensified his contacts with our group. He did subsequently attend and participate in a number of our meetings. I remember one White Institute graduation when Gill was present and sharing a table with Nat Stockhamer, Arthur Feiner, and me. To my utter amazement (the only other "Merton" I knew of was Thomas Merton, the famous literary Trappist monk!), it appeared that Gill spoke a fluent Yiddish and, indeed, came from a New York background.

He was a truly remarkable man; open, respectful, and warm, with an ability to grasp and make coherent muddy issues. In 1982, he gave a talk at White, in defying the then current draconian bans against consorting with us, an act of no small moral courage. He had reviewed the entire corpus of Interpersonal writings; and with his fresh and original intelligence, he saw that there were, as he said, two dichotomies in psychoanalysis and that they did not, as many of us had assumed, run parallel:

> I refer to the distinction between two major cleavages in psychoanalytic thought. One cleavage is between the interpersonal paradigm and the drive-discharge paradigm. The other cleavage is between those who believe the analyst inevitably participates in a major way in the analytic situation and those who do not. I came to realize that I had assumed that these two cleavages ran parallel to each other, or at least that those who adhered to the interpersonal paradigm would also ascribe to the analyst a major participation in the analytic situation.
>
> (Gill, 1983, p. 201)

His two books on transference (the second, coauthored with Irwin Hoffman in 1982) re-examined and explicated his changing perspective on the relationship of resistance and transference, the interpretations thereof, and the nature of the analyst's participation in the transference, thus providing background and perspective for his correspondence with Bromberg (Gill, 1982).

288 Psychoanalytic theory and practice

In traditional transference analysis, transference was seen as a form of resistance—the consequence of projections onto the present. The patient *resists* examination of genetic fantasies by *transferring* them onto the therapist. Consequently, the analyst interprets *away* from transference, to get it out of the way of the authentic inquiry.[2]

> This [classic] view is an integral part of the position that the analysis of the transference is ancillary to the analysis of the neurosis. I argue, on the contrary, that if the analysis of the transference is the analysis of the neurosis, the resolution of the transference must also largely take place in the analysis of the transference.
>
> (Gill, 1982, p. 178)

Although Gill recognized that there was a dimension of reality in the patient's perception of the interpersonal field, and that it needed to be validated by the therapist, the essential coconstructed validity of that perception—and its centrality to the mutative experience—is not fully realized. Thus, in Gill's revision of transference, the patient is perceived as having a real experience with the therapist. It is not fantasy; it is based on real aspects of the interpersonal field and the transference field is used to validate the patient's perceptions. However, the therapist's participation is seen as the therapist, "inevitably enacting the role the patient assigns to him"; surely, a long way from the classical construct but still not arrived at a fully coconstructed interpersonal field (Gill and Hoffman, 1982, p. 4). Without an acknowledgment of the therapist's ongoing and continuous coparticipation, the transference becomes a field rife with mystification; either the patient is misreading the therapist or, if really picking up some participation, overreacting to the event because of unresolved past experience.

The real mutual impact of the patient and the therapist *and the enactment between them of what is simultaneously being talked about*—for me, the absolute core of the mutative process—is diminished or lost entirely. Gill struggled mightily, as do we all, with the antinomy of reality/distortion; but his formulation of the mutative aspects of transference interpretation became somewhat diffused as he reached the limits of his paradigm.[3]

Bromberg, on the other hand, was exploring something rather different; that is, the loosening up of the inherent intellectualization in Sullivan, trying to get to patients' feelings, to get the patient to "let go." Donnel Stern (1995) thought that was Philip's intent: "By 'regression' [Bromberg] does not mean to invoke the concept of transference neurosis, but rather an atmosphere of safety. Bromberg's regression is allowed, not induced and has nothing to do with transference deprivation" (p. 111). That is, not truly regression as Gill would understand it, and he says exactly that in his December 7, 1979, letter: "You are beginning to see the value of *what you conceive of as regression in therapy* [italics added] and I am beginning to question its value as I think it is ordinarily conceived of by Freudian analysts."

Regression seems incompatible with dissociation—a matter of apples and oranges; or, more appropriately, Freud and Proust. Gill may have been rejecting the therapeutic centrality of regression, but his definition of regression is appropriately classical. Gill searches for buried fantasy: Philip for lost time. Gill feels recapture of fantasy releases affect. Philip believes that the recapture of affect opens the door to early memory—but memory of real, albeit early, primitive (for Philip, perhaps a poor choice of term) experience. For Gill, fantasy is the *vis à tergo*; for Philip, it is dissociated memory and affect. Philip is breaking down dissociation, retrieving lost affect, actualizing the links between different states of self, split off from each other: Gill is retrieving repressed—what? Memory? Unconscious fantasy? For Gill, repression and regression are inseparable: "In short, while I would argue that it is important to bring discordant aspects of the transference into awareness I don't think of that as regression" (December 7, 1979, letter).

No, he would think of it as dissociation. Repression/regression is, for Gill, vertical. Dissociation, qua splitting, is conceptualized as a horizontal process. As Stern (2009) put it, "The mind is therefore theorized not as a vertical organization of consciousness and unconsciousness, but as a horizontally organized collection of self-states, states of being, or states of mind, each in dynamic relationship to the others" (p. 169).

In sum, my claim is that these different perspectives—repression and dissociation—are paradigmatically incommensurable. Bromberg does not mean by regression what Gill does. Indeed, he may be inadvertently espousing a classical position. Whether in the pursuit of very early experience or of primal fantasy, the analyst as posited as guide or cicerone, not so much as participant.

By this I mean a state of experienced well being through a deep empathic bond with the analyst that permits the patient to partially

290 Psychoanalytic theory and practice

turn over to the analyst the function that his own self system performed as the guardian of the self representation. This allows the intense re-enactment and re-organization into the self dynamism of the more dissociated preconceptual modes of thinking, feeling, and behaving.

(Bromberg, 1980, p. 244)

Isn't the analyst then necessarily being conceived of as the *container* for this powerfully disruptive re-experiencing? Bromberg makes a clear distinction between interpersonal and interactional; adhering to the former, but conflating *interactional* and *interactive* (Bromberg, 1980). I think he rather means the latter; that the analyst's overactivity blocks the patient's freedom to recapture dissociated split-off experience. I believe this is true; certainly one can be too present out of countertransferential anxiety. I must agree with Gill's critique: I believe there is an inherent incompatibility between allowing regression and being present and interactive.

Alas, there is no coparticipatory free lunch. If one is active, focuses on the present, perhaps one loses the affective intensity of recapturing what Stern (1997) called "unformulated experience." If one acts as container, perhaps one loses the intensity of transference enactments. If one is too "empathic" too concerned with restitution and repair, perhaps one misses the patient's anger and destructiveness (fantasied and real).

I would claim that repression and dissociation and, for that matter, denials are different perspectives on our great core Ur-mystery: "not-seeing-what-is-there-to-be-seen." After all, all psychoanalysis is about what is kept out of awareness, why, and how to retrieve it. But that's another topic in itself, from Freud's interest in hypnosis and the "repression" inherent in hysterical amnesia; thru Sartre's "bad faith"; R.D. Laing's "mystification"; and Sullivan's "selective inattention"; and on to current postmodern, Lacanian versions of not-knowing. Through them all runs the theme of, "How is it possible not to know what is there to be known?" As Wilden (1972) so neatly put it, "At the end of therapy the patient knows what the therapist knows which is, in essence, what the patient has always known" (p. 30).

Psychoanalysis obliges the analyst to become the disease he or she sets out to cure. It may be that nothing one does "works." Perhaps, the key lies not in what one believes is mutative but how one proceeds. Bromberg (1994), it would seem, agrees:

The Gill/Bromberg correspondence   291

Any attempt to turn a therapeutic discovery that emerges from a relational context into a technique that can be "applied" to other patients is an illustration of what I believe to be the single most ubiquitous failing in all analytic schools of thought as methods of therapy, and the shared blind spots in each of their creators (p. 541).

Paradoxically, it is only with the failure of the analyst's power, magic, that the patient gets better. From Freud, on down, there has been a consistent recognition of the dangers of therapeutic ambition.[4]

Gill sees the sine qua non of therapy as the working-through of the transference. So do I and so does Philip, but we really mean different things by "transference." The curse of this field is the glissade of our terms. The same words are used, but meaning slips and slides. The paradigm shifts inexorably but invisibly, since the language remains much the same, fostering an illusion of continuity and ecumenism.[5]

I think of the letters less as a meeting of the minds than as a changing of the guard. Bromberg was a pioneer in effecting a major shift in the psychoanalytic domain. A patient of mine made the distinction between regression and splitting abundantly clear to me when he had a revelation— a genuine state-changing insight. He suddenly realized, he said, that he was not *acting* like a child but he *was* that child at the moment of experience. Thanks to Bromberg, I got it!

Notes

1. This first appeared in 2011 in *Psychoanalytic Dialogues*, 21:3, pp. 259–263.
2. As Meninger defined the therapeutic cycle, it began in the present free-associative field, moved into resistance qua transference and then, on interpretation of the resistance, moved back to the patient's early memories and deeper fantasies. This cycle is still entirely relevant; however, now we move from present inquiry into transference enactment, which leads more or less spontaneously back to early affective-laden history (Menninger and Holzman, 1958).
3. I raised the issue of the limits of Gill's version of transference reality in Levenson (1989).
4. This is the point Wilden was making in my referred to quote; referring to Lacan's use of Hegel's Master-Slave dialectic, wherein the slave cannot win by defying or passive-aggressively submitting to the Master (see analyst) but must replace him.
5. Only H.S. Sullivan invented an significantly different lexicon for interpersonal "psychiatry"—one notes, not psychoanalysis.

References

Bromberg, P. (1980). Sullivan's concept of "consensual validation." *Contemporary Psychoanalysis*, 16(2):237–248.

Bromberg, P. (1994). "Speak that I may see you": Some reflections on dissociation, reality and psychoanalytic listening. *Psychoanalytic Dialogues*, 4(4):517–547.

Gill, M. (1982). *Analysis of Transference. Vol. I. Theory and technique*. New York: International Universities Press.

Gill, M. (1983). The interpersonal paradigm and the degree of the analyst's involvement. *Contemporary Psychoanalysis*, 18(2):200–237.

Gill, M. and Hoffman, I. (1982). *Analysis of Transference Volume II*. New York: International Universities Press.

Levenson, E. (1972). *The Fallacy of Understanding*. New York: Basic Books.

Levenson, E. (1989). Whatever happened to the cat? Interpersonal perspectives on the self. *Contemporary Psychoanalysis*, 25(4):537–553.

Menninger, K.A. and Holzman, P.S. (1958). *Theory of Psychoanalytic Technique*. New York: Basic Books.

Stern, D.B. (1995). Cognition and language. In M. Lionells, J. Fiscalini, C. Mann, and D. Stern (Eds.), *Handbook of Interpersonal Psychoanalysis*. Hillsdale, NJ: The Analytic Press, pp. 79–138.

Stern, D.B. (1997). *Unformulated Experience: From Dissociation to Imagination in Psychoanalysis*. Hillsdale, NJ: The Analytic Press.

Stern, D.B. (2009). *Partners in Thought: Working with Unformulated Experience, Dissociation, and Enactment*. New York: Routledge.

Wilden, A. (1972). *System and Structure: Essays in Communication and Exchange*. London: Tavistock.

Chapter 24

Lost in translation[1]

I very much appreciate the opportunity to comment on the papers of these three psychoanalysts whom I have known and admired for many years. Interestingly, they have parsed out quite different aspects of the Interpersonal position. Hirsch presents an exegesis of transference, countertransference, and, in particular, the nuances of mutual enactment in transference as it is conceptualized interpersonally. Christopher Bonovitz gives two endearing examples: first, of an interlude with his daughter; second, of a spontaneous, intuitive enactment with an adolescent patient. And, by the way, in his exchange with his daughter, he might have commented on the clever way—very Sullivanian—she uses teasing as a strategy for exploring her (primal scene?) experience, without excessively provoking her father's anxiety. An additional Sullivanian dimension might be, neither her fantasies nor his, but the "detailed inquiry," the real events—whatever it was, what really happened, where are the bedrooms, does she sleep in the same room, was a door inadvertently left open, why this night?—that provokes her anxiety. Mark Blechner focuses on the radical aspects of the Interpersonal movement, on gender issues, highlighting an important and overlooked aspect of Interpersonal Psychology. Erich Fromm, in particular, from a Marxist position, focused attention on the immersion of psychoanalysis in its culture. The original members of the William Alanson White Institute included Clara Thompson, Fromm, Florence Powdermaker—a cultural anthropologist—and, of course, Sullivan, who died in 1949 in Paris, after attending a meeting of the World Federation of Mental Health. They all emphasized the cultural relativity of psychoanalysis, its immersion in its time and place. In the days when psychoanalytic training was limited to only the most "normal"—read, conventional—candidates, the White

294 Psychoanalytic theory and practice

Institute actualized Sullivan's dictum that we are "all more simply human than otherwise" by training gay candidates (Sullivan, 1953, p. 7).[2]

Yet for all the excellence of the articles, I perceive, at least in Hirsch and Bonovitz, a seminal drift. Interpersonal Psychology is acknowledged and credited as anlagen of Relational Psychology, but, it is implied, we have gone beyond it. Although this drift may be an inevitable consequence of time and paradigm change, I suspect something is being lost. First, the emphasis on very early experience—i.e., mother/infant attachment—valorizes a kind of psychic determinism, and (implicitly) a consequent belief in an empathic restitution.[3] Second, in explicating the Interpersonal process with a strongly Relational lexicon, they are, I believe, inadvertently transforming it. Inevitably, as a hermeneutic given, *something gets lost in translation.*

As an example: Hirsch (2008) writes, "Sullivan posited an entirely interpersonal picture of human development . . . *dissociation of experiences that were potentially disruptive to creating harmonious equilibrium among various internalized self-other configurations*" (p. 3; emphasis added); and on Clara Thompson, "Her analytic work focuses on the here and now of the transference countertransference matrix, viewing this interaction as an illustration of how *patients construct their current life to conform to the internalized past*" (p. 6; emphasis added).

Or to quote Bonovitz: "A patient with an extremely rigid set of internal images and associated unconscious fantasies *forces* reality to conform to fantasy." These examples all use the lexicon of Relational Psychoanalysis,

> invoking the metaphor of horizontal dissociation with its split-off "self-states"; i.e., aspects of the postmodern fragmented self kept out of awareness of each other. The goal would be integration of the states, not Interpersonal Psychology's semiotic goal of bringing what is mystified into the patient's awareness.
>
> Thus there is no such thing as learning what *ails* a person's living, in the sense that you will come to know anything definite, without getting a pretty good idea of who it is that's doing the living and with whom. In other words, in every case whether you know it or not, if you're to correctly understand your patient's problems, you must understand him in the major characteristics of his dealing with people.
>
> (Sullivan, 1954, p. 13)

According to Interpersonal doctrine, patients develop a "self-system," defined by Sullivan as all the security operations by which people defend themselves against anxiety. It begins in infancy, to be sure, in the nuances of the mother/infant relationship—and continues to develop throughout life as a series of interpersonal strategies for minimizing anxiety in oneself and in the necessary Other.

Is current reality forced (i.e., "muscled") to conform to fantasy? Here is the signal distinction: I believe that defenses persist into the present because the defenses are still relevant—the *present is not that much different from the past.* Bonovitz's case report is about real people—the analyst included—doing real things to and for each other in the real world (see Hirsch, 2008). Yet, I must read his play with the patient as an example of empathic restitution: a lively and powerful corrective emotional experience for the boy, but not, I believe, entirely Interpersonal.

As Hirsch points out, to conceptualize the interchange as Interpersonal, one would have to follow the implications of Bonovitz and his young patient's interaction as an enactment of the verbal content of the sessions. What are they enacting? Has Bonovitz competitively defeated the father? Is he now the better father with athletic calluses? Why does he play "racket games" rather than, for example, squash? Will he pay a price for this interaction? He makes explicit his interest in Field and Chaos theory approaches. If so, then his presumably therapeutic linear progression of interaction, interpretation, and liberating memory and improvement is suspect. God knows, we have all had the experience that no great session goes unpunished! From the perspective of restitution and repair, the outcome is exemplary; from the perspective of defense and resistance, the outcome is overdetermined and must be "worked through" over a period of time—the default labor of psychoanalysis. Would this necessarily be more therapeutic? Maybe not, but it would be Interpersonal!

The problem, as I see it, is that emphasis on early experience and internalized patterns inadvertently reiterates the Freudian doctrine that current difficulties are distortions of the present carried over from the past; not, as Sullivan posited, that real things were being done to real people in the here and now. For me, the crucial queries are: "What's going on around here?" and "How did it come to happen?" The past prefigures the present, but the demystification of Interpersonal process, in the service of modulating interpersonal anxiety, must take place between the patient and therapist, in their interactions, and how they perceive and talk about the patient's past and current world. The analysis of transference and countertransference is all about resolving—in *the present, through the present*—what is essentially the patient's semiotic incompetence: his or her inability to grasp the present

296 Psychoanalytic theory and practice

in an unreified form.[4] To do otherwise co-opts the radicalism inherent in Interpersonal Psychology: the dictum that a cure requires grasping, in their totality, relationships in the current world.

Sullivan said that "no one has grave difficulties in living if he has a very good grasp on what is happening to him." It was clear communication he was after. If a person could clearly articulate and communicate what he is experiencing, he has a grasp on it! (Chatelaine, 1981, p. 411). Note that he says *is* experiencing. Sullivan believed that people were having trouble because intense empathically derived Interpersonal anxiety blocked their perception. One was not allowed to know what one knew, not allowed to see what one knew was there to be seen (see Laing, 1970). Or, as Wilden put it, "[a]t the end of therapy, the patient knows what the analyst knows, which is what the patient has always known" (Wilden, 1972, p. 30), and, to be clear, *not* what the therapist has always known.

To repeat, I believe there is a reality of experience that is obscured because the patient's version of his or her life is distorted by the vicis-situdes of current Interpersonal anxiety. The patient's vision of life is full of avoidances (inattentions), denials, and distortions because not seeing what is there to be seen is necessary to avoid mobilizing the anxiety of the person's significant Others; *not least among these the psychoanalyst*! It seems to me that analysts of different persuasions are more and more in agreement that countertransference is not put into us, but called out of us. We must struggle mightily with our own lack of awareness because it is the heart of the therapeutic praxis.

The current emphasis on the vicissitudes of early mothering, especially as described in attachment theory, reflects a cultural change from the patriarchal, Oedipal-oriented (i.e., conflict and envy) world in which I grew up and became an analyst, to a matriarchal, nurturing one in which early mothering and empathy are valorized.

One also notes, not inconsequentially, that the demographics of psychoanalysis have shifted from largely male and medical to female and psychological, along with a radical shift in the economics. Believe it or not, when I entered the field in the early 1950s, psychoanalysis was the second highest-paid medical specialty and we had waiting lists! Patients were screened for "appropriateness"; i.e., their ego strength and their ability to tolerate the frustration of the long psychoanalytic process. Clearly, this made for a therapeutic milieu that tolerated more frustration and tempted the therapist to assay what seems nowadays overaggressive interventions.

Patients today would not tolerate the patriarchal, stem, and often disapproving tone of the early analysts.

I am so appreciative of the generous remarks about my contributions that I feel somewhat ungracious for raising any caveats at all about these sophisticated articles. Of course, one might question whether my position is entirely congruent with Interpersonal Psychology. I entered the White Institute in 1950 and I remember the sense of excitement and collegiality. Blechner, in particular, has caught vividly the ambience of revolution that permeated the air. I had just come out of the army and the nonauthoritarian and respectful tone of the place carried me away. In truth, the faculty members were strange bedfellows, otherwise hardly teaching the same things, but I didn't really care! There was such a strong, implicit agreement that psychoanalysis should be an instrument of self-realization, not adjustment. Goethe said we spend the first 50 years of our lives trying to get rid of the best things about ourselves. Sullivan, Thompson, and Fromm would surely have agreed with that.

Notes

1. This first appeared in 2011 in *Contemporary Psychoanalysis*, 47(4):588–593.
2. Not to be overly sugarcoating the White Institute's policies, it took a long time for gay psychoanalysts to be openly acknowledged, although they were accepted for training on a "don't ask, don't tell" basis.
3. As Gedo elaborates, Mitchell warned against this assumption (Gedo, 1999, p. 134).
4. For an elaboration of this position, see Gedo, 1999, p. 135.

References

Chatelaine, K.L. (1981). *Harry Stack Sullivan: The Formative Years.* Washington, DC: University Press of America.

Gedo, J. (1999). *The Evolution of Psychoanalysis: Contemporary Theory and Practice.* New York: Other Press.

Hirsch, I. (2008). *Coasting in the Countertransference; Conflicts of Self-Interest between Analyst and Patient.* New York: The Analytic Press.

Laing, R.D. (1970). *Knots.* London: Penguin.

Sullivan, H.S. (1953). *Conceptions of Modern Psychiatry.* New York: W.W. Norton.

Sullivan, H.S. (1954). *The Psychiatric Interview.* New York: W.W. Norton.

Wilden, A. (1972). *System and Structure: Essays in Communication and Exchange.* London: Tavistock.

Chapter 25

Psychoanalysis, the uncanny, and the banalization of evil[1]

As psychoanalysis has—at least for many of us—drifted away from its focus on fantasy (the roiling Unconscious of Freud) toward the more pragmatic interpersonal/relational matrix, we have become less aware of, and pay less attention, to manifestations of the uncanny. Everyone has had experiences with the uncanny, but it is more easily experienced than described. "Uncanny" can mean anything from a mild experience of dislocation, or déjà vu, on to sheer terror. I want to start with a story of my own experience with the uncanny, particularly its relationship to that ultimate uncanny, Evil; and then go on to discuss the consequences of this shift for psychoanalytic therapy.

In 1949, during and after the airlift, when the Russians cut off Berlin from the West, I was, among my other medical officer duties, the American officer for Spandau prison. Spandau held a number of the Nuremberg prisoners who had not been hanged, but given long or, in the case of Rudolph Hess, life sentences.[2] Being there stimulated in me a great deal of interest in the Nazi movement and in its individual participants. I offer this autobiographical bit to emphasize, that despite the difficulty of morally and psychologically struggling with my contact with Nazis I should hate, I found them to be largely very interesting, formidable and—dare I say, agreeable.[3]

This was in striking contrast to the following episode that took place in La Paz, Bolivia, in 1967. La Paz was, at that time, a rather small dreary Indian town at 11,000 feet, with a tiny ex-pat population. I entered a small restaurant. There were two large Nordic men sitting at a table. One looked up at me, quite pleasantly, and I experienced what can only be described as a severe physical shock! I was absolutely jolted by the experience of what felt to me like a contact with some mythic Evil.

As I later discovered, Klaus Barbie, "The Butcher of Lyon," a monster of a sadist and killer, was present in La Paz at that time. He slipped out of Europe in 1957 (with the help of the CIA) in the aftermath of World War II, obtained Bolivian citizenship under the name Klaus Altman, and lived there quite undisturbed until 1971. He was then extradited to France where he died in prison in 1991 at age 77.

I do understand, that at Spandau prison I wore the uniform and I had the power. Also, they were the most benign of the Nazi hierarchy. But even then, my experience in La Paz feels not merely uncanny. It felt—dare one say—telepathic. I do believe it really *was* Barbie—although obviously I can't prove it. It doesn't matter —the experience was certainly real. Oddly enough, there was something *pleasurable* about it, exciting—rather like hearing a ghost story. I had no explanation for why scary and exhilarating should be so co-mingled until— as I shall elaborate—I re-encountered Sullivan's explication of the uncanny.

In any exegesis of the uncanny, of course one, one must start with Freud's 1919 essay on the uncanny, the *Unheimlich* (Freud, 1919). Unheimlich translates as "not familiar." But, as Freud points out, its opposite "heimlich" has two meanings. First, what is familiar, and second, what is hidden or kept out of sight: ergo forbidden. The uncanny, then, is "that class of the terrifying that leads us back to something long known to us, once very familiar" (p. 370–371). Or, "when the primitive beliefs we have surmounted seem once more to be confirmed" (p. 403). It is not an entirely satisfactory exegesis. Although Freud's Oedipus complex, castration anxiety, and vagina dentata surely suggest something approximating uncanny terror, those do not seem to be addressed. At least in this particular article, the focus seems to be on the uncanny experience of the "double"— the me that is not-me.[4]

Kristeva offers a theory of experience-close horror based on the concept of "abjection," referring to the human reaction (horror, vomit) to a threatened breakdown of meaning caused by the loss of the distinction between subject and object or between self and other (Kristeva, 1982). "There looms within abjection, one of those violent, dark revolts of being . . . opposed to 'I'" (1982; p. 1–2). And Lacan in his seminar, 1962–1963 *L'angoisse*, stays close to Freud's vision of the double (Lacan, 2004).

But despite the absence of the cornerstones of Freud's theory in his *Unheimlich* essay, Freud brilliantly conflated his theory to Greek mythology, a European cultural heritage that exploited its intense uncanny

300 Psychoanalytic theory and practice

affects. In Sophocles' *Trilogy*, the focus is not really on the incest; it is on our helplessness and terror in the face of the Gods' implacable and inhuman intent and man's hubris in trying to evade it. Oedipus's lament echoes touchingly across the centuries, when, in *Oedipus at Colonus* the second book of the *Trilogy*, he complains —how could he know she was his mother? How was it his fault? (Sophocles 1941). The Gods' vengeance was transgenerational. Poor, dense Oedipus. The "puzzle-solver" as Tiresias mockingly called him, paid the price for a transgression committed by his father, Laius.[5]

Sullivan presented a far more extensive and detailed exegesis of the uncanny. In addition to the "good-me" and "bad-me," Sullivan described one additional infant state, the "not-me." The "not-me," he believed, was manifested as the unknown, the uncanny, the un-integrated. Because it is dreadful and beyond representation:

> The not-me is literally the organization of experience with significant people that has been subjected to such intense anxiety, and anxiety so suddenly precipitated that it was impossible for the then relatively rudimentary person to make any sense of, to develop any true grasp on, the particular circumstances that dictated the experience of this intense anxiety.
>
> (Sullivan, 1953)

This state is accompanied by intense anxiety such as occurs in nightmares and schizophrenic experiences. Consider Sullivan's famous spider nightmare which describes a terrifying and extremely disorganizing experience of a spider (Sullivan 1953). Note also that, according to Sullivan, "not-me" and its destabilizing affect is an interpersonal event— It is not a reaction to an internal state (Sullivan,1953, p. 334–336).

Sullivan then does an astonishing thing. He establishes a hierarchy of the uncanny, running from "*awe*, to dread, to loathing and horror" (Sullivan, 1953, p. 315). Sullivan goes on at length to describe experiences of awe that are powerful and aesthetic: "awe-some" like the Cathedral at Chartres, or, say, a vision of the Virgin Mary. How did he grasp that progression from awe to terror, the strange confluence of magic and the uncanny, how the extremely disrupting experience of sheer terror makes the experience of the uncanny seductively attractive? Rainer Maria Rilke, in his poem *Duino Elegias* (1923/2001), put the mystery very beautifully:

Psychoanalysis, the uncanny, and the banalization of evil   301

For beauty is nothing
but the beginning of terror, which we can just barely endure,
and we stand in awe of it as it coolly disdains
to destroy us. Every angel is terrifying.

I will turn now, as a clinical vignette, to a dream, not just about uncanny experience, but also something akin to theological Evil. The session prior to the dream centers on this man's profound fear of women betraying him by having ardent sex with someone else. In the process of the telling, he experiences intense severe nausea, quite unlike his usual blandness. That night he has the following dream:

> He is in a room in a hospital (simultaneously his home) with his oldest son, his mother/wife and baby in the next room. They are evil in some terrible way. He has to go in and slit their throats to save himself and his other children. He sees blood, gristle, windpipes, and blood pouring out everywhere. Blood has soaked the carpet. He must cover it up. Then they are alive, coming after him, zombies, he sees his wife's/mother's eyes going blank behind heavy goldfish bowl glasses. He awakes in horror!

I have heard many dreams as horrific as this from rather placid reasonably put-together patients. Sullivan much preferred to finesse any confrontation with uncanny affect or content, since he considered uncanny dreams and nightmares to be momentary psychotic episodes. Contrary to Sullivan's expectation, my experience has been that these dreams are frequently presented blandly—offered up rather like stool specimens — immediately disowned and dismissed, even though, in the dream itself, the affect was overwhelming. Does the patient's response perhaps depend on the analyst's "contagious anxiety"? Is it not occurring in interaction with me because I am less anxious about the patient being anxious; or is it dissociated because I am *more* anxious?

Why are we so inured to the uncanny? You cannot imagine how little visual stimulation we had in the 1930s, when I was a child. We cherished the comic strips, book frontispieces, the arrivals of picture magazines (*Look* and *Life*). There has indeed been a shift from the written to the visual, an incremental increase in visual stimulation, and a progressive desensitization to images of horror, now commonplace on television and the cinema.

302 Psychoanalytic theory and practice

All that was certainly true, but also there has been a paradigm shift from modern to postmodern—with the latter's cultural relativism, its refusal to countenance categorical distinctions like Good and Evil. The shift, I believe, is largely about the flight from an Evil that transcends "the absence of good." The uncanny is unquestionably in the psychoanalytic domain, but Evil, is, strictly speaking, a theological concept. Nevertheless, the traditional Manichean/Augustinian dichotomy—which postulates a split between evil as a real presence and evil as an absence of good—still has great relevance for psychoanalysis, even in our postmodern times. As Delbanco said:

> [despite] the shriveling of the old words and concepts, we cannot do without some conceptual means for thinking about the sorts of experiences that used to go under the name of evil . . . We certainly no longer have a conception of evil as a distributed entity with an ontological essence of its own, as what some philosophers call "presence." Yet something that feels like this force still invades our experience and we still discover in ourselves the capacity to inflict it on others. Since this is true, we have an inescapable problem: we feel something that our culture no longer gives us the vocabulary to express.
>
> (Delbanco, 1955, p. 9)

The death camps were not run by people whose mothers didn't love them enough. The consequence of "opening the eyes," seeing what really look place, what people are capable of, is more than can be endured without emotional flattening. As Stalin is reputed to have said, "A single death is a tragedy; a million deaths is a statistic."

The Freudians' strongest objection to the new interpersonal view was, I believe, its failure to take imagination seriously, bowdlerizing the power of destructive aggression and its fantasy manifestations. If your mother loved you—if there were no attachment issues—would there be no destructive Oedipal fantasy, no castration anxiety, no envy, no terror of the "Dark woman," the vagina dentata, the castrating mother? Are these terrors inherent to the psychic structure or the secondary consequences of emotional deprivation?

One value of engaging the powerful affects of the uncanny is that it brings into the patent's awareness the intense anxiety that, from the interpersonal perspective, leads to avoidances in the present. The present, for all of us, is a Swiss cheese riddled with "absences"—inattentions, blind spots, dissociations that make it impossible to grasp the immediacy of one's experience. It is true that the intensity of the anxiety, and its subsequent avoidances, are based in childhood experience, particularly of helplessness and despair; but the bringing into awareness of these anxieties does assure the patient of a wonderful present. Rather, it equips the patient to know what is going on around here, and to himself or herself—and most neglected perhaps—what he or she is *capable* of. Uncanny experience may be not entirely contagious—not entirely relational, as Sullivan though it to be. It may also be a reflection of human interiority, a capacity for, and even exultation in, the potentials of inhumanity.

Well past the impotence of childhood, one might be able to change the otherwise incorrigible present, come to terms with it, or maybe reconcile to failures and disappointments. Freud dreaded the likelihood that American psychoanalysis would be utopian, espouse a feel-good banality. On the occasion of the Clark lectures, he is reported to have told Ferenczi and Jung, "They don't know that we are bringing them the plague!" Perhaps in our cozier, more gemütlich vision of the psychoanalytic process —by viewing the uncanny, the truly Evil pleasure in destructiveness as being "an absence of good"—we are, as Erwin Hirsch put it, "coasting in the countertransference" (Hirsch, 2008) and, in consequence, diminishing the meaning of being human. Dostoyevsky in *Notes from the Underground* puts the question:

> And what makes you so cocksure, so positive that only the normal and the positive, that is, only what promotes man's welfare, is to his advantage? Can't reason also be wrong about what's an advantage? Why can't man like things other than his well-being? Maybe he likes suffering just as much. Maybe suffering is just as much to his advantage as well-being. In fact, man adores suffering. *Passionately!*
>
> (Dostoyevsky, 1961, p. 117)

It is a telling caveat for those of us who believe that love and repair are enough. As Freud tried to warn us with his much-disputed Death Instinct, life is a lot more complicated than that.

304 Psychoanalytic theory and practice

Notes

1. This chapter was first presented at a William Alanson White conference, Unknowable, Unspeakable and Unsprung in the fall of 2013. It was then published as a chapter in the book *Unknowable, Unspeakable and Unsprung: Psychoanalytic Perspectives on Truth, Scandal and Lies*, edited by Jean Petrucelli, in 2016.
2. Speer, Hess, Dönitz, Raeder, Funk, Von Schirach and Von Neurath were the seven prisoners in the dank ancient fortress. All were eventually released except for Hess who hanged himself after his last prison mate left.
3. This was an extremely common experience. Guards, officers, diplomats became very sympathetic and involved in helping them (e.g., smuggling out notes, etc.) Except for the Russians who would have preferred to shoot them on the spot!
4. Freud based his essay on writer E.T.A. Hoffman's story "The Sandman" which contained a "doubled" doll, Olympia.
5. Parenthetically, I believe that Freud's use of the Greek concept of hubris, its obstinacy in the face of obvious warning of disaster, carried with it anticipations of the death instinct—the desire to self-obliterate, or be destroyed—as a psychoanalytic correlate of Evil.
6. The interview took place on January 24, 2004 and was published in *Contemporary Psychoanalysis*, 2005, Vol. 41, pp. 593–644. The entire issue was dedicated to Edgar Levenson and included articles by a number of his colleagues.

References

Delbanco, A. (1995). *The Death of Satan: How Americans Lost the Sense of Evil*. New York: Farrar, Straus and Giroux.
Dostoyevsky, F. (1961). *Notes from the Underground*. New York: Signet Classics.
Freud, S. (1919). The Uncanny. In J. Strachey (Ed.), *The Standard Edition of the Complete Psychological Works of Sigmund Freud*. London: Hogarth Press, Vol. XVII, pp. 217–252.
Hirsch, I. (2008). *Coasting in the Countertransference; Conflicts of Self-interest between Anayst and patient*. New York: Analytic Press.
Kristeva, J. (1982). *Powers of Horror: An Essay on Abjection*. New York: Columbia University Press.
Lacan, J. (2004). *L'angoisse*. Paris: Seuil.
Rilke, R.M. (1923/2001). *Duino Elegies*. New York: Farrar, Strauss, Giroux: North Point Press.
Sophocles (1941). *Oedipus at Colonus*. New York: Harcourt, Brace and Company.
Sullivan, H.S. (1953). *The Interpersonal Theory of Psychiatry*. New York: W.W. Norton.

Epilogue
Interview with Edgar Levenson by Irwin Hirsch and Victor Iannuzzi[1]

Hirsch:

I want to start by saying that it's an honor for both of us to do this interview with you. As do many, we consider you the key interpersonal theorist following Sullivan, Fromm, and Clara Thompson—the Willie Mays or perhaps the Michael Jordan [laughter] of interpersonal analysts. Seriously, you are the key interpersonal theorist responsible for bringing interpersonal psychoanalysis from them [Sullivan, Fromm, Thompson] to contemporary times. Your uncompromising attention to the inclusion of the analyst's subjectivity has played a seminal role in laying the groundwork for opening up psychoanalysis to include the study of perspectivism, postmodemism, and for what's now widely called the "relational tum" in psychoanalysis. With that said, we feel there is a lot of ground to cover in the interview and so we decided not to focus too much on your personal life history. However, I would like to begin by asking what your personal reasons for becoming a psychoanalyst were?

Levenson:

I arrived at it in a rather desultory way. I had gone to medical school, as a lot of middle-class Jewish kids did, because there weren't an awful lot of things one could do professionally in the 1940s. Once I got through medical school I really wasn't particularly sure what I was going to do with it, since I hadn't figured out what I was interested in really. At that point I went into the army for 2 years and was stationed overseas during the occupation. When I went in, I'd had a neurology residency, so the army gave me a neuropsychiatry specialty rating, and when I came out I was, mirabile dictu, a psychiatrist. I went on to get my boards in psychiatry,

306 Epilogue

and then I went into analysis because I needed an analysis. In those days analysis was a little like syphilology in that it was okay to treat the disease but not to have it. It was still considered somehow moderately embarrassing for me to be in analysis, so I sugarcoated it as a training requirement and it became a lot more acceptable. I went into analysis with Ed Tauber and from there I applied to the White Institute where Ed was one of the people who interviewed me. In other words, I sort of backed into becoming an analyst. It was never anything I'd really planned to do. Probably, if I'd had the analysis earlier I would've been an insurance salesman.

Iannuzzi:

You were in training during the early 1950s, which were pretty exciting times at White. Sullivan died in 1949, but Clara Thompson was around and Fromm was, I guess, in and out. Can you talk a little bit about who your major influences were, both within and outside of the Institute?

Levenson:

Sullivan had died the year before, so I never worked with Sullivan or knew him. Clara Thompson was around, Fromm-Reichmann was around a lot, and I think she was a bigger influence than people tend to consider now. She was working directly with schizophrenics and everybody was fascinated by that. Fromm, living in Mexico, was in and out; I had some group supervision with him. I think the biggest influence—I was thinking about this before—the influences were kind of implicit. I really didn't have a theoretical position, so it wasn't like I was trying to bounce my theories off people. I was simply absorbing a lot of what everybody did clinically. I think probably the biggest influences were Ed Tauber and Meyer Maskin, who was my first supervisor. There were a couple of other things that were floating around at White, but not directly connected. One of them was a lot of this stuff coming out in family therapy, which was extremely lively back in those days. And then the other factor which I've been thinking about, and I'm not really sure how this came about, was Count Alfred Korzybski. Do you know much about Korzybski?

Iannuzzi:

You've written about him, I know.

Levenson:

Korzybski was the founder of General Semantics. The journal is still around and so is the organization. I can't remember how I got to Korzybski exactly. Actually, I think I had a patient who was in the General Semantics group and he got me interested in it and I read some, and the first paper I ever gave was at the General Semantics Society, and the first paper I ever wrote (Levenson, 1961) was published in *ETC* [*ETC A Review of General Semantics*], which was the General Semantics journal. I can't remember how much interest there was in him [Korzybski] at White, but he had studied for 2 years with William Alanson White and he had also spent a summer with Sullivan and [Edward] Sapir, studying psycholinguistics. He was a major influence on me because he developed the concept that as the levels of anxiety go up the levels of abstraction go up. When I was in supervision with Clara Thompson, she used to say that if you started with a patient, and after the first week you found yourself thinking in terms of diagnosis, look to your countertransference. The idea being that the uneasier you became the more you began to diagnose, abstract, generalize, and so forth so. Fromm was at that time a more temporary sort of influence, because he was very characterologically oriented. That was about the time that Wilhelm Reich's book *Character Analysis* (1933) was popular and everybody was very stimulated because it was the first move away from Freudian dynamics to something that had to do with character structure. Fromm was very much interested in character structure too. He was very denunciatory really. So that for a while everybody went around sort of saying to their patients, "Look here, you know, you're the kind of person who blah-blah-blah-blah-blah . . ." It worked for Fromm, but we all lost our patients doing it!

Hirsch:

Erwin Singer was a lot like that, and although I never knew Ed Tauber, I believe he had a similar reputation.

Levenson:

Erwin Singer had a lot of that quality as you say, and so did Ed Tauber who had been analyzed first by Clara Thompson and then by Fromm. He thought of himself as a Frommian and he very much acted as a Frommian. But conceptually he was very much influenced by both Clara Thompson and Ferenczi. So Tauber's [and Green's] (1959) book on prelogical experience really comes down through Ferenczi and Clara Thompson. This whole effort to understand your own participation and the nature of participation really came from Clara Thompson. There was a funny tradition at White of disowning your first analyst I think.

Hirsch:
Was Clara Thompson a big influence on you?

Levenson:
She wasn't really, at least not overtly. Erwin [Singer] and I shared supervision time with her for 2 years, and actually she didn't say very much! [laughs] We used to go afterwards and sit in the coffee shop and discuss cases. If she was an influence, it was through some kind of silent infusion. It wasn't anything that she said very directly. I think it was more the basic structure of White that was influential—there were three things going on at White during that time. One is that the original contingent of White people had left the American, and so they were very companionable, collegial, and interested in getting people to work with them. They were kind of grateful you came to the place and they weren't so judgmental. The whole sense of things was—well, it was very egalitarian I think. Patients were considered human beings, including schizophrenic patients who were treated as people, and candidates—lowest on the pecking order ordinarily—as well were considered people. There was a much stronger sense of egalitarianism than was current in the American. The second thing is that there really wasn't any theoretical coherence. There wasn't a unified theory at White because Fromm and Sullivan were absolutely incompatible really, if you stop to think about it. Clara was presenting a version of Ferenczi's psychoanalytic perspective. So you had the influences of Ferenczi, Sullivan, Fromm, none of whom really fit together, although nobody ever quite said that. Third, the candidates were left, I think, trying to bring these incompatible views together. We all became intuitively postmodern. The feeling around the Institute was very much that there was no system of interpretations that really had hegemony over any of the others. I think the feeling came out that there must be something in what we do. There must be something we all do in common; why else are these people all in the same institute.

Note

1. This is only a short excerpt from the beginning of the interview. The full interview and the entire issue dedicated to Edgar Levenson are accessible through the links below. They are available at no charge to those purchasing this book.

Link to full interview: www.tandfonline.com/doi/abs/10.1080/00107530.2005.10747269

Link to *Contemporary Psychoanalysis* issue: www.tandfonline.com/toc/uucp20/41/4?nav=tocList

The interview took place on January 24, 2004 and was published in *Contemporary Psychoanalysis*, 2005, 41:593–644. The entire issue was dedicated to Edgar Levenson and included articles by a number of his colleagues.

Bibliography of
Edgar A. Levenson, M.D.

1958 Changing time concepts in psychoanalysis. *American Journal of Psychotherapy*, 12:64–78.

1960 The family album as therapeutic tool. *Psychiatry*, 23:219–223.

1961 Jam tomorrow–Jam yesterday: Cultural time perception and neurotic problem solving. *ETC: The Journal of General Semantics*, 18(2):167–178.

1961 Book review. (Psychoanalytic education in the United States by B.D. Lewin, and H. Ross.) *American Journal of Psychotherapy*, 15(3): 473–474.

1961 The treatment of school phobias in the young adult. *American Journal of Psychotherapy*, 15(4):539–552.

1962 Book review. (From adolescent to adults by P.M. Symonds and A.R. Jensen.) *American Journal of Psychotherapy*, 16(1):164–165.

1963 Book review. (On adolescence: A psychoanalytic interpretation.) *American Journal of Psychotherapy*, 17(1):144–145.

1965 and Kohn, M. A treatment facility for college dropouts. *Mental Hygiene*, 49:413–424.

1965 and Kohn, M. Some characteristics of a group of bright, emotionally disturbed college dropouts. *Journal of the American College Health Association*, 15(2):87–85.

1965 Why do they drop out? *Teaching and Learning: Journal of the Ethical Culture Schools of New York*, 25–32.

1966 and Kohn, M. Differences between accepted and rejected patients in a treatment project of college dropouts. *Journal of Psychology*, 63(1):143–156.

1966 Some socio-cultural issues in the etiology and treatment of college dropouts. In L. Pervin et al. (Eds.), *The College Dropout and the Utilization of Talent*. Princeton, NJ: Princeton University Press, pp. 189–206.

1967 Counseling the college dropout. *Journal of the Association of College Admissions*, 12:6–9.

1967 and Stockhamer, N., and Feiner, A.H. Family transactions in the etiology of dropping out of college. *Contemporary Psychoanalysis*, 3(2):134–151.

(Reprinted in *Digest of Neurology and Psychiatry*, Hartford, CT: Institute of Living, and in H.C. Lingren (Ed.), *Readings in Personal Development American Book.*)

1968–1969 and Feiner, A.H. The compassionate sacrifice: An explanation of a metaphor. *The Psychoanalytic Review*, 55(4):552–573.

1968 Discussion of Psychiatry and the Maverick, by I. Goldston. In Masserman, J. (Ed.), *Dynamics of Dissent*. New York: Grune & Stratton, 13, pp. 18–19.

1968 and Feiner, A.H., Fisher, L., and Stockhamer, N. Psychotherapeutic intervention in dropping out. New York State Psychological Association workshop presentation, May 1968. Published 1970 in E.F. Hammer (Ed.), *Antiachievement: Perspectives on School Dropouts*. Western Psychological Service, pp. 79–98.

1972 and Feiner, A.H., and Stockhamer, N. Youth in transition. In M. Levitt and B.O. Rubinstein (Eds.), *Youth and Social Change*, published for the American Orthopsychiatric Association [by] Wayne State University Press, Detroit.

1972 *The Fallacy of Understanding: An Inquiry into the Changing Structure of Psychoanalysis*. New York: Basic Books.

1973 Psychotherapy in the young adult. In E. Witenberg (Ed.), *Interpersonal Explorations in Psychoanalysis: New Directions in Theory and Practice*. New York: Basic Books. Part 3, pp. 149–167.

1974 Changing concepts of intimacy. *Contemporary Psychoanalysis*, 10(3): 359–369.

1974 *Requiem por el psicoanalisis*. Barcelona, Spain: Kairos. Spanish translation of *The Fallacy of Understanding*.

1974 Commentary. (Supervision as revelation of the pattern: I Ching comments on the open door by M. Stambler and C. Pearlman.) *Family Process*, 13(3): 376–398.

1974 Review. (Communicational structure: Analysis of a psychotherapy transaction by A. Scheflen.) *Annals of the New York Academy of Sciences*, 18.

1975 Transforming. (Review of The Transforming Self: New Dimensions in Psychoanalytic Process by D. Shainberg.) *Contemporary Psychoanalysis*, 11(3):376–379.

1975 and Feiner, A.H., and Stockhamer, N. Politics of adolescent psychiatry. In S.C. Feinstein and P. Giovacchini, (Eds.), *Adolescent Psychiatry*. New York: Jason Aronson. Vol. 4, pp. 84–98.

1976 A holographic model of psychoanalytic change. *Contemporary Psychoanalysis*, 12(1):1–20.

1976 The aesthetics of termination. *Contemporary Psychoanalysis*, 12(3): 338–342.

1978 Two essays in psychoanalytic psychology. *Contemporary Psychoanalysis*, 14(1):1–30. And in Stern, D.B. and Hirsch, I. (Ed.) (2017). *The Interpersonal Perspective in Psychoanalysis, 1960s-1990s: Rethinking transference and countertransference*. London: Routledge.

312 Bibliography

1978 Cure or persuasion. In E.G. Witenberg (Ed.), *Interpersonal Psychoanalysis: New Directions*. New York: Gardiner Press, pp. 47–63.

1978 A perspective on responsibility. *Contemporary Psychoanalysis*, 14(4): 571–578.

1979 Language and healing. *Journal of the American Academy of Psychoanalysis*, 7(2):271–282.

1979 Private and universal. (Review of *The Dream and the Underworld* by J. Hellman and *The Innocence of Dreams* by C. Rycroft.) *New York Times Book Review*, August 26, 84.

1980 More different than alike. *Contemporary Psychoanalysis*, 16(1):1–15.

1980 An eye turned in. (Review of *The Adolescent Diaries of Karen Horney*.) *New York Times Book Review*, December 21, 85.

1981 Language and healing. In S. Slipp (Ed.), *Curative Factors in Dynamic Psychotherapy*. New York: McGraw-Hill, pp. 91–101.

1981 Facts or fantasies: The nature of psychoanalytic data. *Contemporary Psychoanalysis*, 17(4):486–500.

1981 The rhetoric of intimacy. *GROUP*, 5:3–10.

1982 Follow the fox: An inquiry into the vicissitudes of psychoanalytic supervision. *Contemporary Psychoanalysis*, 18(1):1–15.

1982 Erwin Singer: in memorium. *Contemporary Psychoanalysis*, 18(3): 307–311.

1982 Playground or playpen. Comments on *The Psychoanalytic Process* by P. Dewald. *Contemporary Psychoanalysis*, 18(3):365–372.

1983 *The Ambiguity of Change: An Inquiry into the Nature of Psychoanalytic Reality*. New York: Basic Books.

1984 Follow the fox. In L. Caligor, P. Bromberg, and J. Meltzer. (Eds.), *Clinical Perspectives on the Supervision of Psychoanalysis and Psychotherapy*. New York: Plenum, pp. 153–176.

1984 Harry Stack Sullivan: The web and the spider. *Contemporary Psychoanalysis*, 20(2):174–178.

1985 The interpersonal (Sullivanian) model. In A. Rothstein (Ed.), *Models of the Mind and Their Relationship to Clinical Work*. New York: International Universities Press, pp. 49–67.

1987 More different than alike. *Contemporary Psychoanalysis*, 23(2):215–220.

1987 An interpersonal perspective. *Psychoanalytic Inquiry*, 7(2): 207–214.

1987 The purloined self. *Journal of the American Academy of Psychoanalysis*, 15:487–490.

1987 Response to review of *The Ambiguity of Change* by Jay Greenberg. *Contemporary Psychoanalysis*, 23(4):704–707.

1987 Discussion of clinical innovation and theoretical controversy. *Contemporary Psychoanalysis*, 23(2):215–220.

1988 Show and tell: The recursive order of transference. In A. Rothstein (Ed.), *How Does Treatment Help?* Madison, CT: International Universities Press, pp. 135–143.

Bibliography 313

1988 Real frogs in imaginary gardens: Facts and fantasies in psychoanalysis. *Psychoanalytic Inquiry*, 8(4):552–556.

1988 The pursuit of the particular. *Contemporary Psychoanalysis*, 24(1):1–16.

1989 Whatever happened to the cat? Interpersonal perspectives on the self. *Contemporary Psychoanalysis*, 25(4):537–553.

1989 Un modello olografico di cambiamento psicoanalitico. (Translator Marco Casonato.) *Psichiatria e Territorio*, 6:57–84.

1990 Memorial to Edward S. Tauber. *Contemporary Psychoanalysis*, 26(1): 186–187.

1990 Reply to Irwin Hoffman. *Contemporary Psychoanalysis*, 26(3):299–304.

1991 *The Purloined Self: Interpersonal Perspectives in Psychoanalysis*. New York: William Alanson White Press.

1991 Standoffs, impasses and stalemates. *Contemporary Psychoanalysis*, 27(3): 511–516.

1991 Back to the future: The new psychoanalytic revisionism. *Contemporary Psychotherapy Review*, 6(1):27–43.

1992 Harry Stack Sullivan: from interpersonal psychiatry to interpersonal psychoanalysis. *Contemporary Psychoanalysis*, 28(3):450–466.

1992 Mistakes, errors and oversights. *Contemporary Psychoanalysis*, 28(4): 555–571.

1992 Help! I am a captive of a psychoanalytic dialogue. *Contemporary Psychotherapy Review*. 7:133–138.

1993 Character, personality and the politics of change. In J. Fiscalini and A. Grey, A. (Eds.) *Narcissism and the Interpersonal Self*. New York: Columbia University Press, pp. 130–43.

1993 Shoot the messenger: Interpersonal aspects of the analyst's interpretations. *Contemporary Psychoanalysis*, 29(3):383–396.

1993 Review: (W.W. Meissner: What is effective in psychoanalytic therapy. The move from interpretation to relation. Northvale, NJ: Jason Aronson) *The Psychoanalytic Quarterly*, LXII(3):489–492.

1994 The uses of disorder: Chaos theory and psychoanalysis. *Contemporary Psychoanalysis*, 30(1):5–24.

1994 Beyond counter-transference: Aspects of the analyst's desire. *Contemporary Psychoanalysis*, 30(2):691–706

1994 Arthur Feiner: An appreciation. *Contemporary Psychoanalysis*, 31(1): 9–14.

1994 A short visit with Jeremiah. *Academy Forum: The American Academy of Psychoanalysis*, 38(1):11–13.

1995 Introduction to E.S. Tauber's Exploring the Therapeutic Use of Counter-transference Data. In D.B. Stern, C. Mann, S. Kantor, and G. Schlesinger (Eds.), *Pioneers of Interpersonal Psychoanalysis*. Hillsdale, NJ: The Analytic Press, pp. 111–113.

1995 A Monopedal version of interpersonal psychoanalysis. *The Review of Interpersonal Psychoanalysis*, 1(1):1–4.

314 Bibliography

1996 Aspects of self-revelation and self-disclosure. *Contemporary Psychoanalysis*, 32(2):237–248.

1996 The politics of interpretation. *Contemporary Psychoanalysis*, 32(4): 631–648.

1998 Awareness, insight and learning. *Contemporary Psychoanalysis*, 34(2): 239–249.

1998 An interpersonal therapist. In J. Reppen (Ed.), *Why I Became a Psychotherapist*, Northvale, NJ: Jason Aronson, pp. 209–214.

1999 Stockhamer, N. and Feiner, A.H. Family transactions in the etiology of dropping out. Reprinted in J. McCarthy (Ed.), *Adolescent Development and Psychopathology*. Lanham, MD: University Press of America, pp. 211–228.

1999 L'interpretazione. *Ricerca Psicoanalitica*, X(3):225–244.

2000 An interpersonal perspective on dreams: Commentary on paper by Hazel Ipp. *Psychoanalytic Dialogues*, 10(1):119–125.

2000 Psychoanalytic love and therapeutic despair. *Journal of the American Psychoanalytic Association*, 48(1):66–71.

2000 The Hero and the Hassid. *Contemporary Psychoanalysis*, 36(2):233–239.

2000 Introduction to A.H. Feiner, Interpersonal Psychoanalytic perspectives on relevance. In *Dismissal and Self-definition*. London: Jessica Kingsley, pp. 9–13.

2000 Interview with E.A. Kuriloff. *White Society Voice*, 11(1):2–17.

2001 The enigma of the unconscious. *Contemporary Psychoanalysis*, 37(2): 239–252.

2001 Freud's dilemma: On writing Greek and thinking Jewish. *Contemporary Psychoanalysis*, 37(3):375–390.

2001 Creativity, genius and divine madness. In J. Petrocelli and K. Stuart (Eds.), *Hungers and Compulsions*. Northvale, NJ: Jason Aronson, pp. 233–244.

2001 Aspects of self-revelation and self-disclosure. *Ricerca Psicoanalitica*, XII(3):299–312.

2002 The first shall be the last: some observations on the evolution of Interpersonal psychoanalysis. *Contemporary Psychoanlysis*, 38(2):277–285.

2003 On seeing what is said: Visual aids to the psychoanalytic process. *Contemporary Psychoanalysis*, 39(2):233–249.

2005 Hirsch, I., Iannuzzi, V. Interview with Edgar A. Levenson. *Contemporary Psychoanalysis*, 41(4):593–644.

2005 *The Fallacy of Understanding and the Ambiguity of Change*. Hillsdale NJ: The Analytic Press.

2006 Response to commentaries. *Contemporary Psychoanalysis*, 41(4):749–750.

2006 Response to John Steiner. *International Journal of Psychoanalysis*, 87(3):21–24.

2006 The pursuit of the particular: On the psychoanalytic inquiry. In A. Cooper (Ed.), *Contemporary Psychoanalysis in America: Leading Analysts Present Their Work*. Washington, DC: American Psychiatric Publishing, Inc., pp. 365–3 s81.

Bibliography   315

2006   *Psicoanalisi Contemporanea*, Ed. Conti, R.P. and Caverni., S. Urbino: Quattro Venti.

2006   A short visit with Jeremiah (reprint). Academy Forum retrospective: Fifty years. *The Journal of the American Academy of Psychoanalysis and Dynamic Psychiatry*, 50(2):20–41.

2007   Oh what a blow that phantom gave me. In J. Petrocelli (Ed.), *Longing: Psychoanalytic Musings on Desire*. London: Karnac Books, pp. 89–98.

2007   Fifty years of evolving Interpersonal Psychoanalysis. *Contemporary Psychoanalysis*, 4(4):557–564.

2007   Controverse psychanalytique. *L'Anneé Psychanalytique Internationale*, 2007(1):36–44.

2008   In search of the person in the patient: An interpersonal perspective on "Roles in the Psychoanalytic Relationship." Commentary on paper by Richard Almond. *Psychoanalytic Dialogues*, 18(1):89–94.

2009   The enigma of the transference. *Contemporary Psychoanalysis*, 45(2): 163–178.

2010   The schism between "drive" and "relational" analysis: A brief historical overview. *Contemporary Psychoanalysis*, 46(1):7–9.

2010   The enigma of the transference. In J. Petrucelli (Ed.), *Knowing, not-Knowing and Sort of Knowing*. London: Karnac Books, pp. 3–20.

2011   Deeper, wider: Some comments on the Gill/Bromberg correspondence. *Psychoanalytic Dialogues*, 21(3):259–263.

2011   Lost in translation. *Contemporary Psychoanalysis*, 47(4):588–593.

2012   Psychoanalysis and the rite of refusal. *Psychoanalytic Dialogues*, 22(1): 2–6.

2016   Re-issue of *The Purloined Self*. London, New York: Routledge.

2016   Psychoanalysis, the uncanny, and the banalization of evil. In J. Petrucelli and S. Schoen (Eds.), *Unknowable, Unspeakable, and Unsprung: Psychoanalytic Perspectives on Truth, Scandal, Secrets, and Lies*. London, New York: Routledge, pp. 209–215.

2016   Remembering Clara. *Contemporary Psychoanalysis*, 53(1):29–31.

Index

alcoholism 270, 271, 273
American Psychoanalytic
    Association 5, 73, 166, 245, 275,
    286
analytic situation 54, 167
anti-hermeneutics 73, 163
anxiety 16, 18, 22, 27–33, 35, 36,
    38, 39, 47, 53, 54, 58, 59, 61, 92,
    104, 118; attack 271; avoidance
    of 212–218; castration anxiety
    299, 302; communicated 28;
    disruptive anxiety 31, 58, 169;
    homosexual 242; social, 181

Bartlett, F. 229
Bass, T. 286
Bateson, G. 3, 161, 270
Becker, H. S. 270
behavior: aberrant 271; addictive
    272; direct motor 229; erotic 67,
    73; self-destructive 95
Berlin, I. 254
Binswanger, L. 274
Bloom, H. 256
Bollas, C. 68, 69, 73, 163
Bromberg, P. 291

Calasso, R. 187
castration anxiety 299, 302
Cavell, M. 245

Chaos theory 77, 187–203
Chessick, R. D. 158
conscious awareness 61
consciousness: Jamesian stream of
    243, 263; ordinary 240;
    phenomenology of 208, 243;
    traditional 244
containment 94–96, 102, 133, 172,
    173
Cooper, A. M. 162
countertransference: incipient 38;
    traditional 46; troublesome 128
countertransference disclosure 216
countertransference reactions 133
countertransference traps 39
Crapanzano, V. 43
creative imagination 40
creativity 269–275
Crowley, R. 226
crypto-Freudians 6
cultural awareness 14
cultural psychoanalysts 64
culture: contemporary 274; feminist-
    aware 189; primitive 4

Damasio, A. R. 229
disruptive anxiety 31, 58, 169; see
    also anxiety
divine madness 269–275
Dostoyevsky, F. 65, 182, 275

Index

Edelson, M. 145
enigma: of human consciousness xx; of transference 161–175; of unconscious 237–249
Erikson, E. 168

Faude, J. 272
fear: of death 60; of destruction 53; of expulsion 181–182; of growing up 182; of helplessness 181; of influence 181; of separation and loss 60
female repression 168
Fonagy, P. 170
Freud, A. 256
Freud, S. 168, 169, 225, 267; ambivalence 259; antiquity collection 258; appropriation 67; archeology 232; bifurcation of theory and praxis 148; claim for psychoanalysis 212; concept of interpretation 213; contemporaries 210; fascination 211, 218, 243; hysterics 12; promotion of sexual libido 259; theory of repression 211
Freudian analysts 76, 166, 286, 289
Freudian mind 226
Freudian theory 65, 189, 240
Freudian unconscious 4, 67, 243
Freudian vision of female dynamics 64
Friedan, B. 64
Friedman, L. 14, 83, 86, 87
Fromm, E. 270; differences 13; jeremiads 14; Marxist sociology 64; rejection 64

Gardner, H. 146, 228
genius 269–275
Gill, M. 75–76, 166, 175, 215
Gopnick, A. 148
Grandin, T. 147
Green, A. 227
Green, M. R. 68, 72, 308
Greenberg, J. 74

Greenson, R. 51
Grünbaum, A. 213

Hadas, R. 242
Handelman, S. 245, 254, 266
Hayek, F. A. 228, 244
hermeneutics 116, 207, 213, 214
hieroglyphics 164
Hirsch, I. 294
Holzman, P. S. 173
human fascination 274

iconic memories 3
imagination 40, 76, 77, 78
impasses 83–89
interpersonal algorithm 60
interpersonal anxiety 28, 29, 39, 169, 295, 296
interpersonal approach 287
interpersonal crises 28
interpersonal intimacy 142
interpersonalism 26, 32, 36, 39, 57, 65, 74, 76, 96, 125, 167, 286
interpersonal matrix 65
interpersonal psychiatry 5, 13, 27, 38
interpersonal psychoanalysis: evolution 72–78; evolution of 63–70; monopedal presentation of 57–62
interpersonal psychoanalytic therapy 61

Johnson, M. 244

Korzybski, A. 151
Krüll, M. 6
Kuhn, T. 237

Laing, R. D. xx, 165, 269
Lakoff, G. 244
language: abstruse 253; coherent 145; left-brain 149
Leary, T. 269
Lubell, S. 283

Mark, D. 272
Marxist sociology 64
May, R. 67, 270
McGinn, C. 237, 241
McLuhan, M. 68, 256
Menninger, K. A. 152, 173
metapsychological assumptions 147
metapsychological theories 187
metapsychology 11, 64, 97, 99, 105, 161; bifurcated 259; canonical 93
Meyer, A. 257
Miller, J. 162, 227, 243
mind: phenomenal 225; psychological 225, 226; unconscious 210, 211, 225; visual 246; wretched 269
mirror neurons 172, 173
Mitchell, S. 74
Morson, S. G. 24
mothering 60, 86, 161

paradigm: basic 46; basic traditional 45; drive-discharge 67; emergent neuropsychological 61
paradigmatic shift 237, 238
patient's problems 51, 59, 92, 113, 214, 228
patient-therapist relationship, 125, 133, 138
personality 7, 16, 32, 33, 36, 38, 110, 189, 215
persuasive psychotherapy 241
phenomenology 157, 161, 162, 172, 208, 233, 238, 239, 246, 247
Phillips, A. 172
Polanyi, M. 228, 244
politics, interpretation 216–221
Popper, K. R. 155, 163, 166, 213
pragmatic psychotherapy 257
psychoanalysis: Chaos theory 77, 187–203; clinical 207; cultural 64; cures 256; developmental 148; evil, banalization of 298–303; existential 189; floats 283; movement 216; rite of refusal

178–184; spectrum 74; taps 221; uncanny 298–303
psychoanalytic concepts 246
psychoanalytic inquiry 7, 208, 271
psychoanalytic love 138–142
psychoanalytic technique 72, 103, 144
psychoanalytic theory 9, 147
psychological mind 225, 226
psychotherapy 14, 15, 31, 60, 118, 120, 122, 152; persuasive 241; pragmatic 257

Rank, O. 270
Reich, W. 307
relational psychoanalysis 294
repression 11, 28, 60, 169, 211, 290
repression/regression 286, 289
Rilke, R. M. 300–301
Rizzolatti, G. 172
Rosen, J. 260
Rothstein, A. 219

Sartre, J. P. 244
Schore, A. 150, 246
self-disclosure 125, 126, 128
self-psychology 23, 86, 189
self-revelation 94, 125–136, 126, 127
sexual repression 12
Siegel, D. J. 149
Sinigaglia, C. 172
social awareness 13
social constructivist 35, 127
stalemates 83–89
standoffs 83–89
Stern, D. B. 226, 289, 290
Stuss, D. T. 149
Sullivan, H. S. xx–xxi, 146, 157, 169, 245; apothegm 261; concept of anxiety 248; formulation 29; interpersonal psychiatry 13; limitations 74; observations 33; vision of interpersonal psychiatry 38

Tauber, E. S. 68, 308
therapeutic ambition 152, 291
therapeutic leverage 119, 134
Thompson, C. 13, 23, 64, 68
traditional countertransference 46
transference: erotic 30; masochistic 49; negative 217; sexual 248; traditional 86, 288
Trilling, L. 219
troublesome countertransference 128
Tulving, E. 149

unconscious mind 210, 211, 225

verbal interpretation 145
virtual desire 277–284
visual aids 144–157

Weiss, R. H. 256
Wheeler, M. A. 149
Wilden, A. 108, 110, 158, 291
Wilner, W. 248

Zornberg, A. G. 255